IRON-JAWED ANGELS

The Suffrage Militancy of the National Woman's Party 1912-1920

Linda G. Ford

UNIVERSITY
PRESS OF
AMERICA

Lanham, New York, London

University Press of America®, Inc.
4501 Forbes Boulevard, Suite 200
Lanham, Maryland 20706

3 Henrietta Street
London WC2E 8LU England

Printed in the United States of America
British Cataloging in Publication Information Available

Library of Congress Cataloging-in-Publication Data

Ford, Linda, 1949-
Iron-Jawed Angels : the suffrage militancy of the
National Woman's Party, 1912-1920 / Linda G. Ford.
p. cm.
Includes bibliographical references.
1. Women—Suffrage—United States—History—
20th century. 2. National Woman's Party—History—
20th century. 3. United States—Politics and
government—1913-1921. I. Title.
JK1896.F67 1991
324.6'23'0973—dc20 91-2073 CIP

ISBN 0–8191–8205–2
ISBN 0–8191–8206–0 (pbk.)

Lucy Branham and Lucy Burns in Prison Clothes
* All Pictures appear courtesy of Library of Congress and National Woman's Party

Dedicated to an unswerving militant

the late Rebecca Hourwich Reyher

and to my ever supportive husband

Ira Glunts

TABLE OF CONTENTS

List of Illustrations

In 1976, years after earning a B.A. and M.A. in American history, I read Eleanor Flexner's *Century of Struggle* and learned to my surprise, that American militant woman suffragists had been jailed under the Wilson administration, during World War I. The year before, I had seen Midge MacKenzie's wonderful documentary, "Shoulder to Shoulder," which dramatically and movingly portrays the struggle of Britain's militant suffragists. I had been incredulous that such a story had remained largely untold for so long. MacKenzie found that most British history works on woman suffrage credited women's war work in WWI for their being "awarded" the vote, exactly paralleling the situation in American history texts. It became apparent that certain British women, radically feminist suffragists, before being "awarded" suffrage, fought very hard for that right, and as a result, had suffered beatings, imprisonment, and forcible feeding. I discovered that 500 American woman suffragists of the National Woman's Party--traditionally assumed to be part of the moderate, even conservative, progressive era reform effort--had also been arrested and jailed, with 168 serving sentences between 1917 and 1919. The purpose of my research was to find out how and why American suffrage militancy developed to the point of government arrests, and to discover who the jailed American militants were.

As to sources on the Woman's Party during the suffrage years, I found the militants have not yet been the focus of a great deal of secondary work. Their activities have been discussed by Flexner, and also by William Chafe and Aileen Kraditor, and more recently, by Janice Law Trecker, Christine Lunardini, Nancy Cott and Ellen DuBois. Susan Becker has done an excellent study on the NWP after suffrage, which is also the major period of focus for Cott. No in-depth study of militancy or the jailed militants themselves has been done, however. Doris Stevens and Inez Haynes Irwin, both participants in the militant movement, did publish (in the 20s) extensive and valuable accounts of their militant activities. The present-day National Woman's Party, luckily for me, decided to microfilm the party papers in 1979 so that a new wealth of material, especially of the suffrage years, was available on the militant movement. This information gives new insight into NWP organizational detail, militant philosophy, leadership strategies, and the personal experience of 168 militant feminists. It proves an invaluable mine of information as a critical starting point on the militant NWP. I supplemented it by searching for biographical detail of lesser known militants and for better, specific information on the peculiar, wartime historical stage on which the NWP operated.

This project began right before my doctoral graduate work and became the subject of my dissertation, and has since been thoroughly revamped and updated. I especially appreciate the combination of pointed criticism and unwavering support from my Syracuse University thesis advisors Sally Gregory Kohlstedt and Cissie Fairchilds. I most recently benefitted greatly from the comments of Leila Rupp. What kept me going were the tremendous, generous help from numerous historical societies and university archives, the courteous women at Schlesinger Library at

Radcliffe, encouragement from Amelia Fry, the wonderful letters from former militants' sons and daughters, and, of course, the meeting with the indomitable Rebecca Hourwich Reyher. A very special thanks is reserved for the heroic, tireless typing efforts of Judy Powers, assisted by Wyatt LaCoss. And most thanks have to go to my sometime editor, typist and cheerleader husband, Ira Glunts.

Introduction: Suffrage Militancy

In 1919, the *Liberator* called the National Woman's Party one of the "leading radical forces in American politics in the near future." Its members were vilified in the New York papers the same year as "seditious suffragists" and "cannibals and Bolsheviks."[1] The woman's suffrage movement is not usually perceived in terms anywhere near the above, but an analysis of Woman's Party suffragists between 1912 and 1920, reveals that they were indeed a "radical force" thanks to a scathing critique of American male-dominated society, an aggressive, evolved strategy of civil disobedience and a very broad-based activist membership encompassing women from left to right politically. NWP women came from all sorts of socio-economic backgrounds, and included scientists, pilots, homemakers, librarians, revolutionaries, and travellers' aides. This study examines the nature of these militants and their militancy: it profiles leaders, organizers *and* recruited (general) members; and analyzes the feminist philosophy behind suffrage as it evolved from petitions, to pickets, to prison.

In most standard suffrage histories, little distinction has been made between the sort of women who joined the militant suffrage movement and those who became members of the moderate, mainstream National American Woman's Suffrage Association (NAWSA). Nor has "militancy" as a developing tactic, been closely analyzed. Since at peak, NAWSA and the NWP had two million and 50,000 members respectively, this is understandable.[2] But the history of the woman suffrage movement cannot be completely understood if it only takes note of the larger group's activities, particularly since it was the smaller, aggressive NWP which pushed and prodded the larger group to more action of its own.

Two statistical studies which analyze late 19th-early 20th century suffragists were written in the 1970s: Barbara Kuhn Campbell's (1977) *The 'Liberated Woman' of 1914* and Andrew and Anne Firor Scott's (1976) *One Half the People*. Both present a picture of woman suffragists as largely wives and mothers who played public roles as clubwoman/suffragists. Campbell wrote using the 1914-1915 *Woman's Who's Who* and *Notable American Women* to look at "prominent women of the Progressive Era." Making no distinction between suffrage organizations, Campbell found suffragists to be ordinarily married, with a small family, often professionals who were college educated and involved in various community club activities.[3] Andrew and Anne Firor Scott's sketch of 89 suffragists taken from *Notable American Women*, includes 26 from the 19th century National Woman's Suffrage Association (NWSA), 15 from the same era's American Women's Suffrage Association (AWSA), 26 from NAWSA (the group formed with the merger of NWSA and AWSA in 1890) and seven from the NWP. The Scotts concluded that suffragists were well-educated, 75% married, 16% divorced and 61% had children.[4] Since no such statistical study of the NWP itself has been done, data was compiled for this study to discover more about the backgrounds of *militant* woman suffragists.

Broader suffrage studies tend to give an impression similar to the Campbell/Scott image, of traditional, moderate clubwomen/wives, chiefly of the educated middle classes. William Chafe, in *The American Woman* (1972) sees the NWP *and* NAWSA as part of the Progressive Era's moderate reform impetus. Chafe argues that "hitherto-uninvolved middle-class women became politicized" through the appeal that women could "clean up" and improve society with the vote. This was more or less in agreement with earlier studies by Aileen Kraditor (1965) and Eleanor Flexner (1959), which stressed the comfortable middle-class backgrounds of NWP members as well, women who were rather conservative and usually reluctant to ally with women of the working classes. Flexner was, in fact, arguing against the notion that the NWP was a "lunatic fringe," the prevailing contemporary view. Observing that the NWP protesters did include woman munition factory workers, she stressed that there were also well-established professional women, wives of prominent men, wealthy women, and women from respectable Quaker families. More recently, Steven Buechler's (1986) fascinating study of the transformation of the suffrage movement in Illinois, which, again, makes no differentiation between the NWP and NAWSA, supports the notion of a national movement which remained class exclusive. His elitist women included both upper class clubwomen interested in progressive reform as "social control," and professional/managerial women from "privileged niches" who desired to rationalize and manage the social order through reform from above. Buechler concludes that the national suffrage movement did make alliances with working women's groups, (and decidedly so in Illinois because of settlement worker dominance) but working women were not influential enough so that a potential argument for the ballot as a "radical" demand "portending major shifts in power relations," could supplant the modest and limited political rights sought by middle and upper class suffragists.[5]

In recent studies that do look specifically at militant suffragists, elitism is still stressed. Ellen DuBois argues, in a 1987 article regarding Harriot Stanton Blatch's New York Women's Political Union (a militant suffrage group which would merge with the NWP in 1917), that working class and union women were courted and were part of the militant movement in New York, but that their influence was "submerged" by that of "elite women." Nancy Cott has observed in her new suffrage studies, that the national militant organization, the NWP, with its "paradoxical" image, "inadvertently or advertently" appealed to left-wing women with its tactics (of 1917-1919), while repelling them with a clique of the prosperous.[6] While the statistics and general data compiled here will, to some extent, bear out the dominance of the upper/middle class of the NWP, particularly in leadership and organizing roles, it will also become clear that the NWP had an incredibly far-ranging appeal as a militant suffrage organization, and that it was, in fact, deeply influenced by its left-wing.

Cott also notes that the NWP women's "enthusiasm and intense determination" set them apart from NAWSA, and made them attractive to a new group of activists. Similarly, Janice Law Trecker mentioned, in her pioneering look at the NWP, that "energetic" women founded the new party. Christine Lunardini, most recently, in her *From Equal Suffrage to Equal Rights,* argues that younger "new suffragists" were drawn to the aggressive NWP. Lunardini calls them "better educated, more career-oriented, younger, less apt to be married and more cosmopolitan activists than "older suffragists" [NAWSA].[7] Young "energetic," "new suffragists" were part of the turn-of-the-century version of the phenomenon of the "new woman," in detail, described in various ways by historians, but basically the new woman was a young working girl, cherishing freedom and independence, "yearning for wider and more significant experience."[8] The militant campaign for suffrage appealed to many such women, but perhaps the most significant factor emerging from the data to follow is that those women who joined the NWP militants were very concerned about and determined to achieve, economic independence from men. That sort of "new woman" feminist emphasis was a potential factor for further democratization of the militant movement. To some degree, new bonds were forged between NWP women who were self-supporting "privileged" professionals and women who were workers in munitions plants.

The independent feminists profiled in this study for specific statistical data as well as broader narrative biographical information, were taken from the prisoners' list in Doris Stevens' 1920 *Jailed for Freedom* (Stevens was an NWP organizer). I believe the 168 imprisoned NWP suffragists chosen for analysis are very much representative of the militants. As women willing to go to prison, they were, of course, among the most militant of NWP members, and represent a good cross-section of party membership, from the national executive committee to the local district. About 2,000 women spent time on the NWP picket lines and in various demonstrations between 1917 and 1919, and 500 were arrested. Of those 500, 168 were actually jailed for their actions, 106 serving terms in 1917. Among these prisoners were virtually all of the major national leaders, all but a handful of their advisors, about half the national organizers (the rest, in the meantime, were speaking throughout the country about the prisoners' plight) a large group of officers and active members from state and local branches, and numerous woman activists (most of them leftist) who joined to demonstrate for feminists' rights of free speech and female solidarity.

There is much more data available about some of the 168 militants than others, more, obviously about the national leaders than the local recruits. The data on the prisoners were collected from various sources. Stevens' list of brief paragraph sketches was supplemented by interviews, university records, hometown directories, historical society publications and newspapers, the correspondence of the NWP papers, NWP photographs, newspaper accounts of NWP activities, information from *Notable American Woman* and *Who's Who of American Women*, *New York Times* obituaries, and correspondence with NWP members and their families. This kind of research data makes it possible to look beyond the most visible party leaders and gain a deeper understanding of suffrage militancy through the lives of ordinary women who risked their reputations to work towards feminist goals. And this study does more than just present the bare statistics on these "ordinary" militants, but also encompasses their feminist motivations, their jail experiences, their families' reactions--the way their militant activities transformed their lives. Certain statistical data areas were collected about each woman prisoner, including family background (class, ethnic, religious), geographic region (of birth, usually residence as well) education, age, occupation, marital status, political orientation and reform activities. This data is summarized in the tables appearing in Appendices A, B and C. Class status, admittedly a difficult area when looking at women in American society, was based upon family background, and occupation and/or husband's occupation, and was broken down into "elite," "middle" and "working." "Elite" is defined as part of the influential wealthy or upper middle, high-ranking professional classes; "middle" as women with what have been called the "semi-professions" of teaching, social work or clerical work, from non-"prominent" families; and "working" as those with factory or domestic service jobs. Data on political orientation and reform activity gave further indication of the breadth of the women's interests, especially in other feminist and progressive issues. And information on age, occupation and marital status helped measure how "independent" the women were, economically or otherwise, when they joined the new suffrage party. As noted, links between economic power and woman's status were continually drawn by NWP spokeswomen: women's economic independence was a basic tenet of their egalitarian feminism, a belief borne out by the data on the militants' own lives.

This new data collected on the prisoners shows the feminist militants falling roughly into three groups: leaders, organizers and recruits. The women who founded and led the new militant Congressional Union, beginning in 1912-1913; who served as political organizers, particularly active between 1915 and 1919; and who were recruited, many as demonstrators between 1917 and 1919, had their militant feminism in common, but would be quite dissimilar in many other areas of their lives. This varied mix of strong-willed woman reformers created a situation with some class tension and personal conflict, especially in the earlier organizing years (1912-1916); but by the time "real" militancy against the Wilson government was reached, the women's differences were submerged in a united effort versus an "autocratic" male power.

Suffrage militancy itself is the other focus here; the feminist philosophy behind it and its developmental stages as a strategy. Christine Lunardini and others have looked at how effective or ineffective militancy was at getting suffrage laws passed, but have not examined its evolution or feminist ideology; while Nancy Cott's recent description of NWP feminism does not give their militancy enough weight.[9] Woman's Party feminists saw suffrage as only one small but essential step of many, towards winning women's full equality with men. As Cott has recently argued, early 20th century feminists were faced with the paradox of recognizing and arguing women's strengths and "sameness" with men when fighting for their "rights," while at the same time appreciating, and sometimes glorifying and making use of, women's differences, particularly traits of peacefulness and nurturance. I would argue that Woman's Party feminists faced the same dilemmas, but as militants, as *angry* feminists impatient with male authorities, they very much tended to stress the importance of women's sameness with men, regarding her strength and power and worthiness; and the need for women's independence, especially economic, from men. Woman's difference was really stressed only in terms of the "female" moral superiority of being anti-violence. Like progressive feminist Charlotte Perkins Gilman, militant suffragists (especially Alice Paul) thought that men and women had evolved certain traits, to woman's definite disadvantage; and that women should use whatever strengths they *did* have to work toward achieving, ideally, a more or less androgynous equality, with *both* men and women strong *and* peaceful. The militants were strong, even radical feminists, believing women should unquestionably, and preferably immediately, have the same political, economic and social rights, status and strengths men had. Moreover, as NWP "Chairman" Alice Paul said in 1910, woman's role should no longer be as merely "comforter" to men. Instead women should develop as a "new race," women whose "ideal is strength."[10] NWP historian Inez H. Irwin wrote of Paul's 1916 political tactics that Paul thought it was "more dignified of women to ask the vote of other women than to beg it of men."[11] Paul's militants developed new strategies based on using the leverage of women's political power as voters in the West, then as women petitioners and pickets, and then as public martyrs. NWP suffragists applied their feminism dramatically, acting upon their conviction that women were quite strong and capable enough to fight--and win--their own battles.

American militant suffragists followed the lead of the liberal women's rights movement of the 19th century which concentrated on winning women's political rights first. The first political feminist was the English Mary Wollstonecraft, who, influenced by the ideals of self-determination of the 18th century's Age of Enlightenment, argues in *A Vindication of the Rights of Woman* (1792), that woman's reason would be equal to man's if she were equally educated in "free enquiry." Women might then apply that reason, "learn their oppression," and then overcome it to " 'wrangle in the Senate' to keep their faculties from rusting."[12] Like the 20th century's English Pankhursts', Wollstonecraft's radical feminism was highly controversial in the United States. Boston essayist Judith Sargent Murray championed her, although Murray's plea for woman's right to education and "competence" was tempered with an assurance that "ideas" would not interfere with woman's skills at the "mechanics of a pudding." The revolutionary John Adams "could not but laugh" at his wife Abigail Adams' similarly tentative attempts to argue for recognition of women's rights in the new republic;[13] and his sarcasm typified what would be the usual response of political authority to the issue of woman's equality for centuries--nothing would be done to further anything so trivial and preposterous. Years of listening to sarcastic male politicians helped lead to female militancy. Susan B. Anthony and Elizabeth Cady Stanton led a movement 60 years after the Adams' exchange to ensure women their rightful place as full citizens of the American democracy, their claims for women's rights, again, largely egalitarian, evolving out of the 19th century outpouring of humanitarian and democratic reform. Anthony argued that only the suffrage could provide women the symbol and fact of equal citizenship. In 1872 Anthony, putting into action her own call for women to finally rebel, illegally voted in Rochester, using civil disobedience to gain public sympathy. Anthony, as the first suffrage "militant," would later be lionized by NWP suffragists.

Woman's rights theorists from Wollstonecraft to Anthony stressed that women had rights of self-determination and self-government, being equal to men in reason and competence, and these same arguments would be used by NWP suffragists to support their impatient militancy. The Woman's Party's feminist militancy for suffrage was not static, but would evolve through several stages to culminate in the "real" militancy of civil disobedience. I am defining "militancy" here as pertaining to aggressive defiance, particularly, to resistance of authority. For American suffragists of the National Woman's Party, militancy would evolve from a militant "state of mind," or their "political" stage, (discussed in Part One) as an aggressive style of action within the political system; to acts of overt or "real" militancy, (discussed in Part Two) steps undertaken with a willingness to break the law and to definitely spurn the usual social rules of behavior for females. This use of the term "militancy" is essentially the way in which it was used by NWP leaders Alice Paul and Lucy Burns. They differentiated, at the time and later, between "feelings" of militancy, or a "militant spirit," that is, a defiant resisting attitude, and overtly militant action. In fact, they would not call themselves "militants" before 1917. "Real" militancy, according to Paul, was reached in June of 1917 when women faced prison for their demonstrations, when, in other words, they became willing to break the law, with all the social consequences, in defiance of authority.

In the late 19th-early 20th century the word "militant" was undergoing an interesting change from meaning that which pertains to the military, to one including a certain state of mind. According to the Oxford English dictionary, militancy was originally taken from the verb *militare*, to serve as a soldier, and used for centuries to describe one engaged in warfare, particularly a "church militant" in the 15th and 16th centuries. By the 19th century, the word also described a person who was "combative," as in a situation so dire as to make the pacific resist, and the militant revolt. By 1900 a militant could be "engaged in strife," which might be the strife of combat or of attitude. Here was, not a soldier, but a person willing to engage in "strife," for a set of beliefs. Obviously, that "strife" could differ in degree, and could take that militant to a stage of militancy which was violent and made militants soldiers again. For some in this period, "militance" still meant only the violence of war and soldiery. In the early stages of NWP picketing, even its organizers were not certain they should accept the label. Interestingly, Hazel

Hunkins would describe the Woman's Party as the "least militant" of groups, one led by a woman who "did not like violence," the Quaker Alice Paul. Hunkins would insist that "militancy" was used "against us, not by us." Organizer Virginia Arnold did not think the NWP was militant since it had not destroyed property, the mark of British suffrage militancy.[14]

For militant suffragists there was some disagreement on exactly what degree of combativeness and resistance was necessary for true militancy, but all agreed that it involved defiance of and resistance to authority, or as the first meaning in the modern definition has it, "pertaining to conflict with opposing powers or influences." Militancy defined as resistance to and defiance of authority and the law make "militant state of mind" or defiant spirit, and "real" militancy or actually breaking the law, useful categories of analysis when examining how militancy evolved in the attempt to achieve women's political equality, the all important 19th (and 20th) century feminist movement's goal.

Interestingly, and in this instance underscoring Cott's feminist paradox, militant strategy as it was developed by the NWP, evolved in particular ways which were consciously feminist and based in woman's strength, but were also determinedly "womanly," that is, nonviolent, to provide a contrast with warlike "male" values. Whether undergoing mob attacks or police violence, NWP suffragists countered with acts of beautiful pageantry, pointed and symbolic banners, and constant picketing and public speeches, in a well-coordinated, nonviolent protest. Alice Paul biographer Amelia Fry, has compared the NWP "Chairman" to Mahatma Gandhi, (and argues, in fact, that perhaps there was some direct Gandhian influence upon Paul) in her pacifism and use of nonviolent resistance.[15] However Gandhian, Paul and the NWP's nonviolent techniques were also taken from earlier feminist protesters, American labor activists, and Quaker pacifists; as well as from Paul's own ideas and her advisors' practical suggestions. The NWP was one of the first American political organizations ever to use methods of nonviolent resistance, using a classically non-violent style which explicitly tried to show "women's" militancy was peaceful. The suffrage militants, as non-violent resisters, set out to accomplish a specific purpose with their defiance, to persuade the government directly and indirectly through public sympathy, to pass a woman suffrage amendment to the Constitution.

As will be seen, NWP resistance fit traditional parameters of civil disobedience, as outlined by Judith Stiehm in *Nonviolent Power,* a type taken by a "population that has been pushed too far," that has no access to (or perhaps desire for) weapons, a commitment to social justice, and a belief that education was no longer enough and compromise on "basic principle" impossible. Specifically, Stiehm describes nonviolent resisters' strategy as graduated actions motivated by an "urge to act morally" with the intention of evading, defying, converting, persuading or coercing a "target opponent" or a third party.[16] Additionally, NWP demonstrators will be seen to follow Richard Gregg's model as outlined in his *The Power of Nonviolence.* Gregg argued that a nonviolent resister's sincerity is proved by her own suffering, causing the attacker to "lose moral balance," poise and self-confidence, particularly if there are onlookers. In the end, the goal is to "convert the opponent." For Gregg's nonviolent resister, continued trust in the decency and reasonableness of the "attacker," leads inexorably to conversion.[17] The NWP would appeal to the best sentiments of their opponent, the government, while at the same time pointing out the hypocrisy of their not acting upon those sentiments. Mabel Vernon reflected the policy clearly when she answered a critic of the June 1917 pickets:

> The conclusion we have reached is that we must stand now for the establishment of a true democracy in this land.... [The sentiments in] the Russian banner have been the same since January 10, [our] purpose is to remind constantly the President and the people of the country [that we] are not enfranchised.[18]

Since America prided itself, based its very existence on, the highest principles of morality, and since Woodrow Wilson himself was reputedly a highly principled man, the technique of pointing out the hypocrisy in his political idealism could be perfectly realized by American suffrage militants.

Generations of political feminists had worked to gain woman suffrage by the time the group of impatient American suffragists who would form the National Woman's Party, turned their considerable talents to the task in 1912. The women and their efforts between 1912 and 1916 are the subject of Part One, Militant State of Mind. NWP militants emerged out of a particular feminist tradition described in Chapter One, Strong-Minded Women: British-American Origins of Suffrage Militancy. Stanton and Anthony's aggressive female egalitarianism and British suffragists who shed Victorian restrictions in a bold demand for the vote, provided the philosophical roots of Womans' Party feminist militancy. Chapter Two, Organizing for Power: Political Phase, describes the birth of the Woman's Party (beginning as the Congressional Union of NAWSA) as a spirited, progressive, political lobbyist organization; grounded in applied, woman-centered feminism which would use woman's power (to NAWSA's dismay) rather than "begging," to move the male body politic. Chapter Three, A New Race of Strong Woman: 'All the So-Called Classes,' 1912-1916, presents a collective biographical study of the early membership based on data collected on the 168 suffrage prisoners, and includes an examination of initial tension generated over race and class issues. NWP founders/leaders and organizers were progressive reform feminists; they were professional and unpaid "clubwomen" reformers, and also young worldly, college-educated "new women." With different priorities as feminists and reformers, disagreements arose, but consensus on working for women's political rights held them together. In Part Two, Real Militancy, unity receives a substantial boost through the extreme situation created by greater militancy and corresponding government suppression.

By 1917, it had become evident to Paul and "Co-Chairman" Lucy Burns, that the usual democratic reformist lobbying was not bringing the quick results they had foreseen. They therefore elected for the "real" militancy described in Part Two, defying authority in civil disobedience, in a consciously "female," nonviolent and dramatic way. In this part, three stages of overt or "real" militancy occurring between 1917 and 1920, are outlined, based on escalating NWP defiance of governmental authority, which, for its part, took no action to pass woman suffrage, while stepping up its efforts to silence the suffrage protests. The growing radicalism of NWP suffragists' attitudes and behavior through the three stages follow Stiehm and Gregg's nonviolent civil disobedience patterns. "Real" militancy for suffrage began in the context of the unsettled and troubled years of the first World War, a time which would prove very dangerous to vocal protesters against the government, whether socialist or suffragist. The war situation definitely shaped the evolution of NWP suffrage militancy and the government's reaction to it. Chapter Four, Defying Authority: Peaceful Picket, Early 1917, presents the first stage. The first level of real militancy began with the "perpetual picket" of the war-beleaguered Wilson White House, a picket which was perceived as threatening the government once the U.S. entered the war. The second stage, the subject of Chapter Five, Resisting Authority: The First Arrests, Mid-1917, describes the escalation of banner rhetoric versus the Wilson government, and the initial arrests and mob violence resulting from the militants' actions. The third and most radical stage, which is discussed in Chapter Six, Radicalization: Political Prisoners, Late 1917, was reached when the NWP declared themselves political prisoners, victims of government administered "terrorism" suffered in November 1917, after the NWP became part of the government's list of "subversives."

The last three chapters of Part Two investigate the NWP at the height of its militancy, late 1917-1920, their maligned members' experience, their strategy as societal outlaws, and eventually, their victory and withdrawal from the fray. At the peak of militant activism, well-to-do clubwomen reformers, impatient at not having citizenship rights, were joined in jail by large numbers of socialist feminists and working women championing the civil rights issues arising here--free speech and the NWP's right to dissent. Data on the recruits, as well as the meeting and combining of these diverse groups of militant women in jail, with their common problems as outcasts, is discussed in Chapter Seven, Jailbirds: A Sisterhood of Struggle, 1917-1919. Chapter Eight, A Victory for Militancy, 1918-1920, describes a thoroughly changed and radicalized NWP, which is linked to other political "radicals." The militants' bold actions, serving to make them a radical feminist vanguard, help keep the suffrage issue alive and controversial. Together with the moderate suffragists' (NAWSA) lobbying efforts, NWP militancy brings the woman suffrage struggle to a successful end. Alice Paul has called the winning of suffrage a "triumph" for women rather than the "gift" from the Wilson government which so many history texts might have us think. The conclusion, Feminist Militancy, looks back at militancy's triumph, the breakdown of the suffrage sisterhood in the 20's, and then looks ahead to the possibilities of militancy for present-day feminism.

The woman suffrage campaign of the National Woman's Party developed in the context of a period featuring an upsurge in reform activity and spirited experimentation, followed by a war atmosphere which ushered in hysteria and suppression of civil liberties. Woman's Party suffragists' demonstrations in wartime led to accusations of sedition, arrests, beatings, and prison. As with MacKenzie's British militants, the feminist nature of their insistent, demanding protests led to even greater hostility. Many in the press and in Congress cried for harsh measures against the militant women, saying that only "their skirts" protected them. It may well be, however, that rather than protecting them, their "skirts" served to raise hackles even more, as their "unnatural," "unwomanly" actions were attacked, and they were called madwomen, Amazons and "iron-jawed angels."

---

[1] *Liberator* quote in *Suffragist*, March 2, 1918; *New York Times*, March 5, 1919, pp. 3, 10.

[2] Inez H. Irwin in *The Story of Alice Paul and the National Woman's Party*, (Fairfax, VA: Denlingers' Publishers, Ltd., 1964), p. 4, gives over 50,000. My study of NWP executive secretary reports shows 28,747 in July of 1917; 29,405 in March 1918 and 32,521 by March of 1919. There was probably much difficulty in keeping track as many women joined to demonstrate and others fell away in disapproval. On the NAWSA numbers, Florence Hilles to Mabel Vernon, May 29, 1917, Reel 42 of the NWP correspondence found on NWP Papers on microfilm, "The Suffrage Years, 1913-1920," Microfilming Corporation of American, 1981 edition. (Hereafter, NWPP)

[3] Campbell, *The 'Liberated Woman' of 1914* (UMI Research Press, 1977), pp. 41, 56, 98, 138.

[4] Scotts, *One Half the People* (Philadelphia: J.B. Lippincott, 1976), p. 164.

[5] William Chafe, *The American Woman: Her Changing Social, Economic and Political Roles, 1920-1970* (New York: Oxford University Press, 1972), pp. 15-16. In this description, they are grouped with NAWSA. Kraditor, *Ideas of the Woman Suffrage Movement* (New York: Doubleday and Co., 1965), p. 106; Flexner, *Century of Struggle: The Woman's Rights Movement in the United States* (Cambridge: Harvard University Press, 1959), pp. 237, 295-296; Buechler, *The Transformation of the Woman Suffrage Movement: The Case of Illinois, 1850-1920* (Rutgers University Press, 1986), pp. 51, 154, 163, 188.

[6] See DuBois, "Working Women, Class Relations, and Suffrage Militance: Harriot Stanton Blatch and the New York Woman Suffrage Movement, 1894-

1909," *Journal of American History,* June 1987; Buechler, *Transformation,* p. 189, Cott, "Feminist Politics in the 1920s: The National Woman's Party," *Journal of American History,* June 1984, p. 43. In her 1987 book, Cott says the NWP had women from both ends of the "economic spectrum," some attracted by labor agitation-type strategies and others who liked to "work from the top," p. 55, *The Grounding of Modern Feminism* (Yale University Press: 1987).

[7] Trecker, "The Suffrage Prisoners," *The American Scholar,* Summer 1972, p. 412. Also see Lunardini, *From Equal Suffrage to Equal Rights: Alice Paul and the National Woman's Party, 1910-1928* (New York: New York University Press, 1986), Chapters 2 and 3.

[8] On the "new woman" see Sherna Gluck, introduction to *From Parlor to Prison: Five American Suffragists Talk About Their Lives* (New York: Random House, 1976), pp. 15-26; June Sochen, *Her Story: A Woman's View of American History* (New York: Harcourt, Brace and World, 1967), p. 174. For another look, see James R. McGovern, "The American Woman's Pre-World War I Freedom in Manners and Morals," *Journal of American History,* September 1968.

[9] Cott, *Grounding,* pp. 4, 20. Also see Lunardini, *Equal Suffrage* or Meredith Snapp, "Defeat the Democrats: The Congressional Union for Woman Suffrage in Arizona, 1914 and 1916," *Journal of the West,* 1975, pp. 131-138.

[10] "The Woman Suffrage Movement in Great Britain," speech to NAWSA in *Annals of American Political Science,* Volume 35, May 1910 supplement.

[11] Irwin, *Paul and the NWP,* p. 12.

[12] See Mary Wollstonecraft, *A Vindication of the Rights of Woman* (New York: W.W. Norton, a 1967 reprint). Excerpted version appears in Alice Rossi, editor, *The Feminist Papers: From Adams to DeBeauvoir* (New York: Bantam Books, 1973), quote if on p. 67. Also see Eleanor Flexner's excellent biography, *Mary Wollstonecraft* (Baltimore: Penguin Books, 1972).

[13] Judith Sargent Murray, "On the Equality of the Sexes," *The Massachusetts Magazine,* March 1790, pp. 132-135, April 1790, pp. 223-226; Rossi, *Papers,* p. 12, note 13.

[14] Hazel Hunkins Hallinan, "A Talk to the Woman's Press Club, Washington, DC, August 23, 1977, transcribed by Angela Ward, Bancroft Library Oral History Project, University of California, p. 5; Virginia Arnold to Helena Hill Weed, July 24, 1917, Reel 46, NWPP.

[15] Amelia Fry, unpublished lecture to a non-violent association, Washington, DC, March 1, 1983.

[16] Judith Stiehm, *Non-Violent Power: Active and Passive Resistance in America* (Lexington, MA: D.C. Heath and Co., 1972), pp. 5, 9, 27.

[17] Richard B. Gregg, *The Power of Nonviolence* (New York: Schocken Books, 1966), pp. 44-51; 55-56.

[18] Mabel Vernon to Kathleen Paul, July 2, 1917. The policy of the NWP was always to send a copy of the *Suffragist* to critics. Reel 45, NWPP. It should be

noted that Alice Paul did go through the NWP papers and remove what she thought might be hurtful or offensive before they were microfilmed.

PART ONE

MILITANT STATE OF MIND

1912-1916

Chapter One

Strong-Minded Women: British-American Origins of Suffrage Militancy

Principle Not Policy, Justice Not Favors--Men, Their Rights and Nothing More: Women Their Rights and Nothing Less.

Motto of *The Revolution* 1868

If men will not give women rights--they will take them.

Emmeline Pankhurst
Washington, DC 1913

Suffrage militancy was a product of women's growing feelings of impatience, frustration and anger against male-run, male-centered government. Calls for women's revolution were not lightly made by militant feminist suffragists like the American Susan B. Anthony or the English Emmeline Pankhurst, and the strong, sometimes violent reaction of government to such threats is not surprising. Late 19th-early 20th century militant suffragists were strong-minded women whose feminism stressed male-female egalitarianism. These feminists focused on the importance of women developing strength and power, with the initial goal of winning political equality and joining the male, public sphere of government. Alice Paul, Lucy Burns and Anne Martin, women who helped found and lead the American militant suffrage campaign, came directly out of an American-British feminist suffrage tradition which defied traditions of sex-role limitations and assumptions of female weakness. The three American feminists, independent highly-educated professionals, became firm militants while experiencing first-hand the amenities of British police and British prisons. Paul, Burns and Martin brought back to America an impatient determination to get "Votes for Women" through passage of the Susan B. Anthony woman suffrage amendment to the Constitution.

Although National Woman's Party activists would reach as far back as Lysistrata to document early examples of "women's militance,"[1] it was the pioneer 19th century feminist Anthony who was the much revered "matron saint" of the militant movement. And it was the aggressive strategies she developed with Elizabeth Cady Stanton, along with the even more aggressive 20th century campaigns of British suffragists, which would provide blueprints for American feminist militants of the NWP between 1912 and 1920. Although Susan B. Anthony and Alice Paul were trying to achieve the goal of political equality for women in very different eras, they had many things in common: most importantly, they shared a feminist philosophy that demanded full equality for women and a belief that moral principles should be committed to action. Paul clearly idolized Anthony: in a 1972 interview in *Smithsonian*, she is pictured gazing reverently at a handsome bust of Anthony at NWP Headquarters in Washington.[2]

Both Paul and Anthony came from Quaker reformist families. They were taught the Quaker maxim that women were equal before God and were entitled, even obliged, to address social problems. Alice Paul was born in 1885 in the Quaker community of Moorestown, New Jersey, the eldest of four children. Her father was a very successful bank president, who died when Alice was quiteyoung. Her mother was reputedly a strong woman, a clerk of the Friends meeting. Paul's maternal grandfather had helped found the Quaker Swarthmore College, where Paul, like her mother before her, would be a student. Since William Penn's founding of Pennsylvania Quaker meetings that emphasized women's spiritual equality and strong leadership, (and interestingly, both Anthony and Paul claimed to be descendants of Penn) Quaker women had played a role in American reform out of proportion to their numbers. Paul would admire not only the Quaker Anthony, but also the remarkable Quaker reformer, Lucretia Mott. Alice Paul biographer Amelia Fry, emphasizes the lasting values of Paul's Hicksite Quaker background, especially the importance given a nonviolent life guided by an inward light, and the strong tradition of gender equality. Paul directly credited her Quaker background for her interest in woman suffrage and the "principle of equality of the sexes." She might also have pointed to it as the source of her highly developed sense of right and wrong. The impression given by Paul's accounts of her childhood is its intense serious-mindedness. There was no music and a great deal of reading, for fun, the arch-moralist, Dickens. In a speech to a group of Quakers in 1910, Paul chastised them for not being more involved in social problems. Following in the steps of Mott and Anthony, she insisted that women particularly, needed a cause. Any other life would be empty.[3]

Susan B. Anthony had first surfaced as a women's rights activist when she voiced her discontent with women's economic opportunities. At an 1853 teachers' meeting, much to the chagrin and disapproval of her colleagues, Anthony rose to advocate equal pay for women. As a single, self-supporting woman, Anthony was very much aware of the importance of securing women's economic independence. Unhappiness with teaching, virtually a woman's sole, respectable occupational opportunity in Anthony's day, turned her toward a career as full-time reformer for women's rights and abolition. Paul, 60 years later, showed the same impatience with the progressive era's version of woman's proper job, social work. Paul's generation of feminists would emphasize the need for women's economic independence more strongly than their 19th century counterparts.

Alice Paul
Figure 2

At age 16, Paul attended the coeducational Swarthmore, where she illustrated an enviable thirst for knowledge by starting with a major in biology "because I knew nothing about it." Through the influence of Professor Robert Brooks she switched. to political science and economics, which she would later practically apply to the "woman's" profession of social work. She received her B.A. in 1905, then did social settlement work in Italian and Jewish neighborhoods of New York City; she received a degree from the School of Philanthropy (now of Columbia) in 1906. In 1907 she earned an M.A. and then in 1912, a Ph.D. in sociology, at the University of Pennsylvania. She knew fairly early on she did not want to remain in the ranks of social workers, because she "did not think they changed anything."[4] Like her hero, Anthony, Paul concluded she would much rather become a full-time worker for women's independence and equality.

As professional feminist activists, Anthony and Paul would follow very similar paths; neither married and had families, both single-mindedly devoting their lives to the feminist cause. Both were intellectual, egalitarian, and highly moralistic reformers. One Anthony biographer called her "a passionate democrat," a woman who stamped her letters with "no just government can be formed without the consent of the governed." Anthony's feminism was the center of her moral reformism: "All the wrongs, arrogances and antagonisms of modern society grow out of this false condition of the relations between man and woman." As for Paul, she based her entire reform campaign in the context of "the great American struggle for democracy" and women's need for equality, her need for "a place of equal responsibility and equal power with men of the nation."[5] Both also concentrated on winning one goal at a time, firstly and most importantly for the two women, the right to vote. Neither woman was a spell-binding speaker, although both had brilliant minds and wrote very well. They were both inspirational leaders in spite of great personal reserve and surprising shyness. NWP organizer, Rebecca Hourwich Reyher, has described Alice Paul as "dedicated and narrow-minded. She believed in loyalty. She galvanized . . . and dramatized." Paul had a great political and tactical sense, with amazing attention to detail. The strong-willed Paul defied any but dramatic description: " 'Napoleon' . . . a genius with beautiful eyes, frail, a low voice . . . still, but with mental swiftness" . . . . "Well under 5'6", a slender, dark woman with a pale haggard face, and great earnest, child-like eyes that seem to seize you and hold you to her purpose despite your own desires and intentions."[6] Leadership ability was evident in both women, as was fortitude.

Susan B. Anthony exhibited great, unbending personal courage when she faced the knives and guns of anti-abolition mobs; Paul showed the same bravery when she was dragged and kicked by police on more than one occasion. Many feminists, both of the 19th and 20th centuries, particularly those who stressed women's "sameness" with men, believed that a whole, free woman had to develop herself to be strong physically. It also helped, of course, in confrontations with mobs and police. Anthony had insisted on wearing the comfortable, physically liberating bloomers. Paul, ill as a child, became a champion tennis player, as well as excelling at basketball and field hockey. Bright's disease, a debilitating kidney ailment, would plague Paul throughout the suffrage campaign, but she doggedly overcame it in the same way she did so many other obstacles.[7] Paul, like Anthony, was renowned for her motto of "no compromise"--Ida Husted Harper's comments about Anthony would fit both militants well: "Theoretically a non-resistant, she fights to the last ditch and never accepts defeat as final."[8] For Anthony, the right to vote embodied the whole question of woman's status, a "symbol of woman's emancipation and independence."[9] Anthony believed that her mission was to help women achieve that symbol of their equal American citizenship; any other feminist goal would have to wait. And this would be precisely how Alice Paul felt about suffrage, and then later, about the Equal Rights Amendment.

Paul and the NWP repeatedly used Susan B. Anthony as an example of heroic suffrage militancy and committed feminism. Ellen DuBois has argued that Anthony and Elizabeth Cady Stanton's demand for suffrage for women was an "important and radical" demand in the mid-19th century because it symbolized the entrance of women into the public sphere from her private, domestic one. The 1848 Seneca Falls convention's most controversial resolution by far, proved to be Stanton's proposal for woman suffrage.[10] Stanton, like Anthony beginning as an abolitionist reformer,[11] was the organizer and prime mover of the convention, and perhaps the most important, radical feminist theorist behind the woman's rights movement of the 19th century. (Although, as Nancy Cott has pointed out, they themselves did not use the term "feminist" yet, they clearly fit Cott's definition of feminist as opposing sex hierarchy, recognizing woman's socially constructed, limited roles and having gender group identity.)[12] Stanton firmly believed that "women should forget tender appeals to man's chivalry," but instead sing "hallelujas to single women, rebukes for spaniel wives, and reasonable denunciations for all flesh in male form."[13] The convention's "Declaration of Sentiments," in which Stanton utilized the language of the revolutionary 1776 Declaration of Independence, protested against the tyranny of men, who passed laws preventing woman from "occupying her proper station in society," maintained a sexual double standard, and branded women inferior. Alice Paul would later state that the 1848 Declaration contained a complete "equality program . . . for women in all fields of life."[14]

The issues of the women's rights program of 1848 became questions of public debate over the next few decades, and eventually the movement would split over the ever controversial suffrage issue. In 1861, in a move which suffragist Alice Paul would consciously *not* imitate, women's rights leaders Anthony and Stanton decided reluctantly to abandon their own struggle for women's rights and instead concentrate on the Union war effort and the great moral issue of slavery. To the women's dismay, when the war was over and the slaves freed, the 14th and 15th constitutional amendments specifically gave black "males" citizenship and the vote. The woman's suffrage movement split over whether or not the 15th amendment should be supported, in 1869. The American Woman's Suffrage Association

(AWSA), led by men and women abolitionists, worked for the passage of the 15th amendment and for Republican party support for woman's suffrage "later." AWSA would tirelessly, and usually futilely, fight, with little money and few workers, in state referendum after state referendum for the next 30 years. The National Woman's Suffrage Association (NWSA) led by Stanton and Anthony was formed in part, as a protest to the first. It was run by women, all the officers and a majority of the members were female, who were more radical, (especially the leaders) and would prove more militant, than AWSA members on a range of women's rights issues; but were primarily dedicated to gaining a national, constitutional amendment for suffrage that included women.[15] In fact, NWSA, as DuBois argues, was the first national feminist organization, and one which was dedicated to gaining for woman the right to "govern herself." One of Anthony's favorite speeches on the NWSA lecture circuit, "Woman Wants Bread, Not the Ballot," is a prime example of decidedly militant feminist rhetoric:

> Insurrectionary and revolutionary methods of righting wrongs, imaginary or real, are pardonable only in the enslaved and disfranchised. . . . Denied the ballot, the legitimate means with which to exert their influence, and as a rule, being lovers of peace, they have recourse to prayers and tears, those potent weapons of women and children, and, when they fail, must tamely submit to wrong or rise in rebellion against the powers that be.

The Stanton-edited *Revolution*, NWSA's aptly named newspaper, echoed Anthony's insistence on woman's strength: "'Woman conquers by her weakness.' Woman's weakness indeed! Woman's nonsense! Woman's weakness is despicable. . . . Every woman possesses the inherent right to the full and perfect control of her own person. . . . This is Revolution. . ."[16] With the Civil War over, Anthony insisted that another "form of slavery" had to be eliminated: "The present agitation rises from the demand of the soul of woman for the right to own and possess herself."[17] NWSA demanded an immediate woman suffrage amendment to the Constitution.

The political tactics of the Anthony/Stanton-led NWSA would later be cited by Woman's Party strategists as an American example of the party responsibility policy usually only associated with British suffrage militants. Throughout the 1870s Anthony and Stanton made countless journeys throughout the country, speaking and successfully gathering signatures on petitions for the amendment. They found many women enthusiastic, especially women in the West, whose states would be the first to grant women suffrage. And thus, in the 1914 and 1916 elections, the NWP could implement an aggressive policy of organizing western women voters to vote in a bloc against the Democrats. After achieving an expanded national power base, NWSA dealt in practical politics, working only for political parties that supported woman suffrage. Anthony declared suffrage a "strict party measure" in 1869; she campaigned for the pro-suffrage Republicans in 1872, the Populists in 1892, and always against any party "that ignore[d] her sex."[18]

NWSA did more than just use aggressive political rhetoric, they engaged in what might be called the first isolated acts of suffrage militancy. As noted, Anthony's radical activism gradually became focused on gaining the ballot, and unfortunately, this estranged her from Elizabeth Cady Stanton, who, by the early 1870s, thought that suffrage was no longer a particularly exciting issue and turned to other projects, such as her controversial critique of the church's oppression of women. Thus Anthony stood alone in 1872 when she was arrested voting for Grant in the presidential election. NWSA officer Matilda Joslyn Gage was virtually Anthony's only ally in challenging the law. Gage also tried to vote, in Syracuse, but was not allowed to actually cast a ballot. At Anthony's trial, when she was finally allowed to speak, she claimed that no one concerned with the trial was her "peer," but all, being men, were instead her "political sovereigns--the most noble woman being considered the inferior of the most ignoble man." Much like Anthony, Alice Paul would argue in 1917 that women could not be considered part of the judicial system, because women, as an unenfranchised class with no say in the law, were not subject to the court.[19] The court case against Susan B. Anthony's civil disobedience gained a great deal of public sympathy for suffrage, as would the 1917 trial of Paul.

Anthony's arrest and subsequent trial for attempting to vote was not the last militant action associated with NWSA. It was again Matilda Joslyn Gage who was threatened with arrest (illegal assembly, no proper license) at the 1876 NWSA Convention. Gage was probably the most purely "egalitarian" in her downplaying woman's "differences," of all 19th century political feminists. She argued that man, throughout history, had treated women as a "degraded beast of burden," and insisted that women "must be recognized as aggressive" in order to break that subordinate tradition. In 1890 she helped found the controversial Women's National Liberal Union, along with a group of woman workers, socialists and anarchists. Gage also, probably because of her radicalism, has been virtually left out of suffrage histories.[20] At the 1876 meeting, Gage spoke about woman's right and duty to "rebel against the tyranny of our present government." Undaunted by police threats to halt the meeting, Gage vowed to move the convention to the jail if they arrested her. The police left.

Later in the year, Gage and Anthony presented a Declaration of Rights to Senator Thomas Ferry, the presiding officer of the Philadelphia Fourth of July Centennial celebration. Refused time to speak, but given five seats in the audience, the NWSA women decided to simply walk on stage and presented the Declaration to Ferry, a suffrage advocate, who bowed and accepted it. The women departed, scattering leaflets of the Declaration as they went, and then repaired to a nearby Unitarian church where the "Declaration of 1876" was read to a crowded meeting. Written by Stanton, this declaration had changed focus somewhat from the one she had written in 1848, describing the "tyranny of government" instead of men.

Appropriately, and foreshadowing the methods of the NWP, the National Woman's Suffrage Association had taken the occasion of the celebration of American government to defiantly denounce woman's unequal status and her continued lack of political representation.[21]

The demonstration NWSA held in 1876 would not have been feasible by 1886. Women's rights activists found that beginning in the post-Civil War decade, America's reform zeal evaporated. Intense arguments for "equality" that were meaningful and acceptable to a relatively homogenous, stable population began to seem too threatening in a changing, rapidly industrializing nation. The days when a perfect society seemed possible grew remote. Arguments for women's rights based on white racism and elitism began to gain precedence. Women of the 1880s and early 90s who had not been part of the earlier 19th century egalitarian, perfectionist crusades often related differently to women's issues than the first, pioneering women reformers had. As more women attended college, worked outside the home, and joined a burgeoning number of woman's clubs, they began to have a sense of having a foothold in a man's world. To many women, NWSA's defiance seemed outdated.

By 1890, when NWSA and the New England-based AWSA merged to form the National American Woman Suffrage Association (NAWSA), it was clear that the old NWSA brand of aggressive feminism had no place in it. Most of the leadership of NWSA vehemently opposed the merger. Gage and Stanton fought Anthony on the move, and both became embittered with "Aunt Susan," seeing her as a traitor for deciding to join forces with the other younger and more conservative group. After the merger, Anthony concentrated all her considerable energies on suffrage, while her fellow radicals chose other women's issues, all the while criticizing Anthony for her narrowness. Similar accusations would plague Paul when she directed the NWP to focus on the ERA in the 1920s. And as in the 1920s, 1880s woman activists were far from militant. To Anthony's disappointment, most of NAWSA's membership, not only were not militant, but were not at all interested in pressing for an immediate federal amendment. They simply continued, as AWSA always had, the exhausting battle for woman suffrage on the state and local levels. In spite of their hundreds of campaigns, only four states passed woman's suffrage in the 1890s (Wyoming, Colorado, Utah and Idaho), and then no more until 1910 when Washington gave women the vote.[22] Although there was activity in the states between 1890 and 1910, even spirited revivals in some cases, virtually nothing was done for a federal suffrage amendment. NAWSA concentrated on working for state suffrage and with their moderate feminist philosophy and strategies, made the issue a fairly respectable one--a cause many women's clubs championed.

The feminism NAWSA espoused in the 1890s and early 1900s, put a ceiling on woman's aspirations to take on "male" roles or adopt "male" (aggressive) behavior, and thus differed quite sharply from the philosophy of earlier NWSA feminists as well as that of the future militant suffragists. All feminists of the period grappled with the sameness-difference issues as outlined by Nancy Cott, but there was a definite divergence between suffragists in philosophical emphasis as to feminist egalitarian radicalism, which created contrasting styles and strategies. Aileen Kraditor wrote that late 19th century suffragists had to decide whether or not women were indeed man's "equal." Had they remained strong and capable, or had they been rendered weak and incapable of self-rule, after years of patriarchal domination? Stanton had pointed to women's lack of educational and professional opportunities as necessarily limiting them, but sought ways to end sex discrimination. NAWSA suffragist leaders, unlike Stanton, used arguments that were not "egalitarian" but, as Kraditor called them, "expedient." They did not stress, as Stanton and Anthony had originally, the need of women, like all of humanity, for full equality. NAWSA suffragists argued for women's rights, but usually within proscribed, traditionally female roles. They tended to stress the non-controversial--that the vote would help wives and mothers to better educate themselves and their children. Their speakers were also eloquent about "elevated," "morally superior" women bringing much needed reforms to American life, particularly in areas like prohibition and child labor. Such arguments could lead directly to elitist and racist ones, which had also been used earlier by NWSA (especially by Stanton) that explained how the white woman was even more deserving of her "hour" than the Negro, and/or that white middle class women should vote before "foreigner" men did. Although women of NAWSA still, at various times, spoke of equality and the "spirit of the (1776) Revolution," for the most part they stressed sex differences which limited women: woman's moral sensibility, pacifism, mother-love, understanding and temperance.[23] This sort of philosophy made them what some historians would call "social" feminists or under Cott's definition, feminists who emphasized "difference." Their outlook could not be called "egalitarian," one which underlined woman's sameness and strength vis-a-vis man, nor was it a feminism which could lead to angry militancy against the government.

The NWP's feminist philosophy was more akin to that of the woman theorist who challenged the moderation of NWSA's woman reformers. In 1900 Charlotte Perkins Gilman argued, somewhat similarly to Stanton, that years of economic dependence had made women as a race, weak, but that "directed evolution" could alter women's lives. She reasoned that women needed the power of the vote to help them gain economic independence and rid themselves of their position as an underclass. The radical Gilman spoke at NAWSA meetings on numerous occasions, converting many women to the cause of suffrage, but she eventually clashed with NAWSA leaders over how much change should be brought to women's existing status as moral arbiter, wife and mother.[24] Gilman became an advisor of Alice Paul and the National Woman's Party, since their feminist philosophies were mutually attractive. The NWP would use both Stanton and Gilman's arguments, and would work, like the earliest 19th century women's rights advocates had, to "empower" women so that they might become at least men's political equals.

In 1913, when NAWSA asked Alice Paul and Lucy Burns to form a "Congressional Committee" to revitalize the drive for a federal amendment, they had no idea they were creating a group of suffrage militants who felt they had a moral mission, women who considered themselves engaged in the same sort of all-out women's rights struggle against male government as their mid-19th century forebears. When NWP organizer Sara Bard Field spoke at the 1920 dedication of the "suffrage pioneer" statues of Lucretia Mott, Stanton and Anthony, she said: "Mr. Speaker, I give you--Revolution." Describing the "blood-red memories" of the 19th century movement for "universal freedom," Field credited, as would many others, the revolutionary spirit of women like Susan B. Anthony as being the "propulsive force," the "dominant spirit," behind the eventual success of the woman suffrage campaign.[25] Anthony's influence upon the Woman's Party was considerable. She may accurately be called their matron saint. She was constantly featured on the cover and in articles in the NWP's publication, *The Suffragist*, and the party called their proposed suffrage amendment the "Susan B. Anthony Amendment," in spite of the fact that it was probably Stanton who drafted the original. Organizer Ethel Adamson nicely summed up the nature of the Woman's Party's feeling of connectedness to Anthony when she wrote: "She certainly was a militant in her day--Thank God we're her 'spiritual children.'"[26] For NWP leader Paul, Anthony and the 19th century's NWSA provided clear American examples of early suffrage militancy, and of egalitarian and highly moral, single-minded feminism, any trace of which had, by 1900, evaporated in the mild-mannered feminism of NAWSA.

Suffrage militancy re-emerged, not in NAWSA, but in the British Women's Social and Political Union. In 1899, the elderly Susan B. Anthony was in London for an International Council of Women. There she met both the archparagon of respectability, Queen Victoria, and the infamous feminist revolutionary, Emmeline Pankhurst. It was five years later, in 1904, on another visit to England, just two years before her death, that Anthony apparently moved Emmeline Pankhurst's daughter Christabel (perhaps the most extreme militant suffragist ever) so much, that she resolved to stage a rebellion for woman's suffrage. Realizing that the aging woman's rights pioneer would die without winning her battle for the franchise, Pankhurst vowed to use "deeds, not words" in a fierce fight to win votes for women.[27] Christabel Pankhurst was inspired by an American suffrage militant, and so too, would American women activists be profoundly affected by the Pankhurst model of supreme defiance.

American suffrage militants identified with the militant Susan B. Anthony, but many would also have very direct connections with the Pankhurst women's revolution in England, particularly NWP leaders Alice Paul, Lucy Burns, and Anne Martin. All three were enthusiastic about the dramatic British militants soon after meeting them. At her first suffrage meeting, Burns was very impressed by the

British militants' "moral ardor, optimism and buoyancy of spirit."[28] Anne Martin reportedly wanted to join the WSPU because it was her "last chance to take part in a movement for the enfranchising of half the English race." Alice Paul found Christabel Pankhurst an "absolutely wonderful speaker . . . a quite entrancing and delightful person." When she first heard Pankhurst speak, Paul particularly admired her for going on when the students attending the lecture tried to shout her down. "When I saw this outbreak of hostility, I thought, 'That's one group now I want to throw in all the strength I can give to help'. . . . [I]f you feel some group that's your group is the underdog, you want to help."[29] Lucy Burns had been accurate in describing the Women's Social and Political Union spirit as one of "moral ardor"--WSPU suffragists saw the rights of women as a distinctively moral and just cause; their feminism, (like Anthony's) was predicated upon strength, action, and complete autonomy for women. A 1914 WSPU fund-raising letter described their purpose as "a great crusade against a hateful and degrading moral system, the fruits of which are prostitution, disease and death."[30] This bold, romantic, and highly moralistic crusade was very appealing to American feminists like Burns, Martin and Paul, all of whom could identify with a movement which sought to "sweep away" everything that "enslaved women."[31]

NWP co-founder Lucy Burns always identified more closely with the WSPU than Paul, both because of her longer association, and her taste for the sort of romantic adventure being a WSPU fighter entailed. The Irish Catholic Burns was a very warm and outgoing woman. She was personally fearless and courageous, pursuing an ideal appropriate to a "new woman" heroine. Alice Paul insisted that Burns was "extremely courageous, a thousand times more courageous than I was. I was the timid type and she was just naturally valiant."[32] It is true that Burns was described by those who knew her in invariably the most glowing terms: "Brilliant . . . the spirit of a revolutionist" . . . "the very symbol of woman in revolt . . . glorious and abundant red hair . . . strong and vital body . . . [She] yearned to play, to read, to be luxuriously indolent." . . . "tall--rounded and muscular . . . blue-eyed and fresh-complexioned; dimpled . . . enormous brilliant red hair . . . [She] speaks and writes with eloquence and elegance."[33] With such a glowing personality, Burns stood in strong contrast to the more somber Paul.

The Catholic Lucy Burns had a very close and devoted relationship with her family. She would on numerous occasions return home to see to their concerns during a suffrage campaign. Like Paul, Burns came from a family which was comfortably well-off. She was born in Brooklyn in 1879 to upper middle class parents. Her father was, like Paul's, a bank president and she, the fourth of eight children, proved an enigma to him with her great desire for study. Sidney Bland, Burns' biographer, has underlined the importance of Burns' early education at Brooklyn Packer Institute, especially the interests she developed there in English classicism, in writing, and in religiously passionate, moral discipline. She also developed her body there. Burns, called a "physical specimen" by her friends, enjoyed calisthenics and cycling, and both coached and played basketball.[34] There appeared in Burns another clear connection between feminists' perception of mental, moral and physical strength.

As a "new" woman of the 20th century, Burns still faced, as did Paul, limited opportunities for applying her talents and abilities. The accepted choices were limited to "women's" areas of endeavor--for Burns, teaching--and she would, again like Paul, feel immense frustration with her chosen career. After receiving a B.A. in English in 1902 from Vassar, Burns studied etymology at Yale. She then taught English at Brooklyn's Erasmus High School, soon feeling bored and restless. Further study in Bonn and Berlin (1906-1909) left Burns still unsatisfied: "I felt wrapped in inpenetrable silence."[35] It was not until she arrived in London that she found the cause to end her silence and release her energies and moral fervor: the Pankhursts' Women's Social and Political Union.

At least one other important future NWP leader, Anne Martin, was baptized into suffrage militancy on the streets of London with the WSPU. Martin was born in Empire City, Nevada, in 1875, like Burns having an Irish banker father, and hers soon to be state senator. She was a favored and privileged child whose family believed her education as important as their sons'. But when her father died, she was "barred from family councils," and she later claimed that at that point "feminist iron" entered her soul. Like her colleagues Paul and Burns, Martin was very well educated, receiving a B.A. and M.A. in history (1896 and 1897) at Stanford, teaching history at the University of Nevada, and then studying art in New York City and London (1899-1901). Anne Martin enjoyed art and made efforts at writing, but was not happy with either endeavor. She showed the same discontent with her seemingly unrewarding life as had the other two Americans, writing: "I am necessary to no useful work in the world . . . . and until I can bring my life into vital connection with some work that is worthwhile, my existence is worthless . . . and a burden to myself."[36] While visiting her friend Lou Henry in London, probably in 1907, (the exact date is uncertain) Martin discovered "worthwhile work" with WSPU.

The British woman's suffrage movement had influenced and been influenced by the American movement. By 1848 England had its first association for the female franchise, in Sheffield, the same year as the Seneca Falls Conference in the United States.[37] The cause was strengthened by the radically egalitarian feminist *Subjection of Woman* (1869), written by John Stuart Mill, a book widely read in America. In fact, Stanton and Anthony sold copies at NWSA conventions. Mill argued that "the principle which regulates the existing social relations between the two sexes . . . is wrong in itself . . . [and] it ought to be replaced by a principle of perfect equality, admitting no power or privilege on the one side, nor disability on the other."[38] Woman suffrage soon became a mass movement which paralleled the American experience. In 1865 Lydia Becker had formed a Woman Suffrage Society in Manchester (joined, significantly, by Richard Pankhurst); and at the end of the 19th century, women were still lobbying for votes under the auspices of centralized suffrage societies like the National Union of Woman Suffrage Societies

(NUWSS). As in America, the British woman's movement had split over whether to pursue "side" issues like prostitution and marriage laws, or to concentrate on suffrage. Suffrage was the choice of most feminists, but the country's, and the government's, interest in such a reform was nonexistent by the 1890s.[39] And then the English produced a wide-spread militant suffrage movement, one which would prove to be shockingly different from the staid "constitutionalists" of the NUWSS.

The links forged between the WSPU and the NWP have been, to this point, underestimated. The most important aspect of the British struggle embraced by American militants in terms of feminist philosophy, was their attitude of complete defiance, their determination to *force* the government to act on women's rights. The British militants of the WSPU had become tired of waiting for political rights, but their rebellion symbolized a great deal more than that. The Pankhursts were not feminists who stressed woman's differing, gentler nature. The Pankhurst revolution sought to smash the rigid Victorian stereotypical image of separate male and female spheres and prove to the world that women were every bit as tough as men, and infinitely their moral superiors.[40] WSPU feminists would show their strength by resisting the government and its man-made laws, in order to "change the evil" done against women: to do something about "maimed children, 'sweated' women and white slavery." English militants insisted that "tradition" had shown them they would have to "suffer and die in order to put things right."[41] In *The Great Scourge and How to End It,* Christabel Pankhurst argued that women needed to persevere in the battle to establish respect for women, end legal and sex discrimination, strengthen women's economic position, and cleanse and purify sexual standards by curbing men's sexual excesses against women.[42] The Pankhurst movement was a movement for woman suffrage, but--at its most militant--was a highly moralistic mission, a battle of Good (woman) versus Evil (man). Such a radical stance against male dominance, which would not be nearly as evident in American militants, would be met with a good measure of authorized official violence against WSPU demonstrators. The WSPU often emphasized woman's equal (to men's) pluck and courage, differing only in her greater desire (than men's) for peace. British militants, and this would be close to American militant attitudes at the peak of their militancy, would be willing to undergo martyrdom for a just cause, but never to harm others, certainly never to take human life.

NWP militants were inspired by the WSPU's feminist moralism, but also borrowed their militant tactics. The major strategist of the WSPU suffrage campaign, the woman at the helm, was Emmeline Pankhurst. She had been deeply influenced by the radical reformism of her husband Richard. Both approved of taking drastic and militant measures to move the government, admiring both the agricultural workers' "burning of hay ricks" to achieve the franchise in 1884, and the Irishman Parnell's policy of "obstructing the government," in order to wear it out and force its surrender on the issue of Irish Home Rule.[43] Emmeline Pankhurst formed a Woman's Franchise League in 1887 (one of its first members was the daughter of Elizabeth Cady Stanton, Harriot Stanton Blatch, then living in England) in order to create "new ways to do woman suffrage." The Franchise League's first project was to hold outdoor meetings in Manchester to reach woman workers and poor women, their plight underlining the need for suffrage, according to Pankhurst. In 1900 she joined the new Independent Labour party, but by 1903, had grown impatient with Labour's unenthusiastic support for women's issues, and with a group of Labour women, formed the Women's Social and Political Union.[44]

The WSPU political strategy, which later would be copied by Burns and Paul to use against the Democrats, was centered in daring militancy. Uniting women who were "prepared to fight for themselves finally," the WSPU put their "suffrage army in the field" and concentrated on winning suffrage from a Liberal Party government which had been obdurate on the question. Demanding to know what Parliamentary Liberal members would actually *do*, "friendly" or not, led to the 1905 arrest of Christabel Pankhurst and Annie Kenney. Since the Liberals were the party "responsible" for not passing woman suffrage, the WSPU would work against and heckle all Liberals to try to force them to make suffrage a government measure (the only way a bill had a chance of success). To this end, they held banners at speeches, unmercifully heckled by-election candidates (like Winston Churchill)[45] and in 1906, descended en masse upon the House of Commons, where the angry women were denied entrance. In an episode foreshadowing the NWP in 1917, Emmeline Pankhurst remembered this moment as the true beginning of their militancy: "[The Women] were awake at last."[46] They had become willing to resist authority.

The years between 1906 and 1909 would be marked with further WSPU protest and resistance, as the Liberal government, very like the Wilson government later, continued to refuse to deal seriously with the women's demands. And, also as in America, the women's militant tactics grew increasingly defiant accordingly. When jailed, the militants remonstrated against their harsh prison treatment--with what historian David Mitchell has called its "overtones of sexual brutality"--and (exactly as Lucy Burns and the New York socialist prisoners would in 1917 in America) demanded political prisoner status. In November of 1906, public outrage finally forced Home Secretary Herbert Gladstone to set free "the suffragettes," but police still regularly charged suffrage deputations. The women were usually tried as "street brawlers"; Emmeline Pankhurst, like Alice Paul later as the "mastermind," was placed in solitary confinement. Militancy's purpose was to gain public attention and support, and in June of 1908, proving its effectiveness, the WSPU organized a suffrage demonstration in Hyde Park, 300,000 strong.[47] In 1909, with the government still unmoved even by mass demonstrations, and after 300 women had been arrested and violently treated, two WSPU women threw stones through Prime Minister Herbert Asquith's windows (stone throwing being a long-standing British political custom indicating displeasure with authorities). Although the first window-breaking was not authorized by WSPU leadership, the strategy was quickly adopted, as was (Miss) Wallace Dunlop's use of a hunger strike to gain political prisoner status. For reasons which will become apparent, the NWP would not quite reach the stage of militant action used in Britain, but as in Stiehm's description of civil disobedience, they would feel a comparable level of desperation.

Christabel Pankhurst explained that for British woman suffragists denied their right of petition, the "only thing left" was "violence." Only "stones could get into meetings" and only hunger strikes in prison, in the end, were left as weapons. The WSPU always distinguished, however, between "male" violence--destroying lives (and women's health and well-being)--and their "violence" for woman's suffrage, which destroyed only property.[48] To many historians, the Pankhurst violence seems terrifyingly drastic, quite possibly because they *were* women, many of them upper class, coming out of a Victorian decorum into a smashing, struggling, aggressive female revolt. By 1909 the Pankhurst-led WSPU had established its reputation as an organization which was clearly militant philosophically and strategically, and dedicated to winning political rights for women by "deeds, not words."

This was the movement which looked very appealing to three restless American college women working and studying in London in 1909. When Alice Paul first met Lucy Burns at the policeman's billiard room at Cannon Row Station, she had noticed her because she wore a little American flag in her lapel. By then Burns had already served the WSPU well, receiving a special medal of valor for her two 1909 prison hunger strikes. Although Burns later admitted fear of the ordeal of forced feeding, she had carried on the work, going to prison for offenses which included slapping a police officer, throwing ink bottles, and breaking police station windows.[!][49] Paul's first participation in WSPU activities was to march in an enormous parade in 1908, which was addressed by Emmeline Pethick-Lawrence, first lieutenant of the Pankhursts, who "thrilled [Paul] beyond words." Thus inspired, Paul, too, felt compelled to become a member of the WSPU and was "thrilled and extremely happy to be part of it." At first she sold *Votes for Women,* attended meetings, and did a bit of street corner speaking; but in 1909, as she was about to go home, the WSPU asked her to join one of its innumerable deputations to Prime Minister Asquith led by Mrs. Pankhurst--since there was a definite risk of arrest, it was decidedly the beginning of militancy for Paul. She remembered "hesitating the longest time and writing the letter [accepting the WSPU summons] and not being able to get enough courage to post it."[50] Her arrest for taking part in the deputation took her to Cannon Row and Lucy Burns.

The ultra-virtuous mission of the Pankhurst struggle appealed to the highly moral feminist Alice Paul, just as its danger and glory attracted the romantic warrior tendencies in Lucy Burns. The series of adventures that Paul and Burns took part in during their terms with the British suffrage militants were of crucial importance: they would inspire similar tactics in their leadership of American suffrage militancy; and philosophically, the severe punishments they underwent for those adventures made them angry and committed feminist militants. In Glasgow at St. Andrew's Hall, on August 19, 1909, Paul hid herself on a roof the entire night in a drenching rainstorm, in order to have a vantage point for interrupting Lord Crewe's speech with a claim for women's rights. At 6:00 in the morning a workman discovered her hiding place, but she pleaded with him not to tell anyone and he obliged. Unfortunately, a second workman (who would apologize to her later, not knowing her purpose at the time) informed the police. "She was in a woefully chilled and drenched condition. . . . Her enterprise, she admitted had been a daring and dangerous one, but she also expressed great regret that her attempt to bring the claims of the women before Lord Crewe had failed."[51] Later that day, Paul returned to the scene, this time with Lucy Burns, Adela Pankhurst (the youngest Pankhurst daughter), and Margaret Smith. Pankhurst addressed the gathering crowd, urging the men to help them gain entrance to the hall where Crewe spoke.

> Miss Pankhurst, Miss Paul and Miss Burns then got out of the waggonette. They each carried a banner aloft, and amid loud hooting and cheering they made a rush for the entrance of the hall at Granville Street, a large crowd following close behind them.[52]

The crowd was very sympathetic to the suffragists and was more than willing to join in the melée with the police which followed, taking place as Smith and Pankhurst tried various entrances to the hall. The tall, fiery Irish-American, "Lucy Burns, 30 years of age, was charged with breach of the peace and assaulting a constable"; and the small, fragile-looking Quaker, "Alice Paul, 24 years of age, was charged with a breach of the peace and with assaulting two [!] constables on Granville Street by striking them on the face with her hand."[53]

Paul and Burns undertook numerous exploits in Scotland and England after this, sometimes accompanied by Emmeline Pankhurst and her woman chauffeur, interrupting such notables as Lloyd George, Churchill, Sir Edward Grey and the Lord Mayor of London. Paul remembered one incident, on November 9, 1909, when she hid in a hall dressed as a charwoman in order to interrupt a meeting addressed by the London Mayor. The police looked for her hiding place; one even touched her hair in his search, but did not find her. Pankhurst herself visited Paul in jail after the arrest and forcible feeding meted out for that particular offense. Paul and Burns were repeatedly arrested (especially Burns), and when they followed the WSPU policy of the hunger strike, were forcibly fed--an experience so horrible neither wanted to discuss it afterward. The hearty Burns remained as a paid WSPU organizer until 1912, but Paul, much the worse for wear, returned home at the end of 1909.[54]

The important thing here is that after working with the British militants and experiencing harsh (male) official government repression, Burns and Paul were irrevocably radicalized and firmly militant. Following the pattern described in Stiehm's study of activists engaged in civil disobedience, after being pushed to a certain point, they became determined to resist authority. The Americans were absolutely incredulous and incensed that women who merely wanted the vote could be treated so harshly. Paul always remembered being dragged through the streets of Berwick-on-Tweed (after interrupting Foreign Minister Grey) and feeling "blazingly angry": "[T]o me it was shocking that a government of men could look with such extreme contempt on a movement that was asking nothing except such a simple little thing as the right to vote."[55] The misery of British prisons described by Lucy Burns in painstaking detail is worth citing at length:

> We remained quite still when ordered to undress, and when they told us to proceed to our cells we locked arms and stood with our backs to the wall. The governor blew his whistle and a great crowd of wardresses appeared, falling upon us, forcing us apart and dragging us towards the cells. I think I had twelve wardresses for my share. In the cell they fairly ripped the clothing from my back, forcing on me one coarse cotton garment and throwing others on the bed for me to put on myself. Left alone exhausted by the dreadful experience I lay for a time gasping and shivering on the floor. By and by a wardress came to the door and threw me a blanket. This I wrapped around me, for I was chilled to the bone by this time. The single cotton garment and the rough blanket were all the clothes I wore during my stay in prison. Most of the prisoners refused everything but the blanket. According to agreement we all broke our windows and were immediately dragged off to punishment cells. There we hunger struck, and after enduring great misery for nearly a week, we were one by one released.[56]

Lucy Burns became a whole-hearted militant after experiencing episodes like this.

Burns and Paul did not work with her in the WSPU, but westerner Anne Martin was also experiencing the trials of joining Pankhurst deputations and with the same radicalizing of attitude. By 1910 she had qualified as a WSPU speaker and described one speech in London in 1911 as given amidst "the hawthorn trees in bloom in May in Hyde Park" and a "swirling mob" fronting the House of Commons. Martin liked the vigorous actions of the Pankhursts, but vigorous understated the WSPU melée Martin participated in on November 18, 1910: "Black Friday." The WSPU had called a truce in the spring of 1910, but the government killed the Conciliation Bill for woman suffrage yet again, and Martin volunteered for the resulting November 18 "rush" on Commons. The bobbies, supervised by Home Secretary Winston Churchill, were ready. "[T]hey laid their hands on the women and literally threw them from one man to another."[57] Martin was in the third row of twelve: "Police used bodies, elbows, and fists with great effect; great rough powerful men, they tossed us all, young and old, from one to the other, hurled, kicked and knocked many down."[58] (After this, Martin wore her fencing armor to deputations.) Martin was soon hauled off by two constables, the only American arrested. She was bailed out by Richard Pethick-Lawrence, though her good friend Lou Henry's husband, Herbert Hoover, had been waiting hours to do so. The charges against her were dismissed. She was still working with the WSPU when they started destroying property in 1911--breaking windows and burning buildings on a regular basis--although she left soon after. Like her NWP colleagues-to-be, undeniably changed by confrontations with authorities in England, Martin was also impressed by the "effectiveness" of militant action. An "ardent feminist" after England, Martin would be more than ready to join the militant movement in the United States.[59]

The Americans' feminist militancy was forged in their British experience and they were determined to bring a few Pankhurst weapons--if not the entire arsenal--back for use in the American suffrage movement. In 1913, Paul wrote Ada Wright, a friend in England: "Please let the English women of the W.S.P.U. know how much our hearts are with them. I am indeed proud to have had even the slightest connection with them" and "I feel the deepest sympathy for militancy, in all its latest phases, and am so glad that you are still working in that line."[60] It should be noted that its "latest phases" consisted of all-out war with the British government, or what the WSPU called "guerilla militancy"--slashing railway cushions and works of art, burning letterboxes and golf courses, and cutting telephone lines. In that spirit of extreme measures, Emily Davison, without the WSPU knowing her plans, threw herself in front of the King's horse at the Derby and was killed. The Pankhursts had decided with "guerilla militancy" that "violence is the only argument [the government] understand."[61] Lucy Burns and Alice Paul would not advocate the Pankhurst brand of "violent" militancy for application in the American suffrage movement, feeling it not necessary, but they did not disapprove its use in England. They most definitely did bring to America, the aggressive and determined stance behind it.

There can be no doubt that the repercussions of the Pankhurst militant revolution were felt in America. Many future American suffrage militants besides those discussed above, acquired their feminist moral outrage by being involved in the WSPU; some only selling *Votes for Women* papers on street corners, or contributing money to the "Cause," while enthusiastically following WSPU exploits at home.[62] Additionally, long before Paul and Burns founded the Woman's Party, some of the milder aspects of the British militant method were tried in the United States. In New York, in 1907, Harriot Stanton Blatch, who years earlier had worked with Emmeline Pankhurst in the Woman's Franchise League, formed the Equality League of Self Supporting Women, later called the Women's Political Union (WPU). It was formed, said Blatch, in order to "introduce new methods of propaganda and to guide the suffrage ship into political channels."[63] Like Pankhurst, Blatch began by recruiting and forming connections with working women and organizations such as the Women's Trade Union League. She also courted prominent New York women to add funds and respectability to the cause of New York State suffrage. In the first year, the WPU acquired 18,000 members. Utilizing dramatic tactics, the WPU did open-air speaking (for which they were arrested, but not jailed), debated from horseback and motorboat, organized mammoth parades (in WSPU purple, white and green), held mass meetings, and were the first in America to use the "voiceless speech" (turning a card with a message) carried by silent sentinels.[64] In their own way, even a few women of NAWSA used WSPU-like tactics in Massachusetts in 1910-1911. For example, the Boston Equal Suffrage Association for Good Government, led by Maud Wood Park, held open-air meetings. One of their members, Margaret Foley of the WTUL, who had served with the Pankhursts, even took it upon herself to heckle Republican candidates.[65] Such ventures, especially those of Blatch's WPU, provide scattered examples of Pankhurst-inspired militant tactics in America before the formation of the Woman's Party in 1912.

More important was the American public's awareness (and apprehension) of suffrage militancy, Pankhurst-style, preceding Woman's Party activism. The WPU leadership, by sponsoring lecture tours, introduced the Pankhursts and other WSPU leaders directly to the American people and press--and the press thereafter had comprehensive coverage of whatever the WSPU was doing. British militants Mrs. Cobden Sanderson and Lady Ethel Snowden were guests of the WPU in 1907 and 1908 respectively; in fact, Snowden was barred from speaking at Vassar by its President James M. Taylor ("too dangerous").[66] Emmeline Pankhurst addressed over 3,000 people at Carnegie Hall in 1909, explaining WSPU militancy by saying that people must fight for their liberties, and that "by going to prison we will eventually win over all England."[67] It was also at that meeting that Pankhurst asked for the American government's intervention for Alice Paul, who was serving a month's hard labor at the time. Visiting "suffragettes" would inspire thousands of American women. As Rheta Childe Dorr, writer and future NWP *Suffragist* editor said, the English suffragists with their tales of arrest, roused a "feeling that the suffrage was a thing to fight for, suffer for, even to die for."[68]

The response to the highly visible English militants could be hostile as well as sympathetic, however, and negative public sentiment would strongly color the way the American militant Woman's Party would be perceived. When Emmeline Pankhurst came to the United States in October 1913, invited by the WPU and Paul and Burns' new Congressional Union, (despite rumors she might be excluded as an "undesirable alien") her visit was a press field day and indicated the sort of emotion she could excite. When Pankhurst arrived in New York, she was "barred out" and detained at Ellis Island. The authorities seemed particularly concerned about whether she was "bringing her tactics here," to which she replied she was not. Lawyers were secured by the wealthy Alva Belmont and by Alice Paul, and after two and a half days, President Wilson ordered the Commissioner of Immigration to release her.[69] New York City Police Commissioner, Frank Waldo, when asked what he would do if faced with arresting "the militant Emmeline Pankhurst," said: "She will be treated exactly like anybody else that preaches riot, or arson, or violence." A *New York Times* article quote a "Sheriff Harburger" as adding: "She's classed with dynamiters, arsonists, seditionists, silly fulminators, nihilistic flourishers and mannish Amazons."[70] The militant Pankhursts may have been admired, feared, or despised; but they were very well known. Any group identifying itself with them would inherit the emotions associated with them.

As will be seen, Burns and Paul's Woman's Party would strongly identify with the British militants well after founding their own organization, and did look to the example and "inspiration" they provided. They used the precedents of militant suffragist policy they set, but, just as importantly, the NWP shared the WSPU attitude of angry defiance, the same sort of rebelliousness which appeared in the aggressive 19th century NWSA. Woman's Party feminists would also share specific WSPU goals of gaining respect for women in society, changing laws regarding women, and, especially, working toward economic independence. They would differ philosophically in that the British WSPU (especially by the end) tended to argue in terms of "justice" for certain sorts of women, whereas the Americans ordinarily stressed equality and opportunity for all women.[71] The clearest element shared by British and American feminist militants would be the importance of women "taking" what they were entitled to, literally fighting against injustice while showing woman's strengths in the process. And, as in America, British militancy escalated in the face of British government inaction and/or violent suppression. One of the favorite slogans of the NWP, which had also appeared frequently in the WSPU's *Suffragette*, was "Who Would be Free, Themselves Must Strike the Blow."[72]

The "blows struck" in America would have clear similarity to those landed in Britain, but only up to a point. The party responsibility and pressure on government policy, would be one of the most important strategies taken from the WSPU, and Blatch's WPU; but the NWP would also imitate their parades, street meetings, pamphlet distribution, sidewalk chalking, banner holding and dropping, "heckling" candidates, suffrage colors green, white and purple (but the NWP changed green to gold), organizing tactics, and using "silent sentinels." When the NWP reached the climax of militancy they would also hunger strike to gain political prisoner status.[73] There would be no "guerilla" militancy, however.

When Paul and Burns began their version of suffrage militancy, they repeatedly insisted that the Pankhurst extreme and "violent" militancy would never be necessary in the United States: "British statesmen jeer and insult women, but American statesmen don't, so American women don't need to be militant." Paul argued in 1913 that "even Mrs. Pankhurst does not believe in militancy for the United States on account of the unusual generosity of American men toward women."[74] The NWP's Mary Winsor, in her survey for the American Academy of Political and Social Science, reported that Britain had an entirely different political situation for women's suffrage than the United States. The public atmosphere, the tone of government, and the man in the street were all "more violent" toward women in England than in America, where men were much more "generous."[75] When Paul and Burns started the NWP, they had to *revive* suffrage as an issue, overcoming indifference and apathy rather than the outright hostility the British suffragists confronted. As Rebecca West has written: "[T]here is nothing that kills an agitation like having everybody admit that it is fundamentally right. . . . [The strategy must be more] to revive the followers than confound the enemy.[76] Such were the sentiments of Burns and Paul. It was not that the American militants would confront no hostility from the American public and government. They would, but it would not be widespread and intense until after America entered World War I, when the Woman's Party suffragists were identified as anti-government troublemakers. Still, the situation would never become quite as extreme as it was in England. Perhaps because the British had a more rigid class and sex role structure, a structure undergoing strain and change in the decade before World War I, there was even greater resistance than in America, to women so obviously and violently trying to cast off their roles. American women's "place" was a bit freer and more varied than Englishwomen's, becoming even more so as the "progressive" era created further opportunities for women to be involved in reform. The NWP would begin as a progressive, political organization, but insofar as it was identified with the WSPU, it would be, even initially, perceived as being as potentially dangerous as the Pankhursts.[77]

When asked in 1972 if she credited Emmeline Pankhurst with her "militant" training, Alice Paul replied that that was not the way it was.

> We were just going in and doing the simplest little things that we were asked to do. . . . I had, of course, a great veneration and admiration for Mrs. Pankhurst, but I wouldn't say that I was very much trained by her. What happened was that when Lucy Burns and I came back, having both been imprisoned in England, we were invited to take part in the campaign over here; otherwise nobody would have ever paid any attention to us.[78]

Alice Paul, Anne Martin and Lucy Burns would often express their "veneration" for the Pankhursts. Anne Martin, in a 1922 essay scornful of American women who were still "drudges," credited bold British women for creating a league to elect women to Parliament, "just as Englishwomen gave us that the final spur that won suffrage . . . ." Paul wrote Emmeline Pethick Lawrence in 1913 how she remembered "with the greatest happiness my years with the W.S.P.U., and think constantly of all of you, who were such an inspiration to us in that movement."[79] When Paul, a graduate student at the University of Pennsylvania, participated in open-air meetings with a group of suffragists in Philadelphia in 1911, the women all privately agreed to resist police arrest, a tactic which came naturally to Paul, recently back from an English prison.[80] Burns, who would (more than Paul actually) remain an ever-constant supporter of the WSPU, thought British women would gain the vote well before "sleepy Americans" because they were part of such a "go-ahead country."[81] And in 1914 she wrote Lady Constance Lytton that the Woman's Party should "be linked more closely than they are to the movement in

England, where the spirit of suffrage workers is so ardent and pure."[82] For Burns, the romance of the Pankhurst adventure, its burning mission, remained a continual source of feminist inspiration.

Emmeline Pankhurst, speaking in Washington for the new militant American suffrage group in November 1913, affirmed the close connection between American and British militancy. Alice Paul told the audience that some of them knew Pankhurst only from "distorted accounts in the daily papers," but would go away "with hearty sympathy [for her]--like mine."[83] Pankhurst began her address by voicing her pride in Alice Paul and Lucy Burns, saying: "In a way, they are my children." She noted first that they had acquired skills like speaking and organizing, from the WSPU. But much more significantly, they had learned the reasons why women rebel and the vital lesson that "if men will not give women rights--they will take them."[84] Suffrage militant Susan B. Anthony helped inspire the British Pankhurst rebellion, and they would, in turn, provide a training ground for American suffragists in their own pursuit of political power. Alice Paul and Lucy Burns would bring the lessons in power politics and militant feminism to their attempts to revive the drive for the progressive reform of woman suffrage.

---

[1] NWP's journal *The Suffragist,* May 24, 1919, p. 9

[2] Lynne Cheney, "How Alice Paul Became the Most Militant Feminist of Them All," *Smithsonian,* Volume 3, 1972, p. 94. Susan B. Anthony is the only pioneer feminist mentioned in Caroline Katzenstein's (NWP officer) work on suffrage -- as one who tested the 14th amendment guaranteeing equal citizenship rights. Katzenstein, *Lifting the Curtain: The State and National Woman Suffrage Campaigns in Pennsylvania As I Saw Them* (Philadelphia: Dorrance and Co., 1955).

[3] Gallagher, Paul interview, pp. 17-18; Katharine Anthony (no relation), *Susan B. Anthony,* p. 18. Amelia Fry, interview with Alice Paul in 1972-73, "Woman Suffrage and the Equal Rights Amendment," Bancroft Library Suffragists Oral History Project, University of California at Berkeley, pp. ix, 11-12. On Penn and women see Linda Ford, "William Penn's Views on Women: Subjects of Friendship," *Quaker History,* Fall 1984; on Paul and Quakerism, Amelia Fry, "The Divine Discontent: Alice Paul and Militancy in the Suffrage Campaign," paper given at Berkshire Conference, Vassar College, June 18, 1981. Paul's speech to the Quakers in *Friends Intelligencer,* July 23, 1910, "The Church and Social Problems," p. 514. She also informed them their lack of involvement in social problems explained why "workers" were "turned off" by the church.

[4] Katharine Anthony, *Susan B. Anthony,* pp. vi-vii; Fry, Paul interview, pp. 17-19, 26. Her dissertation was on the legal status of women in Pennsylvania.

[5] On Anthony: Katharine Anthony, *Susan B. Anthony,* p. vi; Rheta Childe Dorr, *Susan B. Anthony* , 1928 rpt., (New York: Arno Press, 1970) pp. 292, 143. On Paul: NWP Press Release, November 17, 1917 and March 21, 1920, Reels 91 and

92 respectively, in the National Woman's Party Papers, Microfilming Corporation of America, Sanford, NC, 1981, hereafter referred to as NWPP. Historians disagree about how "egalitarian" 19th century feminists were in terms of social class inclusion. On this point, Anthony certainly was much more democratic and egalitarian than Stanton; just as NWP co-leader Lucy Burns was more radically democratic, with fewer elitist tendencies, than Alice Paul. Both Anthony and Paul spoke the language of equality, and in terms of women's overall status in society, unlike NAWSA's view of women's limited role, they stressed women's overall equality and entitlement to have the same roles as men.

[6] Author interview (notes) with Reyher, April 23, 1983; Inez Haynes Irwin, *The Story of Alice Paul and the National Woman's Party,* 1921; rpt. (Fairfax, VA: Denlingers publishers, 1964), pp. 13-16; Crystal Eastman on Paul in Blanche Weisen Cook, editor, *Crystal Eastman on Women and Revolution* (New York: Oxford University Press, 1978), p. 64. When I visited Amelia Fry in Washington, DC, we attempted to visit old CU Headquarters which has since become an executive dining room. Steeling herself with a Paul-like imperious manner, Fry overcame guards and bureaucrats so that we could see it. She remarked how sometimes it was frightening how Paul's personality seemed to overcome her.

[7] Fry, Paul interview, p. 26. Bright's disease (according to Webster's Dictionary) is a kidney disease marked by albumen, a water-soluble protein found in blood plasma, serum or muscle, in the urine. The disease causes degeneration of the kidneys and uric acid is not released from the system.

[8] Ida Husted Harper, *The Life and Work of Susan B. Anthony* (Indianapolis: Bowen and Merrill Co., 1898), p. 954. See accounts of Anthony's life also in Anthony, *Susan B. Anthony.*

[9] Anthony, *Susan B. Anthony,* p. vi.

[10] DuBois, *Feminism and Suffrage: The Emergence of an Independent Woman's Movement in America, 1848-1869* (Ithaca, NY: Cornell University Press, 1978).

[11] In 1910 Alice Paul, soon to become the leader of the NWP, told the NAWSA convention that just as the "women in early abolition days" were vilified and misrepresented, so were the British militants. *The Woman's Journal* (NASWA), May 7, 1910, p. 76. WSPU leader Emmeline Pankhurst was not hesitant to compare her own woman's rights struggle with that of William Lloyd Garrison's campaigns. One of the reasons for Garrison's being the object of mob violence himself was his complicity in the meeting of the Female Anti-Slavery Society. Garrison had insisted upon full participation for women in antislavery agitation and his group split over the issue. See Emmeline Pankhurst, *My Own Story,* (New York: Hearsts' International Library Co., 1914), p. 22. In March of 1918, the, *Farribault Minnesota News* said the NWP suffrage pickets had gone too far, but like John Brown and W.L. Garrison, their names would be enrolled among the prophets. NWP organizer Vida Milholland once wrote to Paul that "you yourself" should be listed with other "fighters for freedom" like Galileo and John Brown. In

the *Suffragist*, March 16, 1918, p. 7. Milholland to Paul, October 30, 1916, Reel 35, NWPP. On abolitionists Anthony and Stanton, see Susan B. Anthony, Elizabeth Cady Stanton and Matilda Joslyn Gage, *History of Woman Suffrage*, Volume I (New York: Fowler and Wells Publishers, 1881, pp. 67-68.
[12] Nancy Cott, *The Grounding of Modern Feminism*, (New Haven: Yale University Press, 1987) p. 4.
[13] Theodore Stanton and Harriot Stanton Blatch, editors, *Elizabeth Cady Stanton As Revealed in Her Letters, Diary and Reminiscences* (New York: Harper and Row, 1922) II, pp. 73-74.
[14] *History of Woman Suffrage,* Volume I, pp. 70-71. Hereafter, *HWS:* Gallagher, Paul interview 1974, p. 94. In 1920 after suffrage was won, the NWP (Paul at least) turned to the Declaration to determine what woman's reform issue to pursue next.
[15] See *HWS,* Volume I, Chapters IV and VI, and Volume II, or excerpts in Alice Rossi, editor, *Feminist Papers* (New York: Banton Books, 1973); Eleanor Flexner, *Century of Struggle* (Boston: Harvard University Press, 1959), Lois Banner, *Elizabeth Cady Stanton* (Boston: Little, Brown and Co., 1980). The decision to postpone the women's struggle Paul thought a grave error and decided to continue to press for a women's right to vote despite the war in 1917. Irwin, *Paul and the NWP,* p. 213. At one time the *Suffragist* (February 2, 1917, p. 8) did erroneously state that Anthony continued the suffrage struggle during the Civil War, as further justification for NWP policy, no doubt. Also see Alice Stone Blackwell, *Lucy Stone* (Boston: Little, Brown and Co., 1930) and Aileen Kraditor, *Ideas of the Woman Suffrage Movement, 1890-1920* (New York: Doubleday and Co., 1965). A more recent excellent work is Nancy Woloch, *Woman and the American Experience* (New York: Alfred A. Knopf, 1984).
[16] Rheta Childe Dorr, *Susan B. Anthony,* p. 143: *The Revolution,* April 9, 1868, p. 214, DuBois, *Feminism and Suffrage,* p. 190. Anthony quote is in Harper, *Life and Work of Anthony,* pp. 1002-1003; Stanton's from *The Revolution,* January 15, 1868, p. 1 and April 9, 1868, p. 214.
[17] K. Anthony, *Susan B. Anthony,* p. 228.
[18] Press release of the Congressional Union, Reel 91, NWPP. In 1915, a Woman's Party pamphlet published in Oregon stated that NWP policy was "to hold the party in power responsible for the use of the sacred power with which it is entrusted. . . . Susan B. Anthony said in 1878 that women should stand shoulder to shoulder against every party not fully and unequivocally committed to Equal Rights for Woman." CU pamphlet 1915, Reel 22, NWPP. Press release written by Helena Hill Weed, February 23, 1917, Reel 39, NWPP; the *Suffragist* (January 19, 1918, p. 8) had a headline on the day suffrage passed Congress which read "Miss Anthony's Vindication," crediting "her theory" of party responsibility for victory.

[19] Banner, *Stanton,* pp. 123-130. See Matilda Joslyn Gage, *Woman, Church and State* (Watertown, MA: Persephone Press, 1980, reprint of 1893 edition). On trial see Katharine Anthony, *Susan B. Anthony,* pp. 289-299. NWP leader Doris Stevens begins her book on her experiences with the "Trial of Susan B. Anthony, Militant Pioneer," *Jailed for Freedom.* On NWP trial see Katzenstein, *Lifting the Curtain,* p. 232; Irwin, *Paul and the NWP,* pp. 300-305.
[20] Gage, *Woman, Church and State,* p. 34. Also see introduction by Sally Roesch Wagner, pp. xvix, xxx, xxxii. In her book, Gage stressed the church's wrongful teaching that women are evil, and denounced wives' treatment as property.
[21] K. Anthony, *Susan B. Anthony,* p. 328.
[22] On 1880s, 90s atmosphere see, for example, Mari Jo Buhle, *Women and American Socialism, 1870-1920* (Urbana, IL: University of Illinois Press, 1981), p. 161. On Gage see her *Women, Church and State,* p. xxxiii; also accounts in Banner, *Stanton,* pp. 117-120; K. Anthony, *Susan B. Anthony,* pp. 315, 350-360; and Flexner, *Century of Struggle,* pp. 223-225; *HWS,* Volume IV; Rheta Childe Dorr, *Susan B. Anthony,* p. 316. A researcher must depend on secondary accounts for Anthony, since her biographer Harper burned Anthony's papers (on her instructions).
[23] Kraditor, *Ideas of Woman Suffrage,* p. 96; Charlotte Perkins Gilman, *Woman and Economics* (Boston: Small, Maynard and Co., 1900); Cott, *Modern Feminism,* p. 4.
[24] Kraditor, *Ideas of Woman Suffrage*, pp. 36, 52. See p. 97 for Shaw-Gilman debate. NAWSA president Carrie Chapman Catt's volume on suffrage discusses the "ignorant and superstitious freedmen" as well as the "venal" Negro vote, bought and paid for in a bloc, by saying: "$5.00, sah -- de Democrats." "Foreigners," the new immigrants, were called ignorant, bribable and "wet" (allies of Liquor, the arch woman suffrage opponent). Catt and Nettie R. Shuler, *Woman Suffrage and Politics* (New York: Charles Scribners, 1926), pp. 73, 162-163. Stanton, Jane Addams and Florence Kelley would all see the value of allying with more liberal "foreigners" and workers as time went on. Working women were not really courted as allies, but their living conditions were used as arguments for suffrage. Only Anthony and Anna Howard Shaw of NAWSA could really identify with working women. Kraditor, *Ideas of Woman Suffrage*, pp. 116, 130-148; Flexner, *Century of Struggle*, p. 225. See Lois Banner's excellent discussion of social feminism and suffrage in *Women in Modern America: A Brief History* (Orlando, FL: Harcourt, Brace, Jovanovich, Inc., 1984) and the equally good Nancy Woloch, *Women and the American Experience*, pp. 332-348.
[25] Adelaide Johnston was the sculptor for the tribute to the woman's movement. Crystal Eastman, "Alice Paul's Convention," in Blanche Wiesen Cook, editor, *On Women and Revolution*, pp. 57-58. Originally in *The Liberator*, April 1921.
[26] Lois Banner, *Stanton*, p. 141; Adamson to Pauline Clarke, November 6, 1917, Reel 52, NWPP. Anthony is called "militant" in the *Suffragist*, March 3, 1919, p.

7; and in Doris Stevens, "The Militant Campaign," p. 26, paper in Folder VI, Stevens Papers, Radcliffe.

27 Dorr, *Anthony*, p. 322; K. Anthony, *Anthony*, pp. 366, 484; Emmeline Pankhurst, *My Own Story*, p. 37.

28 Bland, "Suffrage Militancy of Lucy Burns," p. 7. Burns quote in Irwin, *Paul and the NWP*, p. 289.

29 Fry, Paul interview, pp. 33-34; Anne Bail Howard, *The Long Campaign: A Biography of Anne Martin*, (Reno: University of Nevada Press, 1985), p. 68.

30 May 21, 1914 WSPU letter, Reel 10, NWPP.

31 Annie Kenney speech at Essex Hall, April 13, 1913, Exhibit 15, Rex v. Kerr, WSPU Collection, Radcliffe.

32 Gallagher, Paul interview, p. 12.

33 *Suffragist*, March 2, 1918, p. 12; Stevens, *Jailed*, p. 175; Irwin, *Paul and the NWP*, p. 16.

34 Fry, Paul interview, p. 26; Sidney Bland notes that Dorothy Day remembered sharing a cell with Burns and spending time talking with her about the sea stories of Joseph Conrad which Burns very much loved. See Bland, "'Never Quite As Committed as We'd Like': The Suffrage Militancy of Lucy Burns," *Journal of Long Island History*, Summer/Fall 1981, pp. 4-6; note 51.

35 *Notable American Women: The Modern Period* (Boston: Radcliffe, 1980), p. 124; Bland, "Militancy of Burns," pp. 4-6; Stevens, *Jailed*, appendix.

36 Martin said she was influenced more by her father's populism than her mother's sewing talents. *Notable American Women: Modern Period*, p. 459. From author's correspondence with Anne Martin biographer Anne Howard, October 6, 1982; Stevens, *Jailed*, appendix; Howard, *Long Campaign*, pp. 54-55.

37 Marian Ramelson, *Petticoat Rebellion* (London: Lawrence and Wishart, 1967), p. 81.

38 Mill thought woman suffrage would come to the U.S. first. Stanton thoroughly covered English suffrage news in *The Revolution*. Rossi, *Feminist Papers*, pp. 132, 196.

39 Constance Rover, *Woman's Suffrage and Party Politics in Britain, 1866-1914* (London: Routledge and Kegan Paul, 1967), p. 25. In 1869, the year Wyoming women got the vote, unmarried woman ratepayers in England received the municipal franchise. If women had had the same qualifications as men, the goal of most suffragists of the period, 300,000 to 400,000 women would have qualified between 1867-1884. Rover, *Woman's Suffrage*, p. 3; Ramelson, *Rebellion*, pp. 81; 90-97.

40 Pankhurst, *My Own Story*; Rover, *Woman Suffrage*, pp. 90-93. The most dramatic portrayal of this phenomenon is George Dangerfield's *The Strange Death of Liberal England* (London: Constable and Co., Ltd., 1936).

---

[41] Extract from letter of WSPU member Helen Cragg, in "Who Would Be Free, Themselves Must Strike The Blow," November 1, 1912, *Suffragette* (WSPU journal).
[42] Pankhurst, *Great Scourge,* (London: E.P. Lincoln's Inn, 1913).
[43] Pankhurst, *My Own Story*, pp. 13-19. David Mitchell has argued that Mrs. Pankhurst was a "creation of [her husband's] Pygmalion devotion." She had a "mission to morally cleanse the world and avenge her crucified husband" (who lost his bid for reelection). Mitchell, *Fighting Pankhursts* (New York: The MacMillan Co., 1967), pp. 24-26.
[44] Harriot Stanton Blatch and Alma Lutz, *Challenging Years: The Memoirs of Harriot Stanton Blatch* (New York: G.P. Putnam's Sons, 1940), p. 73; Pankhurst, *My Own Story,* pp. 20, 19-30, 33-40; Ramelson, *Rebellion,* pp. 131-132; Andrew Rosen, *Rise Up, Women! The Militant Campaign of the WSPU, 1903-1914* (London: Routledge and Kegan Paul, 1974), pp. 80-85. Rosen said WSPU speakers depended on the ILP at first for lecture platforms and audiences, but by 1904, they no longer did.
[45] "Heckling" was a policy taken from the Labour party. Pankhurst, *My Own Story*, pp. 37-40, 52. In 40 years, there were 18 debates in the House and three bills passed the Second Reading. Ramelson, *Rebellion*, pp. 84, 132-133. Churchill was so annoyed by the heckling that he considered becoming an "anti," saying he would "not be henpecked." He seemed to agree with his mother that "female suffrage women are too odious." In Henry Pelling, *Winston Churchill* (New York: E.P. Dutton, Inc., 1974), p. 90.
[46] Pankhurst, *My Own Story*, p. 56.
[47] The *London Times*, March 21, 1907, p. 10; Sylvia Pankhurst, *The Suffragette* (New York: Sturges and Walton, 1912), pp. 410-414; E. Pankhurst, *My Own Story*, pp. 94-101; Mitchell, *The Pankhursts*, p. 31; Stephen Koss, *H.H. Asquith* (London: Allen Lane, 1976), p. 102. The *Times* being itself editorially anti. Stating that women were weaker because of their functions as mothers, the paper's editors felt women not responsible on national issues. June 21, 1908, pp. 9, 11.
[48] Emmeline Pankhurst said "property was more important than humans to government." *My Own Story*, p. 265. Also see pp. 115-117, 149. Pankhurst said cabinet ministers had "taunted them to use violent methods of men of 1832 and 1867," referring to two previous British suffrage extension struggles. "The message of the broken pane is that women are determined that the lives of their sisters shall no longer be broken . . . ." In "Broken Windows," a November 24, 1911 pamphlet of Exhibit 102, WSPU suffrage paper #144 by Christabel Pankhurst, WSPU Papers, Radcliffe; also see her *Scourge*, introduction.
[49] Irwin, *Paul and the NWP*, p. 9; Gallagher, Paul interview, p. 18; Bland, "Militancy of Lucy Burns," p. 7; S. Pankhurst, *Suffragette,* p. 411.
[50] Fry, Paul interview, pp. 38, 45-57; Irwin, *Paul and the NWP*, pp. 8-9; Gallagher, Paul interview, p. 18.

[51] The *Glasgow Herald*, August 21, 1909. The account also appears in S. Pankhurst, *The Suffragette*, pp. 416-417 and Irwin, *Paul and the NWP*, p. 11.
[52] *Ibid.*
[53] *Ibid.* When asked about the incident, Paul said she "never hid on any roof in my life. In Glasgow I was arrested, but it was at a street meeting we organized there." Gallagher, Paul interview, p. 18. She also repeated her lack of memory of the incident to Fry in their 1972 interview, p. xiv, although Burns, Irwin and Sylvia Pankhurst all confirmed it. Paul also did not remember the violence at the 1912 parade or much about hunger striking.
[54] Gallagher, Paul interview, p. 18; Irwin, *Paul and the NWP*, pp. 10-11; Fry, Paul interview, pp. 51, 56-57. Burns is listed as a "convicted suffragette" #39, November 22, 1910 for a one month sentence, in exhibit 206 of the Rex v. Kerr Papers.
[55] Fry, Paul interview, p. 53; Gallagher, Paul interview pp. 18-19.
[56] Testimony in E. Pankhurst, *My Own Story,* p. 153.
[57] Howard, *Long Campaign*, pp. 66, 68-69; E. Pankhurst, *My Own Story*, p. 182.
[58] Howard, *Long Campaign*, pp. 68-70.
[59] Martin said she met Paul and Burns in London. Howard writes it is difficult to determine exactly when Martin began with the WSPU. It may well have been through her connection to the Fabian socialists. It may be confused also because she later downplayed her connections with the WSPU, particularly in her Senate race of 1918. Howard, *Long Campaign*, pp. 63-64; 70-72.
[60] Paul to Wright, July 21, 1913, Reel 3, NWPP; Paul to Wright, May 24, 1913, same reel.
[61] Emmeline Pankhurst, January 27, 1913 speech at the Pavilion, London in Rex v. Kerr exhibit; *The Suffragette*, November 1, 1912, p. 29; Howard, "Anne Martin," p. 145; *London Times*, June 5, 1913, p. 8.
[62] For example, NWP advisor Lavinia Dock sold *Votes for Women* in London while at a nurses' conference, while New York NWP leader Dora Sedgwick Hazard, according to her correspondence, contributed to the WSPU and wholly sympathized with their burning of Lloyd George's new house. *Notable American Women, 1607-1950*, Volume I, p. 196; Dr. Louise Garrett Anderson to Dora Hazard, May 6, 1913, Nathaniel Bacon Papers (Hazard's brother-in-law), Rhode Island College.
[63] Blatch and Lutz, *Challenging Years*, p. 91.
[64] Sherna Gluck, editor, *Parlor to Prison: Five American Suffragists* (New York: Random House, 1976) from Laura Ellsworth Seiler's account of being a WPU organizer in central New York, pp. 129, 150, 160, 189, 191. Many future Woman's Party members were organizers and officers of the WPU, including (besides Blatch) Lavinia Dock, Eunice Brannan, Mrs. Henry Butterworth, Louisine Havemeyer, Elizabeth Selden Rogers, Florence Kelley, Rheta Childe Dorr, Mary Beard, Charlotte Perkins Gilman, Dora Sedgwick Hazard and Alva Belmont.

[65] Sharon Hartman Strom, "Leadership and Tactics in the American Woman Suffrage Movement: A New Perspective from Massachusetts," *Journal of American History,* September 1975, pp. 297-313. I would disagree with Strom that such tactics were a "veritable revolution" since Anthony and Stanton also had an occasional open-air meeting, and what Foley did was done on her own. Other links were also formed with Britain -- See Jane Marcus, "Transatlantic Sisterhood: Labor and Suffrage Links in the Letters of Elizabeth Robins and Emmeline Pankhurst," *Signs*, Spring 1978.

[66] Complete press coverage was true not only of papers like the *New York Times*, but also of small town papers. Vassar incident is in *Washington Times*, September 8, 1908.

[67] Blatch and Lutz, *Challenging Years*, pp. 99, 113-114.

[68] *Ibid.*, p. 115; John C. Zacharis, "Emmeline Pankhurst: An English Suffragette Influences America," *Speech Monographs,* August 1971. He argues how much NAWSA was galvanized by the Pankhurst tour, but he overstates it. In the end, they disapproved. See also, Dorr, *What Eight Million Women Want,* p. 297.

[69] Grace Roe, Mrs. Pankhurst's "associate," had written to Paul to arrange bookings at Carnegie Hall, and an appropriate hall in Chicago. August 29, 1913, Reel 4; *New York Times,* October 19, 1913, Section 2, p. 1; Paul to Joan Wickham, October 16, 1913, Reel 5, NWPP.

[70] *New York Times*, September 14, 1913, Section V p. 6. The Tombs warden assured the press that any hunger strikers in New York would be forced fed.

[71] Ramelson argues that, in spite of labor origins, the WSPU seemed most concerned with "picked women, the very strongest and best," while Mitchell has labelled Christabel and Emmeline Pankhurst as becoming "romantic Tories." Sylvia Pankhurst, the middle sister, remained a socialist and pacifist; and the one with whom Alice Paul would stay longest in contact. Ramelson, *Petticoat Rebellion,* p. 148; Mitchell, *Fighting Pankhursts*, p. 75.

[72] *The Suffragette*, November 1, 1912, p. 29. The line is Stanza 76 of Lord Byron's "Childe Harold's Pilgrimage": "Hereditary bondsmen: Know ye not, Who would be free, themselves must strike the blow?"

[73] Irwin, *Paul and the NWP*, p. 203; *New York Times*, June 22, 1908, p. 4; "England's Merry, Militant Suffragettes," *Ms*., November 1978, p. 21.

[74] *The Suffragist*, July 25, 1914, p. 7. Alice Paul to Bureau of Immigration, September 11, 1913, Reel 4, NWPP.

[75] Winsor Report, N.D., Reel 93, NWPP. For more statements on identification with and defense of the Pankhursts, also see Alice Paul to Edna Wilson, April 21, 1913, Reel 1; Lucy Burns to editor, *Washington Post*, May 14, 1914, Reel 10.

[76] Crystal Eastman, "Personalities and Powers: Alice Paul," *Time and Tide*, July 1923.

[77] According to one participant, the Pankhurst movement was "not primarily political, it was social, moral, psychological and profoundly religious. . . . It

became a sex war." In David Mitchell, *Queen Christabel* (London: MacDonald and Jane's, 1977), p. 22. It should also be noted that the U.S. had many more governmental pressure points for lobbying than England where "out-of-doors" activities had more indirect effects. Asquith especially hated out-of-doors agitations. See Koss, *Asquith*.

[78] Gallagher, Paul interview, p. 19.

[79] Anne Martin, "Equality Laws Vs. Women in Government," *Nation*, August 16, 1922, p. 166. Alice Paul to E. Pethick-Lawrence, July 10, 1913, Reel 3, NWPP.

[80] Katzenstein, *Lifting the Curtain*, p. 13.

[81] Bland, "Militancy of Lucy Burns," p. 8.

[82] June 15, 1914, Reel 10, NWPP.

[83] CU pamphlet, 1913, Reel 92, NWPP.

[84] *Ibid.*

Chapter Two

Organizing for Power: Political Phase, 1912-1916

> [Our] policy will be called militant and in a sense it is, being strong, positive and energetic. If it is militant to appeal to women to use their vote to bring suffrage to this country, then it is militant to appeal to men or women to use their vote to any good end.
>
> - CU Policy Statement, 1914

In May of 1910, Alice Paul, just returned home from a London prison, addressed the NAWSA suffrage convention. Sounding very much the WSPU militant, she informed them that although Rousseau's ideal woman, a woman whose sole purpose was "to comfort men," was "still around," a "new race of women" was appearing whose "ideal is strength." The personification of such new women were the British suffrage militants, women who had finally decided after 40 years of patient petition, to "take" their rights: "The cringe was gone from their souls. . . . woman the suppliant had become the rebel."[1] By holding up to them the shining example of the British militants, Paul challenged NAWSA's cautious methods of obtaining political rights for women.

When Paul and Burns began their woman suffrage revival in 1913, gathering together a remarkable group of women, they were highly optimistic about the immediate success of their new, spirited political campaign. As a NAWSA committee, in the first phase of their political strategy, they used traditional, progressive lobbying tactics to effect their democratic reform. Starting in 1914 as the independent Congressional Union, they upped the intensity of their power politics by utilizing a British-style, national "party responsibility" policy, to the shocked dismay of NAWSA. Finally, in 1916, with the first two strategies failing, in the last phase of their "pre-militant" political campaign for woman suffrage, the CU formed a woman's political party as leverage to open the political system to women. Having evolved through a series of stages of frustration, with the Wilson government remaining unyielding for four years, they made the transition from confident reformers to disillusioned and angry protestors. In some ways along with the rest of the country's progressives, their confidence in inevitable "progress" in America, much less in a war-torn world, was shaken. They would decide to forego their political phase and, reminiscent of their sister British militants, apply the "real" militancy of civil disobedience to the suffrage campaign.

Although the Woman's Party eventually went well beyond progressive political methods, they never quite let go of their progressive ideals. In 1913, in the first days of their movement, they had an optimistic faith in democracy and the American people, and confidence that the world's evolution would be "progressive" in bringing new and wider roles for women. The American political reform context was, after all, quite different from Britain's: it featured votes for women as a desirable (eventually) progressive goal, women as important reformers, and a surge of new progressive feminism. Early 20th century American reformers regarded the government as responsible for providing its people justice and economic well-being, wanted reconciliation of groups within society, and wanted national solutions to social and economic problems. With government clearly the base for social change, solutions were, to them, necessarily political first.[2] Middle-class professionals, including a growing number of women, sought to clean up, regulate, moderate, streamline, educate, and improve American society--optimistically believing all things possible and all problems soluble in a modern, progressively evolving world. Women reformers would "naturally" be particularly interested in solving "moral" issues like corrupt city government, children's education, unsafe industrial and sanitation conditions, health problems, or the needs of the poor.[3] But some woman reformers, including the new suffragists, although sharing the general optimism and belief in the democratic process, wanted more change, more quickly, than most progressive reformers.

The Woman's Party, would seek, like most progressive groups, a political solution, the right to the franchise, for improving woman's position in society, but unlike most progressives, they brought to that movement an impatient, militant spirit. After all, American women had been working for suffrage for some 64 years when Alice Paul and Lucy Burns founded a new national suffrage committee for NAWSA in 1912. Paul had drawn the attention of NAWSA through the fame (or infamy) she gained from taking part in the British suffrage drama. After the 1910 NAWSA convention, where she paid homage to the British militant movement as a "new race of women" with the "cringe gone from their souls," she spent two years completing a Ph.D. at the University of Pennsylvania. Her ambitious thesis was on the legal position of women in Pennsylvania. She still found time to be active in the suffrage fight: Paul held street meetings for up to 2,000 in Philadelphia, sometimes helped by Caroline Katzenstein, Inez Milholland, Rheta Childe Dorr, or NAWSA's Anna Howard Shaw. By 1912, Paul had completed her degree and Lucy Burns had returned from England. Anne Martin had also come home to begin suffrage work, in the Equal Franchise League, and with NAWSA, in her home state of Nevada. Sympathetic to the new group from the beginning, she would not officially join until 1915. Hoping to revive the national campaign for woman suffrage, Paul and Burns talked to NAWSA officers Shaw and Mary Ware Dennett, and the WPU's Harriot Stanton Blatch, about going to Washington at their own expense to start working for a suffrage amendment to the Constitution. Finally, with the support of Blatch and the ever influential Jane Addams, the NAWSA Board approved the plan.[4]

The two young suffragists were not taken all that seriously by NAWSA, nor was their task of lobbying Congress for a federal amendment. In fact, their predecessor, Elizabeth Kent, a California Congressman's wife (who would later join the Congressional Union), had been alloted $10 annually for national work and had been told she would have to do nothing but arrange to have the amendment introduced periodically to Congress.[5] NAWSA's efforts had been devoted for years, and largely unsuccessfully, to state suffrage fights.[6] In 1912 NAWSA had no functioning national center, and an ineffective national leader in Anna Howard Shaw. Woman suffrage was a decidedly stagnant issue in Washington: it had never been voted upon in the House of Representatives, been voted on once by the Senate in 1887, had had no committee report since 1896, and no debate since 1887. Neither the Republican party, led by William Howard Taft, nor Woodrow Wilson's Democratic party, advocated woman suffrage, although T.R. Roosevelt's Progressive party did. When Wilson was first approached by the new national suffrage committee in 1913, he said he had given "no thought to woman suffrage."[7]

Paul and Burns, determined to work for a successful outcome, had no idea the sort of tremendous effort which lay ahead. Arriving in Washington in December of 1912, Paul felt that after explaining the logic and rightness of the amendment to every Congressman and Senator, it would pass in a year.[8] After all, woman suffrage seemed a particularly apt and just cause for a progressive administration, and the goal of looking to the federal government to enact a national solution made perfect sense within progressive reform parameters. Burns and Paul were obviously still deeply under the influence of the Pankhurst militant style and spirit, but they would follow a different political path from the Pankhursts, who had given up on the British constitutional process long before 1914. The American women believed that they could work within their political system, relying on its progressive democratic promise, without having to resort to British-style, "violent," militancy.

The progressive spirit of optimism and infinite possibilities for new roles for women gave credibility to the case for women's participation in government. By the early new century, at least some women were growing more independent, especially economically: seven and one half million women were in the labor force by 1910. Women made their presence felt in clubs in every community, were not as subordinate to their husbands, more often kept their own names, got more divorces, and began to enjoy the relative freedom of changing fashions and social and sexual mores. Eventually an entire culture of liberated "new women" was created in Greenwich Village, a community whose unique class of intellectuals advocated freer relations between the sexes along with political revolution.[9] As more and more women gained higher education, there were some real opportunities for change; educated women could be artists and intellectuals, professionals, and, of course, reformers. Many women, including Alice Paul, spoke of the dawn of a "New Era" for women.

No progressive feminist spoke more eloquently of the New Age for Women than Charlotte Perkins Gilman, soon to become NWP advisor and spokeswoman.

One of the key elements of Gilman's feminist (she called it "humanist") philosophy was the need for strong and autonomous women: "Set the woman on her own feet, as a free, intelligent, able human being . . . Woman must stand free with man."[10] Gilman's feminist utopian novels featured women's complete autonomy: the world of *Herland* had no men and was a "beautiful garden world" run by women. Herself a victim of 19th century society's marital and economic restrictions upon women, Gilman insisted that women must "take charge" and "wake up": "Ours the Future, and the Hour, Life is here to do!"[11] Women could first expand their housekeeping skills into paying occupations, while applying these same skills, as Jane Addams had also suggested, "beyond the four walls of their homes" to clean up the problems of the world.[12] She also argued that some "exceptional" women should immediately enter previously male, and thus more "important," fields of endeavor. Gilman was delighted with the new suffrage organization because this was women, finally, "organizing for power": "The Woman's Party [is] in line with all biology and evolution . . . [and] all world progress."[13] The NWP suffragist would be to Gilman the personification of an ideal independent, powerful, "new" woman.

Independent, restless feminists Paul and Burns wanted to effect real change and help usher in the "New Age." Paul even used Gilman's exact language in 1913 when she spoke of woman suffrage as "vitally the very next step in the process of Moral Evolution."[14] Committed to a Quaker moral reform tradition and coming out of a strenuous apprenticeship with the Pankhursts, Alice Paul was well-prepared to carry out a feminist mission in her own country. Her graduate studies had also contributed; she had studied with socialist Sydney Webb in London and was inspired by American economist Simon Patten's ideas of America's ripeness for social reform.[15] Also just back from Holloway, Lucy Burns, a talented, vibrant, and now polished orator, definitely had a well-developed sense of social injustice: her friends had always said she would "die for her ideas."[16] As noted earlier, the two women who originated the new national suffrage organization, were a bit different both in their philosophical and applied feminism. When historian Inez Haynes Irwin asked a Woman's Party activist the difference between the two reformers, she was told: "Alice Paul had a more acute sense of justice, Lucy Burns, a more bitter sense of injustice."[17] Paul, the moral egalitarian, dispassionately demanded much, whereas the passionately idealistic Burns bitterly resented inaction and unfairness. Their combined enthusiasm and idealism helped Paul and Burns provide very effective leadership for the American national suffrage drive.

When they began their work early in 1913, other than working with Congress for a constitutional amendment, Burns and Paul did not have specific instructions from Anna Howard Shaw, and differences soon developed. In regard to fiscal matters, however, Shaw was quite specific. Money would always be a sore point between NAWSA executives and their Congressional Committee (CC). Paul and Burns had to promise to raise all their own money and account for it precisely. Although NAWSA had appointed the committee, it would also be up to Paul and

Burns to enlarge its membership. They were given a list of women to contact for help in the national effort, but since many on the list had died or moved away, the two women turned to their own friends and acquaintances for assistance.

The women they secured to serve on the committee were very talented, experienced progressive reformers, and all committed feminists. Crystal Eastman, a very strong, leftist feminist, was a friend of Burns from Vassar. A graduate of New York University Law School, and at that time, an investigator of industrial accidents, she was also part of the Greenwich Village intellectual community. The brilliant historian Mary Beard would also join the committee. She had worked with the Pankhursts in England and had been very active in the Women's Trade Union League, New York's Woman Suffrage Party (of NAWSA), and Blatch's WPU.[18] Lastly, Dora Kelley Lewis became a committee member and would long serve as an important leader in the NWP,although she hesitated at first, to join. Lewis was a wealthy widow with three children, a friend of Paul's from Philadelphia, who belonged to a mainline Philadelphia family descended from the first Connecticut settlers. In 1916 Lewis would be writing to Paul from Shanghai, where she was on "a visit." Described as "every inch an aristocrat," Lewis's major reform interest (ironically as it turned out) was improvement of prisons, but she had also done a great deal of state suffrage work for NAWSA and was close to Anna Howard Shaw.[19] Left to organize on their own, the committee was free to develop political strategy from a new, militant feminist philosophy.

The first project was to organize a mammoth woman's suffrage parade the day before Wilson's March 4, 1913 inauguration. Such a mass demonstration would hopefully impress the country that woman suffrage was a compelling, national reform issue. From their first staged event, Paul and Burns stressed democratic, progressive and feminist themes, and from the very first they encountered a decidedly hostile reaction from male onlookers and authorities. The underlying concept for the suffrage parade was to unite women in an impressive show of solidarity. The CC called upon women to put aside their reform work for pacifism and child labor laws, or against "white slavery" and venereal disease, to come to Washington and make suffrage their first priority by marching in the parade.[20] Women pursuing political power, 10,000 strong, were to be organized in groups to show how deserving they were of the vote. Even in this parade, the progressive feminist dilemma was expressed: floats showed how women were still restricted and oppressed, while women professionals marched together to indicate that women had already proved themselves capable of success. In both cases, to the parade organizers, the only logical conclusion was that women should vote.

The parade gathered women from the entire progressive reform spectrum. The procession was to be led by the flamboyant socialist lawyer, Inez Milholland, dressed in a white suit and cloak, and riding a white horse. Milholland had spoken to crowds with Christabel Pankhurst in London and had picketed with women shirtwaist strikers in New York, where she had been charged with disorderly conduct.[21] In contrast, among the multitude of women marchers were (and very prominently) women's club members: there were Red Cross volunteers, women from arts clubs, service clubs, political study clubs, the PTA, War Mothers, the WCTU, the Consumers' League, suffrage clubs like the Elizabeth Cady Stanton League, Quaker groups, and Jewish and Catholic club groups. Active political women from the Republican, Democratic and Progressive parties marched, as well as women with more radical causes: Socialist women, the Women's International League for Peace and Freedom and Women's Peace Party and organizations like the WTUL and "Industrial Workers." There was also a contingent from the National Association for Colored Women. Alice Paul was especially happy with the large number of college women who marched (and with whom she would march), and took particular pride in an important middle class suffrage selling point, woman paraders who were organized by profession: nurses, painters and sculptors, "pen women," home economists, federal employees, businesswomen, the Women's Bar Association, teachers, the Medical Women's National Association, and social service workers.[22] Although, as will be seen, complete female solidarity was not achieved, and conflict over issues of class and race did arise, the assembly to symbolize a "new race of strong women" did do a creditable job of presenting a visible, united female front on the issue of woman suffrage.

Women marching for political power, thousands of them, apparently presented a threatening spectacle, if the reaction of male onlookers and police was any indication. A police permit had been secured to march from the Capitol to the White House and then Constitution Hall. But the police proved absolutely useless during the parade, even though they should have been prepared for trouble with such a huge number of people involved. One participant, Suzanne LaFollette, remembered what the crowd was like that day:

> I was invited to be on a float which represented some aspect of repression--I forget which . . . before the avenue came in sight we realized that our movement was extremely slow; also that the noise from the avenue was deafening--and was not cheering. When at last we entered it the view was appalling. There was no division between the parade and the crowd, and the crowd was a seething mob of men who surged around the struggling marchers, shouting obscenities. There were few police in sight, and those who were in sight were making no effort to control the crowd. It was an obscene spectacle, and it lasted from one end of the avenue to the other; that is, it lasted for hours.[23] (See Figure 3)

Finally, Secretary of War, Henry Stimson, had to call in the troops from Ft. Myer to clear a path for the marchers and control the crowd. Mr. Stimson was friendly to the marchers because he was the brother-in-law of the affluent and very militant, Elizabeth Selden Rogers, member of the parade committee. Rogers, a prominent NAWSA and WPU suffragist, as well as educational reformer, was enraged over

The 1913 Parade in Washington
Figure 3

what happened at the parade. She stated that it proved "the lack of respect of men for women. The police were not trying or were laughing and jeering . . . because we were women, working for freedom, the authorities did not *care* what happened to our Parade."[24] The parade experience, with its jeering, hostile male crowd, was a rude shock for the marchers.

Many women and men (some men marched in sympathy with the cause) reacted angrily to the parade spectacle. Carrie Chapman Catt, near the front of the procession, said that that women were "shockingly used," and the police did nothing.[25] An exception to the apparent blanket rudeness of policemen was the one policeman reported to have helped the marchers, a "colored" policeman. Indeed, many women testified that the black male onlookers were not rude, unlike their white counterparts.[26] The women of the Ohio section reported that lewd remarks were made to elderly ladies such as: "I'd like to meet you after dark." Doris Stevens stated that she was told: "You ought to get yourself a man. You can get what you want without that [marching]."[27] Some male spectators were outraged by what they saw. Telegrams of protest were sent to the Washington police by Oswald Garrison Villard (the NAACP founder had himself marched), by the largely male Rochester Political Equality Club and the Progressive Party of Massachusetts.[28] I. A. Sterne, vice president of the Washington, DC Federation of Labor, wrote to his "Friends" of the CC that he "wanted to help bring justice to the police . . . and to arrange resolutions to be sent. . . . I am expressing my heartfelt regards for your movement and those who so gallantly fought to parade."[29] Many later testified in front of a Congressional investigating committee that was set up because of the massive protests, and also no doubt, because Congressional wives and daughters had been among the marchers. Eventually, the investigation led to the police chief's dismissal and sympathetic publicity for the new NAWSA committee.[30] To veteran militants Paul and Burns, the crowd and police reaction did not come as a complete surprise, and in fact, was mild compared to what they had only recently experienced in England. They were gratified that their procession had succeeded in focusing the nation's attention on national woman's suffrage, and already had made women indignant enough to want to intensify the struggle to gain political rights.

The leaders of the future National Woman's Party, with few exceptions, were members of NAWSA's Congressional Union, founded in April of 1913, consisting of an expanded Congressional Committee as "executive" committee of the Union, an advisory board, and other members interested in national suffrage. The women who joined the new organization, firstly in arranging the parade, and then in early delegations to Wilson, represented an interesting blend of old and new egalitarian feminism. There were pioneer NWSA suffragists like Reverend Olympia Brown, who found the new Union "splendid" and would, at age 80, picket the White House. There were mature clubwomen such as Anna Kelton Wiley, active in the Consumer's League; along with younger "new women" activists, friends of Burns or Paul. There were also feminist militants associated with the New York WPU or the British WSPU, like the "fearless" Dr. Caroline Spencer of Colorado, who specifically equated the CU with the WSPU; and the warm "motherly" (and very well-to-do) Eunice Brannan, a New York WPU officer and enthusiastic admirer of the Pankhursts.[31] Impatient with NAWSA's tedious methods, some CU members' angry feminism was very similar to the philosophy expressed by the Pankhursts' wealthier colleagues, reflecting the sense, that as refined and prominent women, used to wielding influence because of their class status, they had more than enough right to take part in the government. The younger progressive reformers, with a different emphasis, optimistically worked for greater democracy and complete independence for all women.

NAWSA leaders tended to be governed by a different progressive feminist philosophy from that of the new CU, one which was much more ladylike. The CU's strong identification with the British militants and with Gilman's "power" feminism was foreign to NAWSA and would eventually estrange them from the CU. Even the beautiful pageantry of early CU parades and demonstrations was designed to make a powerful feminist point. Typical of their "tableaux" was one designed for the Federal Treasury steps in May of 1913. It clearly illustrates the influence of Gilman in its strongly feminist themes. The "Cast" consisted of Woman, Man, Freedom, Justice, Ignorance, Prejudice and Sin, and included an interesting array of "Women of Achievement"; among them were Sappho, Deborah, Queen Isabella of Spain, Joan of Arc, Elizabeth of England, Catherine of Russia, Charlotte Corday, Elizabeth Fry, George Sand and Marie Curie. The action began with Man telling Woman she was "a child" and must be protected. Her hands bound "with silken cord," she told him: "[N]o beast of the forest could have harmed woman more than Man has. I crave full freedom to develop." At that point, the Women of Achievement enter and prove Woman's case to Justice, who rules: "Let her be freed." She then joins Man for "a better love."[32] This clearly presented an egalitarian, feminist point of view: women needed to be strong and powerful, and needed freedom to act for themselves. What a contrast this provided with NAWSA's willingness to use feminine wiles based on weakness, and to depend on male friends for help.

One of NAWSA's major Washington lobbyists, Maud Wood Park, reflected the essential difference when she wrote that her purpose in lobbying was to make and keep friends, in what she described as a necessarily long woman suffrage campaign. Her methods were age-old feminine ones: she found that when she had a good cry in Senator Jones's office, he became a friend to suffrage.[33] Lucy Burns described the CU relationship to Senators quite differently:

> Is it to be wondered at that politicians were puzzled at first by this new development in the suffrage question, that after years upon years of pleas politely phrased . . . they lost their tempers when they found themselves face to face with a protest couched in words of political power?[34]

From the beginning, Burns and Paul insisted on using their own brand of power politics.

It was not long before the militant spirit of the CU approach was all too familiar to the NAWSA leadership, members of Congress and especially, to President Woodrow Wilson. The Congressional Union started lobbying at the top, approaching their "progressive" president about an immediate national franchise for women. Wilson proved an obdurate foe, although Paul said she always had "great respect" for him, calling him "a very great man."[35] Ironically, Wilson was not all that progressive in many of his attitudes. He held a chivalrous, condescending view of women. Mr. Wilson, destined to be (as he would perceive it) continually "harassed" by the Woman's Party, was "repelled" by women who he felt "reversed" the social order. When women spoke in public, he said he had a "chilled, scandalized feeling." A true southern gentleman, he regarded women as purer, finer, gentler, more spiritual, modest and moral than men.[36] He had idealized his first wife Ellen Axson as an angel, and called his second, Edith Bolling Galt, his "little girl." The former president of Princeton University's first job was teaching at the woman's college of Bryn Mawr, where Wilson very much annoyed history professor Lucy Salmon (future NWP advisor), by saying "a woman who had married an intellectual man was often better educated than a woman who had college training." To Wilson, "intellectual power, leadership and logical thinking" were male qualities.[37]

Although he would never quite call out the troops to attack suffrage protesters in the same drastic way the British government had in dealing with its annoying "suffragette" problem, Wilson was irritated at the best of times in his relationship with the Woman's Party, and the measures he took to end their "harassment" would be severe enough.[38] He certainly admired the British government's way of operating in other areas, particularly their system of cabinet government and party responsibility, with elected public servants following a definite policy and platform. Wilson proved a very strong party leader himself, who took responsibility for his party's legislation and was very successful in getting it passed. He was also the first president since John Adams to deliver a political program to Congress.[39] Therefore, although as an individual Wilson proved stubborn and unyielding, for the woman suffragists of the NWP to press such a strong president to adopt woman suffrage as part of his party's platform, particularly as a supposedly "progressive" party leader, seemed a reasonable, even shrewd, strategy.

To early CU delegations Wilson, according to Paul, "was as he always was . . . he gave the impression of being very scholarly, very tolerant and respectful and completely in accord with the idea that women could vote."[40] He may have been respectful, but he was not responsive. At that point, in early 1914, he was fairly amenable to hearing lobbyists regarding various domestic reform issues, but certainly by mid-1915, he was more and more preoccupied with issues of the world war. Even in 1914 he was as stubbornly noncommittal on suffrage as Paul's delegations were persistent. Paul later described it: "And then we sent him another delegation and another and another and another and another and another and another--every type of woman's group we could get."[41] Three delegations were sent in March of 1913. Wilson told the first he was new to the issue; the second, that he thought the issue not important, that the legislation regarding the tariff was paramount at that time; and to the third (The National Council of Women Voters led by Jane Addams) he emphasized again the superior significance of the tariff. It was in this period, on the night of his daughter Nell's wedding to William MacAdoo, that Wilson told his friend and advisor Colonel Edmund House that he "felt unsettled" and bothered by "people with gripes to air . . . The woman suffragists, in particular, were insufferable and he wished he were not president."[42] NAWSA's tiny Congression Union unsettled the President and alerted the public that this was a very bold, defiant and resolute group.

By the middle of 1913 the CU strengthened its national drive. It remained an auxiliary to NAWSA, but launched its own new campaign. It had expanded its advisory board, written a formal constitution and funded its own treasury. In the early CU decisions were made jointly. Various leaders would suggest policies, often, but not always, Paul; which would then be discussed and approved, or rarely, rejected by the executive committee and advisory board. The evidence suggests that the CU (or arguably, the NWP) was not exclusively and autocratically run by Alice Paul: she did often share leadership with Lucy Burns, Dora Lewis and then Anne Martin, among others. After state "chairmen" were in place, they were always consulted and/or informed on every step by Paul. The chairmen secured leaders for each Congressional district, who were then to make contact with women in suffrage societies, and labor and reform associations. The CU worked very hard on demonstrations, letter writing and petition campaigns, and membership drives. Hoping to include all sorts of women in the movement, rather than just the upper class women characteristic of leaders and advisors, Paul and Burns made appeals to all sorts of women's groups, particularly those of working women. Early NWP papers show that correspondence was heavy with groups like the Wage Earners Suffrage League of the WTUL and with socialist party branches.[43] In June of 1913, the CU already had a mailing list of 15,000 and the goal of one paid organizer for every state was becoming viable.[44]

The CU, using progressive political methods along with new sorts of aggressive demonstrations, was beginning to have an impact directly upon the legislators. Their members continued to write pro-suffrage letters and collect petitions; they held mass meetings and conventions, and smaller indoor and outdoor gatherings of up to five or ten a day. Their most effective weapon was speakers like the incredible Mabel Vernon, their first, and probably best ever, officer/organizer. Vernon described herself and the militant suffragists as women "endeavoring to think fearlessly." Organizer Hazel Hunkins would later say there was a leadership "triumvurate" consisting of Burns, Paul and Vernon in the NWP.

The warm, outgoing Vernon had gone to Swarthmore with Paul and would receive an M.A. from Columbia in 1923. She was born in 1883, in Wilmington, Delaware into a large family; her father was a newspaper editor/publisher and a Quaker. She had taught high school Latin and German between 1906 and 1913. Somewhat contradictorily one friend called her a "very quiet personality and very retiring," while another called her "completely selfless" with "dynamism" . . . "very warm and loyal." No doubt Vernon overcame shyness to develop her remarkable speaking talents: Paul called her blessed with a "clear, ringing voice" and a "great, great gift of speaking." In 1913 Vernon brought the suffrage cause to resorts in New Jersey, Long Island, Rhode Island and the South in order to raise much needed funds and create publicity.[45]

After all of Vernon's speeches, after the CU's numerous letter writing and petition campaigns, along with demonstrations and lobbying, the House passed a resolution to form a woman suffrage committee in the spring of 1913 and the Senate made its suffrage committee a majority committee. By June the Senate committee reported suffrage favorably to the full Senate, the first time in 23 years there had been a favorable majority report. A spectacular pro-suffrage auto parade organized in late July to come to Washington from well-chosen Congressional districts was immediately followed by a suffrage debate in the Senate.[46] It seemed indisputable that CU methods of organizing visible, mass suffrage demonstrations, were effective.

The CU's ideal of woman's power and autonomy might have been creating successful strategies, but was, quite obviously, the essence of British militance and anathema to NAWSA. CU militancy would bring to an end the CC/CU's first political phase as a NAWSA organization. Both philosophically and practically, the CU remained closely connected with the Pankhursts until the summer of 1914, when the militants of the WSPU defected from "The Cause" in order to help in the English war effort against Germany. In light of Pankhurst "toughness," it was, perhaps, logical for the British militants to turn from their acts of sabotage against their government to war service; the official reason given was that their militancy was "less effective" in the face of the violence of war, and patriotism demanded their joining the war effort.[47]

Before the WSPU turned from suffrage work, the CU did not, as Nancy Cott has said, disavow their "violence." Paul and Burns consistently answered inquiries about the CU's association with WSPU activities by admitting their sympathies: "[A]s an organization we are not responsible for that [militancy in England], though I believe most of us sympathize and approve of it." In fact, Paul wrote that "[Lucy Burns and I] are working together in Washington, but our hearts are still in the W.S.P.U."[48] CU members continued to join with Paul and Burns because of that "strong suggestion of the Pankhursts" in the new group. Burns was matter-of-fact about the CU plan to follow the "party in power" policy of the WSPU as early as December of 1913, arguing that since both governments were "under a party system," it would be natural to follow their lead.[49] Continuing to support and be associated with the Pankhursts was no small thing in 1913-1914. Guerilla warfare continued: paintings slashed, government members' houses burned, windows smashed en masse, telegraph wires clipped, and red pepper and snuff sent to cabinet ministers. In 1914 the Cat and Mouse Act was passed by Parliament as an alternative to letting the British suffrage prisoners die--or giving them the vote. "G. Doffett" reported to the sympathetic Paul that "the way women are treated in England is intolerable. . . . [and] the men are enjoying it." She asked Paul to deliver Annie Kenney's temporary discharge under the Act to President Wilson so that he might protest to the British government.[50] It was to the CU that British suffragists appealed for help, and they obliged.

CU women shared the militant spirit of the British WSPU, but in 1913 and 1914 were still committed to working within normal American political channels to win suffrage. In an October 21, 1913 speech in Madison Square Garden, Emmeline Pankhurst stated that in a sense, American women did not have to be militant, because the WSPU had done their fighting for them.[51] CU leaders strongly supported the Pankhursts' militant struggle and wholeheartedly admired their strong-minded feminism. Mary Beard wrote an impassioned article that same month (refused for publication by *Pearson's Magazine*) which insisted that "Americans have lost their sense of democracy" in refusing to honor Emmeline Pankhurst. Since Americans had honored Hungarian rebel Louis Kossuth in 1851, she wondered why they did not do the same for the rebel Mrs. Pankhurst, particularly when *she* refused to take human life in her rebellion? The reason, wrote Beard, was because she was a woman.

> What is feminine is hysterical, frenzied, or just idiotic . . . in a man's world. A man's world merely! Ah, ye men who think only the thoughts of your world! And ye women who think only the thoughts of men! May the time soon come when you may be able to think your own thoughts![52]

As horror upon horror appeared in the news from London, the CU assured the press and public that "the actions of Mrs. Pankhurst are absolutely justified by the condition in that country." But the CU affirmed their faith in progressive America: "We have no intention of starting anything like that here because it is unnecessary."[53] Another CU member, Rheta Childe Dorr, Pankhurst's travelling companion, was certainly wholly sympathetic to the aggressiveness of the WSPU feminist cause. Again, she made distinctions between the British and American situations, but wrote Paul a letter of encouragement from England vowing that "we'll give the austere Woodrow the fight of his life, believe me."[54] Such words brought little comfort to more conservative suffragists.

As Christine Lunardini has discussed thoroughly elsewhere, [55] at first, Paul and Burns' visibility as WSPU sympathizers was seen as valuable, but not all that important, to NAWSA leaders. Soon, however, their defiant lobbying techniques became unacceptable to the parent organization. What needs to be stressed is that it was the militantly egalitarian, feminist philosophy behind their technique which really set them apart from from NAWSA suffragists. Catt had been amazed and impressed by the Pankhursts' accomplishments in England, but adament about not using their methods in America and uneasy with their aggressiveness.[56] As the CU became more independent, and stronger, that difference--their strong feminism *and* militant-spirited strategies, obviously influenced by the British--became a liability and an embarrassment to a NAWSA leadership determined not to erode the legislative and public support they had painstakingly won for suffrage. When Paul and Burns were busy handling the Pankhurst visit in October, NAWSA's Mary Ware Dennet wrote a worried letter to Paul about the Congressional Union's connection to the Pankhursts.[57]

NAWSA officers were sure that the aggressive CU was doing damage by pushing too hard, alienating Wilson and antagonizing the public with their incessant, unladylike lobbying. Wilson had already tried to avoid the unending suffrage delegations of the CU whenever possible and failed to mention woman suffrage in his December Congressional message. To counter the impression given by their forceful colleagues, NAWSA began to release to the press statements which were very negative about the CU in order to indicate their displeasure. One release features remarks by Representative Irvine Lenroot of Wisconsin, who regretted suffragist policies that might lead to "militance": "To adopt such tactics in this country would destroy in my judgement all that has been accomplished during the last ten years, and so long as it existed there would be no progress whatever made along the lines or securing the ballot for women."[58] In November 1913 Anna Howard Shaw wrote Burns an irate letter regarding Burns' arrest in Washington for chalking meeting notices on the sidewalk: "We will not be like England."[59] Burns' calm reply was that it would "be unreasonable" for her and Paul to have "a militant spirit" just when the President and Congress were so encouraging. She had paid her $1.00 fine, and the incident meant nothing.[60] Burns tried in vain to negotiate with NAWSA over items like disputed powers of decision-making, sending national organizers into states also working for state suffrage with NAWSA, and the evolving party responsibility policy. Shaw tried to convince Burns, as a presumably more pleasant and malleable personality than Paul, to chair a Congressional Committee in 1914 and disassociate it from the CU. Burns refused to do that, although she was loathe to leave NAWSA.[61] When Paul and Burns were finally asked to be on the Committee with Ruth McCormick in charge, the two objected to not being first consulted. They reiterated their belief in British "militance" in letters to various NAWSA officers, although they stressed that there was "no likelihood of it here."[62]

At the December convention, the problems between the two groups with their conflicting reform philosophies, came to a head when Burns disclosed the CU's plan to begin the controversial "party in power" policy which was so closely associated with the militant Pankhursts. Burns announced that if the Democrats were unwilling to help women gain suffrage, then the CU would work against all Democrats in the coming elections. The militance of this policy was totally unacceptable to NAWSA leadership. Along with these strategic differences, as usual, there was also censure of the CU over money management. The convention voted to make intricate changes in the NAWSA constitution which led to a reclassification of the Congressional Union, the necessity for their re-application, and ultimately, NAWSA's refusal to accept their application.[63] Paul and Burns were honestly saddened and shaken (Paul, in fact, became quite ill) by the entire episode, and seemed to remain conciliatory throughout the split: "[W]e all regret deeply your hostility toward us. We are utterly at loss to understand what we have done of which you disapprove and hope that sometime you will be willing to give us an opportunity of clearing up whatever misunderstanding exists."[64] Apparently, the CU was taking too many active members away from NAWSA, along with money, territory, publicity and power. But the grievances lay beyond issues of money and members. The CU stood for a militancy, an aggressive, unapologetically egalitarian, feminist style, which NAWSA members could not countenance.

In January of 1914, the *New York Times*' headlines announced "Suffragist Rivals Now In The Field" as NAWSA denounced Burns and Paul as women "tinged with militancy."[65] Carrie Chapman Catt, looking back on the suffrage struggle, characterized the CU as a "hindrance . . . [that] annoyed the men . . . [it was] too partisan . . misguided really." Anna H. Shaw wrote that "militant methods were unworthy and unAmerican." The CU, according to NAWSA leaders, made legislators "suspicious of suffragists"; after which they had to be "soothed." Clearly, NAWSA did not want to "be taken over by militants."[66] Mrs. Ruth Medill McCormick stated in the *Washington Herald* that

> [t]he Congressional Union is opposed to every method employed by woman suffragists in America. It is militant clean through. . . . Miss Alice Paul and Miss Lucy Burns . . . have both been trained under the militant methods of Mrs. Pankhurst. . . . Their methods may go in England, but they are no good here.[67]

Rejected by NAWSA, the militant-spirited Congressional Union would now function as an independent organization--still doggedly working within the bounds of the political system. Woman suffrage seemed such a logical goal of progressive democratic reform; why it should take so long to achieve was a mystery to Burns and Paul. As militant feminists, they did believe that women must take it upon themselves to demand suffrage, and use tactics of strength rather than those that cajoled and pleaded.

In 1914-1915, in phase two of "pre-militancy," the newly independent Congressional Union increased the pressure of their political activity by applying a "party in power" strategy. In January 1914, the *New York Times* quoted Lucy

Burns on the "militant" CU policy, which was to "ask from the party in power in Congress the passage of a constitutional amendment enfranchising women, and to hold that party responsible for its answer to this request." By "party in power," the CU referred to the majority party's (Democratic) members' caucus, usually binding; its majority on major committees; its control of appointments; and the power of the majority party to push its own program.[68] Burns realized the party responsibility policy would be even more upsetting to Congressmen than their earlier aggressive lobbying:

> All other mysteries of women faded before this last one, that she should stop asking her 'friends' to give, and attempt, herself, to get. In the most modern of her activities, politics, the old-fashioned woman has persisted longest. No one now looks for the appealing creature of the '80s in the drawing room, or for the helpless amateur needing a lift over fences in the field of sports; but in the political arena there is evidently a certain shock in finding us able to take care of ourselves.[69]

A touch of militancy, bringing to life a feminist philosophy of power, was obvious in this new campaign strategy.

The CU party in power strategy was to be applied to all phases of its operations, beginning with continued, persistent lobbying of the party in power's chief--Woodrow Wilson. In February 1914, a large delegation of working women seemed, to some observers, to move Wilson. He told them, "The strength of your agitation will make a profound impression." Wilson could easily have been impressed by women like CU organizer Rose Winslow. She was born Ruza Wenclawska in Poland, became a factory worker in Philadelphia at age 11, and contracted tuberculosis at 19. The striking-looking Winslow had been a union organizer and worked for the Consumers' League. She was also a poet and an actress, an "eloquent speaker." Winslow told the President that working women needed the power of the vote: "I am one of the thousands of women who work in the sweated trades, and have been since a child, who give their lives to build up these tremendous industries in this country, and at the end of the years of work, our reward is the tuberculosis sanitarium or the street."[70] A report in the *New York World* indicated Wilson was unmoved by Winslow, in fact, that he appeared amused by the women. The article implied that the women were ridiculous, "snubbing" Wilson, some refusing his handshake. The CU press release agreed with the "snubbing," but called the women's anger justifiable. Rebecca Winsor Evans, of the Pennsylvania CU, remarked that some of the President's statements were simply "gunning for votes."[71] The women present at this encounter were dismayed by Wilson's apparently impervious indifference.

The frustrating experience of the working women's delegation was followed by yet more disappointment. In March of 1914, the first suffrage vote in the Senate since 1887 was scheduled. The CU had created a "Congressional Index," which was a file on every Congressman and Senator listing family background, marital status, clubs, religion, profession, community standing, and views on suffrage, labor and other legislation. From the Index it was clear the Senate vote should be postponed until after the fall elections, when suffrage supporters were expected to win. Another complication was added that month when Senator John Shafroth introduced the Shafroth-Palmer Resolution which held that "each state should hold a referendum on woman suffrage *if* more than 8% of the legal [male] voters in the last preceding election . . . signed a petition for it." The CU preferred to continue to work for the federal Susan B. Anthony (or Bristow-Mondell) amendment which simply stated the right to vote could not be denied on account of sex.[72] Woman suffrage did not win a 2/3 majority in the Senate, but the full-scale debate it generated showed the Senators most preoccupied with how woman suffrage related to matters of race, states' rights and the strength of the liquor industry. Idaho's Senator William Borah expressed the sentiments of the majority on women's rights when he worried that women who voted might depart "from the avenues and walks of life for which they are particularly fitted and [enter] a mode of life not in harmony with the highest ideals of womanhood."[73] Aggressive and increasingly impatient CU lobbyists were far from conforming to Senator Borah's ideal.

In fact, CU delegations to Wilson featured a certain unfeminine defiant tone which did not at all please him. A delegation of clubwomen on June 30, 1914, led by Anna Kelton Wiley and Rheta Childe Dorr, seemed to especially upset the President. After hearing his usual "leave suffrage to the states" remarks, Dorr pointedly questioned Wilson as to the existence of precedents for altering the electorate by constitutional amendment. Wilson became distinctly annoyed at being "cross-examined" and then hissed [!]. Such incidents enhanced the CU suffragists' reputation as "hecklers" of Presidents. In the *Suffragist*, Lucy Burns was scornful of the President's refusal to help: "Only fitfully do women realize the astounding arrogance of their rulers."[74] The confrontation of Wilson versus the CU delegation did not go unnoticed. Senator John Randolph Thornton sent Wilson a sympathetic note, to which Wilson replied he "came through the ordeal yesterday, intact, I believe." One supporter told Wilson that a suffragist is a woman "who cannot raise Babies, but who *can* raise Hell." Another thanked him for the "way you shut off the Women Howlers."[75] All his supporters assumed that Wilson's states' rights position was an anti-suffrage position, and were relieved to have "a man" in the White House to stand against the "present 'feminist' movement"--an example they thought should have been taken by English leaders against "the militant outrage."[76] The "Women Howlers" had upset the President, but they were, for their part, also upset and had barely begun to exercise their woman power tactics.

A policy meeting of officers held in late August 1914 at Alva Belmont's opulent "cottage" in Newport, established that CU threats about holding the party in power responsible for inaction on woman suffrage must be carried further. The

Democratic Congress had not been moved to action by the CU organizing throughout the country, nor by their holding mass meetings and demonstrations. Burns, the party theorist, explained to CU officers how the Democrats were effectively "blocking" woman suffrage through their control of Congress and its important committees. Paul then proposed a fall election program, asking, "Who is our enemy and how shall that enemy be attacked?"[77] The enemy, of course, was Wilson's Democrats, and the program suggested to the CU executives was to appeal to the women of the West, of the nine states where women could vote, to vote against the Democrats in 1914.

Paul and Burns, presiding over the newly independent CU, had an expanded executive board to convince. The five-member executive committee (Paul, Burns, Beard, Eastman and Lewis) had been expanded to include Elizabeth Kent, Matilda Hall Gardner (lobby committee "chairman"), Edith Hooker (finance "chairman"), Alva Belmont and Elsie Hill. All of the new officers were of markedly affluent backgrounds, the rationale being they would be invaluable fundraisers; their teas, balls, dinners and lawn parties for suffrage would be sure to attract press coverage.[78] Paul, working closely with Burns on most issues, was gradually establishing herself as the one truly the head of the CU. Burns did exercise leadership, especially for the party in power campaign, but overall strategy blueprints and making sure things got done, became Paul's responsibilities.

Paul was "chairman" of the CU, and then National Woman's Party, for her lifetime. She always drove herself mercilessly to exhaustion with "an airy disdain" for physical ill health and would also have little patience with her colleagues' illnesses or family and work obligations. Often called the "general" of the suffrage campaign, she brought to it her uncanny memory for detail and immense ability as tactician. Paul turned her stubborn impatience into a capability for getting things accomplished; she "brushed aside red tape, and ignored the rules." With a squaring of her jaw and a piercing stare for her victim, she could move just about anyone to do her will. Paul received many laudatory comments for her leadership from her colleagues; in 1916 Katharine Rolston Fisher eloquently called her the "commander of the column, its leader; she was the spring whence arose that irresistible river of women. . . ."[79]

Some women did not respond well to Commander Paul's style. Rheta Childe Dorr was the first editor of the *Suffragist*, the CU journal, but resigned in late April of 1914, because she said Paul "wanted a hired man," and did not consult her about the staff. Paul, ever brusque and businesslike about the loss of her brilliant editor, wrote Dora Lewis: "Mrs. Dorr has resigned. . . . This will save us $100 a month." After losing Dorr through Paul's lack of tact, a bit later, the CU lost a valuable California activist when Charlotte Whitney left the CU because she thought it was an "autocratic organization with its control entirely in the hands of one woman . . . [The] CU is submerging the individuality of the worker into a blind following under hypnotic leadership."[80] Paul did not lead unchallenged or entirely without resentment in some quarters.

In contrast to Paul's iron will, Burns relied on the charm of her "contagious grin" and "sparkling blue eyes." She was "vice-chairman" (through 1917) and was a tireless and brilliant speaker/organizer in the West besides. She served as legislative "chairman" in 1914-1916, directing the drive aimed at persuading women to pass suffrage resolutions and also organizing massive rallies at the Capitol. In her spare time, Burns, after Dorr's resignation, did a very professional job of editing the *Suffragist*.[81] Burns' workload was enormous. Added to it was leading the debate for British-style party in power tactics at the August meeting.

At the Newport meeting, Burns, with Mary Beard, argued that unlike British women, American women already had some significant power politically. American women did not have to resort to "civil militancy because we have the great lever of enfranchised women to help us and the English have none." Englishwomen had little choice but extreme measures: "The struggle in England has gotten down to a physical fight. Here our fight is simply a political one."[82] Again, CU women planned a democratic strategy of exercising existing political rights in order to win their reform. Their chosen way, however, blocking the Democrats, was seen as unorthodox, "foreign" and militant. CU leaders insisted party responsibility was a democratic and American method, citing the Anthony-Stanton precedents of supporting only parties that helped woman suffrage. They admitted, though: "This policy will be called militant and in a sense it is, being strong, positive and energetic." Paul and Burns argued that if it was militant to appeal to western women to use their vote in the cause of national suffrage, then it was militant to ask anyone to vote to further any good progressive end. They wanted all political parties to realize that women, instead of simply counting on individual "friends" of suffrage in both parties to help them, could themselves be a power, and could directly affect the results of an election. Paul saw the CU as having no other course: "[H]ow else were we going to demonstrate that women could be influential, independent voters?"[83] The executive committee at Newport decided to support Paul and Burns in their strategy of holding the party in power responsible, and with that decision showed a growing willingness to be thought, and called, "militant."

In order to implement the party responsibility plan, the CU used an expanded team of organizers to win the women of the West away from the Democrats. Alice Paul tried to use organizers to represent the aggressive Congressional Union who were fresh, youthful, intelligent and attractive. Paul told an interviewer in 1972 that every reform movement needs people "who are full of enthusiasm. . . . I didn't want any lukewarm person around."[84] CU organizers had to be virtually tireless, and independent enough to undertake tasks calling for constant ingenuity and sometimes, courage. The indomitable Mabel Vernon, who worked with close friend Anne Martin in Nevada, described the winning of the West:

> In the West they do not have the feeling that suffrage is an old, old story. They were very willing to go to a suffrage meeting,

> particularly in the mining camps, where to advertise that a woman is going to speak is almost enough to close down the mines in order that they might hear her. . . . We would travel sometimes 120 miles in order to reach a little settlement. . . . There was only the sand, the sage-brush, and the sky.[85]

Using the "voiceless speeches" of hand-held cards, films, handbills, and countless meetings, the CU appealed to women to vote for the rights of women by voting against the Democrats. Organizers told their audiences that national woman suffrage would increase women's power to do something about "women's progressive causes: 'the white slave traffic, the employment of child labor, [and] the sale of impure food and diseased clothing.'"[86] The CU's western organizers' aim was to win suffrage for women, but just as important was to show that women were fully capable of fighting the battle for themselves. As Elsie Hill put it: "Don't ask for pity or special consideration. If you can't do the job, don't take it. Don't have them throw it into your face that women can't do these things."[87] The CU succeeded in making a powerful enough impression upon western women so that it had an impact on their vote in the 1914 elections.

The CU women's exercise of power was not welcomed in all quarters. Democratic party leaders and partisan newspaper editors were up in arms, "intimidating and coercing" CU organizers, telling them to go home, and organizing Democratic women against them. Organizer Elsie Lancaster, working in Utah, was even harassed and cross-examined at Democratic headquarters. Naturally, Republicans were delighted. In the end, of 43 Democrats up for Congressional election in 1914, 20 won. But as Meredith Snapp has argued, the CU, more importantly, had succeeded in making national woman suffrage an issue in the election. From then on, it was hoped, politicians would have to take woman suffrage and woman's power to influence the electorate into account. And, in fact, in December, the House Rules Committee decided to report woman suffrage out.[88]

In 1915 the CU campaign of party responsibility was still within the realm of progressive reformism--particularly the concept of becoming a national organization, with a single reform object. In March, 1915, the CU formally became a national association; and a year later, would form a political party, the Woman's Party of Western Voters. Each step increased the level of political action. After two years of petitioning, national leaders had yet to be convinced of the importance of the woman's franchise. President Wilson politely received a delegation on January 6, 1915, but he wrote a friend that morning that "suffrage for women will make absolutely no change in politics--it is the home that will be disastrously affected. Somebody has to make the home and who is going to do it if the women don't?" Wilson told his new wife that a woman "fit to be a man's counsellor" was one who lived "to warm, to comfort, and command--and yet! not too bright or good for human nature's daily food."[89] When woman suffrage was debated and went down in defeat in the House on January 12, it was obvious that

Congressmen's views of women's rights were still as limited as the nation's leader's. Mr. Stanley Bowdle, Democrat of Ohio, was greeted with appreciative leers and laughter when he commented: "The women of this smart capitol are beautiful--their feet are beautiful, their ankles are beautiful. --But here I must pause."[90] Throughout the rest of 1915, the men of the national government would have little more positive to add for the cause of women's political equality.

Faced with a wall of governmental, male indifference, CU women became ever more self-consciously feminist. As in Anthony's NWSA, under the new CU national constitution, men were excluded from membership: the group would officially and emphatically be women organizing for power. The CU was "open to all women who, regarding woman suffrage as the foremost political issue of the day, will work without considering the interests of any national political party." Under the new national plan organizers were sent out to reach into every state to arrange conventions to promote the national amendment, a tall order for an organization that was very small at the start of 1915, a few thousand at most. This meant enormous effort by a few. In 1915 Mabel Vernon alone went to Delaware, Ohio, Colorado, Utah, Oregon, Washington and Idaho to help arrange state conventions. Vernon also recruited like-minded women to come work in Washington, to interview every single Congressman, Senator and cabinet member in the Capitol, and see the President whenever possible.[91]

Formally a national organization, the CU hoped to have much more leverage on the men in Washington. The CU kept very close track of each party's individual Congressmen and Senators; CU Index files were kept up-to-date and detailed. Alice Paul told a *New York Times* reporter that if a Senator "is for it, we will know, and give ourselves no more concern about him; but, if he is against it we will leave no stone unturned to bring him into line."[92] The staged events in 1915 dramatized a powerful message of woman's solidarity on national suffrage, trying to show Congress and the President that the demand for the franchise was "vigorous and general." Such was the aim of the flamboyant suffrage exhibition at the San Francisco International Exposition; and the eventful fall "auto tour" conducted by Sara Bard Field and Frances Joliffe.[93] Field and a CU delegation met with Wilson on December 6, armed with a petition signed by a half million voters [!]. His response was not encouraging.

In 1915, Wilson proved consistently immovable. Therefore, the CU suffragists were willing to be a bit more militant in strategy in 1915 than in 1914. When in May, a group of Pennsylvania CU members waited for three days to see President Wilson, by then occupied with the world war, he would not give them an audience and said he "deplored" their persistence. Significantly, Lucy Burns wrote to the editor of the *Washington Star*, using an argument which echoed the Pankhursts, that the wait of the Pennsylvania suffragists was a "touch of militancy" created by the government's intransigence. If these women were censured for "militance," then why not censure the much more militant Mexican, English and German men--who were all fighting in wars--as well?[94] Alice Paul wrote two highly significant letters to Burns which discussed the "militant" Pennsylvania incident. In the first letter, she wrote that in the wake of what happened to the "scorned" women, she had had to decide whether to do nothing or use "actual militancy . . . aggressive tactics." Since the event had happened right after the German sinking of the Lusitania with the nation still in an uproar, the decision had been to do nothing at that time.[95] However, in this 1915 letter, Paul showed deep regret that they had done nothing to show their displeasure with Wilson, and suggested a definite willingness to be openly and actively militant well before the 1917 picketing. Still, some tactical advantages were possibly reaped from the occasion, as Paul wrote in a second letter:

> It seems to me that we want to convict him [Wilson] before the country of evading us. We ought to be able to get publicity for a considerable time out of his refusing to see us. And when we have exhausted the possibilities in that line and he has gotten the reputation of refusing to see suffragists, I should think we might go further and *try to make him see us*. [author's emphasis]

With this, Paul predicted exactly what would happen within the next two years. She went on: "[T]he women in the deputation were indignant and were altogether in a wholesome frame of mind." This line neatly characterized a growing feeling within the CU in 1915-1916, an anger and frustration with the government that would give them the emotional strength to eventually withstand arrests and prison. Paul ended the letter with: "Militancy [by which she meant here, active civil disobedience, á la Pankhurst] is not something to be started lightly and without much consideration."[96]

The Pennsylvania delegation incident was decried in the press as another example of the CU's "heckling the president," and worse, in time of war. To that, editorials in the *Suffragist* (written by Burns) replied that people who said the suffragists should not "bother" the president in time of crisis, did not realize that that was a perfect time to "heckle" him, when people were most "awake":

> When the people suffer from a real injustice, the best and most lasting service they can make to their country is to demand that the injustice be ended. The women of the country are suffering under a deep wrong against which they have actively protested for over a century; and their protests have been met with ridicule, with blunt refusal, with tricking and evasion.

Burns was infuriated that the president could not find five minutes to meet with women and warned "anger is building."[97] Paul's admonition to Burns that militancy, or acts of defiance against the authorities, could not be started lightly, may well have been the beginning of her realization that it might become necessary.

Naturally, the "militance" of the Pennsylvania delegation brought forth disapproval and dismay. Within the CU's own ranks, several members resigned over such defiant "heckling." Even a woman as dedicated as Katherine Fisher, who was a CU district officer in Boston and would later be among those imprisoned for picketing, protested this "harassment" of the President and its bad publicity. NAWSA suffragists, already jealous of CU organizing efforts alongside theirs in the states, as might be expected, thoroughly disapproved, passing a resolution at their June 1915 convention against CU actions, and showing concern lest they be linked in Wilson or the public's minds with the "militants." CU advisor Lavinia Dock countered by firing off a letter to Carrie Chapman Catt chastising her for criticizing the Pennsylvania delegation: "Women need to take a more spirited stand and not be absurdly lectured by editors."[98] The CU's aim, however, was not to create rifts between women by their "spirited stand," quite the opposite.

The CU argued that women had to work together, as a power bloc, for suffrage. Their major target, Woodrow Wilson, did vote for suffrage (in a losing cause) in New Jersey in October, but for all the wrong reasons, according to the CU. He said he had voted "not as the leader of my party in the nation, but only upon my private conviction as a citizen of New Jersey." He maintained that woman suffrage was an issue to be settled by the states and "in no circumstance should it be made a party question; and my view has grown stronger at every turn of the agitation." Shaw and Catt sent him their heartfelt gratitude for his New Jersey vote, but the CU "agitators" did not appreciate his states' rights position.[99] In December, at the presentation of Field's petition, Anne Martin reminded the President women were both suffragists and voters: "Speak to your party and as its leader impress upon Congress the importance of passing the [national] suffrage amendment." Receiving the petition, Wilson said it was "an impressive thing" and he hoped he "shall continue to be a learner," but it was much too late to include woman suffrage in his impending Congressional message. The stubborn CU militants asked to have another audience during his January visit to New York; he refused, saying he was seeing no delegations. Hearing that he was seeing 1500 ministers on the 27th, 100 CU women assembled to try to see Wilson as well. He again declined, but the women persisted, waiting for two hours. He finally appeared, saying again he felt the "genius" of the government lay in its state by state method of changing laws. The President then started to leave, but Mary Beard, in inimitable CU style, stopped him by asking if the Clayton Antitrust Act had been gained state by state. He coldly declined to discuss it.[100] Here indeed were most annoying women--women who "reversed the social order" by insisting on their legitimate say as citizens.

As the Congressional Union's party in power phase of political strategy came to a close in 1915, it was evident that their basic, egalitarian feminist belief in acting for themselves was setting them further and further apart from NAWSA suffragists. CU member Marie Jenney Howe wrote in 1915 that the attitude of CU women was unlike that of "other suffragists" who said "please" and "we beg." The CU stance was a "demanding one," informing the government: "Here is what you are not doing for us, this is what we intend to do for ourselves." The essence of the CU was their spirit of insisting on suffrage: "That attitude shows power." What impressed reformer Frederic Howe about a MacKaye tableau of December 1915 was its powerful message of woman's need to be considered whole and strong:

> I feel for the first time the fervor of the movement. The hunger of women to be unshackled and freed for life and opportunity and the power for social and economic justice which the stupid sex qualification now imposes upon all of us. --Not on women alone but on men as well. It is possibly the greatest of all wastes.[101]

Many woman suffragists could sympathize with Howe's sentiments about more freedom for women, but not to extending that freedom to "demand" suffrage and "heckle" the President of the United States. NAWSA remained philosophically opposed to the CU's "negative coercive policy" rather than their own "positive" strategies of patient, "moral suasion." Allies of suffrage must be won as individuals and as "friends" of suffrage; they should not be coerced, but soothed and convinced.

In 1915, given their beliefs, NAWSA leaders were understandably afraid the militant CU was quickly losing them their friends, and driving Wilson further away from suffrage. Beyond the philosophical problems they had with "taking" suffrage, NAWSA suffragists believed the "power" strategy of 1915-1916, ill-conceived. Catt argued that there was "no such thing" as "party responsibility" in America and that to exercise power by convincing western women to vote against all Democrats, "friendly" or unfriendly, was a grave error. She also insisted there was no "party in power" because Wilson and Congressional Democrats simply did not have that sort of control over legislation. Catt and Shaw accused the CU of being "divisive," splitting the suffrage movement and setting suffrage back with their aggressive tactics.[102]

Actually, the dynamic CU, in many ways, had revived the movement. CU activity helped push NAWSA into pursuing strong national strategies of its own. Seven unsuccessful western state campaigns in 1914 had been very discouraging to NAWSA suffragists--enough so that six of nine national officers were changed at year's end. In 1915, four mammoth eastern state campaigns were waged and all were lost. In 1916, when Catt assumed the presidency, she instituted long-range planning and large-scale fund raising to inject new life into NAWSA's national suffrage campaign. She feared, however, that the defiant stance of Alice Paul and the CU might threaten her new "winning plan." Catt described the Woman's Party has having an "entirely separate and often conflicting program."[103] And the major bone of contention which remained throughout the suffrage years was the NWP's stubborn, British-inspired militancy.

The CU/NWP would always be linked in the public eye with the British militants, but there remained real differences between the two groups. *Farm Journal* editor Wilmer Atkin wrote to Wilson expressing fear that CU "militancy" was too much like the Pankhursts. It was "only a matter of time before they throw stones." The *Journal* editor much preferred "pacific" NAWSA women, who understood that male voters must be "handled with delicacy." The CU women were hardly worried about "delicacy," but as was seen in the Paul-Burns correspondence regarding the Pennsylvania delegation, they hesitated over beginning "real" militant acts. Although CU women were growing increasingly impatient, and their actions would begin to show it, they were still very careful not to appear, or at least be labelled, "militant" by the press and public, because militancy had unpopular violent connotations of British stone-throwing. Not until 1917 when picketing started, would they readily accept the label. CU spokeswomen insisted in 1915-1916 they did "not advocate militant methods [for America] ... [but were] strictly constitutional and pacific." Lucy Burns wrote the editor of the *Chicago Post* that the Congressional Union did not have a "counterpart in England ... [that] 'heckling' (the President) is not militant ... Any people ... which dares not rebuke a representative who denies them justice will certainly never be free."[104] Through 1916, CU suffragists firmly believed American representatives would be moved by the public response to their progressive, power strategy.

Congressional Union policy for the election of 1916, as it turned out its final attempt at purely political action, was to have the enfranchised women of the western states form a political party to vote in a bloc against Wilson and his party. In this third and last phase, CU organizers called upon the women of the West to help their "sisters in the East" win political rights. In yet another excellent publicity move, the CU used the device of a "Suffrage Special," a train full of suffragists led by the charismatic Lucy Burns, to make whistle stops in the West to call women voters to the convention where the Woman's Party would by formed. The CU speakers apparently deeply impressed the people they addressed at train stops: Abby Scott Baker reported that formerly amused men changed their attitude to "Bully for you" after hearing the militants. When the train arrived in Salt Lake City in May, a mammoth conference of women voters chose delegates from their new party, who joined the suffrage special crew on the trip back to Washington, where amidst much pomp and ceremony, suffrage resolution were handed to Congress.[105]

The following month, at a convention held before those of the "other" parties, the Woman's Party of Western Women Voters' creation was formally announced. Under a strict party responsibility policy, the Democrats would be held responsible for nonaction on the Woman's Party's one and only plank, "the enfranchisement of the women of America through a Federal Amendment." The decision to form the party and adopt such a policy had not been made easily; as ever, consensus had to be reached and there was a great deal of heated discussion before the entire advisory council could be convinced. In fact, one council member, Vassar professor Lucy Salmon, was so upset over the new policy that she left the party. Paul argued that four million women voted for president; they voted for one-quarter of the Senate, one-sixth of the House, and one-fifth of electoral votes came from woman suffrage states.[106] With that much potential power, the Woman's Party directed its aim at defeating Wilson and the Democrats: The Woman's Party is opposing Mr. Wilson because he is the leader of the party which has used that control to block and defeat the national enfranchisement of women."[107] The founding of the Woman's Party again reflected the militant feminists' belief that women could only gain political power through their own action.

The point of women's necessary self-sufficiency was underscored for the CU when Elsie Hill and Rose Winslow attended a Colorado convention of "labor men" in August, and found the men adamantly opposed to passing a woman suffrage resolution. Winslow, astonished by her fellow workers, remarked: "[N]othing could show more plainly to women ... that the enfranchisement of women is necessarily a woman's fight ... Women must unite to solve their own problems, in their own way, by their own efforts." *Suffragist* editorials also insisted: "Liberty must be fought for. And, women of the nation, this is the time to demonstrate our sisterhood, our spirit, our blithe courage and our will." [108] The resistance of Democratic men was even more apparent, and was making CU suffragists more and more angry, driving them closer to overt, active militancy. Anne Martin, former WSPU warrior, and CU "political chairman" as of 1916, made her anger clear in a *Suffragist* article which insisted men should be "ashamed" to make women come day after day simply to ask for their rights. Waiting upon New York Congressman Walter Chandler, Martin had been given his objections "with considerable heat," to having his time" 'wasted' by suffragist[s]." She told him he was just as much wasting *their* time by blocking suffrage from coming out of the judiciary committee:

> It is very seldom that women pause to consider the abasement of their position when public officers can dare affront them so frankly, not only calmly denying them equal rights with themselves--an injustice so crass as to be ludicrous--but denying to the bill granting them equal rights a chance to be voted on.... [Their] opposition [is] deeply rooted in the belief of the inferiority of women.[109]

CU suffragists wanted to act to change such attitudes.

Woman's Party leaders saw revolutionary implications in their struggle for political rights, and they were not the only ones. A 1916 *New York Times* editorial called the "threat of sex vs. sex" carried out by the new Woman's Party: "Political blackmail . . . an ugly portent, whose possibilities of damage are not limited to politics, but may extend to other parts of the social structure. These [WP] leaders have justified to the extent of their powers, the worst that has ever been said about the danger of giving votes to women." Hostility would not be limited to the *Times*, but also came--in large doses--from the public. A Georgia woman sent Anne Martin this piece of doggerel: "A female creature, queer and quaint, Who longs to be just what she ain't/We cannot efface, - we can't forgive her - We love her still - the stiller the better." [110] Suffrage militants were not at all typical of proper womanhood, and the presentation of their party program to the public would not be easy.

Luckily, the new WP had talented leadership and a dedicated membership. The WP took over CU congressional district organizations in the western suffrage states. By that time, 26 states had CU branches, and CU numbers had been greatly augmented by a February merger with Blatch's New York WPU. The strong-willed Harriot Stanton Blatch would not be particularly pleased with mere lieutenancy in the new party, and she was not alone. The new "chairman" of the Woman's Party was Anne Martin. Although she had been elected to head the Western Woman's Party, the CU remained in charge, and Paul, of course, ran the CU. Martin had been serving as legislative "chairman" and sat on the CU executive committee; she was also used to leading the suffrage forces in her own state of Nevada. She always chafed under Paul's command. Paul responded by handling Martin with kid gloves, but was still resented by Martin. Martin, at this point, was still convinced that state suffrage should be won first in Nevada, and then in New Jersey (a former NAWSA assignment), before a federal amendment was sought. She continually fought Paul on such issues, and was also constantly complaining about not being given proper credit for her efforts as CU legislative chairman. Martin was often upset about what she saw as either inaccurate or unwanted statements about her in the *Suffragist*, and she demanded to be given proper respect. Her friends told her it was "lovely" of her to give way to "Miss Paul" in not taking the credit she deserved. Anne Martin was one who repeatedly challenged Paul's leadership. In an organization which combined women with fiercely independent personalites, clashes were inevitable.[111]

In 1916 Martin and the WP resolved to use their best efforts to convince women of the West to vote "Republican, Socialist, Prohibitionist or Progressive--anything but Democratic." "Wilson Kept Us Out Of Suffrage" was the message brought to the West in a flurry of handbills and banners, and countless meetings and luncheons. The *Suffragist* was another device the CU/WP used to reach as many groups of women as possible, asking them to send resolutions urging the "free" women of the West to use their votes to help their unfortunate sisters of the East. Probably most responsive were, as usual, local socialist parties; and they were joined by groups as diverse as Jewish women, the WCTU, charity organizations and the WTUL. One problem party leaders began to have in recruiting was that many many women were becoming involved in the European allied war effort--or peace effort. As "the war to end all wars," World War I would be a preoccupation for many American citizens, well before the United States entered the war in 1917. The war would have many repercussions for the Woman's Party; in 1916 concerns of war meant fewer volunteers for suffrage. Even Crystal Eastman, who had spent tremendous amounts of energy for the CU as an officer in its early years, was now, in spite of all of Alice Paul's power of persuasion, working only for peace.[112] Again, somehow women needed to be convinced by the CU that only one cause remained imperative--their own.

Woman's Party organizers spared nothing in their attempt to use women's solidarity against the Democrats. Women were sent out from headquarters to all the western states; some were older, experienced suffragists like Harriot Stanton Blatch, but most, as earlier, were college women with much needed youth and energy. All organizers kept daily progress reports, sent to Anne Martin at Chicago headquarters, listing the number of street meetings, indoor meetings, new members, *Suffragist* subscriptions, new committees, the amount of money collected and spent, the number of newspapers stories published, and remarks on the political situation. The organizers were then duly congratulated or chided on the job they were doing.[113]

As in 1914, organizers complained of an uphill fight: Katharine Morey of Boston wrote Burns that "Kansas women have no thinking capacity." She had to tell them why they should vote, and the only way to convince them was with "lurid stories about the white slave trade or women in factories." Anne Martin worked Nevada with Mabel Vernon and Maud Younger, and even pressed her mother into service, having her speak at a Reno street corner. Her mother was heckled by a drunk, but went bravely on until a policeman escorted her home. Even the unshakeable Lucy Burns had difficulty. In October, she wrote Paul from Montana, "I am so nervous, I cannot eat or sleep. . . . I am such a coward, I ought to be the village seamstress, instead of a Woman's Party organizer." Chairman Paul had little patience with negative results or discouragement, singlemindedly concerned with the execution of her strategy, taking little time herself for thought of anything else. When organizer Rose Winslow fell ill, Paul showed little sympathy. She was upset when Winslow cancelled speaking engagements, and urged her to continue, saying it would be "a calamity" if she abandoned the tour. The tour went on.[114]

Mary Beard's husband, the influential Progressive historian Charles Beard, applauded the strenuous WP efforts in the *New Republic* as "nothing but *Realpolitik*," arguing that the WP could very well decide the 1916 elections in the West. He also stressed that it had been Wilson himself who wrote the Democratic platform, so that Wilson could not very well argue he was only following the "dictates of his party" in not supporting woman suffrage. Presidential advisor Dudley Field Malone, reflected Wilson's reaction to "Realpolitik" in a talk to Woman's Party delegates. He remarked that they should be "respectful," (like NAWSA) and gave them "a real dressing down" for their discourteous attitudes.[115]

Wilson obviously wanted nothing to do with disrespectful militants. When asked in a July memo if he would see Mrs. Frank Roessing and Mrs. Carrie Chapman Catt, Wilson demurred and wanted to know, "Are these ladies of the Congressional Union variety?" His aide assured him that the ladies were not from the CU. "NAWSA is regarded as the conservative body and the Congressional Union as the radical body. The CU people are of the 'heckling' variety and their methods are not approved by NAWSA." On July 4, as he addressed the marchers in a Washington labor parade, Wilson assured them that he "stood for the interests of all classes." At this point CU star speaker Mabel Vernon, a member of "the radical body," shouted from the crowd: "Mr. President, if you sincerely desire to forward the interest of all the people, why do you oppose the national enfranchisement of women?" He told her they would have to take counsel over it later. When she repeated her question at the close of his speech, she was hurried away by Secret Service men. A few months later, he showed a new skittishness toward all suffragists. When told that the St. Louis Equal Suffrage League requested an audience with him upon his visit, he wrote in a memo, "It is now evident that I cannot go to St. Louis." As for the WP's western campaign, Wilson did not believe it would have any effect on the election. When a California woman wrote him that women would not be "sex patriots" and that the Congressional Union was wrong, Wilson found that "cheering." He answered her, "I feel properly confident that the belligerent women of the Congressional Union could not command the women of the country how they should vote."[116] Wilson may not have foreseen any success for the WP, but the "belligerents" seemed to be confident of victory in the fall election campaign.

The WP did not convince Wilson to include a woman suffrage amendment in the Democratic platform, although it was included as a "recommendation" to the states. On August 1, Republican presidential candidate Charles Evans Hughes, after being urged by colleagues who had been reportedly convinced by the WP, declared himself for federal woman suffrage. Naturally, suffragists were delighted. Catt urged Wilson to do the same, but he declined. He did agree to come to the September NAWSA convention, where his speech was classic Wilson: "I have not come to ask you to be patient, because you have been, but I have come to congratulate you that there was a force behind you that will, beyond any peradventure, be triumphant, and for which you can afford a little while to wait."[117] No matter how it was phrased, the NAWSA speech was only words to the Woman's Party.

Unwilling to wait, the Woman's Party launched an all-out fall campaign which was met by deep hostility from the Democrats. Apparently the militants' political maneuvering had already passed the bounds of acceptable progressive politics. Elsie Hill was arrested in Denver for distributing "anti-Democratic" literature. One Woman's Party banner was locked up in Colorado Springs--another was unfurled there in front of former Wilson Secretary of State, William Jennings Bryan, courtesy of Dr. Caroline Spencer. In Chicago, Minnie Brooke, wearing a Woman's Party sash, was attacked by two men, who pushed her in front of a car.[118] But the worst outbreak of violence by far was on October 20, 1916 in Chicago. Wilson was addressing a crowd when a group of 100 Woman's Party members with banners emblazoned with "President Wilson--How Long Do You

Advise Us To Wait?", gathered at the entrance to the auditorium. As soon as the President passed by the demonstrators, thugs suddenly attacked the women, destroying their banners, knocking down several women and dragging them along the street. The *Suffragist* reported that there were many women who joined the party after the attack, feeling deeply the CU's call for a "united sisterhood." As a group of Pennsylvania women put it: "We did not understand before the full meaning of your words about 'sex solidarity' and 'loyalty to women.' . . . We are women and belong on the women's side of the fight." Paul remarked that the "disgraceful attack . . . made us more converts than has months of campaigning." She knew how to turn the violence to the women's advantage:

> The violent attack by Democrats upon the demonstration shows the seriousness with which they take our campaigning. Evidently they feel keenly the weakness of President Wilson's suffrage position when they resort to such violence to present his hostility to national woman suffrage being revealed to the people of Chicago.[119]

Feminist militance, even in the mild form of silent banner holding, had shown the enormous antipathy it could provoke, as well as the responsive chord it might strike in women.

Although the ugly incident in Chicago hardened the resolve of the WP to fight for women's political power, it remained to be seen how their "Realpolitik" would actually influence women voters in the West. Lucy Burns was optimistic, writing a Montana newspaper editor that "Wilson was wrong--the women of the West will *insist* on Justice for other women." It is difficult to assess exactly how successful the WP effort was against "the enemy," Wilson and Congressional Democrats, in the 1916 election. Wilson was re-elected and the Democrats did do well, but the Woman's Party contended, as in 1914, that those results were not the entire point. The important element of the election, to them, was that they had, again, made woman suffrage a campaign issue and had been responsible for a significant woman's protest vote. Even the anti-suffrage *New York Times* editorials admitted that the politicians should from then on, consider the Woman's Party. The Paul-Burns strategy of holding the party in power responsible seemed to be vindicated. Some CU lieutenants remained dubious. Anne Martin, her former NAWSA ties showing, was not completely convinced a friendly Democratic senator should be an enemy, and argued that it was the Republicans, not the Democrats, that controlled the states. Even Mary Beard thought the CU had presented "confused statements" about its party policy and wondered if federal suffrage really should come first "in the revolution [she] desired."[120] The revolution was not quite at hand, but the militants did flex some political muscle in 1916, melding pressure, progressive political tactics with a touch of militancy. But would such tactics be enough to win suffrage?

The Democratic President was apparently not yet impressed by women's power. When he failed to mention woman suffrage in his December message to the 64th Congress, the Woman's Party concocted another unpleasant, Pankhurst-like surprise for him. Elizabeth Selden Rogers, Anna Lowenburg, Caroline Spencer, Florence Bayard Hilles and Mabel Vernon faced the Speaker's podium from the front row of the gallery for the occasion. Bunched under Mabel Vernon's cape was an inscribed yellow banner which she would unpin from her skirt after taking her seat. Since she looked as if she were pregnant with her banner, a guard actually got up and gave her his seat! On cue, as Wilson said that Puerto Rican men needed more freedom, the five women dropped the banner over the balcony. The banner read simply: "Mr. President, What Will You Do For Woman Suffrage?" Wilson hesitated a beat, but then went on, the hall buzzing with consternation. Before the guards were able to reach the women, a Senate page tore down the odious banner. Naturally, as planned, the incident made the front pages all over the country. Vernon's close friend Anne Martin warned Paul that Vernon's part in "militant proceedings" was harmful (even though Martin herself had been quite "militant" in London), but Elizabeth Selden Rogers thought the incident absolutely wonderful. "[N]ot only did the honor and self-respect of women demand the act, but it was excellent politics."[121] Vernon's act was at least excellent publicity, but the Woman's Party gained another final surge of public sympathy in 1916 with the death of its own martyr to the cause.

The beautiful Inez Milholland Boissevain was the ideal Woman's Party representative, from her leading of the 1913 parade on her white horse, to her important role as organizer in the western campaign. Her eventual martydom would crystallize the anger of American militants and direct them toward illegal militant acts. Milholland was engaged to speak in the West in favor of women's independence and women's solidarity. Paul knew Milholland's talent as a speaker from working with her at Philadelphia open air meetings in 1912. Her strong feminism was evident in her speeches, one of which informed her listeners that there were those who thought that women were not human beings, such as: "Turks, infidels, the House of Lords in England [and] the *New York Times*! . . . [But] every woman of spirit and independence believes that women are human beings with a definite part to play in the shaping of human events."[122]

When first approached by Paul about a western tour for the party, Milholland was not enthusiastic, explaining she could not afford it and also was prone to be "train sick." She asked Paul not to "feel too hardly toward me." Finally, Milholland agreed to go, but told Paul that her doctor wanted her to include rest on the trip, because she needed a tonsillectomy. Showing what in retrospect seems like incredible callousness, Doris Stevens wired Milholland that she should tell her doctor to give her "a hypodermic of sodium calculate" to keep going. But Milholland collapsed in Los Angeles, late in October 1916. She reportedly fell, dramatically gasping, "President Wilson, How long must this go on--no liberty . . .

[l]et me repeat we are not putting our faith in any man or in any party but in the women voters of the West."[123]

At first, the seriousness of Milhollands' condition, anemia complicated by tonsillitis and exhaustion, was not known. Even though she was told Milholland could not lift her head, Paul, ever adamant, expected her to continue the tour, to at least go to Chicago for "even a word or two."[124] Paul was plagued with ill speakers at this time, Blatch and Winslow, Stevens and organizer Beulah Amidon were also incapacitated, driven to exhaustion by their grueling schedules and insistent commander-in-chief.[125] Vida Milholland, an actress and Inez's sister, wrote to Alice Paul suggesting the Woman's Party use Inez's illness as "grist to the mill." She wrote that it might be cold-blooded, but the "English militants won sympathy and worldwide admiration for their endurance of forcible feeding and the hunger strike." Annie Kenney on a stretcher had produced a powerful effect on a British audience. Vida described her sister's condition before the trip as not good. Her "heart [was] behaving oddly" and her tonsils were "strangely diseased." The doctor in Seattle had given her "more dope," but by California she was "desperately weak . . . . half-dead."[126] Still, Inez Milholland had not given up speaking even when her heart raced wildly when she stood and her gums bled. She died at the end of November. Vida Milholland asked Paul, "Where else was such spirit found? Only amongst Christ's followers, Galileo, John Brown, the Crusaders and sadest of all Emily Davidson . . . . not to mention you yourself and the many other fighters who gave up health, strength & freedom for an idea, the idea of freedom for women."[127] Clearly this political campaign was taking on overtones more resembling a WSPU-like moral crusade than that of an exercise in progressive politics. Gradually the women were entering the state of mind necessary for a campaign requiring much more than gathering petitions.

A memorial was held for Inez Milholland in Statuary Hall in the Capitol on Christmas Day, and a strongly worded Milholland memorial resolution was prepared for President Wilson, who, it was hoped, would be deeply moved by the tragic loss. The invitations to the Milholland Memorial proclaimed it an occasion "to honor her heroic and triumphant death . . . for liberty and freedom." At the ceremony Milholland's friend Maud Younger quoted Milholland: "It is women for women now and shall be until the fight is won! Together we shall stand shoulder to shoulder for the greatest principle the world has ever known, the right of self-government." Younger ended by dramatically calling on all women "to finish the task she could not finish."[128] Alice Paul requested an audience with Wilson to present the emotional Milholland resolution, which read in part: "The struggle requires intense effort and sacrifice . . . [our] health is undermined . . . [but] we will continue until victory . . . . [the President should know] that if necessary many women, whom the Nation can ill spare, will follow in the footsteps of Inez Milholland."[129] Wilson was unimpressed. The memo to his aide regarding Paul's request for a meeting read: "Please say that the days and the hours named are impossible. I would like to avoid seeing them altogether, but if I do see them, it will be at a time of my own selection.[130] Finally the President agreed to accept the resolution, but wanted one person only to make the presentation. Instead, three hundred women came to the White House, and Eunice Dana Brannan used the occasion to ask the President if, in the face of Milholland's "supreme sacrifice," he would use his power over Congress to pass woman suffrage. By then beset by problems of war and ill health, he was plainly irritated. Wilson told them he could do nothing more, he was bound by his party. He advised them "to concert public opinion."[131] For four years Women's Party militants had worked themselves to exhaustion arousing public opinion through political action, but it had not been enough to win suffrage.

After Milholland's death, the suffragists entered another level of determination. Harriot Stanton Blatch expressed what they all felt after the President rebuffed the Milholland memorial delegation: "We can't organize bigger and more influential deputations. We can't organize bigger processions. We can't, women, do anything more in that line. We have to take a new departure." As Rebecca Reyher put it, the women did not become "really angry" until the end of 1916, when they became "exasperated" by their "failed efforts."[132] The political phase of Woman's Party militancy, which took them from a NAWSA committee to a united party of women voters pursuing party responsibility, had been thwarted. The only strategy open to the suffrage militants was to go outside the system of progressive politics and begin the "real militancy" of defying and resisting government authority. Woman the suppliant had become woman the rebel.

---

[1] CU policy statement, August 1914, in Stevens, *Jailed*, p. 34. Alice Paul quote from "The Woman Suffrage Movement in Great Britain" speech to NAWSA, 1910.
[2] The shared goal of these middle class reformers was to "reform," "not revolutionize" society. See Robert Wiebe, *The Search for Order, 1877-1920* (New York: Hill and Wang, 1967); Walter Nugent, *From Centenniel to World War: American Society, 1876-1917* (Indianapolis: Bobbs-Merrill, 1977); Irwin, *Alice Paul and the NWP*, p. 163; Arthur Link, *Woodrow Wilson and the Progressive Era* (New York: Harper and Row, 1954), p. 16; Flexner, *Century of Struggle*, p. 271.
[3] Jane Adams, "Utilization of Women in City Government," in Rossi, editor, *Feminist Papers*, pp. 602-606.
[4] Fry, Paul interview, p. 61; Irwin, *Paul and the NWP*, p. 13. On Martin, see Howard, *Long Campaign*, pp. 74-76, 87.
[5] Kent returned to NAWSA change she had left over at the end of the year. Gallagher, Paul interview, p. 19; Irwin, *Paul and the NWP*, pp. 12-13.
[6] The intense interest and emotion generated in the 1911 California campaign, and WPU's efforts in New York, showed women's readiness for another all-out suffrage fight. Eleanor Flexner does an excellent job on these campaigns in *Century of Struggle*; also see Catt and Shuler, *Woman Suffrage and Politics*.

[7] Irwin, *Paul and the NWP*, p. 3; David Morgan, *Suffragists and Democrats* (Michigan State University Press, 1972), pp. 77-79.
[8] Gallagher, Paul interview, p. 19; Irwin, *Paul and the NWP*, pp. 12-13.
[9] Flexner, *Century of Struggle*, pp. 237 and 177. Her figures include the following:

Women Employed	1890	4,005,532
	1900	5,319,397
	1910	7,444,787

In 1900	domestics	1,800,000
	farmworkers	700,000
	teachers	325,000
	sales clerks	217,000
	clothing factory	671,000
	textile factory	261,000
	bookkeepers	74,000
	clericals	100,000

Also, on this period, Nancy Woloch, *Women and the American Experience*, 1980, is excellent, especially Chapter 12. See Buhle, *Women and American Socialism,* pp. 265-266; Rheta Childe Dorr, *What Eight Million Women Want*, p. 3; also see June Sochen, *The New Woman in Greenwich Village, 1910-1920* (New York: Quadrange Books, 1972), especially pp. 4-6 on suffrage and Village women. Sochen reports on p. ix, in 1909-1910 women earned 10% of all Ph.D.s in American universities.
[10] Quote in *The Forerunner*, August 1916, p. 214; see Gilman's discussion of women's need for autonomy in her *The Home*, (New York: McClure and Phillips Co., 1903), p. 321; and her *Women and Economics* (Boston: Small, Maynard and Co., 1900), p. 330.
[11] Gilman, *The Living of Charlotte Perkins Gilman: An Autobiography* (New York: Harper and Row, 1935). Untitled poem, *The Forerunner*, February 1911, p. 31.
[12] Gilman, *The Home,* p. 87; *Women and Economics*, p. 330.
[13] *The Forerunner*, August 1916, p. 214.
[14] Paul to John Nordquist, Iowa socialist leader, July 23, 1913, Reel 4, NWPP.
[15] Fry, Paul interview, p. 22.
[16] Irwin, *Paul and the NWP*, p. 18.
[17] *Ibid.*
[18] Irwin, *Paul and the NWP*, pp. 13, 52; Fry, Paul interview, p. 63; *Notable American Women*, pp. 543-544, on Eastman. Both Eastman and Beard left the party before the picketing arrests began in 1917; Eastman because she became

involved in the peace movement, and Beard because she did not believe picketing was a good political method. *Who's Who in American Women, 1920-21*; Ann J. Lane, editor, *Mary Ritter Beard: A Sourcebook* (New York: Schocken Books, 1977), pp. 22-24, 27; Blanche Weisen Cook. *Crystal Eastman*, pp. 12-14; Mary Beard to Elizabeth Selden Rogers, November 14, 1917, Reel 52, NWPP.

[19] Lewis to Paul, December 17, 1912, Reel 1, and December 16, 1916, Reel 33, NWPP. Lewis's sister, Mrs. R. R. P. Bradford, was a founder of Philadelphia's Lighthouse Settlement. Irwin, *Paul and the NWP*, p. 321; Stevens, *Jailed for Freedom*, appendix; Louise Page, (Lewis's granddaughter) "Political Prisoner," unpublished manuscript, p. 5. Henrietta Krone, "Dauntless Women: The Story of the Woman Suffrage Movement in Pennsylvania," unpublished dissertation, University of Pennsylvania, 1946, p. 44. The friendship with Shaw would not soften Shaw's attitude toward Lewis's later picketing and imprisonment. Shaw to Shippen Lewis, December 28, 1917, Reel 54, NWPP.

[20] Edith Houghton regretted she could not come to Washington because they were having an important white slave protest meeting. Most women accepted invitations, however. Houghton to Alice Paul, January 8, 1913, Reel 1.

[21] Milholland biographical file, Vassar College.

[22] "Order of Procession," Reel 2, NWPP.

[23] Account by LaFollette, NWP member, of the 1913 parade, in Rossi, editor, *Feminist Papers*, p. 539. Also see Cheney interview with Paul on parade. Paul made light of the hostility and said there had been "no violence."

[24] Rogers to Paul, March 5, 1913, Reel 2, NWPP. Rebecca Reyher characterized it as very hostile. In Amelia Fry and Fern Ingersoll, editor and interviewer respectively, "Search and Struggle for Equality and Independence," Reyher 1973 interview, Bancroft Library at Berkeley, Oral History Project, 1977, p. 327.

[25] Catt and Shuler, *Woman Suffrage*, p. 242.

[26] As in Margaret Wentworth to Paul, March 13, 1913, Reel 1, NWPP.

[27] "Evidence" document from Mrs. J. A. Morley, Mrs. F. S. Hall, Mrs. C. T. Williams and Doris Stevens, March 1913, Reel 2, NWPP.

[28] Villard to Corporal Tanner, March 8, 1912, Reel 2; Equality Club to Washington police, March 19, 1913, Reel 2; Progressive Party of Massachusetts to police, March 13, 1913, Reel 1, NWPP. W. E. B. DuBois bitterly protested, writing sarcastically about the conduct of the white male spectators: "Down on your knees Black man and . . . learn from the Superior Race! . . . Beat them back, keep them down! Shall the time ever come . . . when a free white American citizen may not buy as many women as his purse permits?" *Crisis,* April 1913, p. 267. An R. Bentley Thomas wrote Police Captain W. S. Overton that "police 'protection' has turned me from a passive suffragist into a fighting suffragette." March 7, 1913, Reel 2, NWPP.

[29] Sterne to "Friends," March 5, 1913, Reel 2, NWPP.

[30] Cheney, Paul interview, p.21; Irwin, *Paul and the NWP*, p. 30.

[31] The CU membership will be thoroughly discussed in Chapter 3. Those exceptions who were not founders but did actively participate in the height of NWP militancy in 1917-1919 were Anne Martin, national officer by 1915, Doris Stevens and Mabel Vernon, both leaders and organizers by end of 1914. Agnes Morey became an important advisor by 1917. On Brown, Olympia Brown, to Lucy Burns, February 27, 1914, Reel 7 and to Alice Paul, October 23, 1917, Reel 51, NWPP. On Wiley, *Women's Who's Who in America, 1918-1919*, p. 884. On Spencer, Caroline Spencer to Burns, January 1, 1913, Reel 1, NWPP.

[32] The tableau, written by "Mrs. Hemmick," is dated May 1913, Reel 1, NWPP. The rest of the "Women of Achievement" were: Hypatia, St. Hylda, Lady Jane Grey, Queen Phillipa, Maria Theresa, Mme Roland, Mme de Stael, Florence Nightingale, Zenobia, Countess of Merch, Flora MacDonald, Grace Darling, Kate Barless, Ranke of Imansi and Victoria Colonna. Rebecca Reyher has stressed how very important beauty and pageantry were to Alice Paul and how she filled the office headquarters with beautiful women. Ford, Reyher interview.

[33] Maud Wood Park, with editor, Edna Lamprey Stantial, *Front Door Lobby* (Boston: Beacon Press, 1960), pp. 268-270, 186.

[34] The *Suffragist,* December 25, 1915.

[35] Fry, Paul interview, p. 90.

[36] Edwin A. Weinstein, *Woodrow Wilson: A Medical and Psychological Biography* (Princeton, NJ: Princeton University Press, 1981), p. 83; Thomas Schactman, *Edith and Woodrow*, (New York: G. P. Putnam and Sons, 1981), p. 82; Weinstein, James W. Anderson and Arthur Link, "Woodrow Wilson's Political Personality: A Reappraisal," *Political Science Quarterly*, Winter 1978-79, Volume 93, pp. 585, 592.

[37] Edith Bolling promised Wilson "with all my heart absolutely to trust and accept my loved Lord." Schactman, *Edith and Woodrow*, pp. 49, 78, 85, 99. Weinstein, *Woodrow Wilson*, p. 91. M. Carey Thomas, Bryn Mawr president, never forgave him for his practice of going over her head to the college board in policy matters. According to Thomas, Wilson's attitude toward women was, "Put your sweet hand in mine and trust in me!" Marjorie Housepian Dobkins, editor, *The Making of a Feminist: Early Journals and Letters of M. Carey Thomas* (Kent, OH: Kent State University Press, 1979), p. 20, note 7. Also see Weinstein, "Woodrow Wilson's Neurological Illness," *Journal of American History*, September 1970, p. 326.

[38] Robin Morgan, in "Alice Paul: Mother of the ERA," *Ms.*, October 1977, p. 112, says Wilson called out the troops from Ft. Meyer against the marchers, but they were sent for to help the women parading. Elizabeth Selden Rogers to Alice Paul, March 5, 1913, Reel 2, NWPP.

[39] The young Wilson insisted Congressional leaders should follow the executive will. "English precedent must be followed in the institution of cabinet government in the United States." Ray Stannard Baker and William E. Dodd, *The Public Papers of Woodrow Wilson*, (New York: Harper and Bros. Publishers, 1925),

pp. 109-115 from Wilson's "Committee or Cabinet Government?" January 1884 *Overland Monthly*, Volume III; Arthur Link, *Wilson and the Progressive Era*, p. 35.

[40] Paul had met Wilson's daughter Jessie at Philadelphia's Lighthouse Settlement, and said she was "completely sympathetic to us." Jessie and her sister once came to an NWP reception to see guests. Fry, Paul interview, pp. 90-92.

[41] Gallagher, Paul interview, p. 20.

[42] Thomas Schactman, *Edith and Woodrow*, p. 7.

[43] That committee included the original five: Paul, Burns, Mary Beard, Crystal Eastman, and Dora Lewis. See Leonora O'Reilly to Paul, April 22, 1913; Paul to various socialist party secretaries late in April, and to the Woman's Socialist National Committee, April 28, 1913, Reel 1; Mary Beard to Lucy Burns, January 13, 1914, Reel 6, NWPP.

[44] Paul to Mrs. Ellen Price, June 4, 1913, Reel 3, NWPP.

[45] Burns' political report, May 14, 1913, Reel 87, NWPP; Irwin, *Paul and the NWP*, pp. 36-37, 46, 87; Fry, Paul interview, p. 86; Fry interview with Mabel Vernon, "Speaker for Suffrage and Petitioner for Peace," 1976 (1972 interview), Bancroft Project, UCLA, pp. ix-xii, 6; Mabel Vernon to Katherine Paul, July 2, 1917, Reel 45, NWPP.

[46] Burns political report, May 1913.

[47] WSPU form letter sent to CU headquarters, August 12, 1914, Reel 11, NWPP. Katharine Morey to Paul, January 13, 1917, Reel 37, see also. Included in the list of books the CU recommended for budding suffragists were: "Causes of the Revolt of the Women in England"; the WSPU's *The Suffragette*; and Sylvia Pankhurst's *The Suffragette*. Interestingly, when Emmeline Pankhurst's *My Own Story* was published in 1914, it did not appear on the list, no doubt because Paul "did not care for it." On list, see Gertrude Stone to Frances M. Pierce, Ludlow, Vermont library, March 10, 1913 or Stone to Lloyd Lively, March 17, 1913, Reel 2; October 1913 list "Books of Value to Suffragists," Reel 5, NWPP; Paul quote in Morey 1917 letter.

[48] Paul to Edna C. Wilson, April 21, 1913, Reel 2; Alice Paul to Florence Macauley, July 10, 1913, Reel 3, NWPP.

[49] Jane Bliss Potter to Paul, February 2, 1914, Reel 7; or Caroline Spencer to Paul, February 27, 1914, Reel 7; Burns to Gertrude Hunter, February 24, 1914, Reel 7, NWPP.

[50] The Cat and Mouse Act allowed ill suffrage offenders to be free long enough to gain strength to be reimprisoned. The WPU joined the CU in obtaining signatures to protest the act. See Sylvia Pankhurst, *The Suffragette* for details, or Emmeline Pankhurst, *My Own Story*, especially p. 303; David Mitchell, *The Fighting Pankhursts*, p. 36. G. Doffett to Paul, October 24, 1913, Reel 4, NWPP (on Kenney).

---

[51] Pankhurst quote in Midge MacKenzie, editor, *Shoulder to Shoulder* (New York: Alfred A. Knopf, 1975), p. 250.
[52] October 1913 article on Reel 5; Beard to Paul, September 3, 1913, Reel 4, NWPP.
[53] Eunice Brannan to *New York Times*, April 5, 1913, Reel 1, NWPP.
[54] Rheta Childe Dorr to Paul, December 30, 1913, Reel 6, NWPP.
[55] See Lunardini, *Equal Suffrage to Equal Rights.*
[56] *Syracuse Post-Standard*, May 3, 1913, p. 1; Flexner, *Century of Struggle*, p. 262.
[57] Dennett to Paul, October 30, 1913, Reel 5, NWPP.
[58] An examination of Wilson's mail in late 1913 reveals he was receiving a large amount of "anti" letters congratulating him on his stand against woman suffrage. Most of them were from men and Catholic organizations, but a number were from anti-suffrage clubwomen, deploring the "selfishness" of their sex for demanding suffrage. Letters of October - December 1913, Reel 208, Series 4, Number 89, Woodrow Wilson Papers on Microfilm, Library of Congress, 1958. Lenroot in NAWSA press release, January 19, 1914, Reel 91, NWPP.
[59] Catt and Shaw had participated in the demonstrations of early 1913, but by summer their irritation was showing in their correspondence. Paul and Burns were addressed as upstart secretaries whose only concern should be to arrange sleeper cars on trains for Shaw. Shaw wrote to Paul in November that NAWSA members were confused about CU as opposed to CC jurisdiction. Shaw to Paul, August 26, 1913 and October series of letters, Reel 4; Shaw to Paul, November 10, 1913, Reel 5; Shaw to Burns, November 29, 1913, Reel 5, NWPP.
[60] Burns to Shaw, November 31, 1913, Reel 5, NWPP.
[61] Bland, "Suffrage Militancy of Lucy Burns," pp. 9-10; Burns to Shaw, December 17, 1913, Reel 6, NWPP.
[62] Cora Smith King warned Paul that although Catt might be sympathetic to them, the irascible Shaw "is as destructive as an elephant walking on eggs." King to Paul, December 17, 1913, Reel 6. King always called Paul "Girlie." She assured Paul, "Your own vision of liberty shines undimmed." Mary Ware Dennett to Paul and Burns, December 18, 1913; Dennett to Paul, December 30, 1913, Reel 6; Paul to Mary Hutcheson Page and to Harriet Upton, December 30, 1913, Reel 6, NWPP.
[63] The CU was censured for raising vast sums of money ($27,000), none of which went into NAWSA coffers. This was done even though Burns and Paul had been instructed from the beginning to finance themselves. The CU even paid the costs of the very convention which censured it! Gallagher, Paul interview, pp. 20-21; Morton Tenzer, interview with Elsie Hill, July 30, 1968, pp. 7-10.
[64] Paul to Anna Howard Shaw, January 17, 1914, Reel 6, NWPP. Paul seemed to deteriorate physically when under strain; she certainly did when the CU was being expelled from NAWSA. Her doctors said, in this particular case, her illness was

"not organic." See correspondence between Mary Ware Dennett and Paul and Burns, December 18, 1913, Reel 6, NWPP.

[65] *New York Times,* January 5, 1914, p. 3.

[66] Early members of the CU who had switched from NAWSA would soon return to them over "militant" policies like party responsibility and "heckling" the President. See Kathryn Houghton Hepburn, Mary Beard and Dora Sedgwick Hazard letters (all three were CU) to Paul in late January 1914, Reel 7, NWPP; also see Florence Hedges to Paul in late January 1914, Reel 7, NWPP. Carrie Chapman Catt, editor, *History of Woman Suffrage*, Volume V, p. 476; Anna Howard Shaw, *The Story of a Pioneer* (New York: Harper and Brothers, 1915), p. 316; Catt and Shuler, *Woman Suffrage and Politics*, pp. 244, 248 and 254. Maud Wood Park also decried the "damage" the CU did in *Front Door Lobby*, p. 22.

[67] *Washington Herald*, February 1, 1914, Reel 7, NWPP.

[68] January 24, 1914, p. 4; CU handbill, n.d., Reel 93, NWPP.

[69] *Suffragist*, April - July, 1914.

[70] Irwin, *Paul and the NWP*, p. 60; Stevens, *Jailed*, pp. 187, appendix.

[71] *New York World*, February 3, 1914 appears in *The Papers of Woodrow Wilson*, editor, Arthur Link (Princeton University Press, 1980), Volume 27, pp. 213-214; Congressional Union press release, February 1914, by Elizabeth Glendower Evans, which says women wanted results, but Wilson's position remained unchanged. Reel 91, NWPP.

[72] See March 1914 Congressional Index samples, Reel 8, NWPP; Irwin, *Paul and the NWP*, pp. 55-56. NAWSA leaders decided to support Shafroth-Palmer (which Mrs. Medill McCormick had helped write), thinking it could get around "states-rights" anti-suffrage arguments and make state fights easier. But because of the cumbersome measure's unpopularity, NAWSA lost members to the CU and more friction was created. Gallagher, Paul interview, p. 21; Flexner, *Century of Struggle,* pp. 276-277.

[73] *Congressional Record*, Volume LI, Part V, 63rd Congress, Second Session, March 17, 1914, pp. 4954-4959; on 4959-5103 is the remainder of the debate.

[74] July, 1914; Irwin, *Paul and the NWP*, pp. 61-64; Link, editor, *Wilson Papers*, Volume 30, p. 227.

[75] Wilson to Thornton, July 1, 1914, in Link, *Wilson Papers*, p. 240. Edgar Thompson to Wilson, June 30, 1914 and Fred Barnes to Wilson, July 1, 1914, Woodrow Wilson Papers on Microfilm, Reel 208, Series 4, Number 89.

[76] Charles Reinhard to Wilson, July 1, 1914; Lillian Streeter (NH Children's Commissioner) to Wilson, July 1, 1914 and Glen Stone to Wilson, July 1, 1914, Wilson Papers on Microfilm, as above.

[77] The House Judiciary Committee reported a suffrage amendment to the House, but when the CU tried in early summer to budge the House Rules Committee to act

on it, it was to no avail. Irwin, *Paul and the NWP*, pp. 67-71. Beard to Paul, July 9, 1914, Reel 11, NWPP.
[78] See *Suffragist*, April - July, 1914.
[79] Irwin, *Paul and the NWP*, p. 26; *Suffragist*, "Alice Paul," written January 1916, published January 1918.
[80] Dorr to Paul, April 21, 1914, Reel 9 and Paul to Lewis, June 1, 1914, Reel 10; Whitney to Elizabeth Kent, September 26, 1915, Reel 19, NWPP.
[81] *Suffragist,* December 25, 1914, p. 4; Bland, "Militancy of Burns," pp. 4, 11.
[82] NWP 1921 Report, Reel 84, NWPP.
[83] See CU pamphlet 1915, Reel 22: "Susan B. Anthony said in 1878 that women should stand shoulder to shoulder against every party not fully and unequivocally committed to equal rights for women." Gallagher, Paul interview, p. 23. Organizer Bertha Fowler wrote Paul, for instance, about the need for defiance. "The *Woman's Journal*, speaking of Asquith's treatment of delegations, observes complacently 'We do these things better in America' and upon that follows the President's insulting reception of your women. Why can't the women give up this silly feminine nonsense, and act as human beings?" July 7, 1914, Reel 11, NWPP.
[84] Gallagher 1972 Paul interview, p. 23.
[85] Irwin, *Paul and the NWP*, p. 88.
[86] CU election leaflet 1914, Reel 87. October 20, 1914 press release by E. H. Hooker, Reel 91, NWPP.
[87] Tenzer, Hill interview, Part VI, p. 3.
[88] 1914 CU Congressional Report, Reel 87, NWPP. See Meredith A. Snapp, "Defeat the Democrats: The CU for Woman Suffrage in Arizona, 1914-1916," *Journal of the West*, 1975, for CU western strategy. Pro-suffrage letters to the President, mobilized by the CU, unlike in 1913, were numerous. Wilson Papers on Microfilm, Reel 208.
[89] Link, editor, *Wilson Papers*, Volume 32, from diary of Nancy Saunders Toy, January 6, 1915, p. 21; *Suffragist* on delegation, January 9, 1915. Wilson to Edith Bolling Galt, July 23, 1915 in *Papers*, Volume 34, p. 23.
[90] H. F. Copperberg, "Observations of Suffrage Debate," January 12, 1915, Reel 89, NWPP; *Suffragist*, January 16, 1915.
[91] Report of CU Annual Meeting, January 10, 1915, Reel 14. Virginia Arnold reported that the "famed Mrs. Gilman" was bringing many people into the CU, March 20 and April 3, 1915 letters to the *Suffragist,* Reel 16. See the *New York Times*, April 1, 1915, p. 24; Report on Advisory Council Meetings, 1921, on March 31, 1915 meeting, Reel 87, NWPP; *Suffragist*, February 27, 1915, p. 2. The CU would no longer concern itself with state campaigns, as it had with Nevada and New Jersey. National suffrage could be more economically gained, according to *Suffragist* articles. Woman voters needed to deal with "national woman's problems" such as child labor or "white slave traffic." And if women had a

"national voice" Wilson would have to secure "liberty" and better opportunities for all women workers. Burns asked Lavinia Dock to write about how the white slave traffic could be controlled only through women's national vote. Burns to Dock, March 12, 1915, Reel 15. And the *Suffragist*, March 13, p. 3; March 20, p. 6; Matilda Hall Gardner article, April 24, 1915, p. 4. On 1915 efforts, *Suffragist*, May 15, 1915, p. 4. Paul said *Suffragist* circulation was 3,200. No membership count was recorded at that time, no doubt because NAWSA/CU membership was still in a muddle. The treasury of the CU in January of 1915 had $37,400. *Suffragist,* January 23, 1915, p. 8; *New York Times*, April 25, 1915, p. 6; CU organizer reports, spring 1915, NWPP.

[92] *New York Times,* September 1, 1915, p. 25.

[93] Paul quoted in *New York Times*, August 1, 1915, p. 15. See the *Suffragist,* September 11, and 14, 1915; Amelia Fry, "Along the Suffrage Trail: From West to East for Freedom Now!", *American West*, Volume 6, 1969, p. 16. This is a wonderfully entertaining article on the fantastic auto voyage. The tour had triumphal entries into cities, but also pitfalls, literally of impassable mud and symbolically, of hostile crowds organized by the DAR. One of the two Swedish woman chauffeurs turned out to have been recently released from a mental hospital and threatened to kill Field at the end of the journey. Understandably, Field wrote Paul from Iowa she was ready to quit. Fry, "Suffrage Trail," Field to Paul, October 29, 1915, Reel 10, NWPP.

[94] May 8, 1915, Reel 16, NWPP.

[95] Paul to Burns, May 10, 1915, Reel 16, NWPP. In that letter, Paul also wrote it was wise to have included Anna Lowenburg in the deputation to show the CU was not against "aliens."

[96] Paul to Burns, May 17, 1915, Reel 16, NWPP. I call this the "D'Andrea Effect," named after my own experience of seeing lobbying NOW women livid with anger after being told by their NY Assemblyman, Bobby D'Andrea in 1979, that he had "more important things to do" than speak with them.

[97] *Suffragist*, June 5, 1915, p. 4.

[98] See, for example, Mary McDowell to Paul, June 6, 1915, and several others in June, over "heckling" Wilson; Katherine Fisher to Lucy Burns, June 4, 1915, Reel 17, NWPP. *New York Times*, June 8, 1915, p. 5; Stevens got a letter from Harriet Taylor Upton stating CU federal work was setting suffrage back, in Stevens to Paul, March 16, 1915, Reel 15. Lily Rowe to CU, June 25, 1915, Reel 17, complains of the same thing. Dock to Catt, June 1915, Reel 17, NAWSA leaders were sure Michigan suffrage lost because of the "English militants," but Burns retorted that "there was no cause in America before the Militants secured a world-wide publicity for suffrage." Burns to Katharine Fisher, May 29, 1915, Reel 16, NWPP.

[99] Link, *Papers of Wilson*, Volume 35, October 6, 1915 Press Release, p. 28. He told the DAR a few days later: "I know of no body of persons comparable to a

body of ladies for creating an atmosphere of opinion. I have myself in part yielded to the influences of that atmosphere, though it took me a long time to determine how I was going to vote in New Jersey." October 11, 1915, Volume 35, p. 51.

[100] Link, *Papers of Wilson*, Volume 35, p. 293. He explained he could only talk about one subject at a time and could not speak for himself only but must consult others. Wilson's mind was not on woman suffrage or the war at this time, since the following week he married Edith Bolling Galt. Colonel House, his close advisor, recorded in his diary at that time also, that Wilson's daughter Margaret "desired me to convert her father to her belief that it was desirable for Congress to legislate regarding Woman Suffrage." He thought it "favorable but not advisable" [?] for her father to act as she wished. Volume 35, p. 360. Link, *Papers of Wilson*, Volume 36, January 27, 1916, Message to 200 CU Members, p. 3; *New York Times*, January 28, 1916.

[101] Howe, "My faith in the CU," *Suffragist*, April 10, 1915, pp. 2-3. Elizabeth Kent argued in Oregon in 1915 that "virtues of self-denial and patience were no good in a mother without self-reliance and independence." Report on the Oregon State Convention, September 1915, p. 3, Reel 19. Anne Martin printed posters in the West which equated woman's vote with clean government and "anti-liquor," even though prohibition was an issue with which not everyone in the CU agreed. 1915 Nevada poster, Reel 16, NWPP. Howe to "CU Friends," December 1915, Reel 22, NWPP.

[102] See Kraditor, *Ideas of Suffrage* on the difference, pp. 198-201; Catt and Shuler, *Woman Suffrage*, p. 248. Women who had held membership in the CU and NAWSA had to decide on one group or the other; many CU members did leave over "heckling" and "militance." Catt and Shuler, p. 245. Mary McDowell to Paul, June 6, 1915; Lily Rowe to CU, June 25, 1915 and many others on Reel 17, 1915, NWPP. Abigail Duniway, the western suffrage pioneer preferred to stay with Paul over the "bossism" of Anna Howard Shaw. June 30, 1915, Duniway to Paul, Reel 17, NWPP.

[103] The western states were the Dakotas, Nebraska, Missouri, Ohio, Montana and Nevada; and the eastern were New York, Massachusetts, Pennsylvania and New Jersey. Catt and Shuler, *Woman Suffrage*, p. 266. For best account of NAWSA action, Flexner Chapter 20, should also be seen.

[104] Wilmer Atkinson, in the article, and July 10, 1914 to Wilson, Wilson papers on microfilm, Reel 208; *Suffragist*, May 6, 1916, p.5; Burns to *Chicago Post* editor, July 11, 1916, Reel 29, NWPP.

[105] April 9 the train set off from Washington with Harriot Stanton Blatch, Elizabeth Selden Rogers, Abby Scott Baker, singer Lillian Ascough of Detroit and, of course, Burns. Eugene Debs met the train in Arizona and in Seattle, Burns left the train for a plane, to drop suffrage leaflets from the air. Bland, "Militancy of Burns," p. 11; Irwin, *Paul and the NWP*, pp. 154-155; Paul to Burns, April 21, 1915, Reel 16; Lillian Ascough to Paul, July 2, 1915, Reel 17, NWPP; Stevens,

Jailed, appendix; Sarah Colvin, *Rebel in Thought*, p.2; Katzenstein, *Woman Suffrage in Pennsylvania,* p. 191; *New York Times*, October 18, 1915, p.4.

[106] Irwin, *Paul and the NWP*, pp. 158-160. The Advisory Council included: Florence Kelley, Lucy Salmon, Charlotte Perkins Gilman, Josephine Peabody, Lavinia Dock, Dora Sedgwick Hazard, Eunice Dana Brannan, Elizabeth Selden Rogers, Elizabeth Colt, Inez Milholland, Mary Dixon, Florence Bayard Hilles, Anna Kelton Wiley and Elizabeth Hooker. Council Report, April 1916, Reel 87, NWPP; Irwin, *Paul and the NWP*, p. 160; Paul to Betty Lee, July 17, 1916, Reel 30, NWPP.

[107] *Suffragist*, September 30, 1916, p.6.

[108] Elsie Hill's account of convention, August 26, 1916, Reel 31, NWPP. The women did note that individual labor men had been good about suffrage. *Suffragist*, October 14, 1916, p.8.

[109] Anne Martin, "Begging for Rights," *Suffragist*, April 8, 1916, p. 6.

[110] July 14, p. 10. (*Times*) Nelly Gordon to Martin, February 4, 1916, Reel 23, NWPP.

[111] The meeting which decided the merger took place in the home of Dora Sedgwick Hazard. *New York Times*, February 3, 1916, p. 12. On Martin, Paul to Martin, August 21, Reel 11; Martin to Paul, November 30, 1914, Reel 13; Martin to Paul, July 3, 1915, Reel 17; Paul to Martin, October 28, 1915, Reel 20; Minnie MacDonald to Martin, April 2, 1917, Reel 41, NWPP.

[112] Circulation of the *Suffragist* was over 3,000 in 1916, not large, but it was not unusual for one well-worn copy to pass from hand to hand. Nina Allender's wonderfully descriptive cartoons with their powerful messages of women's powerlessness, frequently featuring a variation of women in chains, were very effective. Burns supplied all of Washington's news correspondents with WP bulletins and then reprinted what the newspapers' reports of the suffragists were. By the end of 1916, *Suffragist* circulation was 4,994. Report on the *Suffragist*, Reel 87, NWPP; Bland, "Suffrage Militancy of Burns," pp. 12-13. See Lynne Masel-Walters, "To Hustle With the Rowdies': The Organization of the Functions of the American Woman Suffrage Press," *Journal of American Culture*, 3, Number 1, Spring 1980, pp. 179, 181-182. Paul had ultimate control over *Suffragist* policies. See Reel 26, NWPP. Eastman showed her admiration for Paul: "I want to say what a delight you are to me. So much humor and honesty, and grasp and quickness--and power!" But, Eastman still refused to work for suffrage. Eastman to Paul, July 12, 1916, Reel 30, NWPP. Eastman was then involved with the American Union Against Militarism with Jane Addams, Rabbi Stephen Wise, Zona Gale and Amos Pinchot.

[113] Organizers' Reports and correspondence regarding details of strategy in the fall of 1916 are largely on Reel 33, NWPP. Anne Martin continued to resent Paul and her Nevada suffragists were confused about whether they were WP or CU. Anne Howard, *Long Campaign*, 109-115.

[114] Morey to Burns, September 24, 1916, Reel 33; Howard, *Long Campaign*, p. 113; Burns to Paul, October 14, 1916, Reel 34; late October 1916 correspondence between Winslow and Paul, Reel 36, NWPP.
[115] Beard, *Nation* July 29, 1916, pp. 329-331. Beard thought it was time for political leaders to rise to "the heights of Lincoln in 1863." Link, editor, *Wilson Papers*, Volume 37, Malone to Wilson, June 7, 1916. WP correspondence with the President was respectful, but did not take a NAWSA-like tone. NAWSA's letters asked and flattered, while the WP presented Wilson with resolutions, appealing to him to use his power. See Florence Manion to Wilson, May 10, 1916: "*I will not* rest until all women of the United States have the same opportunity." For NAWSA see Mrs. Frank Roessing to Wilson, July 14, 1916; plentiful letters of both types are on Reel 209, Wilson Papers on Microfilm. Almost all letters were pro-suffrage in 1916, and the CU deserves much of the credit.
[116] At this point Wilson feared any suffrage group would turn out to be like the Woman's Party. Wilson Papers on Microfilm, Reel 209, July 24, 1916 memos; September 15 and 23, 1916 memos.
[117] The Progressive Party did endorse federal suffrage. Republican Hughes was told by Paul that progressive Republicans would not oppose woman suffrage, and that stand-pat ones would not vote Democratic, no matter the Republican platform. Irwin, *Paul and the NWP*, p. 165. The NAWSA speech is considered by Christine Lunardini and Thomas Knock to have been a major turning point for Wilson away from states' rights on suffrage. The evidence does not seem to me to support his change of heart from that point. See Lunardini and Knock, "Woodrow Wilson and Woman's Suffrage: A New Look," *Political Science Quarterly*, December 1980, pp. 661-662. Address to NAWSA, Link, *Wilson Papers*, Volume 38, September 8, pp. 163-164.
[118] Matilda Hall Gardner, "The Attack of the Suffrage Democrats," *Suffragist*, October 21, 1916, pp. 7-10.
[119] *Suffragist*, October 21, 1916, p. 2.
[120] Lucy Burns to editor of the *Missoulan*, October 30, 1916, Reel 35. The WP stressed that in Illinois, the only state where women's votes were counted separately, 70,000 more women voted against than for Wilson. See Snapp, "Defeat the Democrats," pp. 135-138; *Suffragist*, November 11, 1916, p. 6; Morey to Paul, November 15, 1916 and Paul to Morey, November 17, 1916, Reel 35; *New York Times*, December 24, 1916, p. 8; Howard, "Anne Martin," p. 15, Chapter 1; Beard to Paul, December 9, 1916 and December 21, 1916, Reel 36, NWPP.
[121] Vernon said she always respected Wilson. Her mother told her she was not polite to interrupt him. Fry, Vernon interview, pp. 63-69; Martin to Paul, December 7, 1916; and Rogers to "Editor" for press release, December 1916, Reel 36, NWPP.

[122] She went on: "[A]ny attempt at reconstruction of the world after this war is ended is inadequate and abortive without their help. . . . [In the world, under men] there is too much poverty, war, exhaustion, blasted lives and too little hope, joy, happy children." Report of Convention, June 1916, p. 23, Reel 28, NWPP.
[123] October 23, 1916 telegram, Reel 34; Stevens to Milholland, October 23, 1916, Reel 34, NWPP.
[124] Emily Perry to Alice Paul, October 1916; Paul to A. L. Muhse, October 24, 1916 and Paul to Milholland, October 26, 1916, Reel 34, NWPP: Robert F. Hall, "Women Have Been Voting Ever Since," (On Milhollands) *Adirondack Life*, Winter, 1971. Hall presumed Milholland died of leukemia. But Milholland's death certificate at Vassar, cites aplastic anemia.
[125] Late October correspondence, Reel 34, NWPP.
[126] Vida was, like Inez, a Vassar graduate ('08) and was a singer, actress and athlete. The Milhollands were from Lewis, New York, in the Adirondacks, the daughters of prominent newspaperman and reformer (notably, in the NAACP), John Milholland. Letter to author from Anne Boissevain Nusbaum (Inez Milholland's sister-in-law), March 20, 1983; Hall, "Women Voting." See also Vida Milholland to Alice Paul, October 30, 1916, Reel 35, NWPP.
[127] Her misspellings are included (saddest, Davidson).
[128] Invitations were issued to all the "important groups of women [who knew her], including women lawyers and working women." The ceremony had all the familiar Woman's Party pomp, pageantry, music and speeches of tribute. The speakers were her Woman's Party and socialist friends. December 1916 memo on invitations, Reel 36; Stevens, *Jailed*, pp. 50-51; December Memorial Report, Reel 36, NWPP, *Suffragist*, December 30, 1916, p. 5.
[129] Memorial, December 1916, Reel 36, NWPP.
[130] January 1, 1917 memo, Wilson Papers on Microfilm, Reel 209.
[131] January 8, 1917 memo, Wilson Papers on Microfilm, Reel 209. Field told him that women's "maternal instinct for the preservation of life" -- of a child or of a Cause -- would give them no rest until victory. Stevens, *Jailed*, pp. 55-59.
[132] Stevens, *Jailed*, p. 59; Author interview with Rebecca Reyher.

Chapter Three

A New Race of Strong Women: All So-Called Classes 1912-1916

> We have many noble women of all so-called classes; and welcome all who are in earnest and want to help.
>
> Alice Paul, 1913

> The Woman's Party had from beginning to end--every kind of woman. . . . Women of every experience and every walk of life you find have this same feeling for building up respect for their own sex, power for their own sex, and lifting it up out of a place where there is contempt for women in general. . . . Some people are just born feminists.
>
> Alice Paul, 1976

The rebellious Woman's Party attracted and recruited strong, highly motivated, progressive feminists from all sorts of backgrounds, who were all interested in achieving "power for their own sex." With a militant feminism in common, NWP women still brought contrasting feminist priorities to the suffrage fight, and this created conflict during membership drives to create a "united sisterhood." Recent studies, [see introduction] particularly those of Nancy Cott, Steven Buechler and Ellen DuBois, have stressed the elitist class control of the suffrage movement, but the evidence suggests that the NWP militants do not quite fit into that pattern. With their rhetoric of a "new race of strong women," they had a magnetic appeal which went beyond just an elite upper and middle class. Additionally, Woman's Party "elite" suffragists had the capacity, on some occasions, to move beyond their own class interests toward a collective sensibility with all women. As it sought a "united sisterhood" for suffrage between 1913 and 1916, the CU, unlike the moderate, mainstream NAWSA, sought to reach out to a broad cross section of American women, including working women.

The core membership of the Congressional Union (NWP), officers and organizers, represented two broad areas of progressive feminism: one, the more traditional, mature, "clubwoman" reformers, who often did have fairly elitist desires to wield class power, along with a passion for equal justice and independence from male dominance; and two, younger, educated, liberal "new woman" reformers, often middle class, with a strong desire for economic independence, personal freedom, and a greater, more inclusive democracy, away from patriarchal control. Both sorts of feminists were found among the CU's leaders, chosen to establish the NWP; while the organizers, chosen to help expand the NWP, were predominantly single, independent "new women." Early Woman's Party feminist ideologies spanned the entire spectrum from Alva Belmont's demand for fewer female restrictions, to Rosa Winslow's fight against women having to work in disease-ridden factories. Interestingly, as a leader, Alice Paul tended to be more comfortable with wealthy, mature society women reformers, whereas Lucy Burns was more sympathetic to the younger, CU worker/organizers and the more radical recruits. The coexistence of contrasting feminist viewpoints within the CU was possible because of the women's shared passionate commitment to women's rights; but in the early years of the Woman's Party, when the "political phase" called for a politic use of women's power, there were real clashes over issues of class and race--the inclusiveness of the sisterhood.

CU/NWP suffragists did include Progressive "politicized," middle class social feminist/suffragists as described by William Chafe. Comfortably well-off women who were rather conservative and not at first at ease as allies of the women of the working classes, the sort of suffragists Eleanor Flexner and Aileen Kraditor described, were among the NWP ranks. As for the Woman's Party being dominated by that prosperous elite, as Ellen DuBois and Nancy Cott have argued, it is only partially true, even between 1912 and 1916. Steven Buechler's description of privileged suffragists who were only interested in "social control" from above, is useful in describing the set of CU women who fall into the "clubwoman" section of the feminist spectrum. Women who more or less fit Buechler's description, women who were mature, affluent, club-oriented reformers, joined the CU's "new race of strong women" instead of NAWSA, because they felt they had waited much too long to be able to exercise well-deserved rights as citizens of their community.[1] But they were not the whole story.

A rather different sort of feminist represented in the new party was the twentieth century version of the "new woman." Historian June Sochen's new woman is a "young working girl," probably a clerical worker in a city, possibly well-educated, relishing her freedom away from home. Richard O'Connor called the new woman a "restless heroine . . . yearning for wider and more significant experience," a woman searching for sexual freedom and the overthrow of bourgeois life. Both Janice Law Trecker and Christine Lunardini have noted the energy, youth and worldliness of CU/NWP suffragists.[2] Educated, cosmopolitan, young suffragists brought a fresh, more adventurous, open attitude to the movement. All CU feminists were egalitarian in their views of desirable male-female status, very much action-oriented, and militant on winning women's political rights. Where they differed was over the issue of membership. The new woman feminists were especially liberal toward recruitment of sister suffragists, which sometimes set them apart from the older version of the "new race of strong women."

The women who led and joined the CU between 1913 and 1916 came from all over the country; they were united in their militantly feminist demand for woman suffrage, but differed enormously in background. As noted, the 168 NWP suffragists eventually imprisoned in Washington, true representatives of American suffrage militants, will be profiled in this study. The women on the list of prisoners include all the major founder/leaders (16), many officers and active members from state and local branches who joined in the 1913-1916 period (35), and about half the national organizers (29). As explained earlier, data collected on the militants encompassed both socio-economic and reform backgrounds: age, education, family background (class, ethnic, religious), geographic region, occupation, marital status, political orientation and reform activities. NWP suffragists divide into three groups based loosely upon party functions; the first two will be discussed in this chapter. The first group is the "leaders," that is, members of the national executive committee, (usually founders) active important national advisors, and state CU officers; the second is "organizers," those women, most of them paid by the CU, who travelled throughout the country to speak, agitate and form local branches; and the last is "recruits," (88) the members and sympathizers who came to Washington in 1917-1919 in order to take part in militant demonstrations. The membership study is a collective biography of a sort, based on the data assembled on the 168 suffragists who eventually went to jail for their feminist militancy. (See Appendices A and B)

As is probably already evident, starting with Burns, Paul and Martin, the women who led the militants seemed uniformly to come from comfortable backgrounds, and to have already been reform activists, even with service in other militant suffrage groups. This was certainly true of national leaders, but also held true for the women chairing state and local branches. The two basic types of progressive feminist reformers were clearly present among the leaders--Paul and Burns' college "new women" friends, and older, "clubwomen" types--both groups drawn to the WSPU-style suffragism.[3] National officers were ordinarily founders of the party in 1912-1913. They either had some association with Paul, Burns or NAWSA; or they were secured to give status and respectability to the new group. Certain characteristics in socio-economic background might, therefore, be expected. The 16 national leaders who were among the prisoners were undeniably from affluent backgrounds, for the most part, daughters of high-ranking professional fathers. Twelve of the 16 leaders were of English heritage, with the others Irish, German or Dutch in family origin. Most leaders were probably Protestant, but at least one was Catholic. The two Quakers' beliefs (Alice Paul was the most obvious example) would significantly affect NWP civil disobedience tactics. Four of the leaders claimed distinguished colonial New England ancestry, two were daughters of members of Congress, three were bankers' daughters, three army officers' daughters and three editor-writers' daughters. In terms of geographic region, 14 of the 16 were from eastern cities. Education also attested to their solidly middle and upper class origins and their preparation for future careers. Eight of the leaders were college-educated (mostly in the Northeast: two at Vassar and two at Swarthmore) and five of them had done graduate work. Six had included extensive travel abroad to round out their educational experience. The national leaders, as members of a comfortable eastern elite, were no doubt women who had a certain confidence, and certain expectations born of status and privilege. Many of the highly educated younger women, had the talent and intelligence for professional aspiration, and had family support to develop those aspirations.

National leaders, especially the mature "clubwomen," were veteran activists. Nine clubwomen were married (or widowed) and over 40 by 1915; some of them died in the 1920s. These were independent women, many with years of experience in women-related, progressive reform; they were not, however, all college-educated. These clubwomen's activities ranged from being members of the DAR to working for Progressive prison and labor reforms, to stamping out venereal disease. As a whole, national leaders' politics seem to have been within the moderate range of the traditional Republican/Democrats, but one woman was very active in the Progressive Party and at least three of the younger, new women executives were sympathetic to the socialists. For all, the overriding reform concerns were strictly women-oriented. Twelve leaders had been suffragists before joining the CU; three had left NAWSA for the CU, four had been officers in the militant British WSPU. Nine leaders, then, were already militant suffragists before joining the CU. Five of the woman leaders would remain with the NWP after suffrage was won, most of them as national officers, and many would be involved in international women's rights organizing. In sum, many national leaders already had militant credentials and were experienced activists. They were not uniformly conservative in political outlook and at least a few advocated some of the more controversial Progressive causes.

Paul and Burns loved to call upon mature clubwomen, paragons of affluent respectability, and already highly visible to certain constituencies, to be delegates to political leaders. NWP clubwomen feminists were quite willing to do battle over their lack of the franchise, which many considered, because of their privileged class status, a personal insult.[4] In order to illustrate the makeup of the women who ran this remarkable movement, some of its more important members will be profiled below. The indomitable Matilda Hall Gardner was a well-established presence in Washington, DC, along with her husband, newspaperman Gilson Gardner. She was the daughter of Frederick Hall, Chicago Tribune editor, and had been well educated in Chicago, Paris and Brussels. Gardner once remarked that Washington police were not sure of the "social tone" to adopt while arresting women like herself! (See Figure 4) Anna Kelton Wiley was another widely respected and inveterate progressive clubwoman who resented the fact that capable women had "no share in national life." As a CU National Advisor, Wiley was in the very first delegation sent to Wilson. Born in California in 1877, (a general's daughter) she received her B.S. from George Washington University in 1897, and in 1911 had married famed food expert and chairman of the U. S. Pure Food Department,

Harvey Wiley. Wiley had two sons, and like so many NWP members led a physically active life, including strenuous walks, tennis and camping. She worked in a government office, and volunteered her services for the Elizabeth Cady Stanton Club, the Housekeepers Alliance, the Consumers' League, and, of course, the Pure Food League.[5]

Congressional Union executive Abby Scott Baker's first job "out of the home" was helping organize the 1913 suffrage parade, but after joining the CU, Baker became "chairman" of the National Highway Association's "women's department." Baker's true passion, she said, was for "women's freedom" and for women's rightful power: "Power and responsibility will develop women just as power and responsibility have developed men." As a prominent doctor's wife, she had time to pursue her love of sailing, swimming and the theatre, but she also expressed interest in "getting into the labor fight." Like Wiley, Baker's father had been an army officer, and her three sons fighting in World War I provided excellent press when the NWP's patriotism was questioned. Described as an "alluring personality" and great beauty, Baker was the CU's "diplomat," able to enter the best social circles of Washington politicians.[6]

The CU/NWP needed more talents than the ability to socialize with politicians; they needed to enlist veteran political campaigners in the suffrage fight. Several early officers and advisors advocated or had already engaged in suffrage militancy. These women saw Paul and Burns' organization as the (at least potential) equivalent of British suffrage militancy. Strong, egalitarian feminists, they, like C. P. Gilman, quite explicitly hoped the CU represented a "new race" of strong women, women who could alter the unequal status of the sexes in society. Several of these women provided strong leadership and showed courage in staying with the NWP through its most militant phases, with some actually advocating more drastic steps than were taken. Women who admired the WSPU would logically advocate even greater militancy.[7]

New York WPU suffragists, all with strong ties and sympathies with the Pankhursts, numbered among the CU's most aggressive national leaders. This included Harriot Stanton Blatch herself, as well as many of her most able officers. Eunice Dana Brannan, a former WPU officer, on the CU executive committee, was born in New York, the daughter of Charles Dana, former abolitionist and *New York Sun* editor. Eunice Dana was married to "the eminent Dr. John Brannan," a board member of New York's Bellevue Hospital. Organizer Rebecca Reyher describes her as a good friend, a warm, nurturing woman who liberally dispensed advice on health and affairs of the heart to her younger colleagues. Brannan was also an "ardent admirer" of the Pankhursts. She had helped gather "prominent" signatures for a petition protesting the British "Cat and Mouse" Act.[8]

Another militant WPU officer much taken with the new American suffrage organization was Lavinia Dock. Dock was born in 1858, one of six daughters of a propertied family of Pennsylvania Germans. Although she was living a "free and happy life," at the age of 26, Dock decided to train as a nurse at Bellevue Hospital

Matilda Hall Gardner was the sort of respectable clubwoman sought to lead political delegations.
Figure 4

in New York. She was a visiting nurse for the poor, an army nurse in the Spanish-American War, and then became a nursing teacher, author of nursing texts and well-known advocate of the professionalization of nursing. Dock had already shown her own suffrage militance by having been arrested for attempting to vote in 1896, and by selling the WSPU's *Votes for Women* while attending an International Council of Nurses. In 1896 Dock became one of New York settlement worker Lillian Wald's inner circle. With Leonora O'Reilly and the WTUL, she organized a garment workers local and walked in the 1909 shirtwaist strike picket line. Dock launched an anti-venereal disease and prostitution campaign in 1905. Entranced by the new Congressional Union, she wrote to express her admiration for the parade idea and to send them a contribution in January of 1913. She would write Paul often to offer her support, and her "constant loyalty and devotion to you and your wonderful group of youth-inspired workers--my firm friendship and belief in what you are doing--have done--and will do."[9]

New York WPU women were among the most influential in the country; they often expressed disgust that women of their social rank and prestige had no say in government. Elizabeth Selden Rogers (Wilson's Secretary of War, Henry Stimson's sister-in-law), "Chairman" of the advisory board, was more cynical than most, and perhaps the most militant member of the Woman's Party. An executive WPU officer, she thought a constitutional suffrage amendment "nonsense" in 1913, but was soon won over, writing the *New York Times* that: "It was an impertinent insult for the President to say that it is a matter of no importance that the women be enfranchised."[10] The 45-year-old Rogers (as of 1915) had been a NAWSA suffragist and education reformer. She was the wife of a famous thyroid expert, Dr. John Rogers, with whom she had two sons (one had died) and a daughter, Elizabeth. Paul reported that Dr. Rogers discovered a goiter cure only because Elizabeth Selden refused to marry him as long as she had a goiter problem. With a different background from the leaders who worked as teachers and social workers, Rogers was called by some a "terrible snob," with little understanding of working women's problems. Rogers was very feisty though, and always fuming for militant action: she once wrote Lucy Burns that her "whole soul" was in one rebellious protest and was certain "Emma Goldman is happier than I am."[11]

The New York WPU's Louisine Havemeyer was another prime example of affluent womanhood devoted to the cause. Havemeyer, born in New York in 1855, was the widow of H. O. Havemeyer of American Sugar Refining. A tireless suffrage speaker, contributor and fund-raiser, Havemeyer was probably best known as a patron of the arts, the first American to buy a Degas and to promote painter Mary Cassatt. She was described as a "woman of very pleasing personality, with a good voice, quite pretty, with a good deal of fun . . . amused, intelligent gray eyes and an ingratiating smile . . . totally ingenuous." Her speeches were "salty" with a "type of old-fashioned woman suffrage appeal." She often reflected her indignation against the government, stating that nearly "every Anglo-Saxon government" had given women the vote, but American women "were still deprived."[12] Paul and Burns welcomed these veteran suffrage militants, women with valuable visibility and access to the press and political leaders.

The CU was not entirely dominated by the dowager club types, but was also guided by relatively young college women like Paul and Burns themselves, with bold new ideas and a highly spirited feminism. The younger leaders, many of them friends of the co-leaders, spent a great deal of their time as CU "organizers," but their contributions as CU founders and national leaders and advisors, cannot be overlooked. In 1917 a bit less than half--seven--of the leaders were in their 20s and 30s. Only Doris Stevens was in her 20s by 1917 (the year used to compute the data). Seven national leaders were self-supporting career women in the female-dominated occupations then available to college-educated women. Such careers do not really seem to fall into Steven Buechler's category of powerful, controlling "professional/managerial" women. They were social workers and educators and all single. Six of those seven (Dock was the seventh, a nurse/educator) were in their 20s and 30s, highly educated working "professionals" in the northeastern urban area. Such traits made them prototypical "new women" with the independence necessary to meet the demands of an NWP leader who also served as travelling speaker and organizer.

Among the first on the executive committee with Eastman, Lewis, Beard and Vernon, was Elsie Hill. Hill was the daughter of 22-year Connecticut Congressman Ebenezer Hill. A Vassar graduate, she was a French teacher, and would become a particularly important NWP leader and speaker, highly independent and very engaging. She had been born in 1883 in Norwalk, and remembered a happy girlhood. Hill said her father always deferred to her mother, and "there was nothing of any conflict between them that soured me on men." She was two years younger than Alice Paul, who would become a close friend and whom she would idealize. In fact, after Hill married a lawyer during WWI, he apparently developed resentment toward Paul because of the time Hill spent with her. To Paul, Hill was always "so lovely, so enthusiastic." She remembered the reddish-brown haired Hill dancing in a pageant on the Treasure steps. Hill had been a firm suffragist from her Vassar days, insisting: "They didn't teach us anything at Vassar and they wouldn't allow a suffrage speech on the campus . . . until we got it." She had been brought up to discuss and debate political issues and had been surrounded by Congressmen; her knowledge of Washington's intricacies would be invaluable. After having been "fussed over" by Congressmen her entire life (as her daughter, Leslie Hill Latham, puts it) she knew how progressive reform bills could be fought for and won. She infected everyone with her "good spirits, good health and tireless enthusiasm."[13] Hill typified the progressive era's optimistic style of feminism.

Doris Stevens, a social worker, was further left on the new woman spectrum. She became a member of the executive committee in 1915. Stevens was born in Omaha, Nebraska in 1892; she attended Oberlin and then had gone into teaching and social work. She had spent a year with NAWSA in Ohio and Michigan before becoming CU executive secretary and organizer in 1914. Stevens had become part of the Greenwich Village radical community, forming close friendships with Louise Bryant and John Reed. Stevens espoused a new woman feminism, believing that women should take power for themselves. She told an exasperated young Harvard engineer (male) once, that although men may not "approve" of the militant fight for woman suffrage, women had to "fight for their own liberty": "We're just beginning to get confidence in ourselves. At last, we've learned to make and stand by our judgments."[14] Stevens, socialist democrat that she was, believed the NWP battle was for all women, the "whole race of women."

The evidence suggests that Alice Paul preferred to recruit (theoretically more "powerful") women of the "better classes" to lead CU branches in the period of expansion (1914-1916)--women with a certain aura of respectability. The state and local officers recruited provided many of the most militant NWP members: women like the "lovely" Amelia Walker of Baltimore, one of Paul's Swarthmore friends; Josephine Toscan Bennett of Hartford, Connecticut, DAR member and lawyer's wife; and Chicagoan Lucy Ewing, niece of Cleveland's Vice President, Adlai Stevenson.[15] Walker, Bennett and Ewing were fairly typical of the women Paul preferred to head state branches--women of status in the community. All but two of the 35 state officers analyzed were white, native-born and of western European, Protestant background. The class status of the officers is not quite as striking as with national leaders, but 11 of them were wealthy women, while 12 had fathers in the upper-levels of the professional classes: army officers, Congressmen, doctors, bankers or businessmen. One woman traced the inevitable colonial New England ancestry and two came from old southern families. Nearly all the rest of the state officers had middle class family backgrounds; one older woman had farmer parents. The 25 officers were not as urban and northeastern as the national leaders, since they obviously were representing their various regions. Only about half were from the East. Twelve of the state officers had had a college education (that we know of); some went to single sex women's schools like Bryn Mawr and the rest to coeducational universities. The large majority of branch leaders, wherever they came from, matched national ones in their middle to upper class status, in a time when class consciousness and the achievement of community standing was considered important--and thus very useful to the Congressional Union.

State leaders tended to be older than national leaders and on average, just as likely to have spent many years in reform work involved in a wide range of "women's issues." Their political views seem to have been comparable to the national leaders, with one woman in the Midwest-based Farmer Labor Party, three socialists and one Progressive Party member. Thirteen had been involved in community work, social reforms, government leagues or the Women's Trade Union League. Seven of the 35 officers were former suffragists, five from NAWSA and two connected to the WSPU. Unfortunately, information on the state officers' lives after suffrage is scant, but three *were* NWP officers in the ERA period, and at least three were involved with peace and/or labor reform work. What evidence exists underscores the fact that state officers appointed between 1914 and 1916 were much like the more mature national leaders in social background, and had wide-ranging reform and political interests, with a strong commitment to feminist issues.

The evidence suggests that some state officers were independent "new women." Sixteen of the 35 officers were well over 40, but 13 were in their 20s and 30s. (Six are unknown.) Half were single and half married. An extraordinary number, about half, were self-supporting--12 of the 17 single women earned a living, and five of the 18 married women earned a wage outside the home. Fourteen of the married women volunteered a great deal of time in club activity. Of the 17 who worked for wages, 12 of them were, again, "semi"-professionals, usually social workers or teachers; but two were doctors and one a government administrator. Like national leaders, the branch officers were not entirely older clubwomen, nor were they exclusively youthful, more liberal college women. State officers *were* confident, economically independent women--women used to playing public roles.

These were mature women with a sense of duty and civic responsibility, but who felt a great deal of impatience, even anger, at their lack of political power and equal citizenship. Some, as very strong feminists, would question other kinds of social restrictions and become supporters of more liberal, even socialist political ideologies. The CU branch leaders had their share of eminent doctors and lawyers' wives who thought Wilson "impertinent" and "disgraceful," and fully expected their due as women of the elite class. They were not about to await the result of NAWSA's tedious state suffrage fights. In some ways, perhaps it was easier for wealthy, self-sufficient women of leisure to be outrageous feminists. One example of this sort of feminist was the outspoken (some said "tactless") Sarah Tarleton Colvin, a CU officer in Minnesota, who had long lobbied for nursing legislation in the Midwest. Brought up as a southern belle of the Alabama Tarleton family, Colvin rejected her family's notion that women should be taught only "prayer and instinct." After not being allowed to train as a singer, Colvin chose nursing and had been a graduate nurse at Johns Hopkins and a Red Cross nurse in the Spanish-American War. Colvin was married (with no children) and her doctor husband did not share her CU sympathies. This never stopped Colvin, who held firmly egalitarian feminist views which challenged traditional domestic roles for women. She argued that women should be self-reliant, have more than "their husband's interests" at heart, and direct their own lives. Colvin understood the difficulties of a woman "who did not find it easy to conform."[16]

Dora Sedgwick Hazard, CU "Chairman" for Central New York in 1915, was not outwardly nonconformist, but was attracted to the CU early on, and was able, through her social position, to greatly help the effort in New York. Hazard, born in Syracuse in 1864, was married to Frederick Hazard, the wealthy owner of a soda ash processing plant. When he died he left his wife with four million dollars. Described as "lovely, cultured . . . a lady," and "charming, very intelligent," Hazard lived the life of the very wealthy--with two chauffeurs, four or five maids, a cook, a butler and a "mammy." Hazard believed woman suffrage a paramount issue because women were "needed to help maintain high standards in politics, [without them] the riff raff will reign."[17] She had been NY Women's Political Union Vice President, and her CU district recruited a very large number of members. Hazard herself was a generous contributor, even though she was hesitant to support the party in power policy. Social pillars like Hazard were valuable, according to former WPU organizer Ramona Baxter Bowden, because they could help their "less powerful sisters."[18]

Other CU officers did not think in terms of "riff raff," and some were far from wealthy. Minnie D. Abbott was Secretary for the CU district in Atlantic City, New Jersey, and would hold down a "man's job" on the railroad after the war broke out. The 45-year-old French-speaking Alice M. Cosu, NWP Vice Chairman of New Orleans, had "no prestige socially, a diamond in the rough. She's poor." Cosu was married to a Belgian cabinet maker, a firm suffragist. Alice Cosu was called "so militant as to be unpopular [in Louisiana]." Although far from socially influential, Cosu "worked like a little galley slave" for Paul.[19]

The CU District Chairman of Worcester, Massachusetts, a single (she said she never wanted to marry) 55-year-old artist, Camilla Whitcomb, was the daughter of an affluent machine-shop owner. Whitcomb was a socialist and pacifist, who used to arrange for anarchists to hold meetings at her stable. Her eyes, at age 80, would "still blaze at injustice." Whitcomb would (to her mother's dismay) cast her hard-won first vote for socialist Norman Thomas.[20] Leaders like Cosu and Whitcomb shared the shaping of policy with mature and independent, (and less radical) affluent social reformers.

Even when looking only at leaders, the view that NWP suffragists were much like mainstream NAWSA suffragists in upper/middle class elitism, needs some qualification. They were definitely of comfortably well-off eastern backgrounds, and well-educated; this leading to a certain insularity in some, and freedom and adventurousness in others. They were also independent because they were economically self-supporting or self-sufficient. And the CU's self-supporting women were likely to sympathize with all working women. Although Steven Buechler argues that early 20th century feminist suffragists did not question women's subordinate domestic status, some NWP militant leaders, with their new woman feminism, provide exceptions.[21] Independence and power for women in every area, were very important to progressive, feminist professionals. The Woman's Party was led by older clubwomen, disenchanted, impatient former NAWSA members and WPU-WSPU suffragists, *and* by classically progressive, liberal, "new women."

Although the leadership included new women feminists with fairly liberal tendencies, it was the organizers who brought political radicalism into the very working core of the NWP. CU organizers of the expansion period of late 1914 to 1916 represented a widening spectrum of social class. The 29 imprisoned organizers who were analyzed do not differ a great deal in socio-economic background from party leaders. They were basically of native-born families from the East with six from wealthy families and five from the upper middle class. But there were two women from working class origins, and the remainder from the lower ranks of the middle, indicating a real opening up of the Woman's Party in the 1915-1916 expansion period. Twelve of the 29 organizers had fathers who were businessmen, lawyers or engineers; four others had fathers who held government office. Half of them--14--were known to have been college-educated and six with graduate school educations. Seven went to Vassar or Bryn Mawr, and the rest to coeducational institutions. Although the majority of organizers had familiar-sounding backgrounds, there were important exceptions.

Real contrast begins with the relative radicalism of organizers' politics compared to that of national leaders, which would lead to some major differences of opinion. There were 13 socialist organizers, with one more in the Farmer-Labor Party. Jailed organizers worked for peace, labor reforms (two in the WTUL), even for the infamous Industrial Workers of the World (IWW or "Wobblies.") There were also two women who were members of the less than radical DAR. The large majority of the organizers were too young to have been very politically active in suffrage before joining the CU, but four of the 29 were former NAWSA suffragists. In spite of Alice Paul's stern disapproval of their not putting the amendment first, at least three organizers left NWP work temporarily to help in Anne Martin's woman issue-oriented campaign for the Nevada Senate seat in 1918.[22] Six organizers are known to have remained active in the party after suffrage was won, and many became affiliated with the World's Woman's Party. At least four worked for birth-control and other woman-related reforms after 1920. These were hardly stereotypically conservative suffragists.

Organizers were highly mobile and independent, likely to have the classic characteristics of free, "new women." The rigors of life on the road for their cause almost demanded it. Unlike most leaders, they were certainly youthful, with 87% of them between the ages of 19 and 29 in 1917. Again, they were self-sufficient; twenty-four were single and all earned their own living. Twenty-five of them were either professional working women, mostly teachers or social workers in eastern urban areas, (18 were in the East) or working for the first time (eight) as (low) paid organizers for the CU. Significantly, the other four were factory workers and/or labor organizers.

CU organizers were picked by Alice Paul to project an image of youth, beauty, intelligence and freedom--personifications of progressive, new women. Former organizer Rebecca Reyher relates that Paul wanted "good looking women" as suffrage organizers. She would not allow them to indulge in unhealthy and unladylike cigarette smoking at Washington headquarters, since it might "hurt the amendment."[23] From differing backgrounds, but largely well-educated and likely to be involved in numerous controversial reforms; organizers were independent, self-supporting and self-reliant women. These women stressed democratic equality, and tended to care about injustice in society, particularly class-based injustice, but on occasion, also race-based discrimination. These were open, optimistic, liberal feminists.

Again, it will be illustrative to look more closely at examples of hard working CU organizers dedicating themselves to converting all women to the cause of women's political equality. It was not always easy, even for the tiny, "young, beautiful and brilliant" Hazel Hunkins, who could convert almost anyone to nearly anything. She did have a definite problem moving Baptist women in California, however: "[They are] like so many bodies without minds or feelings. I never saw such stones."[24] Hunkins was probably one of the CU's most colorful and radical members, another comrade of the Bryant-Reed Greenwich Village circle. She was, for instance, determined to have a "eugenic baby" by a father she picked, and she eventually did, to Alice Paul's disgust. Hunkins was born in Billings, Montana; appropriately, her father's ancestors were New England Puritans. She was a Vassar graduate, had been a chemistry instructor and researcher at the University of Missouri, and then got a high school job teaching botany and geography (chemistry was taught by men only) when her mother became ill. Hunkins thought it unfair that a "girl's path was a channel that converged as it grew with the times," while a "boy's expanded." Thoroughly disgruntled by her teaching experience, she welcomed the "full philosophy of feminism" taught her by the CU organizers, and enthusiastically joined the "Cause."[25]

Another organizer, Lucy Gwynn Branham, 24 years old, (pictured in Figure 1 with Lucy Burns) was also driven by the reform urge typical of young progressives. She joined her mother in suffrage work. Branham was born in 1892 in Kempsvill, Virginia, and brought up in Baltimore; her father was a physician. A student of history, Branham was as well-educated as Paul, with a B.A. ('11) from Maryland's Washington College, an M.A. from Johns Hopkins ('14) and Ph.D. from Columbia. When teaching school in St. Petersburg, Florida, Branham was on the scene when two girls were drowning in the surf. Beating three men who had a head start in the rescue, she saved one of the girls and then helped save one of the three male rescuers. Branham had received a bronze Carnegie hero medal and $1,000 for the rescue (the number saved was from one to six depending on which newspaper account). Branham was called "a stormy petrel" by her colleagues, but had difficulty explaining her new cause to most of her family: "My family are so bitter toward Federal Suffrage and the Union. It is uncomfortable but interesting to be ostracized by your nearest and dearest relatives: especially when they are so prejudiced that they refuse to listen to logic of justice."[26]

Progressive new women feminists like Hunkins and Branham, much like Lucy Burns, saw injustice around them and wanted to change it. Many of the organizers had such sentiments: Mary Gertrude Fendall worked for the Farmer-Labor Party; the CU drew the radical socialist Katherine Morey of Boston; they had, of course, former factory worker, organizer and actress, Rose Winslow; and then there was Julia Emory who worked for the WTUL. Emory was the daughter of a Maryland state senator. Although Emory's mother cautioned Alice Paul that Julia was a "dear child with more energy than strength," her daughter's complete loyalty to Paul and "the cause" continued to drive her to further effort. As with many organizers who saw their political lobbying go for nought, Emory's growing fury provided strong motivation: "By Gummie! I long to start a feminist revolution . . . if only the *women would* revolt! When I see the men so perfectly willing to accept the unstinting services of women [for the war effort] and let suffrage fail . . .!"[27] Emory worked to change that injustice.

Organizer Gladys Greiner, also of Baltimore, provided another clear example of youthful, dedicated feminism. Rebecca Reyher describes Greiner as then a "laughing college girl . . . long-legged and unconventional." Greiner was a Maryland tennis, basketball and golf champion who had studied at Forest Glen Seminary and then at Johns Hopkins and Harvard. She had also done settlement work in Kentucky. Greiner's father, John Greiner (an engineering expert), wrote Alice Paul that he would like her to find a safe desk job for his "abnormal" daughter, who took "no interest in home," wanted to reform the world, thought the servants in the house "should be treated as well as guests," and in short, was "inclined to Bolshevism."[28] The CU corps contained women who could not see beyond their garden parties, but those women had to contend with other CU members within the fold, both leaders and organizers, who believed in a more literal sisterhood of all women.

One of the still debated questions of the progressive era is whether or not any real, wide-reaching democratic reforms actually were achieved, and if reformers were, as ordinarily portrayed, purely the affluent, concerned with maintaining "stability" and pursuing only their own power interests. Steven Buechler is one who forcefully argues that privileged suffragist women, like other progressives, were trying to manage the social order through reform from above.[29] But Woman's Party suffragists attracted more than one sort of reformer with their strong, woman-centered philosophy and militant policies. They attracted feminist women with all sorts of political agendas and class-based outlooks. For the CU/NWP, and especially for Alice Paul, the *only* important issue was winning suffrage. Whatever could be done to expedite the amendment was usually done. Paul and Burns wanted suffrage for *all* women and believed their fight was for all women, but also wanted to use any weapon they had, including the relative power of wealthy women, to get it. The NWP courted wealthy "elite" women as national advisors, officers and branch leaders, in order to finance the group, make it respectable, give it publicity and make "important" men take more notice of the group. The "new women" feminists, college women, socialists and union women in the CU, shared a strong feminism with the wealthy clubwomen , but were *not* in agreement on every class--or race--issue. Many of them were from middle class backgrounds, and, as Buechler points out, did not have the class consciousness of the upper *or* working classes, but many did, in this case, tend to sympathize with working women trying to be independent in a male-run economy.

Woman's Party leaders had to deal with feminists from an entire spectrum of social class and reform background, with differing perspectives, priorities, and agendas, all the while doing what they felt best for the amendment. As leaders, Alice Paul and Lucy Burns, both middle class, straddled the line between a more elitist feminism and a more liberal, democratic one; with Paul leaning toward the elite and Burns toward the socialists. Both favored using the power of prominent women to help in the suffrage fight; although Paul, more than Burns, wanted them as NWP officers. Both also were sensitive to the issue of representing *all* women, including working women, in the struggle for women's political power, but Burns felt this more deeply than Paul.

In a correspondence which is nearly always business-like and to the point, Alice Paul, in the summer of 1913, had written Iowa socialist leader John E. Nordquist a long, revealing and rare explication of her class philosophy. Nordquist had wanted to know if Paul's party had any socialists, and if it had any interest in "the downtrodden." She replied that they had many socialists, but stressed that the Congressional Union represented no particular political party, but only the cause of woman suffrage. Paul explained (and it is worth quoting at length from this letter):

> We feel that this Woman Suffrage question is above every question of the time, because; for one thing, it is so vitally the very next step in the process of Moral Evolution. We have many noble women of all so-called classes, and welcome all who are in earnest and want to help. We have many who work all day, in government offices, and shops, who are Chairmen of Committees and who come after work hours and do all they can to forward the Cause. If you mean the ultra wealthy class, we have a few of those, and those we have give generously, both of their time, and means and I think that I may answer, in the name of every woman who is a Suffragist, to your question, regarding our interest in the downtrodden and oppressed, that the main and first reason for Woman's awakening to the need for an instrument in her own hands, for helping in affairs of state, is her devotion to the whole Human Race, and the women who have given the best of their lives to this work, have ever been those whose work has been to give a fairer opportunity to the real workers in the world, to enjoy that world, and to reap the benefits of their lives of labor.[30]

Paul insisted here, as she did thereafter, that the Party's concern was the "whole Human Race"; all women were represented in the Woman's Party, women "of all so-called classes" helped with CU suffrage work. She also assured Nordquist that many NWP suffragists were more than likely women who had been, if not socialists, then at least active in labor rights organizations. Many women, such as Lavinia Dock, (and Alva Belmont, for that matter) had worked with the WTUL.

"Chairman" Paul herself was no socialist, that was not her cause. She argued that her task was to work to benefit all *women.* Steven Buechler's argument that middle class women were not really class conscious can be applied to many CU militants, in that class issues were not seen as all that important--arguably, freeing them to concentrate on women's issues. This was surely true of Alice Paul: Crystal Eastman called Paul "sex-conscious, not class conscious."[31] Paul did not see the Woman's Party as an elite and self-involved group of women, but one which represented and worked for all women. Paul did not concern herself, therefore, with working class issues, or sensibilities at times, as when she insisted on securing "prominent" women as branch officers.

It became clear during the 1914-1916 organizing period, that Paul's outlook on class issues contrasted, to some degree, with that of Lucy Burns. Perhaps Burns' larger "sense of injustice" made her more in tune with class grievances. It was Burns who was responsible for editing the *Suffragist* by 1915, and she diligently tried to include all points of view, feeling that all women, regardless of class, needed a voice in government. The journal regularly had articles, for example, by Crystal Eastman on "voteless women and the labor problem" or Matilda Hall Gardner on "women workers and the federal government." It also carried news of women's unions, Burns, as editor, stressing the import of the issues of women of the working classes.

Burns and Paul were in agreement that woman workers should continually be asked to wait upon President Wilson, and that socialist women constantly be requested to send suffrage resolutions to western women's groups and to the White House.[32] They thought it important that the CU show it represented all women--immigrant workers along with blue-blood socialites. The militants argued that sex discrimination should be something all women would want to combat. It was the ultra-wealthy Alva Belmont who in 1915 called woman suffrage "a great spiritual movement . . . a permanent union between all women to make each woman realize that her interest is the interest of all women."[33] Quoting Susan B. Anthony, the CU called upon western women that same year to "stand shoulder to shoulder against every party not fully and unequivocally committed to equal rights for Women."[34] But when the CU suffragists stood shoulder to shoulder in the cause, would some be more equal than others?

Courting the rich, and therefore, relatively powerful, was done, but was controversial, even among top CU officers. Lucy Burns wrote organizer Virginia Arnold in 1915, if she could not get a Congressman to make an appointment with her, then she should get a delegation of "important women" to ask him and he usually "would succumb."[35] Women of "wide social influence" were courted at fund-raisers featuring a "thé-dansant" or lawn party. According to one account, Alva Belmont, herself the wealthiest of CU advisors, was a "Vikingess" with extraordinary energy and capacity. Of the over $28,000 taken in by the CU in 1914, almost half of it came from Alva Belmont. With such a stake in the CU, Mrs. Belmont made her presence felt, to say the least, and was generally consulted for her approval of policy. Belmont was, it seems, a difficult woman to please and was known to sometimes treat suffrage workers unfairly. Additionally, some labor organizers would feel understandably alienated by affluent suffragists like Alva Belmont, who they felt, along with the WTUL, took too much credit for organizing the 1909-10 New York shirtwaist workers strike.[36] Doris Stevens once wrote Paul that everything was done to placate Mrs. Belmont and keep her with them, but it was no easy task.[37] Some CU leaders were not at all comfortable with the arrangement with Belmont, nor with the "prominent women" philosophy generally, thinking suffrage must include both "working and leisured" classes. National officer Mary Beard was especially worried that associating with such "plutocratic" types as Alva Belmont and Louisine Havemeyer, would hurt her in labor circles. Finally, Beard decided that the Congressional Union had to have Belmont and her circle in order to thrive and wield power, although she remained uneasy. She always insisted that suffrage was not more important to her than labor issues.[38]

There was consensus that working women should at least be part of political delegations, but there was not always complete harmony regarding the sort of women who should lead or join the CU, or on the sort of (class-based) arguments organizers should use in the western election campaigns. For their part, as Mari Jo Buhle has written, there was controversy among women in socialist organizations over whether the sex struggle was as pressing as the class struggle. There was agreement with suffragists that a woman on her own in the work force needed political rights as added leverage, and that women as mothers in a modern industrial state needed a voice in politics. To many socialist women though, those concerns had to be subordinated to the workers' power struggle. Still, Buhle also points out that socialists, and especially western socialists, remained among the most amenable, helpful and constant friends of suffrage. This was particularly true of socialists and the militant suffrage fight. Numerous socialists joined the militants, and CU organizers and fundraisers repeatedly sought and received their help throughout the suffrage period.[39] Nancy Cott has noted that the CU attracted members from "both ends of the economic spectrum," and appealed to socialists because it was "neutral" on socialism.[40] The CU/NWP *did* attract socialist women, but they joined for more than neutrality, they experienced a strong feeling of solidarity versus common male oppressors with other women in the party, and this would be even more true by 1917.

NWP leaders reflected the view that working women, or more specifically, factory workers or "industrial women," were valuable in the very first 1913 parade. Socialist "Red" Kate Richards O'Hare, later given a five-year sentence under the Espionage Act for her anti-war speeches, was a marshal in that Washington parade. But from the first, some friction between classes developed. One float was proposed based on the old suffrage argument that any "inferior" man could vote, but not well-to-do women; it featured a "hobo" with a sign, "Hoboes kin vote." Paul told irate socialists it had been "only a suggestion."[41]

On the other hand, socialist influence was apparent in one 1916 CU election appeal which used the Marxist sounding "Women of these states, unite. We have only our chains to lose, and a whole nation to gain."[42] Some CU members would be much more comfortable than others with the political issues of the laboring classes. Organizer Rose Winslow was a true working socialist, a former factory worker and union organizer, who naturally wanted to speak to groups of workers in the West. In fact, the CU billed her as "one of [the workers'] own people." She eventually complained to Paul, however, that perhaps the woman suffrage issue was "too upper and middle class" and that fellow organizer Elsie Hill would not let her speak to coal miners. Paul countered by asking her not to be "difficult" and "destructive."[43] In this early period, the class alliance could be shaky.

Paul's good friend Margaret Whittemore, like Winslow, preferred speaking to a labor audience. Whittemore, daughter of a Detroit attorney, had a Quaker grandmother who pioneered suffrage work in Michigan. The 30-year-old organizer found it tough going bringing suffrage to Seattle in 1914, but she kept at it. Whittemore wrote Paul that she hated outdoor speaking, was poor at it, and her throat soon gave out. Yet another organizer who showed "socialist" tendencies, Whittemore reported to headquarters that the working class was much more responsive than the wealthy in Washington state.[44]

The organizer for Idaho, Helena Hill Weed, found great enthusiasm for an aggressive suffrage fight from woman workers. Weed reported: "I began with a meeting which was organized by the working women in the hotel where I was stopping. I told them of our work and what it meant. Many of the women had worked in the East, and they knew what conditions were among the laboring women there, and they said they never before realized that they could do anything to help the women in the East."[45] Weed, a 40-year-old geologist (in 1915), highly intelligent and idealistic, was married to a fellow geologist; she worked with him as his "field assistant" in scientific explorations. She was also one of the very few married organizers. She, like sister Elsie Hill, had attended Vassar (M.A. '02), but then went on to the Montana School of Mines. Weed loved to travel, and said she had the "curse of the wandering hoof." Sure of the suffrage cause, Weed was still insecure about her own abilities, and wrote Paul from Idaho very discouraged about the work she was doing. (Happily, she was able to report in the end that no Democrats won in Idaho in 1914.) Organizing in the West strengthened Weed's socialist outlook and her impression that women needed more power in society. She protested to Secretary of Agriculture Houston that farm women, particularly, were "made to be drudges and slaves . . . and kept ignorant."[46] Unlike Weed, Paul's rhetoric about the "whole Race" of women was not colored by a socialist perspective.

One of the clearest examples of the different class outlooks held by Paul and Lucy Burns, was the conflict created between them when Margaret Wood Kessler ran for Woman's Party office in 1915. Kessler was from Denver, where her father was a doctor. She had attended Denver University and was vice president of the

Woman's Progressive Club of Colorado.[47] In March of 1915, she wrote to Paul to introduce herself and tell her that she had taken the place of Colorado organizer and "Chairman" Ruth Noyes. She presented Paul with her credentials: she was an acquaintance of Jane Addams, was a hospital fund-raiser and had run for office on the Progressive ticket. A few weeks later, Paul wrote Burns that she did not want Kessler as Colorado chairman because "she is not a person of much importance" and they needed "a more influential name."[48] Organizer Ella Thompson was sent to Colorado to see what the situation was, and reported to Paul that Kessler "prevented" her from seeing women of wealth and was openly opposed to the "evils of capital and wealth."[49] But Caroline Spencer, Colorado CU secretary, had a very favorable opinion of Kessler, writing that Kessler was "a frail little body, all spirit and fire,--a dauntless lover of liberty and justice," who was very good with "labor." In spite of Spencer's support, Kessler was asked to leave office. However, she stayed with the NWP as a member; and, in spite of very poor health, she would picket and be jailed in 1917. Several CU women were angry that Kessler's credentials should be questioned: Organizer Rose Peacey wrote Paul that Kessler's treatment was unfair and caused entirely by "her pro-labor views." Burns answered this particular letter (not Paul), assuring Peacey that the CU "appreciated the services of Mrs. Kessler."[50] The CU, on Burns' authority, then released a bulletin admiring Kessler's pro-labor work and citing that work and the burdens it put on Kessler's schedule as the reason for her leaving office. Paul, however, disowned that bulletin, stating that the CU wanted to take no position on labor issues. She reminded Burns that the CU had one issue only. Yet at the same time, she suggested to Burns that "respectable" people in Colorado leaned toward the mine operators' position, not the miners'.[51] Obviously, saying suffrage was the only issue was a rather neat way, perhaps the only way, of uniting women whose views on other social and economic issues sharply divided them.

The CU leadership, with its democratic rhetoric, was ambivalent about race. Citing woman suffrage as the only issue would prove as useful a method of getting around problems of including black women, as working women, in 1914-1916, and would be the same method that had been used in the 1913 suffrage parade. Paul, who had handled the situation for the parade committee in 1913, reflected a fairly typical (for her era) middle-class view on the race issue. In fact, her own personal views were very similar to those of many NAWSA leaders, although not as extreme as Catt's, who always wrote it had been a mistake to quickly enfranchise "ignorant black men, fresh from slavery" before more deserving, "moral" white women. It would be Paul's CU lieutenants who would prove to be liberal on the race issue. Paul later admitted that perhaps her position on matters of race was not well thought out during the suffrage years, but explained that the issue of race was "unimportant" to her--only sex discrimination mattered.[52]

Incidents occurring at the time of the 1913 parade clearly reflected Paul's consistent wish not to deal with the matter. According to the *Crisis*, edited by black leader W. E. B. DuBois, black women who called at Congressional Committee headquarters about the parade were "received cooly." They were told to register, only to find that the clerks were out. The "order went out" to keep them segregated, but they protested and were therefore allowed to march by state and occupation.[53] This account is more or less verified by NWP documents. Answering one letter protesting the "prevention" of black women's participation, Paul wrote:

> As to the colored women--I can see no reason why they should not be in the procession, we are expecting to include them and I have written to an official of the colored women's organization asking her to call at the office so that we could talk over plans for their disposition in the parade.[54]

A few days later, Paul, answering a note from Alice Stone Blackwell, the editor of NAWSA's *Woman's Journal*, wrote that they did not want "colored women as such" organized, but wanted to scatter them with northern women, since southern suffragists had objected to marching with them. She agreed with Blackwell that suffrage would help black women, but, forecasting her position on this matter for the remainder of the campaign, said that that was not the time to bring up the question, and raising it would ruin the parade. Blackwell answered that black women should be "allowed, but not encouraged to participate." Marie Hardwick of the Howard University suffragists secured a place for herself and five other college women, and Ida Wells Barnett led the National Association of Colored Women. Black women were also represented by "one artist, one musician, two professional women, one teacher, twenty-five students, three homemakers, one nurse, and one mammy," all of whom reported, in spite of rumors, "courteous treatment" from parade marshals.[55]

Unsatisfied with the treatment black women had received at the hands of the parade committee, DuBois, who himself advocated woman suffrage as a "democratic" measure, had protested to Paul. She wrote him that black women could and did parade, and not in a segregated order. However, Paul was honest enough to admit to him that although she did not want the question of race to be brought up, "It was excellent that the Negro race should be represented."[56] That same day, Paul had written to a Virginia woman that she did not understand why the woman would not support a federal suffrage amendment. "[T]he question of the negro woman's vote can be disposed of the same as that of the negro man's vote."[57] In matters of class and race, the Woman's Party, and Paul in particular, continued to want to include all manner of women in demonstrations, but their stand was equivocal in terms of who was to be included as fellow workers or what the practical recruiting policy would be regarding a woman's class or race.

In the context of the times, the CU stand was not surprising. The "progressive" period was hardly that when it came to racial harmony. In 1915 Thomas Nixon's *Birth of a Nation* was published, with its portrayal of blacks as sex-mad animals;

lynchings and mutilations of blacks were a regular occurrence in the South at this time. The NAACP had been formed by blacks (including W. E. B. DuBois) and whites to defend blacks' civil and political rights, and they had had some hope that Wilson, the progressive president, might do something for blacks. But Wilson, as also evident with the woman suffrage issue, was very concerned about the southern Democrats' majority in Congress, so he segregated federal offices and appointed few blacks.[58] NWP women generally had predictable views on race: some were overtly racist; a few objected to racism; and most wished to avoid the issue of whether or not to include black women in a suffrage "sisterhood."

Alva Belmont, born in Alabama, gave $1,000 to Kate Gordon's white supremacist "Southern States Woman Suffrage Conference," sharing their view that black women should be excluded from suffrage and white women have "parity with men." Gordon had broken from NAWSA in 1914 because of her opposition to any sort of federal suffrage amendment and, as a good Southerner, also did not like the CU's "pro-Republican" policy.[59] The CU, therefore, had two rival suffrage organizations in the South. NAWSA, as noted, had always freely used racist arguments to protest the exclusion of white women from the franchise, and the CU would also use those arguments, although not quite as explicitly or consistently.[60] Organizer Virginia Arnold was citing accepted official CU policy in 1915 when she wrote southerner Ida Porter Boyer (and three other southern women the same day) that "white supremacy will continue and be strengthened with woman suffrage."[61] Being, like Wilson, very well aware that Congress was predominantly southern, CU delegations to senators and the President would often bring up the fact that "Negro women" could remain unenfranchised; the women assured these gentlemen that statistics showed that there were more white women than black men and women together. The February 1915 *Suffragist* contained an article by Helena Hill Weed, "The Federal Amendment and the Race Problem," which made a clear public statement that showed Weed's socialism did not extend to the black working classes. Weed argued that a federal amendment would enfranchise no one directly, and that the "grandfather clause" could be applied to black women. The article also included the oft-repeated assertion that "white supremacy" would be increased through the large influx of white woman voters.[62] These were hardly calls for solidarity with black women.

But objections to official racist CU policies, from the membership, though fairly rare, did occur. For example, Weed's article stirred some in the party to resign. Theresa H. Russell wrote Paul she was sorry that the *Suffragist* had assured a prejudiced South that suffrage would not imperil "white supremacy." She then told Paul about five innocent black men lynched in a county in Louisiana.[63] Other CU women also embraced the issue of black woman suffrage.

Sixty-year-old CU officer L. J. C. Daniels of Grafton, Vermont, wrote Paul so many times concerning the inclusion of black women in "the Cause," that Paul suspected, until informed differently by witnesses, that Daniels was herself black. Daniels, a very interesting woman, had studied law and was a long time women's rights activist before joining the Woman's Party. Ironically, her father Francis Daniels, had amassed a fortune in cotton in New Orleans before the Civil War. Lucy J. C. Daniels was born in 1858. As a single woman, a "suffragette," and a vegetarian, she was considered "rather eccentric" in Grafton. To save money, she always travelled by bus; even on a trip to California, she took the bus and sat up the entire way. She had painted on the side of her house "A Square Deal--Votes for Vermont Women" in huge white letters. Daniels insisted on coupling the issues of sex and race discrimination, at one point sending Paul a copy of a letter she had written to Vermont Congressman Carroll Page stating that women would "solve our problem just as for the Negroes--with a federal amendment." Paul responded with no comment on the race issue, but she did compliment Daniels on refusing to pay her Vermont taxes to protest her unenfranchisement.[64]

Pennsylvania CU officer Ellen Winsor also reacted strongly against CU racism. Winsor and sister Mary were from Haverford, Pennsylvania, with a family background of Quaker/Huguenot pacifism. Mary Winsor did the study of English militant suffrage cited earlier and had founded the exclusive "Limited Suffrage League" in Pennsylvania. Her sister Ellen apparently had developed a bit different perspective. She was on the board of managers at Sleighton Farms Girls Reformatory and criticized the CU for not seeking true democracy. She angrily objected to a *Suffragist* cartoon that classed Negroes with criminals. "To demand from the present administration the ballot for colored women as well as for white women may retard the progress of Votes for Women, but it will never retard the arrival of justice and democracy."[65] Some members did, then, insist on a complete application of democracy. Daniels and Winsor wanted to explicitly include black women in the cause of women's rights, but Paul was not willing to deal with race discrimination; she remained unwilling to take up any cause but sex discrimination.

The militant suffragists had not escaped the prejudices of their age; more often than using blatantly racist arguments, however, they tried to ignore the problems of their black sisters, seeing that as the only practical way politically. Lucy Burns wrote to an author who had compared the similar situations of blacks and women that she agreed, but she did not "want to rub in the point so hard."[66] Similarly, Burns tried to appease a Mrs. A. Freschers of New Orleans by assuring her that "property and educational qualifications" within the states would remain the same with a federal amendment, *only* the "sex qualification" would change. (She also told Freschers that Senator Ransdell of Louisiana, a white supremacist, favored the suffrage amendment.)[67] As organizer Rebecca Hourwich Reyher has said, women like Alice Paul (and most CU activists were much like her in this) simply looked at issues of race as unimportant; it was rather like the way Wilson and the Democrats looked at suffrage. Paul later admitted that she had written editorials in support of white supremacy, but said that at the time she "didn't think it a serious matter."[68]

Beyond the objections to racism, there were occasionally a few hints in the CU hierarchy that black women should be included in the 1914-1916 organizing efforts. A letter from CU New York headquarters encouraged the Colored

Woman's Republican League to work with the Woman's Party in Colorado. In 1915, permission was given to Howard University students to march in a suffrage procession, by none other than Helena Hill Weed.[69] The sentiment more typically expressed regarding black and white sisterhood, however, appeared in a official 1915 CU pamphlet: "The *Negro problem* is no argument against a Federal Amendment, *for such an amendment would force suffrage on no one* because there are MORE WHITE WOMEN in the South than there are COLORED MEN AND WOMEN TOGETHER. With the enfranchisement of women the white supremacy would be greater than now."[70] Since suffrage for women was the CU's only issue, then a southern Congress must be convinced of the merits of the issue, and this appeared to be the first concern. Few white women reformers of the time would argue for black women's issues at any rate, although the CU did contain some of those few. Once white women became prisoners with black women in Washington jails, a great deal more fellow feeling would be generated.

Exclusivity was a source of conflict between conservative national leaders and "new woman" leaders and organizers whose liberal democratic views and sympathy with working women's concerns superseded their desire for upper class support for their political struggle. In terms of class, clearly NWP leaders, and many organizers, were from a privileged portion of American society. But elitist tendencies were broken down between 1913 and 1916 by the Woman's Party need to expand, democratize and develop a mass national base and appeal. Between those years, when they were engaged in a battle of power politics, the leadership argued that they were chiefly directing efforts toward achieving a democracy of men and women, making sure women were not discriminated against because of sex. But policies which seemed to exclude certain women from the "sisterhood" did not remain unquestioned or uncriticized, particularly by the CU's liberal or socialist, "new women" leaders and organizers. It would not be until the Woman's Party called upon all women to demonstrate their support during the most overt suffrage militancy of 1917-1919, when respectability became useless to the militant pariahs, that the party would achieve something that more nearly resembled a group which united, if not both races, then "all so-called classes." By then the women who wanted "power for their own sex" were united against the common male enemy of the Wilson government.

---

[1] William Chafe, *The American Woman*, pp. 15-16; Kraditor, *Ideas of Woman Suffrage*, p. 106; Flexner, *Century of Struggle*, pp. 237. 195-196; Dubois, "Working Women, Class Relations, and Suffrage Militancy"; Cott, *Grounding of Feminism*; Buechler, *Transformation of Woman Suffrage*.

[2] Sherna Gluck, introduction to *Parlor to Prison*, pp. 15-26; Sochen, *Herstory: A Woman's View of American History* (New York: Alfred Publishing Co., 1974), p. 242; Richard O'Connor and Dale Walker, *The Last Revolutionary: A Biography of John Reed* (New York: Harcourt, Brace and World, 1967), p. 174. Russian revolutionary Alexandra Kollontai, a contemporary of Paul and Burns, described the 20th century New Woman, world-over, as a single city worker, "sober and self-reliant." Her most important characteristic, however, was that she be independently on her own: "Not a mate--a whole and human woman." In Cathy Porter, *Alexandra Kollontai* (New York: The Dial Press, 1980), p. 198, taken from Kollontai's "Autobiography of a Sexually Emancipated Woman." Lunardini, *From Equal Suffrage to Equal Rights*, Chapter Two; Trecker, "The Suffrage Prisoners," p. 412.

[3] As mentioned, Belva Lockwood and the Reverend Olympia Brown, both pioneer professionals, and both early suffragists, welcomed the NWP warmly. Progressive stars also served on CU boards, including Jane Addams, C. P. Gilman, Florence Kelley, and history professor Lucy Salmon. Olympia Brown to Lucy Burns, February 17, 1914, Reel 7 NWPP. See Fry, Paul interview, p. 71; *History of Woman Suffrage*, Volume II, p. 241; *Suffragist*, May 25, 1917, p. 4, April 25, p. 4, July 24, p. 6, September 22, p. 3, 1914. Salmon left the NWP in 1917 because she disapproved of picketing. See Salmon to Paul, June 15, 1914, Reel 10, 1914, NWPP. Salmon influenced many Vassar students to embrace woman suffrage, and nine CU prisoners attended Vassar: Elsie Hill, Helena Hill Weed, Lois Warren Shaw, Martha Shoemaker, Hazel Hunkins, Gertrude Crocker, Elizabeth McShane, and Vida Milholland.

[4] Sherna Gluck, editor, *From Parlor to Prison*, p. 26.

[5] Stevens, *Jailed for Freedom*, appendix; Irwin, *Paul and the NWP*, p. 400. Wiley's parents were General John and Josephina Campbell Kelton. On Wiley see *Suffragist*, January 30, 1918, p. 7; *Woman's Who's Who of America*, 1918-1919, p. 884; Stevens, *Jailed for Freedom*, p. 22 and appendix; *New York Times* (obituary), January 7, 1964. Fry, Paul interview, p. 190. Paul listed Baker with Lewis, Dock, Belmont, Hilles, Beard, Kent and Younger as among her good "older" workers, and as testimony that theirs was not simply a "youth movement."

[6] Stevens, *Jailed for Freedom*, appendix; Baker to Ruth Pickering, January 14, 1918, Reel 55, NWPP; *New York Times*, May 25, 1919, Part VII, p. 1.

[7] One new Philadelphia member had written Paul that Mrs. Pankhurst should, as a matter of course, have been asked to be in the parade: "Our co-workers in the British Isles are justifiably militant. Most American women are ignorant of the true

type of character 'John Bull' asserts when dealing with women, by law. In such matters he is Lord and Master, the women have always had to obey him." "Mrs. Snyder" to Paul, January 30, 1913, Reel 1, NWPP. In a February 1914 letter to Burns, Dr. Caroline Spencer of Colorado Springs, as noted, equated the CU with the WSPU. January 1, 1913, Reel 1. In Mary Winsor's account of the British and their methods, she argued that WSPU actions served generally "to make women feel at ease in the streets of the city and helped to break the sex dominance that man had set up." She also invited visiting Irish militants to speak at suffrage meetings. Winsor report, N.D., Reel 93, NWPP. Katzenstein, *Lifting the Curtain*, p. 58.

[8] Brannan's father, Charles Dana, taught German and Greek at Brook Farm, (where he met a woman he admired, Margaret Fuller) and then became disillusioned with political reform after the 1848 revolutions in Europe. Dana was an abolitionist, as many NWP parents and grandparents were. Stevens, *Jailed for Freedom*, appendix; Ford, Reyher interview; *New York Times*, September 14, 1913, Part V, p. 6; Brannan to Burns, September 9, 1913, Reel 4, NWPP.

[9] The quote cites what British suffragist Alice Park was to have said to Emmeline Pankhurst. In New York, Dock was active in intellectual society, rejecting Social Darwinism for social evolution as advocated by anarchist Kropotkin. *Notable American Women*, Volume I, pp. 195-197; Stevens, *Jailed*, appendix; April, 1956, *New York Times* obituary, p. 31; and Dock to Paul, December 21, 1916, Reel 36, NWPP.

[10] Elizabeth Rogers to Paul, March 5, 1913, Reel 2, NWPP; *New York Times*, November 28, 1915, Part II, p. 10. And see DuBois, "Blatch and New York Suffrage" on WPU elitist feminism.

[11] Fry, Paul interview, p. 167; Morton Tenzer interview with Elsie Hill, July 30, 1968, Center for Oral History, University of Connecticut, Storrs, Part VI, p. 22; Ford, Reyher interview, April 23, 1983; Rogers to Lucy Burns, N.D. 1917, Reel 54, NWPP.

[12] Havemeyer only showed her collection for suffrage. She had three children--Horace, Adaline and Electra. Adaline was encouraged to go to Bryn Mawr, but instead married. Aline Saarinen, *Proud Possessors: The H.B. Havemeyers* (New York: Random House, 1958), pp. 167-169; *Notable American Women*, Vol. II., p. 156. Havemeyer's WPU speeches were very colorful, featuring the "suffrage torch" held aloft, and the illuminated "ship of state," a ship needing the ballast of women." Abby Scott Baker to Elsie Hill, October 3, 1916, Reel 33, NWPP: Saarinen, "Proud Possessors," pp. 145 and 150; Louisine W. Havemeyer, "The Suffrage Torch: Memories of a Militant," *Scribner's Magazine*, May 1922, p. 535. Irwin, *Paul and the NWP*, p. 415.

[13] Irwin, *Paul and the NWP*, p. 135; Tenzer, Hill interview, Part VI, p. 7; Part II, p. 1; Ford interview with Leslie Hill Latham, April 24, 1982 and November 4, 1990; Fry, Paul interview, p. 72.

[14] Stevens, *Jailed*, Appendix; Biographical File, Stevens Papers, Radcliffe; Betsy Schmidt and Leah Freed, "A Tribute to Doris Stevens," *Oberlin Alumni Magazine*, May/June 1977, p. 29; Virginia Gardner, *Friend and Lover: The Life of Louise Bryant* (New York: Horizon's Press, 1982), p. 16; *Omaha Daily News*, June 29, 1919.
[15] Stevens, *Jailed*, appendix.
[16] Sarah T. Colvin, *A Rebel in Thought* (New York: Island Press, 1947), pp. 2, 34, 47-48, 57, 104, 142.
[17] Hazard would picket in 1917, but would not be arrested. Interview with Mary Cooper and with Hazard's granddaughter Sarah Auchincloss; *Syracuse Post-Standard*, July 31, 1935; *Buffalo Express*, March 28, 1918.
[18] Author interview with Bowden, the then 90-year-old daughter of New York WPU and CU leader Blanche Weaver Baxter, March 29, 1983.
[19] Abbott to Paul, August 3, 1918, Reel 63; Ella Thompson to Beulah Amidon (on Cosu), October 20, 1917, Reel 45 and Thompson to Paul, June 20, 1917, Reel 44, NWPP.
[20] Meta Wade, "A Tribute to Miss Camilla Whitcomb of Worcester," unprocessed manuscript collection, Schlesinger Library, Radcliffe.
[21] See Buechler, *Transformation of Suffrage*, p. 184.
[22] *Suffragist*, October 19, 1918, p. 4. Paul to Alice Henkle, May 24, 1918, Reel 61, NWPP.
[23] Ford, Reyher interview, 1983.
[24] Hunkins to Doris Stevens, October 14, 1916, Reel 34, NWPP.
[25] Gluck, on Jessie Butler, *Parlor to Prison*, p.90; Virginia Gardener reports that Hunkins once rebuffed John Reed when he tried to "make love" to her because she was a loyal friend of Louise Bryant, his wife. In *Friend and Lover: The Life of Louise Bryant* (New York: Horizon Press, 1982), p. 142. Hunkins, "A Talk to the Women's Press Club, Washington, D.C.," August 23, 1977, editor, Angela Ward, Bancroft Oral History Project, pp. 1-3.
[26] Two other suffrage prisoners campaigned in the West in 1914 and 1916. One of the youngest was the "small but strong" Joy Young from New York and Dover, New Hampshire. The other was Iris Calderhead from Marysville, Kansas, whose father was a congressman. She was a graduate of the University of Kansas and Bryn Mawr and an English teacher. Irwin, *Paul and the NWP*, pp. 230, 336; Stevens, *Jailed* appendix; *Topeka Journal*, November 18. On Branham, *The Baltimore Evening Sun*, and her Johns Hopkins University biographical and admissions file clippings in The Ferdinand Hamburger, Jr. Archives, Record Group Number 13.010, Office of the Registrar, Applications for Admission, "Branham, Lucy Gwynn." Presumably Branham would not include her mother in antisuffrage sentiment. I have not corrected any speaking or grammatical errors in quotations. Branham to Paul, December 1, 1916, Reel 36, NWPP.

[27] "Mrs. Emory" to Paul, August 1918, Reel 63; Julia Emory to Abby Scott Baker, April 22, 1918, Reel 59, NWPP.
[28] Reyher interview 1983. Greiner worked for the labor movement before 1920. February 4, 1919, Reel 68, NWPP.
[29] Beuchler, *Transformation of Suffrage*, pp. 154-157.
[30] Paul to Nordquist, July 23, 1913, Reel 4, NWPP.
[31] B. W. Cook, Eastman, "On Personalities and Powers," p. 63.
[32] *Suffragist*, May 22, 1915, p. 6; and April 24, 1915, pp. 4-6; on unions, see for example, June 19, 1915, p. 2; and see Reel 36, 1916, NWPP.
[33] Belmont to Mrs. Hugh R. Rood, May 3, 1916, Reel 17, NWPP.
[34] Oregon CU pamphlet, 1915, Reel 22, NWPP.
[35] August 19, 1915, Reel 18, NWPP.
[36] See See Mari Jo Buhle, *Women and American Socialism*, p. 217. The methods used in the shirtwaist strikes would also be used by the NWP. Leaders like Inez Milholland and Lavinia Dock, as well as Belmont, participated in that strike, walking the picket line. Like the NWP pickets later, the striking pickets were subject to thugs, police brutality and mass arrests. Buhle, pp. 219-225. Socialist and future NWP member Maud Malone, defended Belmont and the suffragists, saying labor and suffrage groups both needed money and should be grateful for Belmont's generosity (and that *she* was not a capitalist.) Like Belmont, Malone advocated "militant methods" for suffrage. *New York Times*, December 20, 1909, p. 5. Seven hundred women were arrested in the 1909 ILGWU strike and some women were sent to the Blackwell Island Workhouse. Gladys Boone, *The Women's Trade Union League in Great Britain and the United States* (New York: Columbia University Press, 1942), p. 82; Dye, *WTUL*, pp. 89-93.
[37] See the *Suffragist*, August 7, 1915, p. 3; and February 27, p. 5. Organizers were always sent to wealthy resorts, as when Isabella Mott was sent to "convert the wealthy" in Newport in the summer of 1915 (she did), *New York Times*, July 20, 1915, p. 11. Also see Inez Irwin, *Angels and Amazons*, p. 8; Treasurer's Report 1914, Reel 87, NWPP. On Belmont, Alva Belmont to Paul, September 7, 1914, Reel 12, NWPP. Stevens to Paul, April 23, 1915, Reel 16, NWPP. Harriot Stanton Blatch, another well-to-do advisor, was described by one suffragist as "autocratic and arbitrary." Laura Seiler left the WPU because of Blatch, in Gluck, editor, *Parlor to Prison*, p. 209.
[38] Alice Paul to Beard, August 18, 1914 and Beard to Paul, August 21, 1914, Reel 11, NWPP. Interestingly, the anarchist Alexander Berkman wrote the *Suffragist* editor asking: "Why your peculiar silence on the American woman Hunger striker?" (Becky Edelsohn). He assumed their ignorance and sent the August *Mother Earth*, thinking the group should be aligned with the far left apparently. August 14, 1914, to Paul, Reel 11, NWPP.
[39] Buhle, *Women and American Socialism*, p. 217. Many letters were exchanged with socialists, largely from Oklahoma and Iowa. See Reels 3 and 4, NWPP.

[40] Cott, *Grounding of Feminism*, p. 55.
[41] "Order of Procession," Reel 2, NWPP; F. P. O'Hare, *Kate Richards O'Hare: Selected Writings and Speeches* (Louisiana State University Press, 1982); Alice Paul to "Concerned Socialists," January 1913, Reel 1, NWPP.
[42] 1916 pamphlet, Reel 93, NWPP.
[43] Irwin, *Paul and the NWP*, p. 181. Late October 1916 correspondence, Reel 36, NWPP.
[44] Stevens, *Jailed*, appendix; Whittemore to Paul, November 1914, Reel 13, NWPP; Whittemore to Paul, August 6, 1915, Reel 18, NWPP.
[45] Irwin, *Paul and the NWP*, p. 86.
[46] *Women's Who's Who, 1914-1915*, p. 262; Stevens, *Jailed*, appendix; Weed to Paul, October 20, 1914, Reel 13, NWPP; *Suffragist*, May 20, 1915, p. 6.
[47] Stevens, *Jailed*, appendix.
[48] Kessler to Paul, March 30, 1915, Reel 16; Paul to Burns, April 20, 1915, Reel 16, NWPP.
[49] June 25, 1915, Reel 17, NWPP.
[50] Spencer to Paul, June 30, 1915, Reel 17, NWPP; Peacey to Paul, July 15; Burns to Peacey, July, 1915, Reel 17, NWPP.
[51] Official CU Statement, August 15, 1915, Reel 18; Paul to Burns, August 22, 1915, Reel 18, NWPP.
[52] Catt and Shuler, *Woman Suffrage*, pp. 199, 205, 491-492. See Fry, Alice Paul interview, p. 134.
[53] "Parade Procession," March 1913, Reel 2, NWPP. *The Crisis*, April 1913, p. 267.
[54] Alice Paul to Mrs. C. L. Hunt, January 9, 1913, Reel 1, NWPP.
[55] Alice Paul to Alice Stone Blackwell, January 15, 1913, Reel 1; Blackwell to Paul, January 23, 1913, Reel 1, NWPP, NAWSA Headquarters to Congressional Committee, February 8, 1913, *The Crisis*, April 1913, p. 296.
[56] *Crisis* editorial, April 1915. DuBois spoke at the Pennsylvania NAWSA suffrage convention in November of 1912. Katzenstein, *Suffrage in Pennsylvania*, p. 85. Also see *The Crisis*, April 1913, p. 14; Paul to DuBois, July 12, 1913, Reel 3, NWPP.
[57] Paul to Mrs. E. M. Valentine, July 12, 1913, Reel 3, NWPP.
[58] See August Meier, *Negro Thought in America, 1880-1915: Radical Ideologies in the Age of Booker T. Washington* (Ann Arbor: University of Michigan Press, 1978); August Meier and Francis L. Broderick, eds., *Negro Protest Thought in the 20th Century* (Indianapolis: Bobbs-Merrill Inc., 1965), particularly the essays by W. E. B. DuBois.
[59] Kenneth R. Johnson, "Kate Gordon and the Woman Suffrage Movement in the South," *Journal of Southern History*, August 1972, p. 374. Christabel Pankhurst spoke at the group's first annual convention in November of 1914, pp. 372-373, 377.

---

[60] See Catt and Shuler, *Woman's Suffrage and Politics*, pp. 97-101. For example, Inez Boissevain argued in the *New York Times*, August 28, 1916 Part V, p. 5, that "aliens" might vote, "yet good American white women cannot." They also objected (*New York Times*, May 15, 1916, p. 9) to Sioux Indian males receiving the vote from Wilson before them.

[61] April 19, 1915 and April 20, 1915, Reel 16, NWPP. It was Arnold again, who, when reporting on the meetings she held in Oregon in June of 1915, wrote that Mrs. Lee Davenport of New York, a guest of the assemblage, assured her audience that a woman's vote would bring social and moral changes such as an end to child labor and to "do-nothing workers," lazy men personified by "a big nigger sitting on a bale of cotton," June 15, 1915 Report, Reel 17, NWPP. Ella Thompson, southern organizer (and native southerner), always used such arguments and language in her letters.

[62] October 16, 1915 political report, Reel 19, NWPP; Irwin, *Paul and the NWP*, p. 171. The grandfather clause prohibited anyone from voting whose grandfather could not vote before 1867. *Suffragist*, February 6, 1915, p. 3. Harriet Stanton Blatch told President Wilson that women's votes would increase the white domination of the South. Also see Maud Younger, speech to mass meeting at National Theatre in Washington, D.C., March 4, 1917, Reel 40, NWPP.

[63] Russell to Paul, February 14, 1915. Mary and Isabel Miller left the CU because of Weed's article. February 17, 1915, Reel 15, NWPP. Neither Russell nor the Millers' letter had answers contained in the NWP correspondence.

[64] She was told they made no special effort to recruit blacks, but many marched in the parade. Paul wrote NAWSA's Maud Wood Park that Daniels' presence would "not be good" at a 1914 CU banquet, but Daniels received her tickets within a week so apparently CU leaders found out from Park she was white. "Corresponding Secretary" to L. J. C. Daniels, March 19, 1913; Paul to Park, July 23, 1913 and Paul to Daniels, July 28, 1913, Reel 4; Daniels to Paul, May 5 and 12, 1914, Reel 10; Paul to Daniels, June 19, 1914, Reel 10, NWPP; Helen M. Pettengill, *History of Grafton, Vermont, 1754-1975* (published by Grafton Historical Society, 1975), pp. 52-56.

[65] Henrietta Krone, "Dauntless Women, The Story of the Woman Suffrage Movement in Pennsylvania, 1910-1920," University of Pennsylvania, unpublished dissertation, 1946; Winsor to *Suffragist* editor, September 23, 1917, Reel 49, NWPP.

[66] See Rosalyn Terborg Penn, "Afro-Americans in the Struggle for Woman Suffrage," unpublished dissertation, Howard University, 1978; Burns to Leavitt Stoddard, July 17, 1915, Reel 17, NWPP.

[67] September 20, 1915, Reel 18, NWPP.

[68] Reyher said that she herself never used racist arguments or black "sandwich men"--men carrying advertising signs--when organizing in the South. She said her

mother punished her as a child when she said "nigger." Reyher sadly told me there are "always people who hate people." Ford, Reyher interview.

[69] George Cook to Helena Weed (October 27, 1915) said permission was given to Howard University students to march in a November procession, "as per your phone call," Reel 22, NWPP.

[70] 1915 CU pamphlet, Reel 22, NWPP.

PART TWO

REAL MILITANCY

1917-1920

Chapter Four

Defying Authority: Peaceful Picket, Early 1917

We Shall Fight for the Things Which We Have Always
Held Nearest Our Hearts--For Democracy, For The
Right Of Those Who Submit To Authority To Have A
Voice In Their Own Governments.
-Wilson's War Message
April 1917

On January 10, 1917, 12 women wreathed and sashed in suffrage purple, white and gold--"professional women, working women, society women, women of all parties"--silently walked the short distance between NWP LaFayette Park Headquarters and the iron White House gates. They held aloft two bold banners: "Mr. President What Will You Do For Woman Suffrage?" and "How Long Must Women Wait For Liberty?"[1] The NWP strategy of "womanly" non-violent resistance, their own unique style of suffrage militancy, had begun, with a "perpetual delegation" to the president.

Amongst the columns of news of the European war that month, the *New York Times* reported a strong spirit of indignation in the American Woman's Party. In the wake of the Milholland memorial, NWP suffragists were "very upset" with the Wilson government and had told the press that "no price was too great to pay for liberty and democracy."[2] Having reached the point of exhaustion with progressive political lobbying for suffrage by 1917, the NWP feminists changed from merely "militant-spirited" strategy to tactics which would be decidedly defiant of male authority and overtly militant. Woman's Party suffragists had been aggressive, militant-spirited lobbyists within the political system and more or less within the bounds of socially acceptable female behavior, through 1916. But by 1917, having failed to achieve their goal, Woman's Party feminists were ready to defy and then resist the male, government authorities who had blocked them every step of the way, by going outside normal political and social channels into the realm of civil disobedience. They had reached the point described by Judith Stiehm in *Nonviolent Power* of a "population that has been pushed too far who believed that education was no longer enough and compromise impossible."[3] They stood at the edge of a whole new dimension of their fight, beginning a series of actions intending to "defy, convert and coerce" their male government opponents.

Woman's Party militancy was applied feminism; more specifically, their suffrage militancy was applied political feminism. NWP feminist demonstrators, as in Stiehm's description, had "no access to weapons" except for the potent weapon of their own "moral" action: public displays of female, defiant, resistant strength versus male, heavy-handed, authorized power. The NWP's action-oriented progressive feminists, directly applied their egalitarian feminist ideology. Their militant tactics to win suffrage reflected their belief that women were worthy of political power both because of their shrewd use of women's existing political leverage and their obvious courage and iron-willed determination. Increasingly resentful of the men who held power over them, NWP suffragists would use graduated militant actions against an unyielding government. At the same time, they sharpened their feminist critique. They slowly shifted from just insisting on a greater democracy which included women, to a condemnation of an oppressive, autocratic, patriarchal society. In the context of this critique of male-run society, NWP demonstrators made a conscious effort to show the "women's" militancy of picketing and civil disobedience was different from and highly superior to, the manifestation of "men's" militancy--war. Ironically, NWP leaders would sometimes use the language of military campaigns popular at the time, especially words like "execution" or "campaign." Doris Stevens wrote that the "militant campaign was based on [the] well-established political and military strategy" of concentrating forces at "the enemy's weakest point."[4] Paradoxically, the Woman's Party used the weapon of nonviolence very effectively to illustrate their enormous strength as women.

The Woman's Party strategy in 1917 to use "real" militancy and resist governmental authority was incremental both in the level of radical action taken by the NWP and the growing seriousness of government efforts to suppress that action. The militancy of 1917 consisted of three distinct stages: first, displaying defiant messages in peaceful picketing (early 1917); second, picketing using passive resistance techniques in the face of mob attacks and the first arrests (mid-1917); and third, using the hunger strike to obtain political prisoner--and martyr--status for jailed, radicalized pickets (late 1917). The subject here is the first state, peaceful picketing, which moved from an early phase of perpetual picketing of the White House begun in January, to a closing phase of peaceful picketing after the U.S. entered World War I in April. The initial decision to begin the overtly militant, defiant policy was not made easily. It was a significant departure which deeply affected the women on the picket line, as well as an onlooking public and government. After April, NWP leaders had to decide whether suffrage work should yield to war (or peace) work, and had to deal with the consequences--or make use of the fact--that a government and a nation at war reacted very differently to NWP persistence than a nation at peace.

Silent picketing of the White House began in January as a constant protest delegation; the pickets were a reminder to Wilson and the world that American women wanted their political rights. After the president told the Milholland delegation on January 8th that he could do nothing about suffrage until his party and public opinion seemed more favorable, Harriot Stanton Blatch advised the dejected delegates: "It rests with women to go on with their fight. We have got to bring to the President individually, day by day, week in and week out, the fact that great numbers of women want to be free!"[5] Alice Paul described the Milholland delegation as "quite disappointed," a decided understatement, after their meeting with Wilson. She said that Wilson had made it clear that he wanted no more audiences with their lobbyists, but the militants "made the decision to have a perpetual delegation, six days a week, from ten in the morning until half past five in the evening, around the White House. We began the next day." As Eunice Dana Brannan wrote in a letter to the *New York Times*, Woman's Party suffragists would "back up their displeasure" with a perpetual picket line.[6]

Actually the decision for a continual delegation was made at least by the end of December, 1916. Mabel Vernon, then serving as Woman's Party Secretary, had written to Marie Ernst Kennedy on December 30, "We have decided that it will be an excellent thing to have a silent guard of suffragists stand at the gates of the White House." Vernon asked Kennedy to be a guard as part of a planned Pennsylvania delegation of women on January 24th, and she agreed.[7] The executive committee had apparently decided on extended picketing on January 5th, before the Milholland delegation met Wilson. The committee did not disagree over whether or not the CU/WP should picket, but only over whether or not western members who were already voters should picket, since they could vote to express their political views. It was finally decided that they too should picket, but then, according to Paul, they "had quite a long discussion" on how picketing would be executed. Following a pattern common to many Woman's Party executive meetings, Paul recommended the course of action and the rest voted to support her suggestion.[8] The Committee members were in complete agreement on the new militant policy, and all but four of the 14 women on the committee would pay the consequences of that militancy by going to jail.[9] The January picketing was not spontaneously begun simply because of the refusal of Wilson to satisfy the Milholland delegation, but was a carefully determined policy; one which would build upon the militant-spirited earlier actions, from the "heckling" of Wilson in 1913 to the banner unfurling in Congress in 1916.[10] Still, the picketing decision was a departure for the NWP, a step up into real militancy, directly defying authority.

The direct target of the new militant policy was the Wilson administration. Rebecca Reyher described the picketing strategy by recalling Paul's oft-quoted statement: "If a creditor stands before a man's house all day long, demanding payment of his bill, the man must either remove the creditor or pay the bill." Paul felt "that pickets outside the White House would be the best way to remind [the president] of our course."[11] As Anne Martin wrote for the *Suffragist*, the militants felt their responsibility was to symbolize and dramatize the injustice of woman's unequal position and put the blame for inaction on suffrage firmly upon Wilson. Martin argued that with "enthusiasm high" the time was right for new militant policies:

> The justice of suffrage is acknowledged. The idea we now have to overcome is that there is injustice in woman's having to struggle for suffrage for an indefinite time. We must show people that justice delayed is justice denied. . . . To go on having the same kind of demonstrations would make people feel that suffragists expected to go on having them.[12]

The Woman's Party had always impatiently demanded immediate action: since political action had been unsuccessful, then stronger pressure would be applied. Again, Woman's Party feminists believed in exerting their strength, their power as women united against this symbolic and actual, male opponent. Wilson had said the NWP must convert his party, but they felt *he* controlled his party and insisted he had the authority to compel a "supine" Congress to pass woman suffrage. The women also knew Wilson had just been re-elected (on a peace platform) and was under no obligation to deal with any political problem but the war.[13]

Although the WP lobbying committee continued to canvass Congress in 1917, trying to impress them with the potential power of women voters in the West, and although the organizing and petitioning functions of the Party remained; the militants' primary commitment was to highlight the plight of unenfranchised women by a vigil of silent sentinels. The sight would become a familiar one in Washington, and as Alice Paul said, "We always tried to make our lines as beautiful as we could and our banners were really beautiful."[14] The picket line kept woman suffrage in the news and served as an ever present reminder to Wilson and Congress of how seriously the Woman's Party regarded their cause. Paul's special talent for pageantry was at its best here. In February, the Woman's Party had special picket days: Women Voters' Day, Patriot Day, state days, starting with Maryland Day; and days for various professional women, like teachers, doctors, nurses, authors, artists, lawyers and "wage earners." College Day brought women from thirteen schools including Bryn Mawr, Leland Stanford, University of Kansas, Oberlin, Smith and Swarthmore.[15]

The banners were very shrewd, and often quoted Wilson himself, as in "Liberty Is A Fundamental Demand Of The Human Spirit." On Lincoln Day the banners asked Wilson, "Why Are You Behind Lincoln? Lincoln Stood For Woman Suffrage 60 Years Ago."[16] Again showing ties to nineteenth century feminists, the militants were especially fond of quoting their matron saint Anthony on banners: "The Right of Self-Government For Half of Its People is of Far More Vital Consequence To The Nation Than Any Or All Other Questions." Other messages read on Susan B. Anthony's birthday (which showed awareness of war clouds gathering over the Atlantic) were: "We Press Our Demand For The Ballot At This Time In No Narrow, Captious Or Selfish Spirit But From Purest Patriotism" and "At This Time Our Greatest Need Is Not Men Or Money, Valiant Generals Or Brilliant Victories, But A Consistent National Policy Based Upon The Principle That All Governments Derive Their Just Powers From Consent Of The

Governed."[17] Again, egalitarian Woman's Party feminists used the democratic language typical of the American Revolution, the mid-19th century reform age, and Woodrow Wilson.

Thousands of women took their turn on the picket line, all sorts of women, "all ages and classes," who wanted to be involved if only for a few minutes in the NWP's dramatic campaign to gain women's political rights. Some were wealthy tourists on honeymoon or visitors from foreign countries, thinking the whole struggle "exciting."[18] Others, like women who participated on "Labor Day" took a more serious view of women's political situation. On the day office workers and factory workers picketed, Yetta Gabin of the WTUL was solicited for her views: "I believe the working women's need of the ballot is a vital one and that is why we are here. . . . [We need] self-defense in industry to change low pay and hard conditions."[19] According to Rebecca Reyher, *everybody* took a few hours on the picket line, but it was the NWP regulars who found the job less than exciting and inspiring day in and day out. Supposedly, when Sara Bard Field, who had fought tuberculosis for years, told Alice Paul that to picket with her health record "would mean a very possible death," Paul replied, "Well, that would be very good for the cause."[!] Picket Ernestine Evans described how the "sockets of their arms ache from strain." And Doris Stevens said the usual lofty thoughts of a picket were, "When *will* that woman come to relieve me?" She remembered of her own experience that "anything but standing at a President's gate would be more diverting."[20] The pickets particularly remembered the acts of kindness of many women who would offer warm coats, mittens, galoshes, or hot bricks. Elizabeth Kent, of California, who had already contributed money for the picket campaign, ($100 a month) would come out "in her little electric coupe and bring hot coffee."[21]

Within the larger membership of the party there was a mixed reaction to the defiant picketing policy of Paul and the executive committee. Letters of disapproval and cancelled *Suffragist* subscriptions flowed into headquarters from women questioning the merits of picketing while the world was at war.[22] On the other hand, Sara Bard Field collected $3,000 in fifteen minutes after a talk on the pickets. Money was pouring in and new party branches were founded. The Detroit branch wrote the *Suffragist* that they "appreciated the brave strong work on the picket line." Many of the more militant Woman's Party members were particularly thrilled with picketing. Elizabeth Rogers wrote Paul, "I think the picketing is *splendid* and I will come and do it myself." Matilda Hall Gardner stated in the *Suffragist* that "[t]he picket line is part of the eternal truth we all believe in, and we must make our demand for liberty plain to every one."[23]

Many members were incensed at the Wilson government's continuing inaction. CU District Chairman Eleanor Calnan of Methuen, Massachusetts wrote Paul that she supported picketing, but was having difficulty recruiting pickets there; other Massachusetts members not being "hot on it." "They make me sick with Red Cross work, I tell them the political double cross is as much as I can carry."[24] Calnan's friend Agnes Morey, who was Massachusetts NWP Chairman as well as on the

National Advisory Council, wrote "Chairman Paul" regarding Wilson, "I trust he is *thoroughly uncomfortable*. He will act when he has to for his political life--not before."[25] Morey, from Brookline, Massachusetts, was one of the first founders, with daughter Katharine. She was an enormously gifted speaker and administrator. She was "anxious" about picketing for suffrage on the eve of war. She still wanted to come "right off," but needed to consult her husband. Doris Stevens reported that many "good suffrage husbands" were now growing uncomfortable with the necessity of their wives going to Washington.[26]

Picket "Mrs. Richard" Wainwright, an admiral's wife, made a statement which reflected her insistence on picketing because of her continuing frustration at being left out of American political life. It also showed the rather comfortable class status she, along with many NWP leaders, enjoyed.

> While standing there, the thought that came to me was that we were in very much the same position as is a person who is locked out of her own home. You know how it feels to go to the theatre and get home late without a key and find the door locked and the other members of the family asleep. You ring the bell, you whistle, you knock, you call. You stand outside, while inside are the servants who need your direction, the children who need your care, the man of the house who can't get along without you. Finally you rouse the neighbors and they help you wake the family. . . . We women are shut out from the government in which we have a right to participate.[27]

Woman's Party pickets were insisting on their rights, no matter the government's war concerns, and were now called upon, in larger numbers, for more intensive action.

David Morgan stated in his study of American suffragists, that in 1917 the Woman's Party started picketing "to the distaste and resentment of a great many Americans of all kinds."[28] Indeed the NWP did experience resentment, even within their own party, but "distaste and resentment" were not the only reactions of the public, press and even members of government, to the suffrage pickets. According to Doris Stevens, the vast majority of people who actually saw the pickets were "filled with admiration." A few would argue with the woman sentinels, but the "serene, good humor" of the pickets' answers quieted debate. In fact, the WP found it a valuable "educational tool" for pickets to answer questions from the "rank and file."[29]

At first the press was, if not approving, then at least neutral in its coverage of the pickets. The *Suffragist* reported that some newspaper coverage was initially sympathetic to the NWP, but as time went on, reporters began to call them "crazy women," "unwomanly," and "shocking."[30] The *New York Times* reported that the White House was "beleaguered" by "hostile suffragists" performing "mild militancy." The militancy itself, and its frequent association with things military, was an occasion for poking fun at the women, as the *Times* described it, the "order issued for the day by Commandant Alice Paul," was given, there were "privates and bugler" involved, and the "challenge" of the day was, "Mr. President, What Will You Do For Woman Suffrage?"[31] "Unnatural" women engaged in such aggressive action inevitably drew fire from the press.

As for governmental reaction to the militant feminist pickets, at first it too, was at least neutral. The President, on the first day of picketing, regarded the women with a face "stern and unsmiling" and "an impassive stare." By the second day he "laughed openly" and "lifted his hat." A *Suffragist* editorial retorted that lifting his hat to them was good publicity for him. His feelings towards the militants remained unchanged and unfriendly. When Congressional Union leaders asked for an audience in early February, Wilson told his aide to tell them it was impossible for him to see them: he was too busy.[32]

After a week of picketing, the touchy subject of the women pickets came up in the House of Representatives. Even the friends of the Woman's Party were not willing to directly champion them in the ensuing debate. NWP member Bertha Fowler's telegram to Congress which protested "against the undemocratic blocking of the Federal Suffrage amendment by the President and the party in power," was read into the *Record* by NWP supporter Congressman Charles Timberlake with no comment. Typical of the voiced sentiment of unfriendly legislators was Congressman Henry Emerson's, who objected to "certain persons who think they are working for the cause of woman suffrage by annoying the President of the United States by placing pickets about the White House . . . [It is] unbecoming . . . and retards The Cause." He further stated that the President had nothing to do with the fate of suffrage, and, interestingly, if men did what the women were dong, they would be jailed.[33]

Anna Howard Shaw firmly distanced her group from the militants: "No one can feel worse than I do over the foolishness of their picketing the White House."[34] To Maud Wood Park's assertion that the WP pickets were losing votes for woman suffrage in the Congress, head lobbyist Anne Martin replied that it was not true. She insisted that any Congressman who said the picketing had made him become "anti" was already opposed to the amendment. According to Martin, the picketing had helped them gain votes from the uncommitted.[35] Whether or not the picketing was having an effect on government, and what the effect was, had yet to be clearly determined. What was certain was that Woman's Party suffragists had proved themselves willing to take the step leading into real militancy, using their physical presence in a demanding bid for their rights. To cries that the picketing was too extreme a tactic, Rheta Childe Dorr answered, "But does anyone suppose that a large masculine class barred from citizenship, absolutely discountenanced by the President, would do anything half so mild as stand at the gates of the White House carrying banners?"[36] Even the earliest "mild" militancy had definitely raised masculine hackles.

A more serious phase of the first stage of overt militancy began in the spring of 1917: at that point the NWP policy of standing at the gates of the White House put the women in a potentially grave situation because of the United States' entry into the World War. Since the war between the Allies and Central Powers had broken out in August 1914, President Wilson had tried to maintain U.S. neutrality, and hoped himself, as "missionary diplomat," to arbitrate between the warring powers. But both our traditional ally Britain, and Germany, had harassed our neutral shipping. A very tense incident occurred in May of 1915, when the Germans torpedoed the British Lusitania carrying a large group of American passengers. Still, America's sentiment for peace was firm at the start of 1917. Then, in February, Germany began unrestricted submarine warfare and war cries began to get louder throughout the country, smothering reformers' cries for internal political change.[37] Wilson himself perceptively forecast what involvement in the war would mean for political reformers like the NWP, and for free speech itself:

> Once lead this people into war and they'll forget there ever was such a thing as tolerance. To fight you must be brutal and ruthless, and the spirit of ruthless brutality will enter into the very fibre of our national life, infecting Congress, the courts, the policeman on the beat, the man in the street. . . .[38]

The militants resolved to go on picketing in spite of the threat of war, because of their still strong resentment of government attitudes toward women's political rights, the pacifist tendencies of their leaders, and the belief that women especially needed their rights in wartime so that they would have a say in whether or not their family members went to war.

Early in February Ethel Adamson, a New York CU officer, expressed the thoughts of many members when she wrote CU headquarters that she was fearful lest the Congressional Union split over the war into pacifists and patriots. She advised party leaders to take no stand on the war. Alice Paul's policy letter to state "chairmen" on this issue showed total agreement with Adamson, declaring the Congressional Union was united for only one thing, woman suffrage. Women could work for peace or war through other organizations, but the CU/WP would continue to press for women's participation in government. Women's consent was necessary, said Paul, for a declaration of war.[39] The Votes-For-Women-First policy was officially adopted by a majority at the Congressional Union-Woman's Party Convention held March 1-4, 1917, in Washington. The resolution read:

> Whereas the problems involved in the present international situation, affecting the lives of millions of women in this country, make imperative the enfranchisement of women. - Be it resolved that the National Woman's Party, organized for the sole purpose of securing political liberty for women, shall continue to work for this purpose

> until it is accomplished; being unalterably convinced that in so doing the organization serves the highest interests of the country. And be it further resolved that to this end we urge upon the President and the Congress of the United States the immediate passage of the National Suffrage Amendment.[40]

It was decided at the convention that the Woman's Party and the Congressional Union should merge and become the National Woman's Party; in uniting the two, the militants hoped they could more easily realize the goal of power for women in a war-town world. In arguing for the merger, Paul discussed the merits of the "powerful" combination of the "active, determined, well-financed" Congressional Union and the respected, politically visible, Woman's Party. Alice Paul suggested they keep the name of Woman's Party "because it stands for political power" and "throws the emphasis more than does the Congressional Union on the political power of women." Harriot Stanton Blatch disagreed with the decision to merge thinking it "lessened political power."[41] Blatch, never completely satisfied with her subordinate role in the CU, was among the first of many who left the NWP in order to work for the war effort.

The strategy adopted by the Woman's Party differed from their militant antecedents, both NWSA and the WSPU, in one very important area, that of continuing the fight for women's rights in wartime. When America finally entered WWI on April 2, hostility towards the suffrage pickets would markedly increase. Many NWP members would quit the organization over the issue of "patriotism" or suffrage. But Alice Paul remained firm on not leaving the suffrage battle and insisted that Susan B. Anthony had made a grave mistake in not pursuing woman suffrage after the Civil War broke out. She believed it was imperative for women to have a voice in time of war, and moreover, that if there were "universal suffrage [male and female] throughout the world, we might not have wars."[42] Paul, like Charlotte P. Gilman, believed that women had, through evolution, developed a desire and love for peace which had to be balanced with man's aggressive tendencies. Such a philosophy, coupled with Paul's Quaker background, led to creative strategies for militancy carefully orchestrated for beauty and non-violence. Alice Paul, engaged in fighting for woman's full equality in society, still believed she may as well use the one socially evolved major difference between men and women to her moral advantage.

The Quaker Alice Paul was a pacifist, and so were many--but not all--of her colleagues. Some, like Crystal Eastman and Vida Milholland, belonged to Jane Addams' Woman's Peace Party.[43] Hazel Hunkins and Paul, in fact, "unofficially" visited Congresswoman Jeanette Rankin and "tried to get" her to vote against the war: "We told her we thought it would be a tragedy for the first woman ever in Congress to vote for war, that the one thing that seemed to us so clear was that the women were the peace-loving half of the world and that by giving power to women we would diminish the possibilities of war."[44] As it happened, Rankin agreed with that point of view, and voted accordingly. Paul stressed that she made the request of Rankin as an individual. The NWP's only object was suffrage, not world peace. Indeed, many powerful individuals in the NWP would be very supportive of the war effort. New Yorkers Alva Belmont, Eunice Dana Brannan and Dora Sedgwick Hazard all diligently worked for the war effort. Louisine Havemeyer wanted to leave the Advisory Council because she did not think the cause of suffrage should be pressed during wartime, but was convinced by Elizabeth Selden Rogers to stay on in a less visible capacity.[45]

Of course, unlike their British counterparts, American militants did not feel their country was in a life-threatening situation; and the tone of NWP militancy, certainly thus far, had been mild in comparison to the desperate guerilla warfare waged by the WSPU. Alice Paul was willing to be increasingly militant until women achieved their political goal, but would be more comfortable with Quaker-like non-resistance--and American labor protest methods--than the British tradition of political violence. During the debate on the war and the pickets at the March convention, Abby Scott Baker argued that the American and English situations were "not analogous." England was "stripped for a death struggle." Englishwomen had "held the government in their hands," but had let go because of the war.[46] Lady Constance Lytton renewed her subscription to the *Suffragist* in March, writing that perhaps American women were closer to suffrage than English women, but "much good would the vote do to men or women if the Germans landed victoriously in our country."[47]

Some English suffragists like the Pethick-Lawrences, Annie Kenney and Kitty Marion, would come to the United States for a few months to work for woman suffrage when they could not do so in their own country. A major split occurred in the WSPU when pacifist/socialist Sylvia Pankhurst disagreed with her older sister and mother, first on issues of close links to workers, and then over the war. Thereafter, Paul admired Sylvia Pankhurst a great deal for remaining with the suffragist struggle during the war. For her part, the younger Pankhurst frequently requested news of the "American woman's suffrage movement" for her suffrage paper, saying she was "full of admiration" for them. Paul insisted [in September 1917] the British "would have suffrage now had they not ceased their campaign when war broke out."[48] Paul received a letter from a woman who had once joined her in one of her WSPU escapades, confiding that she was very upset that Mrs. Pankhurst was so pro-war. She thought perhaps the hunger strike might have "unhinged her mind." On January 13, no doubt disapproving of her abandonment of the cause, Paul was cited as saying she "didn't care for" Emmeline Pankhurst's autobiography, *My Own Story*.[49] The WSPU had decided their militancy was not effective in the face of war violence. Although they often argued that when women were in power it would mean a world at peace, beginning in 1914, with Britain in great peril, the WSPU had turned its militancy "to the service of war patriotism."[50] It would not be so in America, three years later. As Alice Paul put it: "...[W]e continued picketing the White House, even though we were called traitors and pro-

German and all that."[51] The militant NWP continued to press for women's rights in spite of the war.

The convention merger created a new National Woman's Party, with new officers, but there was no question about the real power in the NWP. In the early organizing period, Paul shared leadership with Burns, and to some extent, with other officers. But, early in 1917, Alice Paul was clearly in command; she was joined by Anne Martin as vice-chairman, and Mabel Vernon as secretary.[52] Lucy Burns was noticeably absent among the top officers. In January, at home in Brooklyn, and obviously seeking to recover a family life and her career, Burns had told Paul she wanted to resign from the CU executive committee. Paul asked her to at least attend the March convention lest members think there was internal dissension over "near militant" policies. Burns returned to active duty, but in July, exhausted from years in the suffrage cause, would again express a desire to retire, saying no one could doubt her agreement with militance. As it happened, she would not leave the party until after ratification. Anne Martin, as ever, felt at odds with her leader; she never felt she was involved enough or given sufficient credit. She was not surprised that Paul was formally in charge after the merger, since she and not Martin had made the decisions for the Western Woman's Party. Paul knew that Martin was not happy that she did not become "Chairman" of the new National Woman's Party, although Martin said nothing to her.[53] Martin was instead appointed "legislative chairman" in charge of lobbying, but she was still jealous of Paul's authority. Martin was upset, at any rate, at this time, having just seen her brothers off to France. She complained that lobbyists like Maud Younger and Mabel Vernon surpassed her to report directly to Paul. She insisted (and she was perhaps the only one to address "Miss Paul" in this tone) that Paul "recognize the department responsibility principle."[54] The three American leaders, much like the Pankhursts, could not easily balance authority within the organization.

Personality conflicts were submerged in work when the National Woman's Party organized a thousand woman procession to the White House just weeks before America entered the war. Following the NWP convention, Dudley Field Malone informed the newly inaugurated Wilson that the women would visit him with the demands of the new NWP. The pageantry of a line of women of all ages and "classes" with their colorful banners, would have been impressive at any time, but the sight of 1,000 women marching in a freezing downpour was even more moving. In ironic symbolism, the women found that all the White House gates were locked against them. Thus they continued to march and then waited for two hours in the rain. The President and his wife drove out of the White House, through the picket line, both looking straight ahead. Some undersecretaries, watching, laughed.[55] The women were furious. The *Suffragist* reported that "Mrs. Frederick Thompson of California," a former Wilson supporter, was so angry that she declared she "would travel up and down California until women were free." Matilda Hall Gardner's husband, the journalist Gilson Gardner, wrote: "It is a poor business."[56] According to Doris Stevens:

> All the women who took part in that march will tell you what was burning in their hearts on that dreary day. Even if reasons had been offered--and they were not--genuine reasons why the President could not see them, it would not have cooled the women's heat. Their passionate resentment went deeper than any reason could possibly have gone. This one single incident probably did more than any other to make women sacrifice themselves.[57]

The women's resentment over having their presence ignored by their government was the same sort of anger that frustrated women's rights activists in NWSA felt, and the same emotion that led Britain's WSPU to guerilla militancy. The NWP did not, like the British, resort to dynamite, but did persist in presenting their case, world war or not.

Actually, in some ways, Woman's Party leaders thought wartime better than peacetime to press their cause. On the one hand, the militants knew a country primed for war might not be happy with the NWP's continued insistence on attention to other issues. But in wartime, there was, along with the argument of women's valuable services for a country at war, an emphasis on the ideals of democracy that could be very useful to the NWP. Doris Stevens wrote Alice Paul directly after war was declared that it was "arrogant" of Woodrow Wilson's administration to fight for "democracy" abroad "with [the] big task that lies right at their feet. It's *too* depressing."[58] Freedom and democracy would be the operative words for the governmental Committee on Public Information's new propaganda drive. The counterside would be that the "Huns" were diabolical and had their spies everywhere, unions were treasonous and most significantly for the NWP, (and as Wilson himself had prophesized) soon all dissent was considered unpatriotic. In wartime, "[f]eelings rose . . . everywhere tending to merge into stereotypes that made optimism and rationalism alike remote."[59]

NWP militants were proud of the fact that in the face of the horrors of war, they were still optimistically fighting for women's political freedom. Kate Heffelfinger, a new member, was an art student from Shamokin, Pennsylvania. Her mother was an invalid and her brother was in an army machine gun unit in France. She wrote Paul early in May, "You know that the 'concerted' sanity of the Woman's Party, with the country gone war mad is a great thing to have maintained." Florence Bayard Hilles, NWP officer and organizer from Newcastle, Delaware, seemed a fair choice to remain a "patriot," being the daughter of Thomas Bayard, former ambassador to Britain and Cleveland's secretary of state. She wrote "Chairman" Paul that perhaps the call to national defense would "make women realize that woman's place (duty) is in the home and that the home is not limited to four walls and a roof." Hilles would eventually work at Bethlehem Steel for the war effort, and then in reconstruction work in France. Doris Stevens declared, "We must not let our voices be drowned by war trumpets or cannon. If we do, we shall find ourselves, when the war is over, with a peace that will only prolong our struggle, a democracy that will belie its name by leaving out half the people." Elizabeth Rogers displayed sadness over the war, but found hope in their own struggle for the vote. "I am heart-sick over this war and this awful militarism--cannot find a way to bear it. My soul revolts and my *mind*--Well-it's Votes for Women *first* anyway -."[60]

It was Massachusetts NWP "Chairman" Agnes Morey who really summed up the women's feminist ideology on war and women's power:

> So far as democracy and liberalism goes it is for men--that politicians speak--women are outside their cosmos. And until more women wake up to the fact--the goal will not be won. The whole situation today is of man's making--and the solution will be man's--unless women themselves demand something else. It is all sickening--and confusing. . . . I look for nothing from men--but only hope that conditions will force upon women the conviction that 'who would himself be free, he first must strike the blow!'[61]

Although all suffrage lobbyists had been told that only "war measures" would be considered by Congress until the war was over, Women's Party members would not give up. They were in a power struggle they did not want to lose.

Anne Martin argued to many Senators that woman suffrage should be passed as a war measure since women wanted to do their "part in carrying out and helping to solve the problems that lie before the government when our country is at war." The NWP spent a great deal of time lobbying that spring ascertaining the stand of individual Congressmen, but many legislators insisted they were busy with war issues or other matters.[62] As for NAWSA suffragists, they were indirectly aided by the NWP when legislators who were irritated with the militants were happy to do favors for lobbyists who were so friendly and polite. NAWSA women were working for the war effort *and* for woman suffrage, and, as usual, tried hard to distance themselves from the militants. In fact, Helen Gardener wrote Wilson she wanted "to clear the hostility to a great cause" engendered because of "the conduct of a few women."[63] Whoever caused it, and the NWP's keeping suffrage in the papers had to be a factor, there was movement on women suffrage in April and May; the Susan B. Anthony amendment was introduced into the House and Senate on April 2 and 4 respectively, and on April 26 the Senate Woman Suffrage Committee held hearings. On May 1, the President wrote the Chairman of the House Rules Committee, Edward Pou, that he "approved" of the formation of a standing House Woman Suffrage Committee.[64]

Carrie Chapman Catt feared the NWP's policies would prevent further positive Congressional action; she wrote Paul to ask her to withdraw the pickets because they jeopardized the establishment of the House Committee.[65] The NWP remained unmoved by such pleas and scornful of NAWSA's style of petitioning. Florence

The White House Pickets--including Pauline Adams in middle
and Betsy Reyneau at right
Figure 5

Bayard Hilles wrote Mabel Vernon, "[Catt] doesn't *see* or *know* how ineffably weak and poor-spirited her policy of making '2 million' of women regular foot mats for politicians is."[66] With some political success, spirit was high on the NWP picket line as spring approached summer, but the women were not unaware of real problems brewing.

One concern was that with the withdrawal of some NWP members, and with people's money going to the war effort, funds were not coming in as in former times.[67] Numerous appeals continued to be sent out to women "who want to do suffrage first" from Anne Martin, and Mary Beard appealed to a potential leftist contributor by writing she had to ask "the more radical elements in our society, since the conservatives' money all goes to the war."[68] The NWP also tried other fundraising schemes, such as sending out "The Suffrage Ford" piloted by Margaret Whittemore and Marjery Ross. The NWP still reached out for alliances for suffrage, too; they wrote, for example, to the WTUL, the WCTU, the American Association for Labor Legislation, and The Farmers' Education and Co-operative Union to send suffrage resolutions to the President.[69]

Maintaining the picket line remained the most important concern for the NWP despite whatever else was occurring, including the world war, and banner messages were growing ever more defiant.[70] When Arthur Balfour visited the president to discuss the war, the pickets brought out: "We Shall Fight For The Things Which We Have Always Held Nearest Our Hearts--For Democracy, For The Right Of Those Who Submit To Authority To Have A Voice In Their Own Governments"--Wilson's war message.[71] (See Figure 5) To critics who charged that such an action was not "womanly," NWP member and botanist Agnes Meara Chase replied, "We are only repeating Woodrow Wilson's words . . . it isn't 'unwomanly,' for telling a man what he *said* is what every woman from Eve down has always done!"[72] But obviously, such defiance was not considered within the bounds of normal female behavior: it was much too aggressive--too militant.

Months of picketing had changed the attitudes of the women in line in front of the White House; they had developed a rebellious spirit which they would sorely need to withstand the events about to befall them. From the first pickets of January upset over Wilson's refusal to receive them, to the women soaking wet and freezing in front of the locked White House gates in March, to the sentinels reminding Wilson he had done nothing for democracy at home; all these women underwent a conversion toward greater militancy--from defiance to resistance. Elizabeth Selden Rogers said that they must keep holding their banners: "The fundamental rightness of it brings comfort to the mind and helps us bear the rebellion that is rising in our souls." Picket Florence Boeckel reflected that the administration was asking women to sacrifice for the war, but was giving them nothing back.[73] Florence Bayard Hilles thought it was incredible that so many kinds of women picketed: "business, society, professional, but all there for just one thing; to make a demand for political freedom." The first time Hilles picketed she though it a "joyous lark"; the second, she though of the long years of waiting; and the third, she was filled with "hot rebellion."[74] The perpetual picket began as the women's defiant continuation of their suffrage petitioning, and after months of being quite literally overlooked, they were bitter.

Picketing with inflammatory banners, even after America joined the world war, was daring, but in June, in the second stage of the evolution of 1917 militancy, the women faced the risk of arrest. Early that month, Lavinia Dock, veteran reformer and valuable NWP advisor, congratulated Paul for keeping up the picketing: "Stick to it--I think it is getting under the skin!"[75] Indeed it was, so much so that government authorities warned the NWP that pickets would be arrested if they continued. NWP feminist militants deeply resented their disadvantaged position in society in relation to men, and saw their struggle for the vote as the first necessary step toward full equality. To win that goal, angry militant suffragists became more than willing to do battle with male government authorities. The militants' arrests and confrontations with mobs would parallel the experience of other groups of dissenters, but unlike other groups, Woman's Party protests took the form of organized nonviolent resistance.

---

[1] Ford, Reyher interview; Irwin, *Paul and the NWP*, pp. 202-203, 206; Blatch and Lutz, *Challenging Years*, p. 276; *Suffragist*, January 17, 1917, p. 7.
[2] In the *New York Times*, January 2, p. 11 and January 10, p. 1, 1917.
[3] Steihm, *Nonviolent Power*, pp. 5-9.
[4] Stevens, "The Militant Campaign," *Omaha Daily News*, June 29, 1919 in Folder VI, Doris Stevens Paper, Schlesinger Library, Radcliffe.
[5] *Suffragist*, January 17, 1917, p. 6. Blatch, like Paul, also called this the beginning of militancy. She recalled she had "called for more drastic action, for militancy, to focus the attention of the entire nation on the President's unfavorable attitude and his stubborn resistance to woman suffrage." Blatch would change her mind on the wisdom of picketing once the war started. Blatch and Lutz, *Challenging Years*, pp. 275, 284.
[6] Robert Gallagher, Paul interview, p. 24; Fry, Paul interview, p. 274; *New York Times*, February 25, 1917, p. 10.
[7] Vernon to Kennedy, December 30, 1916 and Kennedy to Vernon, December 31, 1916, Reel 36, NWPP.
[8] Fry, Vernon interview, p. 22; Minutes of Executive Committee, January 5, 1917, Reel 87, NWPP. Fry, Paul interview, p. 174.
[9] *Suffragist*, January 24, 1917, p. 2; Stevens, "Militant Campaign," Doris Stevens Papers, Radcliffe. The executive committee were, at this time, Paul and Burns, Harriot Stanton Blatch, Alva Belmont, Eunice Dana Brannan, Dora Lewis, Anne Martin, Mabel Vernon, Matilda Hall Gardner, Florence Bayard Hilles, Elizabeth Selden Rogers, Maud Younger, Elizabeth Kent and Edith Houghton Hooker. Technically Younger, Hilles and Rogers were not on the executive committee, but as important advisors took part in the decision. Other members of the Advisory Council in January (whose approval was sought and gained) were Mary Beard, Reverend Olympia Brown, astronomer Annie Wells Cannon, Lavinia Dock, Rheta Childe Dorr, Crystal Eastman, Charlotte Perkins Gilman, Phoebe Hearst, Mrs. Randolph Hearst, Mrs. Frederic Howe, Inez Haynes Irwin, Dr. Cora Smith King, Folla LaFollette and Mrs. Julius Rosenwald. In the *Suffragist,* January 24, 1917, p. 2.
[10] Picketing itself was, of course, not novel for U.S. political protests. American labor unionists had used the device for years. English and Dutch suffragists had picketed their parliaments, and the WPU had picketed and used "silent speeches" as early as 1914. In 1916, in Chicago the WP had displayed banners reading, "Vote Against Woodrow Wilson, He Opposes Woman Suffrage" and "President Wilson, How Long Do You Advise Us To Wait?" Sara Bard Field in the *Suffragist*, January 17, 1917, p. 6; Blatch and Lutz, *Challenging Years*, p. 275; Sarah T. Colvin Report, N.D., Reel 91, NWPP.
[11] Ford, Reyher interview; Gallagher, Paul interview.
[12] *Suffragist*, January 31, 1917, p. 6.

[13] Maud Younger, "Why Picket?", *Suffragist*, February 7, 1917, p. 5; and January 17, 1917, p. 6; Stevens, *Jailed*, p. 65.
[14] *Suffragist*, February 7, 1917, pp. 708. Lynne Cheney, "How Alice Paul Became the Most Militant Feminist of Them All," p. 97.
[15] Alice Paul to Elizabeth Rogers, January 29, 1917, Reel 38, NWPP. The other schools represented were George Washington University, Goucher, University of Pennsylvania, Washington College of Law and Western Reserve. *Suffragist*, February 7, 1917, p. 4.
[16] From his *The New Freedom*, in Irwin, *Paul and the NWP*, p. 204; Stevens, *Jailed*, p. 72.
[17] *Suffragist*, March 3, 1917, p. 5.
[18] Ernestine Evans, An Hour on the Suffrage Picket Line," *Town and Country*, March 20, 1917, p. 10; Stevens, *Jailed*, p. 66; *New York Times*, January 12, 1917, p. 8, reported women from Berlin and Liverpool relieving the sentinels.
[19] *Suffragist*, February 24, 1917, p. 5.
[20] Ford, Reyher interview. Field quoted in Howard, *Long Campaign*, p. 116. Evans, "On the Picket Line," p. 10; Stevens, *Jailed*, p. 66.
[21] *New York Times*, January 10, 1917, p. 1; Elsie Hill interview, Part VII, p. 5; Stevens, *Jailed*, p. 70.
[22] See Correspondence, Reels 37-39, NWPP. CU board member Eugenie Nicolson resigned over picketing. Nicolson to CU Secretary, February 10, 1917, Reel 39, NWPP.
[23] *Suffragist*, February 17, 1917, p. 5; January 15, 1917.
[24] February 14, 1917, Reel 39, NWPP.
[25] January 16, 1917, Reel 37, NWPP.
[26] Stevens, *Jailed*, p. 69; Morey to Paul, February 8, 1917, Reel 39, NWPP.
[27] *Suffragist*, January 31, 1917.
[28] Morgan, *Suffragists and Democrats* (Michigan State University Press, 1972), p. 114.
[29] Stevens, *Jailed*, p. 68; *Suffragist*, January 17, 1917, p. 8.
[30] *Suffragist*, January 24, 1917 and January 31, 1917, p. 11. The *New York World* was reported as especially "anti," Stevens, *Jailed*, pp. 63-64.
[31] *New York Times*, January 11, 1917, p. 13.
[32] *Suffragist*, January 24, 1917, p. 5; Wilson to Joseph Tumulty, February 8, 1917, Reel 209, Wilson Papers on Microfilm.
[33] *Congressional Record*, Volume LIV, 64th Congress, Second Session, House of Representatives, January 18, 1917, pp. 1801; 1618.
[34] Anna Howard Shaw to Alice Edith Bisnnse Warren, March 9, 1917, Link, editor, *Wilson Papers*, Volume 38, p. 399.
[35] Martin to Park, February 28, 1917, Reel 39, NWPP.
[36] *Suffragist*, February 17, 1917, quoting Dorr in the February 7, *Chicago News*, p. 10.

[37] See Arthur Link, *Woodrow Wilson and the Progressive Era, 1910-1917*, (New York: Harper and Row, 1954).
[38] As he reportedly told editor friend Frank Cobb, in Ray Stannard Baker, *Wilson*, VI, pp. 490, 506-507.
[39] Ethel Adamson, Vice Chairman, New York City CU Committee (Eunice Brannan was Chairman) to "Abbie" (Abby Scott Baker), February 8, 1917, Reel 39; Alice Paul to state chairmen, February 8, 1917, Reel 39, NWPP.
[40] Irwin, *Paul and the NWP*, p. 207.
[41] Irwin, *Paul and the NWP*, pp. 206-207; Blatch and Lutz, *Challenging Years*, pp. 278-287; Fry, Paul interview, p. 93.
[42] Gallagher, Paul interview, pp. 91-92.
[43] Eastman would also soon be a founder of the American Union Against Militarism. Howard, *Long Campaign*, p. 173. Paul herself, much against the war, had written pacifist Crystal Eastman on January 4, thanking her for asking Emmeline Pethick-Lawrence to speak at a peace meeting organized by John Milholland (father of Inez and Vida Milholland, and an early NAACP member), Reel 37, NWPP.
[44] Fry, Paul interview, pp. 161, 175. Interestingly, NAWSA urged Rankin to vote *for* war.
[45] Morton Tenzer, Hill interview, Part VI, p. 5; Anne Martin to Elizabeth Rogers, March 26, 1917; Rogers to Paul, March 29, 1917, Reel 40, NWPP.
[46] Convention Report, March 10, 1917, Reel 40, NWPP.
[47] Lytton to Elizabeth Smith (*Suffragist* editor then), March 3, 1917, Reel 40, NWPP.
[48] Kenney to Paul, September 19, 1914, Reel 11; Marion May to Paul, June 12, 1917, Reel 44, NWPP; Mitchell, *Fighting Pankhursts*, pp. 42-47. On Sylvia, Alice Park, "What Are the Militants Doing Now?" in October 24, 1914 *San Francisco Bulletin*; Paul to Janet McCallum, September 19, 1917, Reel 48, NWPP. Sylvia Pankhurst to Doris Stevens, December 22, 1915, Reel 22. Press chairman promised her press releases to keep in touch in April 1916, Reel 26, NWPP.
[49] C. Cullen to Paul, from Victoria, Canada, July 2, 1917. Cullen also said that Adela Pankhurst was there in Canada to help the woman's movement, but "they're hopelessly conventional and middle-class and nonparty." Reel 45; K. Morey to Paul, January 13, 1917, Reel 37, NWPP.
[50] They did not change their policy until all their women were out of prison. WSPU war policy letter, August 12, 1914, Reel 11, NWPP.
[51] Gallagher, Paul interview, p. 92.
[52] The rest of the officers were Gertrude Crocker, treasurer; and executive board members Lucy Burns, Alva Belmont, Eunice Brannan, Matilda Gardner, Abby Scott Baker, Elizabeth Kent, Maud Younger, Florence Bayard Hilles, Edith Houghton Hooker, Allison Turnbull Hopkins, Dora Lewis and Doris Stevens. All

but Belmont, Hooker and Kent would go to prison in 1917. Report of officers, March 1917, Reel 42, NWPP.
[53] Bland, "Suffrage Militancy of Lucy Burns," pp. 18-19; Anne Howard, *Long Campaign*, pp. 120-121; Fry Paul interview, p. 212.
[54] Martin to Paul, June 12; Martin to "Mother," Louise Martin, June 11, 1917, Reel 44, NWPP.
[55] *Suffragist*, March 10, 1917, p. 6; Stevens, *Jailed*, pp. 75-79.
[56] March 10, 1917, p. 6.
[57] Stevens, *Jailed*, p. 79.
[58] April 4, 1917, Reel 41, NWPP.
[59] John Morton Blum, *Woodrow Wilson and the Politics of Morality* (Boston: Little, Brown and Company, 1956), p. 118.
[60] May 13, 1917 Reel 42; September 23, 1917, Reel 48, NWPP. Heffelfinger would be jailed by October. Hilles' is, again, a truly Gilmanesque argument. Hilles to Paul, April 19, 1917, Reel 41; Betsy Schmidt and Leah Ford, "A Tribute to Doris C. Stevens," *Oberlin Alumni Magazine*, p. 30; Rogers to Paul, May 1, 1917, Reel 42, NWPP.
[61] Morey to Mabel Vernon, May 3, 1917, Reel 42, NWPP.
[62] Irwin, *Paul and the NWP*, pp. 307-308. On lobbying see Reel 42, NWPP. In May a coalition of liberal groups, "The National Party," called on President Wilson to ask his help for passage of the suffrage amendment. The NWP sent Mabel Vernon with the delegation unofficially. They included socialist John Spargo, labor unionist Samuel Gompers, prohibitionist Virgil Hinshaw and Progressive J. A. H. Hopkins. The president made no promises. J. A. H. Hopkins to Vernon, May 1, 1917, Reel 42, NWPP.
[63] May 25, 1917, Reel 210, Wilson Papers on Microfilm.
[64] Wilson to Pou, May 14, 1917, Reel 210, Wilson Papers on Microfilm.
[65] Catt to Paul, May 24, 1917, Reel 42, NWPP.
[66] May 29, 1917, Reel 42, NWPP.
[67] Stevens to Paul, April 1, 1917, Reel 41; Paul to Mary Bakewell, June 12, 1917, Reel 44, NWPP.
[68] For instance, see end of March, early April, Reel 40, NWPP.
[69] *Suffragist*, May 12, 1917, p. 5; alliance letters, end of May from NWP headquarters, Reel 42, NWPP.
[70] Some women at headquarters rarely picketed themselves, but spent a great deal of time organizing pickets. Grace Needham, for instance, did a gracious job of arranging everything and answering letters that came in damning or praising pickets. Particularly poignant were the several letters from Mr. John Price at the Old Soldier's Home, who backed them "100%." Needham answered all of his letters with courtesy. See, for example, June 16, 1917, Reel 44, NWPP.
[71] Irwin, *Paul and the NWP*, p. 214.
[72] Chase to Alice Paul, May 26, 1917, Reel 42, NWPP.

[73] Speech by Elizabeth S. Rogers, May 29, 1917, Reel 42, NWPP; Boeckel, "Reflections of a Picket," *Suffragist*, March 3, 1917, p. 6.
[74] *Suffragist*, May 26, 1917, pp. 4-5.
[75] June 12, 1917, Reel 44, NWPP.

Chapter 5

Resisting Authority: The First Arrests, Mid-1917

President Wilson and Envoy Root are deceiving Russia.
They say we are a democracy, help us win a world's war
So that democracies may survive.
The women of America tell you that America is not a democracy.
20 million women are denied the right to vote.
President Wilson is the chief opponent of their national
enfranchisement.
Help us make this nation free.
Tell our government that it must liberate its people
before it can claim free Russia as an ally.

-The "Russian" banner, June 1917[1]

According to Alice Paul, the defiant picketing of the President in early 1917, "this going out and standing there with our beautiful banners," was not "anything very militant." But, said Paul, when the "Russian" banner appeared in front of the White House in June, and the women who held it knew that they faced arrest, "[t]hat's when our militancy really began."[2] That was the point of "real militancy" to Paul because that was when women became willing to break the law in civil disobedience--to resist authority. In fact, Emmeline Pankhurst made exactly the same distinction in England, matching sufficient female anger with readiness for civil disobedience. Pankhurst stated that in 1906, when British suffragists demanded entrance to the House of Commons and were refused, that was the "start of their militancy": "The women were awake at last."[3] By mid-1917, NWP petitioners had displayed their bold suffrage banners before the White House gates for months, only to be ignored or ridiculed. For Woman's Party feminists, who believed in carrying out the logic of female strength, there was nothing for it but to move further down the road of militancy, from defiance to a second stage of actual resistance. Unlike Pankhurst's WSPU, they would not use "violence" against property; they would not smash windows and blow up buildings in their resistance. They would instead use their own bodies, sacrificing themselves--their health, their jobs, and their reputations--for women's rights. Spurning "normal" female behavior, they would now quite literally fight their own battles in a still frustrated power struggle with stubborn male government authorities.

Once the women made the decision to stand their ground under threat of arrest, jailing, and brutal attacks by crowds of onlookers; they became fully ("really") militant, but militant in their own way and in a particular, wartime context. The militants' object was to force the Wilson government, through public pressure, to pass woman suffrage, using the most effective weapons available to them. They worked to keep suffrage in the headlines and create public sympathy for them as opposed to the Wilson government. And for the NWP, the means were as important as the end; that is, they would operate as strong, capable opponents, with the "same" strengths as men, while employing nonviolent resistance techniques to point out a very useful "female difference." To quote Richard Gregg's *Power of Nonviolence*, a nonviolent resister

> does not respond to the attacker's violence with counter-violence. Instead, he [sic] accepts the blows good-temperedly, stating his belief as to the truth of the matter in dispute, asking for an examination of both sides of the dispute, and stating his readiness to abide by the truth. He offers resistance, but only in moral terms.[4]

The Woman's Party, already experts at using the media, utilized this technique masterfully. And, as described in Stiehm's *Nonviolent Power*, NWP dissenters used graduated actions to coerce their targeted opponent. In 1917 the women put their bodies on the line: the pickets held fast to their banners, "obstructed" traffic, staged outdoor pageants (the street theater of 1917), and used wave upon wave of banner holders or speakers while those in front were attacked or arrested. They stood stubbornly until forcibly moved, and marched until physically prevented, offering only passive resistance to mobs and police. They would become more and more non-cooperative in court and in jail. Such "moral jujitsu" methods, as Gregg calls them, were the classic techniques employed by Mahatma Gandhi in South Africa and India, and, later, by the Reverend Martin Luther King in the American South. And, reportedly, Gandhi was inspired by the Pankhurst struggle, which he observed while in London.[5] Woman's Party feminists were America's first political dissenters to use the nonviolent resistance method, and they did it very well.

The reasons for the NWP militants' arrests; the effects of the "resisting" stage of militancy, with its surly mobs and jail sentences, on the public, Congress and the President; and the significance of the NWP's self-consciously nonviolent militant style; all have to be put into the context of a war-frenzied atmosphere. As William Preston argued in *Aliens and Dissenters*, periods of stability in America were periods of tolerance, but:

> Depression, class conflict, increasing social and geographic immobility, [or] war or the threat of it . . . developed tensions and fears that sought release in retaliation against the supposed enemy within, alien or radical. . . . In a war atmosphere, any 'Christian tolerance' was swept away by patriotism.[6]

The over-heated atmosphere of America in wartime, in a way only accentuated the points the militants were making against a government fighting a "war for democracy." But war hysteria also meant they had to come face to face with enraged patriots who considered them just as treasonous as other "radical," subversive (leftist) dissenters. By fall, the NWP would develop strong identification with other "radicals," while at the same time, attracting them to *their* civil liberties struggle. As female dissenters, the pickets also had to face men who had developed militarized "macho" attitudes about militant women who obviously did not know their place.

The NWP's second, very crucial stage of militancy, was framed by the highly critical June "Russian" banner, with the first arrests; and the August "Kaiser" banner, accompanied by a repressive and violent police crackdown. The arrests began when NWP suffragists called Wilson a hypocrite on the occasion of a visit of the Russian delegation. On June 20th, Kerensky's new Russian republic, which had just passed woman suffrage, sent diplomats to visit Wilson. They were met with the sight of Lucy Burns and Dora Lewis holding a banner which charged Wilson and Envoy Elihu Root with deceiving "free Russia" when they called America a democracy. The women were soon surrounded by a crowd of men that ripped the banner from its poles. The Wilson government, deeply embarrassed by the banner, instructed Chief of Police Major Raymond Pullman to warn Alice Paul that if pickets continued to be sent out, they would be arrested. Paul argued with Pullman, reminding him they had already been picketing perfectly legally for six months.[7] The militants did not see the "Russian" banner itself as a major new departure, since they had been holding banners depicting Administration hypocrisy for months. Apparently it was Elizabeth Selden Rogers who had the original idea for the Russian banner, and Paul stated at the time that they had "spent many hours on the wording and did the best [they] could."[8] Even a group of visiting Russian women joined the pickets, carrying banners inscribed with an appeal to the United States to make itself "a real democracy in relation to women, as Russia has." The women of "free Russia" were then invited to a reception in their honor.[9] Paul herself relished the fight at the start of the arrests, calling the "Russian incident" an "exciting time."[10]

To Paul it may have been exciting to resist the authorities, but for women facing angry mobs and jail, excitement could be tempered with dread. On June 21st Lucy Burns again, this time with Katharine Morey, brought out another Russian banner and, as Morey described it, it was immediately ripped down by a group of boys while the police looked on. Lucy Burns was on the front lines, as usual, and Katharine Morey, of Brookline, Massachusetts, was consistently up there with her. Katharine A. Morey, with her mother, Agnes H. Morey, were early leaders of the NWP branch in Massachusetts. Katharine Morey had also been a tireless organizer in Kansas in the 1916 campaign, and served as an assistant at national headquarters. After Morey lost the banner she carried with Burns that day, new

Russian banners were secured, while Morey ventured out this time with Hazel Hunkins, carrying a banner stating "Democracy Should Begin At Home." All was quiet for awhile, and then, as Morey was having lunch at headquarters on her break, she suddenly "heard a great roar," and saw a mob attacking Hazel Hunkins and the other pickets.[11]

The first FBI (then called Secret Service) reports on the NWP came on that day of the first mob attacks. Agent W. W. Grimes reported on the charge of "Mrs. D. Richardson" on Hunkins. Grimes, like Morey, was on lunch when he observed the "heroic" Richardson lunge at Hunkins. The throng and the police cheered Richardson on as she left Hunkins to then lead a charge at the western gate, where she engaged in a "physical struggle" with the pickets. He granted the pickets the "stoicism of martyrs," as they immediately sent in reserves. "But," Grimes concluded, "they cause the riots and it's bad publicity for the country." He feared shots could be fired at the White House in the melée.[12] A member of the mob wrote the President assuring him he had done his best to uphold the country's honor in the face of the pickets' challenge. The letter gives some idea of what was in the "minds" of the mob. After Wilson was reportedly called a hypocrite by a picket, the letter writer claimed that:

> [W]ith the assistance of a little group of '*real men*', [I] tore down all the banners which had been placed in front of the White House. Colonel Bryan was leaving at the time and smiled. I love this country and the American flag, and in the name of the group of men who helped me to defend your good name, I appeal to you to put an end to their offensive and outrageous doings. A distinguished Russian congratulated me and informed me that if the women in Russia would do such a thing, they would immediately be 'spanked' on the street. Now, millions of young men must leave for France and die for their country's honor. Is it right, is it justice to them, that at the same time females, who are no women are permitted to disgrace and insult the government and the manhood of this country?[13]

Clearly the combination of unpatriotic banners and the temerity of women being militant for feminist purposes was too much of a threat to this fellow's manhood--to him the picketers were "females, who are no women." The police finally intervened to stop the mobs of "real men," the first the women had experienced.

The first six women jailed all knew when they went out to picket they faced more crowd violence and arrest. On the 22nd, Paul informed Chief Pullman that the pickets were going out. Katherine Morey and Lucy Burns were immediately arrested, for "obstructing traffic," but their case was dismissed by the court. Four more women were arrested on the 23rd, 12 on the 25th and nine on the 26th of June. Six of those nine were tried the following day, found guilty of "obstructing the highways," and after refusing to pay a $25 fine, were sentenced to three days in jail. The first suffrage prisoners were organizers Katharine Morey, Mabel Vernon and Virginia Arnold; advisor Lavinia Dock, state officer Maud Jamison and "recruit" Annie Arniel.[14] They were the first ever to be incarcerated for advocating women's rights.

All the prisoners had willingly answered appeals from headquarters to picket and all refused to be treated as "heroines."[15] Two who were jailed, Annie Arniel, a munitions worker from Delaware, and Maud Jamison, a teacher from Virginia, were called upon to speak at the breakfast held for them upon their release. Arniel, who had "played tunes on a comb" in jail to amuse the others, had picketed many times before her arrest. She said she had spoken to the "poor women in prison" many of whom were there not "from any cause of their own," but "through lack of justice . . . We didn't go [to jail] for fun. . . we are standing for liberty, if we must lose every drop of our blood for it."[16] NWP Assistant Treasurer Jamison was a twenty-seven-year old "new woman" who wore her black hair "bobbed." She was reported, however, to be "as earnest as Alice Paul." Jamison had a flair for the dramatic, what she called "a romantic turn of mind." She called the pitching of the police van taking her to jail "just like the dungeon of a prison ship." She echoed Arniel in her "blood" metaphor, saying, "[There is] no better training school for NWP leaders than jail . . .[I] love every drop of blood shed for liberty.[17] Even a three-day exposure to prison had these women emphasizing women's solidarity in oppression and expressing a firm resolve to fight for their rights by "shedding blood" if necessary.

Governmental authorities hoped that the June jail sentences would discourage the radicals from persisting in their picketing of the White House, but soon saw that the militants were not ready to cease. In fact, on the eve of the nation's celebration of its political liberties, Alice Paul was considering how far the militants might have to go so that women could gain theirs, writing a fellow suffragist: "The hunger strike is a desperate weapon, which should only be used as a last resort in resistance of authority."[18] As in her 1915 letter to Burns about resorting to greater militancy, this letter indicates she was thinking of using more serious militant tactics before actually suggesting them as party policy; and three months later the first hunger strikes, the ultimate weapon of nonviolent resistance, would begin.

Many women in the NWP saw irony in the July 4th pronouncements that summer, considering their own situation. Katharine Fisher stormed from a celebration at Grant's tomb when the speaker started discussing "the political equality which we are all so used to that we take it as a matter of course."[19] Therefore, on the Fourth of July in Washington five pickets left NWP Headquarters bearing the sign "Governments Derive Their Just Power From The Consent Of The Governed." This time, before the demonstrators had proceeded very far down the street, the crowd and police had seized their banners and arrested the picketers. The angry crowds yelled, "Send them over to the Kaiser," "They are idiots," and "They ought to be sent up for life." Hazel Hunkins tried to wrest back her banner from a man in the crowd who had taken it and was immediately arrested. Many of the women fought to hold on to their banners. Joy Young was one of the women exhibiting that sort of resistance. Young was originally a New Englander (Dover, New Hampshire) who had come to New York and eventually worked for the leftist publication, *The Masses*. She had served as an assistant on the *Suffragist* and an organizer in the CU western campaigns. Tiny Joy Young wrestled with her attacker as she led a second group of seven pickets to replace the first. The second contingent was also taken into custody. According to Doris Stevens, orders had been received at the District Jail to be ready for the July 4th pickets before they had even gone to trial.

Such summary justice for the women demonstrators was deeply resented. Stevens bitterly noted that the judge and district commissioners were directly appointed by President Wilson, and that the commissioners appointed the chief of police and jail warden. Stevens concluded, "No one would notice a few 'mad' women thrown into jail."[20] It was Lucy Burns who argued their case in court. She noted that it was the police and not they who attracted the crowd, that the Judge had previously stated marching pickets were not unlawful, and that the police acted differently from day to day. In summation, Burns asserted: "It is evident that the proceedings in this court are had for the purpose of suppressing our appeal to the President of the United States."[21]

Burns and the other jailed demonstrators thought it ironic to be sentenced for asking for political liberty on the Fourth of July. The ten women detained were organizers Margaret Whittemore, Vida Milholland, Helena Hill Weed, Iris Calderhead, and Joy Young; officers Lucy Burns and Dora Lewis; new members Frances B. Green and Elizabeth Stuyvesant from New York, and Lucille Shields--all the way from Amarillo, Texas for the July Fourth demonstration. Shields was a "33-year-old housekeeper" married to merchant Alexander Shields (he sold "gents furnishings." [?]) She had considerable singing talent, and reportedly went to France in 1919 to sing under the auspices of the YMCA. She had picketed enough to be considered a "regular" by the time of her arrest. Shields' hometown paper had headlines reading "Amarillo Suff Taken in Riot at Washington--Spends Night in Lockup." Maintaining a sarcastic, humorous tone throughout, the article states that the "demonstration resulted in a comedy riot, and much amusement for a holiday crowd." The women were said to have denied contemplating a hunger strike. In fact, the friends of the pickets reportedly sent them "flowers and baskets of fruit and dainties to ease the rigors of imprisonment." A later report said the women chose to serve three days in jail rather than pay the $25 fine Judge Mullowny "pleaded vainly that they accept . . . and offered to advance them the money." He told them to "keep away from the White House. You know the times are abnormal. We are at war and you should not bother the President."[22]

Undeterred by the judge's advice, the militants continued to demonstrate against the President. Similar treatment awaited the NWP in its next picket on July 14, Bastille Day, another appropriate occasion for the pickets to carry banners, this time of "Liberty, Equality, Fraternity," to the White House. Elizabeth Stuyvesant, on her way from New York to work at Washington headquarters, wrote to organizer Iris Calderhead, "May the America Bastille fall Saturday!"[23] Again, the pickets only travelled a short distance from headquarters before arrest occurred, in front of a fairly quiet crowd; there was "no manhandling this time." Sixteen women were booked for "unlawful assembly" and sentenced to a stiff *sixty* days at Occuquan Workhouse for "obstructing traffic." Among their number were some of the NWP's top leaders: Anne Martin, Doris Stevens, Matilda Gardner, Eunice Brannan and Elizabeth Selden Rogers. Anne Martin asserted that the sidewalk was "unusually spacious," and at any rate, she occupied a "vast area perhaps one foot square." She said it was the gawking crowd which obstructed traffic, not she. Martin relished the chance to tell the court a line something like (it was oft-repeated): "So long as you send women to prison for asking for justice, so long will women be willing to go in such a cause." The Administration vainly hoped the longer sentence given would "deter other women."

The sixteen "Bastille" prisoners, after three days at Occuquan, and after a good deal of public pressure, were pardoned by President Wilson and released. At first the prisoners refused release, stating they would not accept a pardon unless Wilson promised to press for woman suffrage. Minnie Abbott, who worked for the railroad during the war, was secretary for her district branch in Atlantic City. Abbott insisted "we acted entirely within our rights." When she went out to take part in the celebration of the fall of the Bastille, it had been with fear of the much publicized threatening crowds, but she found the crowds much thinner than those she had often faced in suffrage demonstration on the boardwalk. She learned from fellow inmates that preparations for their arrival were made well before the trial had begun. Abbot did not want a pardon, but justice: "[I]t was not personal liberty but political freedom that we asked." But their warden, Raymond Whittaker, told them they had no choice in the matter, so after deciding protests must have been strong to force the pardon, the women left prison.[24]

They were released on that occasion, but the angry reaction to their aggressive banners insisting on democracy at home was serious, and was echoed by crowds already charged with war hysteria. Because of their insistence on showing what they saw as government hypocrisy in its use of democratic rhetoric the women were considered "unpatriotic, if not seditious and treasonable."[25] A double charge of treason and unwomanly behavior was repeated in various places. Congressman J. Thomas Heflin of Alabama called the June pickets "monstrous, disloyal, unpatriotic" and agreed with the crowds who yelled "treason" and "take it to Berlin." The *New York Times* reacted favorably to Richardson's attack on the pickets, calling organizer Hazel Hunkins and the pickets "traitors," a "disgrace to womanhood" and "white feathers." The *Times* accused the women of going against their own natures; the picketing was "more irritating when done by women . . . men expect women to be wiser and better-mannered than themselves and are angry when they show themselves to be no better." The *Washington Post*'s coverage was sarcastic: "The picketing nuisance" was handled well. The "women were arrested just like men would have been." No more "leniency and tolerance" could be afforded women who held banners with inscriptions that were "unpatriotic."[26]

Those "unpatriotic" militant suffragists were soon equated in the minds of loyal Americans and the authorities, with other American anti-war radicals, just as they had been (and still were) with the Pankhursts. A *New York Times* editorial had "socialists, draft resisters and suffragettes" engaging in activities whose purpose was to "incite rebellion," either "active or passive."[27] Other "radicals" would begin to be more supportive of the militants, since they were experiencing similar treatment by government and the public. On July 1st, 8,000 "Labor organizers, socialists and Jews" had held a parade in Boston carrying banners saying "Democratize Germany?" and "Six-Hour Day in Socialist Russian, Why Not Here?" They were attacked by soldiers and sailors (on command), beaten, their red flags torn; and they were forced to kiss the American flag. According to an H. C. Peterson and Gilbert C. Fite study, during the war crowds attacked pacifists, the IWW, anti-war politicians, blacks, "aliens" (German, Irish and Puerto Rican-Americans), and leftist professors, high school teachers and ministers.[28] Since people were harassed if they did not buy Liberty Bonds, militant suffragists calling the President a hypocrite were in very grave jeopardy. It also seems a reasonable assumption that if the women had continued to picket in a time of peace, they may well never have been mobbed, arrested or jailed. It was not a proud moment for American civil liberties, but the NWP, a group engaged in nonviolent resistance, thrived on the government's bad publicity, and their own resulting martyrdom.

The NWP had most definitely stirred the country with the bold Russian banner, and subsequent arrests, but did it hurt or help their cause? Lillian Ascough, the singer on the 1916 "Suffragist Special" train and an NWP officer in Connecticut, wrote Paul that she had approved of the Russian banner, but that the Connecticut Executive Board did not. "Dismayed," Advisory Council member Edith Bigelow left the NWP immediately. NWP headquarters received many letters of resignation from its own members, along with many unfriendly letters from the public, (running about 5 to 1 against the pickets in early July) saying their actions were treason.[29] Congressman John Small wrote them that their picketing was "vulgar" and "unworthy of your sex." NAWSA members frantically wrote to try to stop them "from damaging suffrage prospects."[30] Far from discouraged by detractors, the NWP were determined to continue their resistance.

Unfortunately for the militants, hostile "onlookers" of the press continued to hurt the crucial fight to win over the public. From Chicago, an NWP member wrote that the local papers said "ugly unjust things" about the party, and that women were losing faith there. In Oregon the members were reported to be "disaffected," the local papers "bitter in condemnation"; Caroline Spencer reported "all the papers" in Colorado were against them. A *Philadelphia Inquirer* editorial was scathing: "They cannot be regarded as women. What a pity that their poor intellects cannot be stretched to a comprehension of their degradation."[31] "Degraded" or not, the NWP still had a following.

NWP supporters who were left were strongly behind the Party. Elizabeth Cahill wrote Paul wishing she could send "thousands of dollars." Five thousand new *Suffragist* subscriptions came in. Colorado's Caroline Spencer warmly congratulated them. Crystal Eastman (and socialist brother Max) "loved the [Russian] banner." John Reed spoke at the breakfast honoring the first suffragist prisoners. Contributions poured in, along with new memberships. Although Lucy Burns said she was often told that the women were "going too far," many women "looked up to" the Woman's Party.[32] This was never more true than when "real" militancy began in June.

It had hardly gone unnoticed that the militant suffragists' civil liberties were being suppressed. Protest meetings were held all over the country and NWP prisoner speakers were very much in demand. Professor Charles Beard voiced strong public objection, as did Amos Pinchot. Even though no longer with the party, Harriot Stanton Blatch wrote for the *Suffragist* that "short-sighted and foolish governments give imprisonment instead of votes. . . . Protests cannot be stopped by criticism of their form or by suppression, but only by doing justice." Commissioner of Immigration Frederic Howe cabled Burns, "This is not the only time when truth has been on the scaffold."[33] The rebellious NWP was certainly not without friends at the end of July. And Anne Martin insisted that their illegal arrests had "created strong reaction in our favor in Congress," particularly among Republicans.

Woman's Party supporters admired the strength and courage of the militants' resistance to government efforts to stop them. Mabel Vernon outlined NWP militant policy to resist authority when she answered a critic of the June pickets:

> The conclusion we have reached is that we must stand now for the establishment of a true democracy in this land. . . . [The sentiments in] the Russian banner have been the same since January 10, [our] purpose is to remind constantly the President and the people of the country [that we] are not enfranchised.[34]

Similarly, writing to New York NAWSA members, Martin tried to explain the political merits of NWP tactics:

> The National Woman's Party must continue to picket. We must maintain our constitutional right 'to petition the government for a redress of grievances' . . . . There could be no law against it, as the right of peaceful petition is guaranteed by the United States Constitution. . . . The President and the President alone, can secure its [the suffrage amendment] passage, when he lifts his finger, Congress will act. As long as the Government and its

> representatives prefer to send women to jail on petty and technical charges to giving American women justice, we will go to jail. . . . Prosecution has always advanced the cause of liberty.[35]

Probably the most quoted retort to the question of the wisdom of picketing was that of one of those jailed in June, 60-year-old Lavinia Dock, who herself personified the "fearless spirit of youth" she wrote about:

> What is the potent spirit of youth? Is it not the spirit of revolt, of rebellion against senseless and useless and deadening things? Most of all, against injustice, which is of all stupid things the stupidest? . . . . Can it be possible that any brain cells not totally crystallized could imagine that giving a stone instead of bread would answer conclusively the demand of the women who, because they are young, fearless, eager and rebellious, are fighting and winning a cause for all women--even for those who are timid, conventional, and inept? . . . Obstructive reactionaries must move on. The young are at the gates![36]

The women at the gates continued to press their demands, but the rebel ranks did suffer some setbacks.

With the public furor surrounding the arrests, and many women resigning from the NWP, the number of militants were reduced, but Alice Paul did not see this as necessarily a bad thing. "So we sort of emerged from all this with, maybe, the sturdier feminists, people who wanted to continue anyway." In that sense, rather like other revolutionaries, the NWP would be a radical vanguard well out in advance of their feminist contemporaries, advancing strong radical feminism, both philosophically and tactically. Still, Paul was not such a hardened combatant that she was insensitive to the "general feeling over the whole country that you were the scum of the earth and all that."[37] The strain of maintaining a militant posture under much criticism did take its toll, and Paul, ordinarily the last to appear fatigued, began to show definite signs of stress. In the heat of her summer battle for women's rights, she became very ill; by mid-July she contracted what was originally diagnosed as "Bright's Disease," and then later called "not organic." If nothing else she certainly badly needed rest. Her condition was at first judged so serious that the doctor feared for her life, but after retreating to a Philadelphia sanatorium, she recovered within a month. Lucy Burns, despite wanting to withdraw from the NWP at the start of the year, became active "chairman," helped by Mabel Vernon and Hazel Hunkins. Meeting with Paul at her bedside, the executive committee voted to keep picketing, one day a week. On July 23rd daily pickets resumed.[38] Concerned about the stricken Paul, her fellow militants were determined to carry out her bold strategy against a yet immovable Wilson government. Pennsylvania NWP chair, Mary Hall Ingham described it that summer as a government that would "beg for our gifts and despise our intelligence and distrust our patriotism." Elsie Hill wondered, "Can't we have it [suffrage] as justice accorded not as a price paid for so much servitude to a warring government?"[39] Paul's sturdy feminists would not win justice from the Administration quite so easily.

The Administration was in no mood to give in to the NWP; they had decided that the banners had become more than just a joke or nuisance, but an embarrassment and real problem to an administration trying to conduct a war. Wilson's attitude toward women of the "Congressional Union variety" had not grown more charitable over the years, and by mid-1917 he seemed convinced that they were mentally unbalanced. The volume of mail he received in June only confirmed his belief that the NWP was not favored by the public. A few letters protested against the women's arrests, but most were against the pickets, and most were from women.[40] Therefore he had no problem making moves to disperse the pickets. The *New York Times* reported that, supposedly, the federal district attorney had received requests by "five businessmen," to arrest the pickets initially, but "the impression" was that the D.A.'s office had "been instructed by the President" to arrest them on the 22nd, but to take no more legal action. Washington journalist Gilson Gardner in strongly condemning the arrests, placed the blame directly on Wilson: "When President Wilson's administration ordered the arrest of the suffrage pickets--and of course the police have taken their orders in this matter directly from the White House--the administration did a very stupid thing." Gardner stated that because the President "was irritated" he answered words "with force," and that was an abuse of power: "tyranny."[41] Wilson's forceful efforts to dissuade the pickets with a few days in jail had had no such effect. The sentences given on June 27th by Federal Judge Raymond Mulowney were made light (three days) intentionally, reportedly so that the women could not hunger strike or do some "other form of desperation or deviltry" like their fellow English militants, as rumor had it they would.[42] But by the July trials, the authorities thought 60 days would stop the protests.

As has been seen, the public would not stand for the 60 day sentences, and the women served only three days. And Wilson had indeed received protests. Mabel Vernon had helped by writing all the NWP district members to urge people to send hundreds of telegrams to the White House.[43] As Doris Stevens wrote, "For the first time . . . our form of agitation began to seem a little more respectable than the Administration's handling of it."[44] The President had received direct personal appeals from his friends Dudley Field Malone and Gilson Gardner; J.A.H. Hopkins, Progressive party leader and Wilson supporter, had conferred with Wilson after visiting his wife in jail.

Allison Turnbull Hopkins, 37-year-old daughter of a naval officer, said she could not remember "a time when she did not believe in rights of women." Hopkins was educated by private tutors and was active in charity work for years, which, she said, taught her that "only through political power could women secure the reforms they wished for in our government and in our labor laws." She was New Jersey state NWP chairman and on the executive committee. She had three children, two sons and a daughter, was active in the Progressive party and had been in the WPU. The Morristown native also indulged in "notable civic activities" such as the State Charities Aid Society, Women's Town Improvement Committee and the Morris County Corn Growing and Industrial Contest Committee[!]. Husband J.A.H. Hopkins asked Wilson: "How would you like to have your wife sleep in a dirty workhouse next to prostitutes?" (The Hopkins had only recently been Wilson's dinner guests.)[45] Wilson told Hopkins he was "shocked" over the jailings and "might" advocate suffrage as a war measure.

But the suffragists insisted that far from being sympathetic, their jailing, in July as in June, was Wilson's idea. A "suffrage husband" reported "he had information that a cabinet officer" was directing the police and D.C officials "in their repressive measures."[46] The brouhaha caused the President to issue a pardon, but his views on the merits of the case for woman suffrage remained unfavorable.

If the women could not be deterred by jail, the Administration considered other means. Joseph Tumulty suggested to Wilson that they arrange a press black-out. The editors of the *Washington Times* and *Washington Star* agreed to conspire not to cover news of the NWP. One of them had talked to Dr. John Rogers, husband of Elizabeth Selden Rogers, who had supposedly confided to him that "some of the women were unbalanced mentally . . . [and] if they were encouraged with publicity, they would go on, getting worse each day and finally do something desperate."[!] Tumulty warned Wilson that if they were not "gently ignored" they might get violent. Wilson replied that a compromise was in order. "[Total press] [s]ilence might provoke the less sane of these women to violent action." Wilson suggested they be given no headlines, but "bare, colorless chronicle [which] need not be made interesting reading."[47] Wilson and his men seemed to simply dismiss the NWP as madwomen. Louis Brownlow, Wilson's District Commissioner, remembered that "hardly a day [went by] when the problem [of the NWP] was not brought to my attention." He insisted the NWP picketed "in the hope of arrest and martyrdom," and that, moreover, the "suffragettes themselves threatened the use of firearms if we did not arrest them."[!] Brownlow confirmed that Wilson wanted to limit the NWP's publicity, and that he had made the arrests on his own. When the women were sent to Occuquan Workhouse, Brownlow said that the President was absolutely furious. However, it is difficult to take Brownlow's word seriously when he follows this statement by saying he had to arrest the "suffragettes" because they were "belaboring members of the crowd with the staffs of their banners."[48] The viewing of militant suffragists as lunatics reveals how very "unnatural" these strong-willed women were thought to be. As unfeminine women crazies they were dismissable, but since they were also "treasonous," it called for governing authorities to use oppressive measures.

One month after the aggressive demonstrations of July, Lillian Ascough wrote Lucy Burns that she hoped Burns would "think up some ripping big stunt to keep the good work going, and if so, send for me."[49] Burns did think of a good stunt for August, the "Kaiser banner," a stunt which brought the suffragists into a violent confrontation with a government which had hoped that the July presidential pardon would put an end to further picketing. New spirit had been shown with the arrests following the Russian banner, an overtly militant and aggressive spirit, and a willingness to resist authority. NWP suffragists were still not quite sure of what militancy meant though. Some equated militancy with the violence of the WPSU. In a July *New York Times* article, organizer Virginia Arnold wondered why they were called militant, since the British were not called that until they started destroying property. (NAWSA's Mrs. James Laidlaw stated that if Alice Paul had "transplanted" English militant methods in America then she should follow their example and do war work.) Anne Martin continued to deny the NWP used "militant" tactics, saying militancy was "used against them." Alva Belmont mocked the horror shown at the NWP's "mild" militancy in the face of war in Europe.[50] Paul and Burns felt that in defying authority they had become "really" militant, and to most NWP pickets "militancy," by August 1917, was an acceptable term to describe their strategy.

Women of the NWP were furious over the unjust, illegal arrests and imprisonment since the Russian banner. "The whole procedure has been so outrageous that one simply choked with rage over it . . . [The released prisoners'] faces were all haggard and drawn, their hair uncombed and their hands unclean because they had not been allowed to use the toilet articles they had taken with them."[51] If rage was one side of militance, the other was pride. A woman wrote to the *Suffragist* that she admired the NWP for "enabling women to hold up their heads . . . Men have to admire you [too] for your intelligence and aggressiveness."[52] Marie Howe described the new militant spirit of resistance:

> The National Woman's Party has created a new spirit. We used to be so anxious to please, so pleasant and ineffective, so frightened and smiling. . . . Where is the anxious fear we used to see at every legislative hearing? Has it disappeared off the face of the earth? Not at all. You see it's still at every legislative hearing, only now that fear is on the faces of the legislators. If you could gather up Alice Paul, Lucy Burns, Anne Martin, Mrs. Belmont and send them all to Siberia, the NWP would live on in all of us who are here today, in thousands of women who are not here. This new attitude of the woman who respects herself and her cause is unquenchable.[53]

Women of the "Congressional Union variety" had evolved a distinctive militant style of nonviolent, civil disobedience; moving from January's defiant, peaceful picketing to the summer's jailings for resisting Administration attempts to end their protests.

At the close of the second militant stage, in August, the NWP militants decided to emphasize what they believed to be the hypocritical and autocratic nature of the Wilson administration. In so doing, the NWP's "resisting" stage manifested a willingness to engage in a more radical critique of "male" government than ever before, and as a direct result the women were faced with much more violent confrontations. On August 14th a new banner was carried out of headquarters reading: "Kaiser Wilson, Have You Forgotten Your Sympathy With The Poor Germans Because They Were Not Self-Governing? 20 Million American Women Are Not Self-Governing/Take The Beam Out Of Your Own Eye." [54] Pickets after Bastille Day had gone out weekly since July 23, including the day before the Kaiser banner went out, asking Envoy Elihu Root, "Whose Liberty Is America Fighting For?" But the new banner ushered in a more serious confrontational style of NWP message. Lucy Burns had drafted the Kaiser banner, and later explained that she meant no personal abuse of Wilson, but merely meant that Woodrow Wilson was an autocrat to *them*. "He refuses to be in a democratic relation to us . . . but is in an autocratic one . . . [And the idea] has to be administered to the public with a slight shock or they do not get it at all."

Burns was not alone in her sentiments regarding Wilson. Alice Paul wrote that "toward women, President Wilson has adopted the attitude of an autocratic ruler."[55] Pennsylvania's Mary Winsor told the *New York Times* that the President "hypnotizes himself into thinking that what he believes in must be so and that what he disapproves is wrong. . . . The President is an autocratic ruler over Congress."[56] Doris Stevens explained the NWP's militant resistance to administration authorities by saying that they did not regard Woodrow Wilson as *their* president. He had no moral or political claim to their loyalty and waged war without their consent. They deeply resented what they saw as his hypocrisy of fighting for democracy abroad but not at home. "They were stung into a protest so militant as to shock not only the President but the public. . . . The truth . . . had to be told."[57] "Autocrat" Wilson had made it clear to the Woman's Party that they had no part--no rights--in government. So the method for the second stage of resistant militancy was that of the civil disobedience of protest demonstrations--going outside the bounds of law, since *they* had no say in the law and no loyalty to the president.

Unfortunately, the crowd that gathered that August day was not particularly happy to be told such "truths" about the President's mistreatment of women, and in fact set about to do some brutal mistreating of women themselves. The police did nothing as rowdies set upon Elizabeth Stuyvesant, a dancer and socialist activist from New York. Stuyvesant was a settlement worker, originally from Cincinnati, who, in addition to her social work, ran a studio where she taught "interpretive dancing." She had been busy in the birth-control movement before joining the NWP demonstrations. Stuyvesant was the first to leave headquarters bearing the Kaiser banner. In the scuffle surrounding the banner, she was struck by a sailor and had her blouse torn off.

After all the pickets had lost their banners, they retreated to headquarters, but the mob followed them and allowed none of them to leave the building. Some of the men in the mob got a ladder and pulled down Kaiser banners which appeared on the NWP balcony, and which Burns and Virginia Arnold struggled to hold in place. Suddenly, a shot was fired into the second floor, nearly hitting two of the women. In spite of the gun fire, the indomitable Katharine Morey, who was first to hold the Russian banner, and Catherine M. Flanagan, whose father had fought in the Irish Revolution, then decided to take out the Kaiser banner, and stood on the sidewalk almost 20 minutes before being dragged down the street. Flanagan, from Hartford, Connecticut, had been a very active organizer (in Idaho, especially) and state officer for the NWP. (Pictured in Figure 6.) She struggled hard to hold onto the banner in spite of the policeman's nails digging into her hand. Flanagan and the other pickets made repeated charges towards the White House with very little police protection. According to Flanagan's account:

> While the crowd was milling its thickest before Headquarters, somebody said to a policeman standing there, "Why don't you arrest these men?" "Those are not our orders," the policeman replied. . . . During all the early evening, men were trying to climb over the back fence of the garden to get into Cameron House. None of us went to bed that night. We were afraid that something--we knew not what--might happen.

Not only the "regulars" were hurt that day, but women in Washington for the first time.

Madeleine Watson, a state officer from Chicago, had been anxious to come to Washington to picket for some time, saying "her time was her own." (She is in Figure 7.) Her first day on the line was terrifying, but she stood fast. Her husband told the local papers after the Kaiser mob attack that she was "willing to stand abuse and endanger [her] life in order that the spirit of American democracy may be brought into real life. . . . [She] has truly displayed great courage in facing a howling mob without any protection." Watson was knocked down and kicked by the mob that day.[58]

In a grim new twist for the August protests, the women pickets began to be knocked down by government police. During the three days after the battle on the 14th, NWP pickets stubbornly marched out with their Kaiser banners. The rioting continued; Alice Paul was knocked down repeatedly and had her neck gashed. On the 16th, according to Doris Stevens, the police led the attack, injuring Virginia Arnold, Elizabeth Stuyvesant and Lucy Burns, and arresting men who tried to help the pickets. In light of this, it is understandable that once arrests and violence were imminent, organizer Rebecca Reyher would not picket once she became pregnant. Not wanting special treatment at headquarters, she did not tell Paul, who was not happy with her absence from the picket line. Twenty-two-year-old Natalie Gray from Colorado Springs had been sent to Washington by her mother, Colorado NWP treasurer, to "fight for democracy at home" since she had no son to "fight for democracy abroad." Gray had not been worried about jail, and was "most radiantly happy to go." On her first outing, she was attacked by a police officer. Hundreds of banners were destroyed by the police, not all of them Kaiser banners. Ada Davenport Kendall, a Buffalo newspaper columnist, was an observer of the summer actions and was soon to be arrested herself as a new recruit on the line. Kendall described the pickets in a way which clearly defines their nonviolent resistance at this stage:

> There is nothing hysterical or violent in their method. Although men have thought it glorious to slay their brothers and raze cities for liberty, these women have raised neither hand nor voice. They speak no word and do not attempt to defend themselves if attacked. With their silent appeal they have made woman suffrage the vital issue from coast to coast.[59]

The government, target opponent of their battle, continued to cooperate with their plan, by infringing on their perfectly legal right to picket.

Showing a greater willingness to criticize the administration, Alice Paul insisted that (like the "Kaiser" he was) President Wilson was directly responsible for the police attack, and encouraged the crowds to attack the pickets. If nothing else, the President clearly saw the pickets' situation, as he passed directly through the August 14 riot. *Suffragist* editorials insisted that the government was definitely behind the suppression of militant suffragists' rights. Elizabeth Rogers wrote Elizabeth Stuyvesant with a hope "that all you dear women are not killed by Wilson's police." On August 17, six women were arrested: Natalie Gray, Lavinia Dock, Catherine Flanagan, Madeleine Watson, Edna Dixon of Washington (a teacher and doctor's daughter) and state officer Lucy Ewing of Chicago (an NWP state officer and niece of Cleveland's Vice President).[60] They were sentenced to 30 days at Occuquan and this time, not pardoned. Obviously, these sentences ushered in a more severe phase of official punishment for the feminist dissenters.

Although organizer Joy Young thought the violent Kaiser episode a "glorious situation for us," and Martin always insisted the publicity was helping suffrage in Congress, "real" militancy's effects on the Woman's Party itself were yet to be measured by the end of the summer of 1917. *Suffragist* circulation did increase and some large contributions came in. Large contributor and Connecticut NWP officer Kathryn Houghton Hepburn, was very active in August, sending lots of money and numerous pickets, whom she would recommend by saying, "She's a corker!" On the other hand, there were many members' resignations after the Russian and Kaiser banners. Allison Turnbull Hopkins, herself just out of jail, thought the Kaiser banner "undid so much of our good work." CU founder Mary Hall Ingham agreed, objecting to "illegal acts" such as the Kaiser banner. Elizabeth Rogers

Organizer Catherine Flanagan suffered violence
at the hands of the police.
Figure 6

feared the Advisory Board would "melt away," five members leaving in August. At the end of the month, they had lost 48 members, and gained 224, "sturdy" new women.[61]

The violent public reaction to the NWP's Kaiser banner paralleled what was coming from administration authorities. The *New York Times* found the statements of the "militant suffragettes" on the "Kaiser," nothing short of seditious. In Congress, Senator Charles Culberson of Texas introduced a bill to supplement a newly proposed Espionage Act bill, to prevent "loitering" near places important to National Defense, and Senator Henry Myers of Montana introduced one to make picketing the White House illegal (this after 39 were already in jail).[62] Neither passed.

Not everyone in Washington condoned the Administration's methods. Congressman John Baer introduced a resolution protesting the violence of the crowds and police, signed by, among others, Congress members Meyer London (socialist) and Jeanette Rankin. In the Senate, William Borah presented a similar resolution.[63] Colonel C.L. Lindbergh (aviator Charles Lindbergh's father), a Minnesota Congressman and eyewitness, sent a detailed account of the violent Kaiser banner riots to the President, citing Jefferson and Lincoln as examples Wilson should be following in passing woman suffrage.[64] William Bayard Hale, former envoy to Mexico, angrily protested about being attacked by sailors when he tried to help Katharine Morey. Though many objected to the violence used to suppress the Kaiser banner pickets, neither the government nor the Woman's Party had reached the upper limit of escalation in their battle of wills.

Woman's Party militancy of the second stage had been greeted initially with the first few women's arrests and three-day sentences, and then, by summer's end, with 60-day sentences and violent police attacks. In July, Alva Belmont wondered, "Why all this fuss about woman's militancy when men are at war?"[65] Belmont raised an interesting question about the range of acceptable sex-typed behavior. "Real" militancy was met with real suppression and real violence against the "unwomanly," "treasonous," women's rights demonstrators. The women pickets had been subject to verbal and physical abuse, and then jail, which they faced with classic nonviolent techniques of stubborn standing fast, refusing to cooperate with authorities. "Judge Pugh," who sentenced the Kaiser pickets, told them: "You are doing your cause no good. You are simply seeking publicity, and in so doing you push a method which violates the law."[66] NWP women at the end of stage two of their militancy, *were* violating the law in resistance of authority; they therefore were suffering violent consequences while gaining valuable publicity, the non-violent resister's goal. The second, serious confrontational stage of the resistance resulted in a growing disillusionment with the government, and a readiness to escalate militancy yet again.

---

[1] The "Russian" banner is in an anonymous letter to the Secret Service from one of the men (there were many) who helped destroy the banner on June 20, 1917. He copied the message and sent it to the Federal Bureau. FBI File 108-250, Document 25025, Reel 208. Microfilm Publication of the U.S. National Archives, 1981.
[2] Fry, Paul interview, p. 214.
[3] Emmeline Pankhurst, *My Own Story*, p. 56.
[4] Gregg, *Power of Nonviolence*, p. 43.
[5] Stiehm, *Nonviolent Power*, pp. 5-6, 9, 27. Stiehm also discusses the American, New England Non-Resistance Society founded by William Lloyd Garrison in 1838. Their Declaration read: "We expect to prevail through the foolishness of preaching--striving to commend ourselves into every man's conscience." Garrison is said here to have influenced Tolstoy, who influenced Gandhi. Stiehm, pp. 60-62.
[6] *Aliens and Dissenters: Federal Suppression of Radicals, 1903-1933* (Cambridge: Harvard University Press, 1963), pp. 3, 6.
[7] Stevens, *Jailed*, pp. 92-93; Fry, Paul interview, p. 214.
[8] Mabel Vernon to Elizabeth S. Rogers, June 13, 1917; telegram from Paul to Lillian Ascough, June 21, 1917, Reel 44, NWPP.
[9] Elsie Hill to Beatrice Castleton, June 16, 1917, Reel 44; Abby Scott Baker to Madame B. A. Bakhrnetieff, June 20, 1917, Reel 44, NWPP. N. A. Bessaraboff, the "Junior Inspector of the Russian Artillery Commission" wrote Paul: "From all my heart and soul I am proud of the courage of American women, who so boldly defends real liberty and democracy. . . . In Russia, different kind of oppressors did the very same thing as American police does now . . . Your high ideals are an unlimited source of joy." June 20, 1917, Reel 44, NWPP. (Grammar unchanged.) Letter released to public by NWP.
[10] Alice Paul to Marion May, June 21, 1917, Reel 44, NWPP.
[11] Katharine Morey, "A Statement From a Picket," *Suffragist*, June 30, 1917. In 1915 the WP had moved its Washington headquarters from a dark, cramped space on F Street to the gracious Cameron House (thanks largely to contributions from Alva Belmont and Dora Sedgwick Hazard) on 21 Madison Place. Irwin, *Paul and the NWP*, p. 125. It is now an executive dining room--the one Amelia Fry and I stormed in 1983.
[12] Grimes report, June 21, 1917, FBI File 108, 250, Document 21025, Reel 208.
[13] John Theurer to Woodrow Wilson, June 23, 1917, Reel 210, Wilson Papers on Microfilm.
[14] Stevens, *Jailed*, pp. 92-96; Irwin, *Paul and the NWP*, pp. 227-228. The arrestees were: on June 22, Katherine Morey and Lucy Burns; June 23, Dora Lewis, Gladys Greiner, Mabel Vernon, Virginia Arnold; June 25, Vernon, Burns, Greiner, Morey, Dock, Arnold, Jamison, Arniel, Vivian Pierce and Hazel Hunkins. Nearly all were NWP officers and organizers.
[15] *Suffragist*, June 27, 1917, p. 9.

[16] Report of breakfast on June 17, Reel 44, NWPP; Irwin, *Paul and the NWP*, p. 487; Stevens, *Jailed*, appendix.
[17] *Norfolk Ledger-Dispatch*, July 20, 1917; Stevens, *Jailed*, appendix; NWP Report on jailings, June 1917, Reel 89, NWPP.
[18] Paul to Grace Henshaw, July 3, 1917, Reel 45, NWPP.
[19] Fisher to Mabel Vernon, July 2, 1917, Reel 45, NWPP.
[20] *New York Times*, July 5, 1917, p. 9; Stevens, *Jailed*, p. 96. On Young, Stevens, appendix; Paul to Joy Young, December 27, 1917, Reel 53, NWPP; Irwin, *Paul and the NWP*, p. 230.
[21] Irwin, *Paul and the NWP*, pp. 231-232.
[22] *Directory of Amarillo, Texas, 1907,* Volume I, p. 189; NWP Press Release, January 23, 1919, Reel 92, NWPP; *Amarillo Daily News*, July 5, p. 1; July 7, p. 1.
[23] July 12, 1917, Reel 45, NWPP.
[24] *Suffragist*, July 21, 1917, p. 4. The sixteen "Bastille" prisoners were: Allison Hopkins, Betsy Reyneau, Julia Hurlbut, Minnie Abbott, Anne Martin, Beatrice Kinkead, Amelia Walker, Florence Bayard Hilles, Matilda Gardner, Janet Fotheringham, Eunice Brannan, Elizabeth Rogers, Louise Mayo, Doris Stevens, Mary Ingham and Eleanor Calnan. Anne Howard, *Long Campaign*, p. 118; *New York Times*, July 20, 1917, p. 1; Stevens, *Jailed*, pp. 115-116. On Abbott, *Atlantic City News*, July 21, 1917, pp. 1-2.
[25] *Washington Post*, June 21, 1917, p.1. The *Post*, after this report, would have very scanty coverage of the pickets, probably because of government censorship.
[26] *New York Times*, June 21, 1917, p.1; June 22, 1917, p.5; June 27, p. 8. White feathers of cowardice were given to men who, because of their conscientious objections, refused to go to war. *Washington Post* quote, June 23, 1917, p.1. The *Post* reported Lucy Burns shifted her position so a movie cameraman could get a better shot of her.
[27] June 21, 1917, p. 12.
[28] *Opponents of War* (University of Wisconsin Press, 1957), pp. 45-46.
[29] *Suffragist*, June 27, 1917, p. 12; Lillian Ascough to Paul, June 21, 1917; Edith Bigelow to Paul, June 21, 1917, and late June correspondence, to early July, Reel 44, NWPP.
[30] Congressman John Small to Sophie Meredith, July 7, 1917, Reel 45, NWPP.
[31] At the end of July, 101 members were gained, 70 lost, for a total number of members of 27,747. *Suffragist* circulation was 4,895. July 1917 Executive Secretary Report, Reel 87; July correspondence, Reel 45, NWPP. On NAWSA, David Morgan, *Suffragists*, p. 120; Madeleine M. Watson to Virginia Arnold, July 19, 1917; Florence Manion to Anne Martin, July 7; Spencer to Hunkins, July 7, 1917; *Philadelphia Inquirer*, July 9, 1917 all on Reel 45, NWPP.

[32] Cahill to Paul, June 21, 1917; C. Spencer telegram to Burns, June 21, Eastmans to Burns, June 21, 1917, Reel 44, NWPP; Lucy Burns quote in *Suffragist*, June 27, 1917, p. 9. Also see late June correspondence, Reel 44, NWPP.
[33] *Suffragist*, July 28, 1917, pp. 7-10; Howe to Burns, July 20, 1917, Reel 45, NWPP.
[34] Mabel Vernon to Kathleen Paul, July 2, 1917. The policy of the NWP was always to send a copy of the *Suffragist* to critics. Reel 45, NWPP.
[35] Anne Martin, statement to Mrs. James Laidlaw, Mrs. Frank Vanderlip, and Mrs. Guilford Dudley of the New York Campaign Committee, July 11, 1917, Reel 45, NWPP. She used passages from this statement at her July 16th trial.
[36] *Suffragist*, June 30, 1917, p. 5.
[37] Fry, Paul interview, pp. 218, 225.
[38] Iris Calderhead to Margaret Whittemore, July 20, 1917, Reel 45; Minutes of executive committee meeting, July 13, 1917, Reel 87, NWPP. The committee: Paul, Burns, Martin, Vernon, Belmont, Brannan, Baker, Gardner, Hilles, Hooker, Hopkins, Lewis, Stevens, Younger, Mary Gertrude Fendall and Elizabeth Kent (who tried to resign).
[39] Mary Ingham to Iris Calderhead, July 10, 1917, Reel 45; Hill to Abby Scott Baker, July 12, 1917, Reel 45, NWPP.
[40] Late June and early July correspondence, Reel 210, Wilson Papers on Microfilm.
[41] *New York Times*, June 22, 1917, p. 5; Gardner, "Why Arresting Pickets is Stupid," *Suffragist*, June 27, 1917, p. 7. Gardner further argued that arresting the pickets violated the Clayton Act, and that the pickets were allowed to march for five months unmolested, so should not suddenly be subject to arrest.
[42] *Washington Post*, June 24, 1917, p. 2; *New York Times*, June 28, 1917, p. 6.
[43] Week of July 14, 1917, see Reel 45, NWPP.
[44] Stevens, *Jailed*, p. 11.
[45] *Scannell's New Jersey First Citizens, 1917-1918*, pp. 267-268; Irwin, *Paul and the NWP*, p. 110.
[46] *New York Times*, July 18, 1917, pp. 1, 5; July 12, 1917, p. 1.
[47] A. Brisbane to Joseph Tumulty, July 20, 1917; and Tumulty to Wilson, July 21, 1917; Wilson to Tumulty, July 21, 1917, Reel 210, Wilson Papers on Microfilm.
[48] Louis Brownlow, *A Passion for Anonymity* (University of Chicago Press, 1958), p. 74. He said he and Pullman were originally CU members! His wife was a local NAWSA officer, and he often consulted with Catt and Shaw, pp. 76, 79. The *Washington Post* showed similar hysteria when reporting on "draft riots," saying the demonstrators "threatened violence and even murder on the 50 or more police." June 24, 1917, p. 1.
[49] Ascough to Burns, August 2, 1917, Reel 46, NWPP.

[50] Virginia Arnold to Helen Hill, July 24, 1917, Reel 46, NWPP; *New York Times*, July 12, 1917, p. 11; Martin to James and E. M. Garrett, July 9, 1917, Reel 45, NWPP; *Suffragist*, July 21, 1917, p. 9.
[51] Iris Calderhead to Margaret Whittemore, July 20, 1917, Reel 45, NWPP.
[52] Maude Sorrels to Editor, *Suffragist*, July 31, 1917, Reel 46, NWPP.
[53] Katzenstein, *Lifting the Curtain*, pp. 208-209.
[54] *Suffragist*, August 18, 1917, p. 7.
[55] Burns to Aline E. Solomons, August 13, 1917, Reel 46, NWPP; Paul, in the *Suffragist*, August 18, 1917, p. 7.
[56] *New York Times*, August 10, 1917, p. 8. J. A. H. Hopkins told Wilson his "government had been autocratic." He listed, along with no action on woman suffrage, the closing of newspapers, preparation of a "Secret Black List," and the persecution of hundreds of IWW men in the West. Hopkins to Edwin Webb, Chairman House Judiciary Committee, August 9, 1917, Reel 46, NWPP. At that time, Hopkins urged Wilson to make suffrage a war measure and told him it could be passed. Hopkins was told by Wilson he did "not object" to and was "not annoyed" by the pickets, also in the *Suffragist*, August 25, 1917, p. 6.
[57] Doris Stevens, *Jailed*, pp. 122-124.
[58] Stuyvesant to Catharine Flanagan, November 23, 1917, Reel 81, NWPP; *Chicago Tribune*, August 19, 1917, p. 3; Irwin, *Paul and the NWP*, pp. 237-239; Stevens, *Jailed*, pp. 125-126, appendix; Watson to Virginia Arnold, July 12, 1917, Reel 45, NWPP.
[59] Irwin, *Paul and the NWP*, p. 480; *Colorado Springs Gazette*, August 3, 1917; Spencer to Hazel Hunkins, August 3, 1917, Reel 46, NWPP; Ford, Reyher interview, Kendall's "Garrett Philosopher," *Buffalo Express*, September 1917.
[60] Rogers to Stuyvesant, August 24, 1917, Reel 47; *Suffragist*, August 25, 1917, p. 6; Stevens, *Jailed*, pp. 125-127; appendix.
[61] Young to Iris Calderhead, August 29, 1917, Reel 47; Hurlbut to Lucy Burns, August 16, 1917, Reel 46; Hopkins to Katharine Morey, September 7, 1917, Reel 48; Ingham to Paul, August 20, 1917, Reel 47, NWPP. In September it was a gain of 84 and a loss of 58 members. Executive Secretary Report, August and September 1917, Reel 87. Rogers to Paul, September 2, 1917, Reel 47; *Suffragist* Circulation Report, September 21, 1917 said circulation was 17,000, Reel 49; Hepburn to Paul, August 1917, Reel 48; Advisory Council Report, 1921, Reel 87, NWPP. Mrs. William Prendergast, Mrs. John White, Mrs. Nina Proctor, Mrs. William Lemar and Mrs. Lewis Delafield resigned.
[62] *New York Times,* August 15, 1917, p. 3.
[63] Anne Martin, August Legislature Report, 1917, Reel 87 and August 20, 1917 Martin report, Reel 47, NWPP. A vaudeville manager in Indianapolis asked Margaret Whittemore to go on the circuit with the picket story [!] but Whittemore suggested Vida Milholland would be better. Whittemore to Burns, August 14,

1917, Reel 46, NWPP. Whittemore was not at all sure it was a proper thing to do, in any case.

[64] Elizabeth Stanton's son Theodore voiced his warm support for the women who were suffering jail for an ideal. Stanton to Elizabeth Rogers, September 12, 1917, Reel 48, NWPP. He was still upset it was the "Anthony" woman suffrage amendment though. On Lindbergh, Lindbergh to Wilson, August 27, 1917, Reel 210, Wilson Papers on Microfilm; on Hale, *New York Times*, August 26, 1917, p. 22.

[65] *New York Times*, July 9, 1917, p. 8.

[66] *Chicago Tribune*, August 19, 1917, Part I, p. 3.

Chapter Six

Radicalization: Political Prisoners, Late 1917

> We are put out of jail as we were put in jail--at the whim of the government. They tried to terrorize and suppress us. They could not, and so freed us. The administration has found that it dare not imprison American women for asking for a share in the democracy for which we are fighting. . . . [T]he arrests were unjust, arbitrary and gross discrimination made in an attempt to suppress legitimate propaganda, an attempt which failed.
>
> NWP Press Release, November 27, 1917

By the fall of 1917, National Woman's Party militants had travelled a long way since marching in the suffrage parade on Wilson's 1913 inauguration day. In October the jailed pickets demanded to be treated as political prisoners, and refused food until the Wilson administration granted them that status. The government's response was what the women called "administration terrorism": prison beatings and forced feeding. This third stage of militancy, reached in late 1917, was the height of the suffrage militancy: the women became radicalized in their view of government and of men. The government crackdown of late summer, the 60-day sentences at the workhouse, and the police attacks, all for "obstructing traffic," illustrated the administration's view that the women were not only "madwomen," but political subversives, threats to national security. In the face of public, government-sponsored male violence, the NWP countered with the most potent weapon of their "womanly," nonviolent, "passive" resistance--the hunger strike. Woman's Party feminists demanded political rights for women, and had been beaten and jailed for their persistence. As far as they were concerned, this made them *political*, not criminal, offenders and they endured a terrible ordeal to make this point.

In September, the NWP fight was already perceived as a struggle against a repressive government: by the party itself, by an increasingly sympathetic public audience, and especially, by its large contingent of leftist supporters. Radical leftists were not drawn by "tactics" (as Cott has argued) so much as by a shared critique of an oppressive, undemocratic, unjust--male--government. The suffrage radicals continued to make headlines, gaining more friends *and* detractors, with the hunger strikes for political prisoner status in October. In November, the struggle reached its most dramatic point, with the government-sponsored "Night of Terror" against the suffrage prisoners, followed by whole-sale forced feedings of militant hunger strikers. As Richard Gregg wrote in *The Power of Nonviolence*, to suffer for a cause is very impressive, proving sincerity.[1] The suffering of the suffrage prisoners proved a powerful technique for the militants in converting "onlookers." By December, the radicalized Woman's Party had unreservedly embraced the label of "militant."

Being militant political radicals in late 1917 and 1918 was very brave and also foolhardy. The war against Germany, coupled with the November internationalist Bolshevik revolution in Russia which overthrew Kerensky's liberal government, had made Americans, especially American government authorities, very nervous about political dissent. Possible "Bolshevik" or "Red" new immigrants were deported after being rounded up and held incommunicado until "confessions" were extorted. Mobs would soon be roaming the streets looking for "war opponents" and "traitors": spies would seem to be everywhere. A German-American was lynched in Missouri, the "American Protective League" called anyone who picketed treasonous, and "Boy Spies" watched their families and neighbors for any false moves. Benjamin Salmon, a "violent" conscientious objector, was put into solitary confinement and then organized a hunger strike for which he was put into an insane ward and forced fed. As Lucy Burns and Alice Paul would soon find out, this was apparently standard for leaders of inhouse political rebellions. In October of 1917, Congress passed the Espionage Act which provided penalties of up to 20 years in prison and a $10,000 fine for "abetting the enemy," obstructing recruiting or inciting rebellion within the armed services. On November 22, the *New York Tribune* reported that the Department of Justice was looking into links between militant suffragists and "pacifists, anarchists and anti-war agitators."[2]

By autumn, the militancy of the NWP suffragists had brought them and their cause new fame (or infamy) in the wake of serious government attempts to suppress their demonstrations for women's right to the franchise. There was also a recognition of what their strongly held egalitarian feminism meant in terms of their staying power. Radically feminist Woman's Party actions evoked fear and disgust in upholders of (patriarchal) societal tradition. In September, Joseph Walsh of Massachusetts, a firm opponent of woman suffrage, refused to consider giving women the vote because it would seem

> . . . to yield to the demand of some iron-jawed angels who have been picketing the gateways to the Executive mansion and flaunting in the face of the Chief Magistrate of this Nation banners seemingly treasonable and seditious in character. . . . [They are] poor, bewildered creatures, [who] after their disgusting exhibition can thank their stars that because they wear skirts they are now incarcerated for misdemeanors. . . . [They are reprehensible], posing with their short skirts and short hair. [Applause][3]

Antifeminist sentiment like Walsh's combined with the war frenzy in the air, evoked an escalation in the battle between the "iron-jawed angels" and the administration; it led directly to November's "days of terror."

The "Kaiser" banner pickets had continued in the wake of the August riots, and so had the frantic efforts to stop them. In an infuriating twist, banners often carried the President's own radical words. One of them quoted from his book *The New Freedom*:

> I don't wish to sit down and let any man take care of me without my having at least a voice in it; and if he doesn't listen to my advice, I am going to make it as unpleasant for him as I can. . . .
>
> [Or] We have been told that it is unpatriotic to criticize public action. Well, if it is, then there is a deep disgrace resting upon the origin of this nation. . . . We have forgotten the very principle of our origin if we have forgotten how to object, how to resist, how to agitate, how to pull down and build up, even to the extent of revolutionary practices, if it be necessary to readjust matters.[4]

On September 4th, in punishment for reminding the president what he had said, 13 women agitators were arrested and sent to Occuquan Workhouse for 60 days. On September 13th and 22nd, six and then four more, received 30 days.

If six of the thirteen "revolutionaries" jailed on September 4th are considered, they seem to be from quite bourgeois backgrounds. They were veteran NWP leaders and organizers Lucy Burns, Abby Scott Baker, Lucy Branham, Mary Winsor, Eleanor Calnan of Massachusetts and Edith Ainge from Jamestown, New York. Ainge said she was determined to give herself for the cause of democracy in America as her brother was in France. The other seven, quite respectable seeming women, were all veteran suffrage workers in their home states. One, Pauline Adams, a doctor's wife from Norfolk, Virginia, echoed Ainge, saying she was "ready to suffer for the cause of American democracy." Fifty-one-year-old newspaperwoman Ada Davenport Kendall stated that if she died for women's rights in prison, it would not have been in vain. She wanted to focus the attention of the world on the fact that as an unenfranchised citizen she was denied the right to have any voice in the decision to wage the war in which her sons lost their lives in the trenches.[5] The women jailed for picketing were more than willing to fight for what they thought was right, and against what they perceived as an autocratic government.

In mid-September it was suggested that men picket, but Paul vetoed the idea, saying there were not enough of them "willing to make a show." Besides, jailed militants knew their fight was a women's fight. Organizer Julia Emory may have been outwardly "frail" and slight, but she was "outraged" with the arrests and wanted to "break the judge and the lying witnesses."[6] In the third stage of militancy, many feminists from families far removed from the comfortable classes took part; this included a burgeoning number of leftist women, who were drawn to the militants' campaign as an important civil liberties struggle, as well as an all-out female struggle for power in a male-run society. The September 13th prisoners included labor organizers Nina Samarodin and Anna Gwinter, government worker Ruth Crocker, and social worker Katharine Fisher, along with Ada Davenport Kendall and "Mrs. Mark Jackson" (who turned out to be an FBI "plant"). All the women arrested on September 22nd had socialist leanings; these recruits perceived the NWP fight as a radical fight against a repressive government for free speech, and for equal rights for all women. They were: Hilda Blumberg, Ernestine Hara, Peggy Baird Johns and Margaret Wood Kessler (the woman who had caused Paul such concern in Colorado in 1915). Russian immigrant Blumberg, a teacher of "ethical culture," and one of the youngest pickets, described the pickets as "all working women, professional and otherwise." Student Ernestine Hara, a Rumanian-American Jew said when arrested, "As a radical, I believe in justice." Socialist Peggy Baird Johns, a newspaperwoman and magazine writer, was one of the first to suggest the women demand status as political prisoners. The ever vigilant FBI cited suffrage prisoner Ruth Crocker at the end of September: "They may think they can scare us into giving up. I guess they can make us sick but they can't make us quit."[7] Woman suffrage had evolved into a radical cause.

Repressive actions by government authorities convinced the jailed suffragists that their view of the hypocritical and autocratic nature of the government had been proven correct, but they also obviously realized the publicity value of the repression. Government violence just gave nonviolent woman suffrage protesters added public visibility and increased sympathy, even among Congressmen. On September 15th, suffrage was reported out of committee, and on the 24th the House finally created a standing woman suffrage committee. It is no doubt debatable why these moves happened when they did, but woman suffrage *was* voted out of committee the day after its chairman visited Occuquan Workhouse. The debate in the House on the 24th included a great deal of comment about the pickets, not always favorable to be sure, but the pickets had undoubtedly made suffrage newsworthy. The resignation of Dudley Field Malone, Wilson's campaign manager and then collector of the Port of New York, also affected Congress. Malone had become increasingly upset with the Administration's handling of the pickets, influenced no doubt by the fact that he was very much in love with Doris Stevens. In his resignation letter Malone wrote that if American *men* demanding the vote had been ignored by government for 50 years, their "inevitable impatience and righteous indignation" would be understood.[8]

The "inevitable impatience" of the NWP was not completely comprehended in the House of Representatives. Even their friends could not quite bring themselves to condone picketing. Congressman Andrew Volstead did not approve of picketing, but he strongly disapproved of the "hoodlum methods used in suppressing the practice," and argued it was obvious that women did need the vote to protect themselves. New York's socialist Meyer London gave a moving speech which began with "a woman is either a human being or she is not," but ended with his usual long lecture on the evils of property qualifications.[9] The general consensus was, that although the pickets themselves "might not deserve" the vote, women like Carrie Chapman Catt did, and should not be denied because of the "iron-jawed angels." So, although many in Congress denied that the pickets and their treatment did influence them, and worried that passing suffrage would be "yielding to the outrageous nagging of these wild women," NWP "Political Chairman" Abby Scott Baker said that the adamant opposition of the "antis" was a "great tribute" to their efforts, and that it was the NWP that had caused the administration to yield.[10] The arrests and longer jail sentences with their publicity, had escalated the NWP's war for democracy, but they still had a range of militant, nonviolent weapons from which to choose.

In October, schooled by the campaign of the British militants and influenced by fellow American dissenters, Lucy Burns and the socialist suffragists led a campaign in prison demanding that the suffragists, jailed as criminal offenders, be treated as political prisoners. They soon backed up their demand with the threat of a hunger strike. The Administration's point of view seemed to be that the NWP suffragists were seditious madwomen who had to be stopped. For all their efforts to make them cease their demonstrations, the Woman's Party continued to protest their lack of political power as women outside and inside prison. According to Ernestine Hara Kettler, (arrested on September 22nd) when she, newspaper writer Peggy Baird Johns, Margaret Wood Kessler and Hilda Blumberg (all socialists) were in the city jail right after sentencing, it was Johns who suggested they demand to be political prisoners. Sympathetic socialist women had begun to be much more apparent among the prisoners by mid-September. Although they were well aware of class differences within the party, socialist suffragists were quick to note the political nature of incarceration for protests demanding *women's* rights, and demanded recognition of the militants as *political* prisoners. The women they later joined at Occuquan Workhouse, including Lucy Burns, and later Alice Paul, all readily assented to the plan, agreeing that they were not criminal "traffic obstructors" as charged, but in reality, just like the jailed anti-war socialists, political offenders imprisoned by their government. This decision also exactly paralleled the action the British militants had decided upon 10 years earlier. After the four women had arrived at Occuquan, and Lucy Burns and the other pickets jailed there accepted the strategy of insisting on political prisoner status, they drafted a letter for the district commissioners asking for political offender privileges. The women stated they would refuse to work like the other offenders, and wanted legal counsel, food, writing materials, books and letters from the outside, opportunities to see each other and Burns taken from solitary confinement. They said they were protesting their unjust and erratic sentences, which ranged from suspended sentences to 60 days for the same offense. The letter was never answered, but the suffragists decided they would not work, stubbornly insisting they were political prisoners.[11]

The radical socialist prisoners were particularly eloquent in describing the plight of women and their lack of freedom in prison. Anna Gwinter, a socialist from the Bronx Waistmakers' Union, said she was "more revolutionary than the Woman's Party" but wanted "to help in the work": "We are enslaved here."[12] Hilda Blumberg called the NWP women "Noble Women," stating that a small group of women by uniting and standing together could accomplish great things. She quoted Alexandre Dumas: "As long as Royalty imprisoned the Nobles, the Bastille stood, but as soon as Royalty attempted to imprison thought the Bastille fell, for thought cannot be imprisoned even behind bars."[13] Nina Samarodin was shocked to find there was "no industrial and political democracy" in America when she came from Russia. In her youth Samarodin had been told women and men were not equal mentally, and hence not politically. She wondered why American women were so slow to go to the White House gates. Samarodin had a brother and many cousins fighting on that Russian front, and she said she was "fighting for American democracy here." Samarodin felt all American women should demand their rights under the Constitution, not beg for them, and should use force if necessary: "Working women of this country arise now and demand your political rights, and prove, that the American woman is strong enough to help herself."[14] The demand for political prisoner status, instigated by Lucy Burns and the radical socialist pickets, was quickly adopted by many of the militants in and out of prison.

Paul's approval of the plan resulted in the remarkably harsh action of her being placed in a psychopathic ward, and being forced fed when she decided to hunger strike alone, in protest. A month before Paul actually went out on the picket line herself, Doris Stevens, ever protective of the "General" warned Paul that she should not picket because it would be an excuse for the authorities to give her a six-month sentence. But as soon as she thought she could spare the time, on October 6th, Paul led 11 women on a picket of Congress's Emergency War Session. There is a photograph (See Figure 7) of women on that picket line in the NWP papers, that speaks volumes about feelings of those banner-holders. They have very tense white mouths. Their poles are held rigidly and their eyes are filled with dread, as an arresting officer and a crowd of men look on. The crowd and police were very rough that day, tearing up all the banners, even that held by "the pale little leader."[15]

When she was tried two days later, Paul insisted (echoing Susan B. Anthony) the pickets were not subject to the Court, since they were without voice in the making of the law. Sentence was suspended then, but not when four of the October 6th pickets--organizers Maud Jamison and Rose Winslow, Pennsylvania art student Kate Heffelfinger and Minnie Hennesy, a self-supporting business-woman from Connecticut--returned to picket a week later. They were sentenced to six months at Occuquan. On October 20, Alice Paul led out organizers Gertrude Crocker (sister of Ruth) and Gladys Greiner, with Colorado officer Caroline Spencer, bearing a very timely banner, a slogan from the Liberty Bond drive: "The Time Has Come To Conquer Or Submit, For Us There Can Be But One Choice.

The pickets are arrested. Catharine Flanagan is on the left and Madeleine Watson on the right.
Figure 7

We Have Made It." On October 22nd, they were sentenced to six months at Occuquan--Spencer and Paul got seven months. That day, Alice Paul wrote her mother: "Dear Mother: I have been sentenced today to seven months imprisonment. Mrs. Lawrence Lewis is going on with the work in my place and will be at headquarters. Please do not worry. It will merely be a delightful rest. With love, Alice." Perhaps she did think it would be a rest. After all, according to Virginia Arnold, "She was working and dictating practically until the Black Maria came!"[16]

In jail, in true nonviolent resistance non-cooperation, Paul led a militant rebellion from the inside. The first thing she wanted to reform in the District Jail was the lack of fresh air. Finally the prisoners succeeded in breaking a window, and followed this with other actions, determining on "rebellion . . . to make it impossible to keep us in jail." Ernestine Hara Kettler remembered that time as "raising Cain . . . I remember that after we ate, we'd take the tin plates and throw them . . . at the windows. . . . We raised so much hell."[17] After two weeks, only seven women, those with longer sentences, remained at the jail. Too weak from illness and poor food to move, Rose Winslow and Paul were taken to the prison hospital and together decided to hunger strike.

Paul wrote Dora Lewis a letter composed on the fly leaves of her *Oxford Book of English Verse*; she explained that she and Winslow wanted to be treated like political prisoners "in accordance with the plan started by the 60 day group." Arguing with prison officials proved useless, so after arriving at the hospital: "We thought we'd try this method." Showing how conscious she was of her sister British militants, Paul wrote that to feed them well and then starve them was a different form of the Cat and Mouse Act of England. She had thought of the hunger strike as "short term" so that "we could direct the affair, and just ourselves knew of it." However, since the world found out, "I suppose we are committed to the plan and must go forward!" Paul never wanted her followers to have to go through the ordeal of the hunger strike. In this, Alice Paul, as NWP leader, again foreshadowed Gandhi in the use of the hunger strike. As Stiehm has described it, the behavior of nonviolent resisters has "gradations of actions," and the hunger strike is the pinnacle. Caroline Katzenstein's book on the militant suffrage struggle includes this quote from Mahatma Gandhi to begin her chapter on prison: "A fast is the sincerest form of prayer . . . . It stirs up sluggish consciences and inspires loving hearts to act. Those who have to bring about radical changes in human conditions and surroundings cannot do it without raising a ferment in society." And Paul intended to raise a ferment. Paul wrote Lewis that "things took a more serious turn than I had planned, but it's happened rather well because we'll have ammunition against the Administration, and the more harsh and repressive they seem the better." Paul instructed Lewis to make the most of jail experiences in the "onlooking" press and the *Suffragist*: "We certainly cannot afford to miss a trick during these next few weeks." She said that she and Winslow were having "an interesting time" and it was better than collecting money. Concluding, Paul stressed that their purpose in hunger striking was not to be taken from the hospital to be with the others in jail, but to gain food and political prisoner rights for all suffrage prisoners.[18]

According to the NWP, even "17 murderers" were granted special food, fresh air, exercise and newspapers; but not the NWP pickets. The suffrage prisoners were given bad food until ill and hospitalized, then fed well and put back in prison--exactly what Paul and Winslow struck to prevent. In an "underground" letter, the prisoners wrote organizer Beulah Amidon to tell Paul that they were receiving food and exercise and were considering hunger striking to get Paul and Winslow back, but it would only work with publicity. They instructed the women at headquarters to refer to the hunger strike as "attitude" since their mail was opened.[19] Alice Paul and the Woman's Party had turned the passive resistance technique of the hunger strike into a powerful weapon against Wilson, but the Administration soon struck back.

The government authorities, according to Paul, at this point went to great lengths to try to discredit her, thinking the rest of the NWP would "disown this crazy person." After a week of hunger striking and being threatened with forced feeding and the insane asylum, Paul and Winslow were force fed. One day a Dr. William White appeared by Paul's bedside to make an "investigation." He was a psychiatrist, what was then called an "alienist." Paul told White, when he asked, the entire history of woman suffrage up to the status of the amendment at that time. What White was really waiting for apparently, was for her to say she was persecuted by the Wilson Administration. White brought District Commissioner Gwynne Gardener and another doctor to "examine" her. (Gardener later falsified his report to Wilson, as will be seen.) Gardener gave the order to begin forcible feeding and to place Paul in the psychopathic ward. Kept there a week, she was not allowed to sleep and was threatened as if insane. She and Winslow were force fed three times a day for three weeks. The *New York Times* reported that Paul had gone on hunger strike, and that she "already had a reputation as a striker in England." They reported she was forcibly fed to "prevent her dying." The article also said her sister Helen Paul was not allowed to see her, and was horrified that such a brutal thing was being done: "She has never been able to tell me about her experience in England, it was so horrible . . . I can't believe the President or the men he has appointed would risk her life."[20] Dora Lewis protested to Commissioner Gardener about Paul and Winslow's treatment and insisted that NWP prisoners, as "government enemies," should be treated as political prisoners. She also told him forcible feeding was inhuman and unnecessary--it was being used to discipline and not to save life. Testimony of many of the suffrage prisoners regarding Superintendent Raymond Whittaker's threats uphold Lewis's belief. Margaret Wood Kessler reported that Whittaker told her, "We are going to stop this picketing if it costs the lives of some of your women and it will cost the lives of some of these women but we are going to stop it."[21] The strategy of stopping the

NWP picketing through intimidating their leader had not succeeded, nor did threats of further punishment.

The violent attacks and arrests, and the harshness of life in prison, had not fazed the militants, now intent on achieving political prisoner status. The women, at the height of their militancy, stood ready to suffer new government attacks; and with their publication, ride a wave of public sympathy to victory. November's "Night of Terror" in prison, and large-scale hunger strikes and forced feedings, did make headlines. Knowing the sort of punishment they faced, the Woman's Party turned out in large numbers on November 10th to register their displeasure with the incarceration and treatment of Alice Paul. The night before they marched and were arrested, 41 women had gone to the District Jail, to Paul's window. There they had managed to call out their names, the sum of money coming into the treasury, and the news of the protest picket they would hold the next day. The pickets were applauded by a crowd of onlookers, particularly 73-year-old suffrage pioneer, Mary A. Nolan from Jacksonville, Florida. The Irish Catholic Nolan had been a teacher and education activist in the South and was then prominent in "Confederate organizations." Nolan, a descendent of the Revolutionary War heroine, Elizabeth Zane, told the judge at her trial, "I should be proud of the honor to die in prison for the liberty of American women."[22] The 41 pickets were dismissed without sentence, but only an hour later, 31 women were again picketing the White House. The crowd was not so friendly this time. Two soldiers attacked Boston leader Agnes Morey and jabbed her splintered banner pole between her eyes. Grandmother Dora Lewis was knocked about by three youths. At court, the women were again told to wait, so the next day went back out to picket. On the 14th these 31 women were sentenced. Nolan was given six days, three women got 15 days, 24 received 30 days. Lewis and Brannan got 60 days and Lucy Burns got six months.[23] On November 17, three more women received 15 days on the November 10th charges. This group of November pickets would suffer the most terrifying period in prison.

The 33 protesters who served their sentences (Elizabeth Kent's husband paid her fine against her wishes) were a wide-ranging group of women, but all were remarkable, strong feminists, quite willing to undergo the harshness of a jail sentence. Five were veteran NWP leaders: Lucy Burns, Anna Kelton Wiley, Lavinia Dock, Dora Lewis and Eunice Dana Brannan. Five were new NWP organizers (four organizers were already in jail, the rest were busy telling the prison story to the country): Julia Emory, Alice and Betty Gram from Oregon, Traveller's Aide worker Kathryn Lincoln, and the youngest picket, Matilda Young, sister of organizer Joy Young. Five of the pickets were state officers: Boston's Agnes Morey, Minnesota's Mary Short, pacifist Camilla Whitcomb from Worcester, Massachusetts, Nellie Barnes from Indianapolis and Alice Cosu from New Orleans. Nine were longtime woman suffragists and reformers: Mary Nolan; Vermonter Lucy J. Daniels, so concerned about black women's participation in 1914; Quaker Rebecca Winsor Evans of Pennsylvania; New York City craftswoman and civic leader Mrs. Henry Butterworth and her companion Cora Week; Smith graduate and settlement worker Phebe Persons Scott from Morristown, New Jersey; reformer and mother of six from Oklahoma City, Kate Stafford; and from Salt Lake City, Utah, LaVerne Robertson and socialist Minnie Quay. Quay later said she had wanted "to do her bit for the freedom of [the] enslaved millions of sisters in . . . our fair land." [24] Such sentiments were shared by all the suffrage prisoners, veteran and novice alike.

The suffrage fight was fairly new to the remaining feminist pickets sent to Occuquan. Four of the November pickets took time from pursuing professional careers to protest in Washington: aviator Mrs. L. H. Hornsby, from New York City; physician Dr. Anna Kuhn from Baltimore; playwright Paula Jakobi, also from New York, author of "Chinese Lily" and an activist in prison reform; and diminutive teacher Amy Juengling from Buffalo, who had taught in Puerto Rico and the North Carolina mountains. The last group of five women to undergo the November ordeal were all radical socialists: New York socialist Hilda Blumberg; New York University student Belle Sheinburg; Ella Findeisen from Lawrence, Massachusetts, who worked for her milk dealer brother and who feared getting ten years for being a "pro-German" socialist; Buffalo probation officer Hattie Kruger, who would run for Congress as a socialist in 1918; and the famed founder of the Catholic Workers' Movement, New Yorker Dorothy Day, then on the staff of the *Masses*. Day had been recruited by Peggy Baird Johns, who said Day "did not really believe in suffrage, but picketed for the cause of free speech." [25] Obviously, this was a very diverse group of women, but united in rage against the suppression of the NWP's demonstrations for women's political rights.

It was this diverse group of prisoners that experienced a particularly rough reception at the hands of prison authorities which they would later call "The Night of Terror." It was when the suffrage prisoners began to demand rights as political prisoners rather than common criminal offenders, that they were subjected to what Doris Stevens called "administration terrorism." Prison and government officials seem to have had lost all patience with the stubborn "suffragettes."[26] Following the lead of the October prisoners, the women jailed in early November 1917 had decided to demand to be political prisoners and refuse food if they were denied that status. When the prisoners arrived at Occuquan on the evening of November 15, Dora Lewis demanded to see Superintendent Whittaker before she and the women would give their names and be processed. After a wait of some hours, Whittaker came in with some guards who were later described by a picket as "a band of wild ruffians." According to Inez Haynes Irwin, Whittaker had just come from a White House Conference of district commissioners; he was in no mood to listen to Lewis's demands and did not hesitate to give the women the treatment he thought they deserved. As mentioned, Whittaker had already told Kessler they would stop the picketing if it cost the lives of some of the women. LaVerne Robertson testified that Whittaker said that night that Lucy Burns and Dora Lewis should be locked into solitary for life, if not shot, and Lucy Burns confirmed he had made threats to kill them.[27]

The demands for political offender status were not even delivered to Whittaker before his men seized Lewis and began what Betty Gram Swing called "the most terrible night of my life." The guards seemed in a frenzy of rage. Lewis had just begun to ask that they be treated as political prisoners, when Whittaker yelled, "You shut up. I have men here to handle you. Seize her!" The women were dragged, carried, and shoved to the cells, including the aged and lame Mary Nolan.[28] Sixty-year-old Lavinia Dock fell down some steps, badly injuring her leg. Alice M. Cosu reported that she was shoved by a man with a club against a cell wall, and had her right leg bruised. "I was completely unnerved. . . . I was sick all night long from the treatment." The other prisoners were afraid she had had a heart attack, but the guards ignored their cries for help. Cosu was so frightened she could barely speak to Whittaker, but he told her "in her work she could stand anything."[29]

New York artist Cora Week had studied art in Boston and exhibited in Paris salons. Week was originally from Wisconsin, of Norwegian farmer background. Week testified that that night at the jail was "one of threat and terrorism":

> [A]s I was sitting in a chair quietly reading a paper two rough guards rushed into the room from the dark night outside, fell upon me from the rear, seized my arms, bending them sharply backward, dragging me backward over the chairtops and suitcases and so out into the darkness. . . I asked what was the necessity of so much violence? [30]

Week's experience was hardly unique; apparently the women had to be taught a lesson about criticizing the government in wartime. Julia Emory was dragged away as she tried to come to the aid of the injured Dora Lewis, whose head had hit the iron bed. When Emory tried to secure her travel bag, Whittaker threatened to slap her face, and when she attempted to get water, she was thrown against a wall and "choked" by guards. The guards were particularly rough with Lucy Burns, a vocal leader at Occuquan, and singled out for special treatment. When she resisted being hauled away, she was beaten. When she refused to stop calling to the other women to determine their injuries, she was threatened with a strait jacket. Then they handcuffed her wrists to the door, high above her head. Julia Emory stood in the same position as Burns all night, in sympathy. Gladys Greiner's waist was covered with blood from the guards who assaulted her for opening a window. Dorothy Day stated she "naturally . . . tried to pull away" from the guards so they pinched her arms, twisted her wrists, then wrestled her down over an iron bench, bruising her back and shoulders. One guard's hand was at her throat. No one treated her injuries. None of the women were treated; they were not even allowed to use the bathrooms. By morning Day was "in an hysterical and sick condition." Hattie Kruger said she had had "several heart attacks" with no treatment and was "terrified." LaVerne Robertson also said she "was in a terrified condition"; and Belle Sheinberg was "terror stricken" at the actions of the guards.[31] Such violence was calculated to intimidate the women into ending their stubborn protest, inside and outside the prison walls. But when the night was over the women were still insisting on their rights as political prisoners.

Still denied the rights they demanded, 16 of the women went on hunger strike. With their nonviolent style of civil disobedience, the only practical resistance to the authorities seemed to them to be, as in the struggle outside, to use publicity, this time through the hunger strike. But hunger striking had its own horrors. As Dorothy Day wrote:

> I would have preferred the workshop to hunger striking--to lie there through the long day, to feel the nausea and emptiness of hunger, the mental activity that came after. I lost all consciousness of any cause--I had no sense of being a radical, making protest against a government, carrying on a non-violent revolution. I could only feel darkness and desolation all around me . . . the bitter awareness of the need to endure somehow through the days of my imprisonment.[32]

Lucy Daniels remembered that on the fourth day of her fast, a rat took the toast they left her. Organizer Kathryn Lincoln said a "spirit of calm determination" at first pervaded her while she fasted, but soon the days "became an eternity." She saw "shadows--corners of the room moving together," and would throw herself on the bed sobbing.[33] The hunger strike was bad enough in itself, but as a weapon against the authorities, as Alice Paul and Lucy Burns knew only too well, it had an even worse counter weapon: "forcible feeding."

Forcible feeding of some of the hunger strikers that November was done ostensibly to save lives, but the procedure was so cruel that it can only be seen as a further punishment, another inducement for the NWP to stop picketing and stop their political prisoner demands. At least six were regularly forced fed--the first were Paul and Rose Winslow after their hospital hunger strike, and then Kate Heffelfinger after she refused food.[34] Rose Winslow reported that when forced fed she had "a nervous time of it, gasping a long time afterwards . . . I heard myself making the most hideous sounds. . . . Don't let them tell you we take this well. Miss Paul vomits much. I do, too. . . . It is horrible."[35] On November 21 forcible feeding of Dora Lewis and Lucy Burns, the ring leaders, began, and then Elizabeth McShane was fed, after attempting to speak to Burns (the other Irish rebel) while Burns was in solitary confinement. Lewis wrote her daughter that she told the doctor the second time she could not and would not "take the stuff" because of the pain, but he brought three men and three nurses, and they wedged her mouth open.[36] Lucy Burns, a veteran of Holloway, was held down by five people and refused to open her mouth, so that the doctor pushed the glass tube up her nostril.

She said "it hurts nose and throat very much and makes nose bleed freely."[37] Organizer Elizabeth McShane was a Vassar graduate, a former school principal in Indianapolis and businesswoman in Philadelphia. She had once helped the Pennsylvania AMA do a health survey. McShane wrote a report which was graphic, and is worth quoting in full to show the extent of the horrors of this "medical treatment":

> I know I sound insane, but I've just had the most revolting experience possible. I've been forcibly fed, and I feel that every atom of American self-respect within me has been outraged. . . . They said they would check my heart, but didn't. . . . Dr. Ladd appeared with a tube that looked like a hose, and a pint of milk in which two eggs had been stirred up. Without any heart exam, he put the tube in my mouth and told me to swallow it fast. I did it as fast as I could, but he pushed it down so fast that I gagged and choked terribly. Finally the tube was at what felt like the bottom of my stomach, and my heart was beating so fast that I couldn't get my breath. The he poured the liquid rapidly down the tube. Of course a stomach that has been unaccustomed to food for a week cannot take so much liquid cold, all in half a minute. That was the actual time. So before he was half through, it began, to come up, out of the corners of my mouth and down my neck until my hair was stiff with it. Tried to bite the tube and to pinch it with my hands, to check the flow for a second, but it poured on until all was finished. When he pulled the tube out, it was followed by a large part of the food. Thereupon the matron and he walked away, leaving me in that messy condition, to die if I chose. I couldn't bring it all up at once, . . . as my muscles were all trying to do, for other prisoners were eating just outside . . . Lucy Burns comforted me. It was her *fifth* time.

McShane developed stomach ulcers and a gall bladder infection, but the feeding was repeated.[38]

Besides using forcible feeding, the doctors and matrons "tried to persuade, bully and threaten" the suffragists out of "sticking to their purpose," the hunger strike.[39] The terror and brutality in prison, with the ordeals of hunger striking and forcible feeding, did not force the militants to give up their protest.

In the end, under public pressure, it was the President who had to give in, to release the prisoners. On November 23, Judge Edmund Wadill decided the 31 suffragists had been illegally committed to Occuquan (they were supposed to be at the District Jail), and they could either be paroled on bail or finish their terms at the District Jail. Twenty-two decided to return to jail. It seemed clear that the militants' spirit was not broken. They were all released on November 27-28.[40]

When she was freed, Alice Paul stated that the pickets were released just as they were arrested--at the whim of the government, in a futile attempt "to suppress legitimate propaganda." The government had "tried to terrorize and suppress" women for "asking for a share in the democracy for which we are fighting." But, she said, the Administration "found it dare not" imprison them.[41] Christine Lunardini has argued that if Wilson had "kept a tight rein" on district officials, then things would not have gotten out of hand.[42] The testimony of the suffragists themselves, however, and of historians such as Inez H. Irwin, give Wilson personal responsibility for the pickets' treatment. Wilson had become more and more convinced that NWP women were beyond the pale. He wrote Carrie Chapman Catt in October that he hoped no voters were influenced by the "so-called pickets": "However justly they may have laid themselves open to serious criticism, their actions represent, I am sure, so small a fraction of the women of the country who are urging the adoption of woman suffrage that it would be most unfair and argue a narrow view to allow their action to prejudice the cause itself."[43] Even New York Secret Service head W. G. Flynn reported to Wilson that he thought the jailed women were "being treated very harshly" after receiving a letter from NWP prisoner Ada Davenport Kendall. Wilson replied he did "not think that this lady is in the condition of mind to discuss the matter." But then Wilson wondered if District Commissioner Louis Brownlow knew the real conditions at Occuquan, and wanted to be certain there was no foundation for Kendall's statements.[44] The President was already inclined not to believe women like Kendall.

After receiving more such letters of protest and the *Suffragist*'s open letter hotly protesting Paul's forcible feeding (along with some letters saying the NWP was working for the Republicans), Wilson ordered an investigation. As mentioned, Commissioner Gwynne Gardener visited Paul and saw the conditions under which she and the others were being held, but still chose to tell the President what he wanted to hear--that everything was fine. Gardener's prison report said there was good food, conditions were sanitary; and Winslow and Paul were well, in clean, well-ventilated rooms. Forcible feeding, an "every-day occurrence" in many institutions, was done to a "willing" Winslow and Paul--a true contradiction in terms! All the matrons and guards had acted with "good order and discipline," but the NWP women had "beforehand a set purpose and plan to violate very rule of these institutions," breaking windows and striking walls with their shoes. District Commissioner Brownlow characterized (even later, in 1958) the DC jails as wonderful, comfortable places, and proudly described forced feeding as "our edition of [the British] Cat and Mouse."[45] Obviously, the NWP "madwomen" were imagining things.

The Wilson administration consistently stated that the NWP's prison situation was perfectly fine. When Mary Beard with 50 New York woman suffragists, mostly from the WTUL, protested against the suffragists' treatment at the White House, Wilson suggested to Joseph Tumulty that he tell Beard "that the treatment of the women picketeers has been grossly exaggerated."[46] Even some NAWSA members wrote worried letters to Wilson about the forced feeding, but Wilson's reply reflected wholehearted belief in Gardener's report. "[N]o real harshness of method is being used, these ladies [are] submitting to the artificial feeding without resistance." He insisted that no abuses had been disclosed, but any that were would be corrected, "there being an extraordinary amount of lying about the thing." Wilson concluded that the United States had no political prisoners, and that the NWP suffragists "offended against an ordinance of the District and are undergoing the punishment appropriate in the circumstances."[47] In other words, Wilson thought disobeying a traffic regulation, a misdemeanor, should be punished by harsh treatment at the workhouse.

The NWP put the responsibility for the women prisoners' harsh jail treatment squarely on Wilson. Doris Stevens wrote on November 16 that there was a rumor (and the *New York Tribune* confirmed it) that "President Wilson met with the commissioners yesterday afternoon to decide what to do about the suffragists," and was satisfied with their reports of the way the situation was being handled. They agreed no one was to see Alice Paul. The NWP had (and we have) no proof that the President *directed* the campaign against the suffragists, but it certainly appeared he consented to it. This meeting was the same that Superintendent Whittaker was to have left when he came back to the institute the "Night of Terror" at Occuquan. Stevens was aghast at "the lengths the commissioners . . . are going in order to force us to retreat from our position."[48] An NWP organizers' handbill printed at the time, read: "Who appoints the District of Columbia Board of Charities which controls Occuquan and the jail? Woodrow Wilson.--Who appointed the judges who sentenced the suffragists? Woodrow Wilson."[49]

By this time the authorities certainly considered the NWP seditious and dangerously radical; the Administration took steps beyond forcible feeding to keep the militants suppressed. W. J. Flynn wrote Leland Harrison at the Department of State that William Randolph Hearst [whose wife Phoebe Hearst was in the NWP] was about to start a "vast peace propaganda" drive in his paper. This propaganda would be "conducted in such a fashion as to appeal to the Jewish, Socialist, Pacifist, Militant Suffragists and Russian elements in this country."[50] He then suggested the Administration "make some discreet use" of information it possessed regarding Hearst's "connection with German propaganda in this country."[51] NWP leaders felt that their flamboyant actions were probably the only way to get front page news, and "attract the wild war mad people," even if press coverage was negative, and felt, even with NWP speakers out to give their side of events, that the press was antagonistic because it was predominantly "under government control."[52] Rebecca Hourwich (Reyher) stated that the local postmasters in Pensacola, Florida were "kowtowing to Washington" and only printed stories approved by propaganda minister George Creel. In Washington, DC, wrote organizer Iris Calderhead, censorship of the press was rigorous, "by a gentleman's agreement amongst the correspondents in Washington, only comments favorable to "the administration pass."[53] Some NWP women were slandered as individuals:

the *New York Tribune* published two letters, apparently received through the Administration, to socialist Peggy Baird Johns. One was from her father joking about the salary she was receiving from the Germans; the other was from a friend called "A. Turner" who (also in jest) suggested Johns should blow up the White House. Doris Stevens scoffed at the charges, saying "the pro-German accusation has gotten so pale that it makes very little impression." Still, the *Rocky Mountain News* reported that "German propaganda sent Mrs. Kessler [another socialist] to Washington." Kessler sued.[54] The government, determined to end the "seditious" picketing, used the power of the press as well as its new security organization.

Ever vigilant, the Secret Service kept tabs on the NWP all over the country, starting in 1917. By then, "The Bureau" had become a valuable part of Wilson's Justice Department, with 300 agents out investigating espionage. It is just possible that one of its agents infiltrated the picket line. The FBI files contain a *Baltimore Evening Sun* article on "Mrs. Mark Jackson," who was arrested for picketing in September and was released after three days. Jackson said that the pickets were treated well and if they were not, it was because of their own "bad behavior." Jackson went on to say her fellow pickets were "anarchists and revolutionaries" and that five of them attacked her. NWP leaders found out Jackson was an infiltrator and her husband was a long time "scab" and anti-union agent.[55] Mr. Wilson's brother alerted the FBI that he had also been informed that the women were anarchists, that two of the pickets were pro-German and one was associated with Emma Goldman. The FBI kept track of Matilda Gardner after she protested to Louis Brownlow, and they were sent a letter to Wilson from a Mr. Morton Schanberg protesting against the treatment of suffrage pickets to Wilson.[56]

The administration's Secret Service also kept a close watch on NWP organizers out on the speaking circuit. Rebecca Reyher says that she was followed by Secret Service men, perhaps particularly because her father was a Russian Jew; Ella Thompson said the Service kept an eye on her. Their watchful presence in New Jersey caused Abby Scott Baker to argue at a public meeting that Alice Paul was not against Liberty Bonds, the war or conscription. Charlotte Perkins Gilman helped win over that hostile group by praising the pickets' courage and comparing the crowds watching the picket arrests to those in front of bulletin boards with the World Series scores[57]--yet another source of news to keep the NWP off the front page. Anne Martin was especially plagued by the Secret Service, several of them attending many of her meetings; one even listened at her door. One reason for such vigilance may have been Martin's willingness to make statements such as "Russia fears World War I is only a capitalistic war" because the United States "democracy" jails its women. In Los Angeles the Bureau man told her there would be no meeting, but she told him there was freedom of speech and assembly, and he could come arrest her if she said something seditious. "The hand of the administration is certainly reaching out after us. The prison story gets the women and they fear it." Martin argued that criticism of President Wilson for blocking woman suffrage was not treason--not an overt act against the country.[58] To the government, however, the NWP speakers were wild and treasonous radicals, dangerous enough to be spied upon.

NWP militant feminism had become anathema to the Administration and to right-thinking American patriots, but a cause célèbre to "other" American radicals. It was November 22nd when the *New York Tribune* reported a link between the NWP and "pacifists, anarchists and anti-war agitators." The NWP's connection with socialists Peggy Baird Johns, Crystal Eastman, Sara Bard Field, Vida Milholland and Joy Young were supposedly incriminating. Elizabeth Selden Rogers denied any links with anarchists but voiced gratitude for the support of socialists.[59] When the NWP searched for support and speaking platforms from various groups that fall--Baptists, Jewish women, high school business teachers, milk producers and brick layers--most of them put off the NWP request,[60] but this was not so of fellow dissenters and other "minorities." Rabbi Stephen Wise condemned the Wilson administration for jailing the women pickets. Pacifist Lola Hennacy wrote to "comrade" Alice Paul that her brother was a conscientious objector in an Atlanta federal prison and asked "to send you and your fellow prisoners greetings, commending you all for your noble fight."[61] The National Negro Congress passed a resolution in December praising the NWP and stating that "the evil of American Democracy is its restrictions on liberty."[62]

But as fellow "radicals," the NWP's most vocal allies by far were the socialists. Since June, parallels had been made between "unpatriotic" socialists and militant suffragists. The District attorney for the District of Columbia compared the NWP "trial of 6" in June, for the "Russian banner," to the case of Indiana socialists who had paraded with a red flag and slogans on banners. They too had been charged with causing a crowd to gather and thus obstruct traffic, and were given the choice of $25 or three days. They served the days. Many socialist leaders were arrested in the summer and more would be under the October Espionage Act, often for "discouraging enlistment." Many congratulatory telegrams had been received from socialist party branches since the Russian banner and the NWP's "stand on democracy." Socialist Max Eastman had wired the NWP: "Magnificent. Perfect from every point of view. Accept our warmest admiration." Radical socialist leader John Reed spoke at the prisoners' breakfast, and wrote in an impassioned article for the *Suffragist*: "[O]ur government is primarily a government by coercion. It makes no difference what the constitution says. . . . The only thing that makes any difference is power. . . . [The government] is an instrument of the rich." He also wrote that "the police show contempt for the law" when they let the women's banners be trampled and then themselves attack the women. Reed admired the pickets for giving "a plucky struggle" against the mobs.[63] Among the many letters of sympathy which came to headquarters from socialists, one came from John Spargo. Vernon answered him with the thought that men might have to drop what they were doing and "join the protesting women."[64] The socialist journal *The Call* began to cover the militant suffragist stories daily and Morris Hillquit's speakers always mentioned them. John Milholland stated in *The Call* that the NWP had "indomitable persistence" and that nowhere in the civilized world were women treated so harshly.

NWP picket and socialist Elizabeth Stuyvesant wrote, also for *The Call*, about war-crazed American society's harsh treatment of IWW people, socialists and "the suffrage pickets [in] prison."[65] One way to see how radical the NWP was considered by the public was the constant parallels drawn between the NWP and the IWW--The Industrial Workers of the World. Originating in the Colorado mines, the IWW sought better working conditions for all workers, using strikes and pickets, always violently put down, to protest against "capitalist greed." The IWW fought for labor issues throughout the war, insisting, as did the Woman's Party, on their right to free speech. Although the IWW had no official policy on the "capitalistic" war, the membership was persecuted for antiwar conspiracy. When 113 "Wobblies" were convicted after criticizing the government during strikes and jailed, the newspapers implied that the strikes, like the NWP pickets, were "backed by German gold." In jail, IWW members were brutally treated, receiving poor food, filthy cells, no medical treatment, and often solitary confinement. The IWW, like the NWP, tried to argue they were not antiwar, but had only one goal, in their case, economic justice. Alice Paul had said women were not part of the American government and had no say in its laws; Bill Haywood said that workers had no country--if they were stepped on by all and had nothing, there was no reason to be patriotic. (Unlike Alice Paul, however, Haywood, as apparently a greater threat to American society, would be sentenced not to seven months, but 20 years in prison.)[66] The *Colorado Gazette* equated the IWW's unpatriotic, harmful methods with those of the Woman's Party. Lillian Kerr, answering the editorial for the NWP, defended their reputation by listing all of the "prominent" women and wealthy supporters involved in the organization. The accusation never did go away. The *New York Times* would quote Mary Garrett Hay, powerful New York NAWSA leader, as saying the NWP was "the IWW of the Woman Suffrage movement."[67]

The NWP organizers left on the outside had the unenviable task of trying to tell the story of the radical NWP prisoners versus the federal government in a war-charged patriotic atmosphere. Women were sent to each region of the country: Joy Young went to the South; Anne Martin, Natalie Gray and Margaret Whittemore to the Northwest; Vivian Pierce, Iris Calderhead, Clara Snell Wolfe and Rebecca Hourwich to the South and Midwest; and Catharine Flanagan, Virginia Arnold and Doris Stevens were in the Northeast (when not running headquarters).[68] Organizer Hourwich was called at that time "young, unusually brilliant and with a well trained mind, rare charm and personality." She remembers that many people were hostile to the NWP because of the war.[69] (She herself was a pacifist.) Hourwich did say her "campaign" was made simpler because the NWP had already thoroughly researched her region and had ready arguments for her use. Still, the organizers had no easy assignment. Some towns would not let the NWP speakers in because of their "questionable loyalty." Pauline Adams stated that "[s]entiment [in Virginia] is awfully against picketing and some say we ought to be *tarred and feathered*."[70] Tar and feathers was seen as a proper reception for antigovernment, "suffragettes."

At times everyone seemed united against the feminist militants. As ever, even within their own ranks, the militant policy of demanding political prisoner status took its toll. Although membership numbers did rise over all, five more advisory board members left that fall, among them Dr. Josephine Baker, Mrs. Amos Pinchot and Mary Ritter Beard. Beard withdrew quietly after her protest to the White House, writing Elizabeth Rogers, "I can't fight the battle the picketing way . . . or the war work way." NWP headquarters received many letters from the public, many finding the pickets unpatriotic, dishonorable, or mad.[71] One writer scolded Alice Paul for her "fatuous hunger strike": "[Y]ou and your associates are all wrong. Act like a woman a son, father, husband or brother would be proud of, and you will be gratified with the results obtained." A lawyer from Peoria wrote Lucy Burns that he was in hearty sympathy with their punishment, and that they were receiving "almost universal censure [for their] course of notoriety-seeking conduct." Another letter scolded them for "embarrassing the government at a time when any relaxation of its energies means death to thousands of our boys abroad."[72] When NAWSA's Anna Shaw was implored by Shippen Lewis, Dora Lewis's son, to protest the jailing and the treatment of his mother, once her friend; Shaw refused in no uncertain terms. Shaw wrote Lewis that "no sane person" could think picketing had been good for suffrage. She assured him that the horrific statements made about the prison were "without foundation," and that the "government has been more mistreated than the pickets." She told him that she had spoken to the heads of police and secret service, and telegraphed the President for leniency, but the NWP did not appreciate it.[73] The American militants were not quite scorned by all.

There were supporters who sent sympathetic letters. Meta Cohn had read about the pickets in the *New York Call* and wrote Burns: "[Y]our sufferings . . . shall not be in vain. It is ever so, the great and idealist must live an uncomfortable life. . . . We 'new citizens' won't forget." J. A. H. Hopkins wrote Paul to compliment her "sterling courage and the extraordinary loyalty of all your fellow prisoners," and added that their treatment was a stain on Wilson's record. At a rally in New York, several black women volunteered to picket. One, "Mrs. M. M. Young," a dressmaker, wanted to picket because "there were women of her race at the prison."[74] (Whether or not she ever picketed is unknown.) After news of forcible feeding and the "night of terror" was out, many more letters of admiration were received. The martyrdom of the nonviolent resistance in prison created a good deal of sympathy, especially among other women; it also created front-page publicity. Both of these elements would have their effect on Congress in 1918.

How "radical" had the militant feminists of the NWP become? The Woman's Party had gone to radical extremes, both in tactics and in suffering, for their fight for women's rights. They were radicals for women's rights who were feared by the administration as subversive, and would be embraced by fellow dissenters for their civil rights fight and for their criticism of the lack of real democracy in America. The militants were willing to break the law in resisting government authorities. These were feminist, sex-conscious, political radicals, not leftist, class-conscious, political radicals. The militants were suffering public censure and physical danger in prison, and many were "radicalized" by the experience. It would be difficult for women jailed by their society for exercising their rights of free speech to ever look upon that society in the same way again. Ada Davenport Kendall testified that Occuquan was "a place of chicanery, sinister horror, brutality and dread," and she knew exactly whom she blamed for her experience: "No one could come out without just resentment against any government which could maintain such an institution."[75] The indignities, the suffering, the violation the militants felt in prison, had fallen upon them by order of their own government.

Furious at the Wilson government's hypocrisy in denying them their rights as citizens, Woman's Party suffragists vowed to keep up their resistance. When the Congressional Union was founded in 1913, progressive reformers Paul and Burns had believed strongly in the promises of American democracy and the superiority of the generous and fair-minded American male when compared to the British brutes responsible for the sufferings of the WSPU. By 1916, when it had become apparent to CU leaders that it would take more than patient lobbying to persuade Congress to pass a woman suffrage amendment, the women had organized to use their existing political power in election battles, the "progressive," American democratic thing to do. But in 1917 the promises of American liberty seemed empty to the feminist radicals. Again and again the NWP protesters insisted they were only fighting for "real democracy." At the end of November Alice Paul wrote: "How is it that people fail to see our fight as part of the great American struggle for democracy, a struggle since the days of the Pilgrims. We are bearing on the American tradition, living up to the American spirit."[76] Dorothy Bartlett, from Connecticut, stated that if going to jail was "what we must do in America for liberty than I guess I'll be there, but I really can't believe it."[77] Organizer Mary Dubrow found her prison experience "utterly unbelievable," and was sure the Wilson administration "could not keep it up without the world's censure." Elizabeth Selden Rogers wrote Burns, fearing peace would come before they got suffrage, since the war was so useful for their tactics. She felt it would be an excellent idea at that point to "block Woodrow Wilson in the White House."[!] Anne Dorris Chisholm angrily wrote Wilson to ask him what her rights were as a "pseudo-citizen."[78] To the militants it seemed that there was no justice, no real democracy in America in 1917; not for women, in any case. For some of the suffrage prisoners, despair may have stopped them from continuing their struggle against the government, but for most of the militants their anger further radicalized them into a willingness, even an eagerness for further militant action against the Wilson administration.

NWP militants were swept into prison along with other dissenters on a wave of war hysteria. Obviously, many of the middle and upper class Woman's Party suffragists did not wholeheartedly embrace the anti-government causes of Wobbly or socialist dissenters, but at least for a time these disparate political radicals were united in feeling alienated from American society and united in grievances against the Wilson government for suppressing their civil rights and for sustaining a war about which they felt they had no say. By November of 1917, instead of being thought of as a respectable, middle-class movement, through its militancy, the NWP had become a radical group.

On December 6, the NWP held a conference and mass meeting in Washington, passing out prison pins to all who had been jailed. It was a changed organization from the one that started silent picketing on the eve of war--certainly not as innocent. The cover of the December 15 *Suffragist* was blazingly entitled "The Militant," and the NWP was thoroughly militant by that December.[79] The nonviolent resisters had escalated their struggle for political rights by demanding to be treated as political prisoners, and had taken the drastic step of the hunger strike to try to force the authorities to act on the issue. The government had not flinched from inflicting punishment on the protesters, but in the end had had to make concessions. Leo Kuper, writing about passive resistance in South Africa, stated that "[c]ivil disobedience . . . works by converting the opponent through an emphatic process. The foe is made to feel uncomfortable, by having to witness or even to inflict suffering, and therefore he acts to alleviate the primary suffering in order to reduce his own suffering."[80] The NWP had found that militant, nonviolent resistance worked well to create public sympathy and force the government to act.

Thoroughly established as militants and radicals after the jailings of 1917, the National Woman's Party would not shrink from further acts of militancy when woman suffrage was still not won. On the contrary, when the House passed suffrage early in 1918, the NWP credited the public pressure created by the suppression of their militant protests. Having won a major battle, the militants retreated, hoping victory was at hand. When it became apparent by the summer of 1918, that further pressure on the government was necessary, and convinced that the fight for women's suffrage was "a vital part of the struggle for democracy," the NWP determined to keep fighting with a "spirit of doing 'til it's done."[81] The "real" militancy of civil disobedience would begin once more.

---

[1] Richard Gregg, *Power of Nonviolence*, p. 47.

[2] H. C. Peterson and Gilbert C. Fite, *Opponents of War, 1917-1918*, (Madison: University of Wisconsin Press, 1957) pp. 294, 202, 262; Joan M. Jensen, *The Price of Vigilance*, (New York: Rand McNally and Co., 1968) pp. 47, 79, 106; William Preston, *Aliens and Dissenters* (Boston: Harvard University Press, 1963) p. 11; Zechariah Chafee, Jr., *Free Speech in the United States* (Cambridge: Harvard University Press, 1946) p. 52; *New York Tribune*, November 22, 1917 and November 23, 1917, Reel 95, NWPP.

[3] *Congressional Record*, Volume IV, Part 7, 65th Congress, First Session, House, p. 7379.

[4] Record of Picket Arrests and Trial, August 28, 1917, Reel 87, NWPP.
[5] Kendall was arrested September 13. The rest of the jailed were Annie Arniel, Ann Dorris Chisholm, Margaret Fotheringham, Julia Emory, New York socialist Maud Malone and Dorothy Bartlett. Ainge affidavit, September 4, 1917, Reel 91. Dorothy Bartlett felt giving up a month or two of her life was the least she could do. Bartlett to Dr. Paul Pearson, September 8, 1917, Reel 48, NWPP. Dr. Walter Adams, Jr. to author, November 1, 1982. On Kendall, "Mrs. Clark" to "Mrs. Pitzer," N. D., Folder 20, Box 2, Sue White papers, Radcliffe.
[6] Alice Paul to H. E. Brennan, September 18; Emory to Paul, September 5, 1917, Reel 48, NWPP.
[7] These socialists joined Maud Malone, already in jail. Katharine Fisher statement, September 17, 1917, Reel 49; Blumberg affidavit, October 26, 1917, Reel 51, NWPP; Gluck, editor, *Parlor to Prison*, on Kettler pp. 228, 242; Crocker, in *Maryland Suffrage News*, September 29, 1917, p. 17; in FBI File 108-25, Document 25025. Crocker also said at an October dinner for the prisoners, "Everything was being taken away from everybody and it was time for everybody to stand up for everything . . . the least I could do was picket." A great quote. October 13, 1917 Report, Reel 89, NWPP.
[8] Stevens, *Jailed*, pp. 160-163, 165, 171; Anne Martin, September Legislative Report, Reel 87, NWPP. Malone's letters to Stevens are in Folder 36 Carton 2, Doris Stevens Papers, Radcliffe. Apparently even Carrie Chapman Catt applauded Malone's actions (p. 16, Stevens). Malone's letter to Wilson in *New York Times*, September 8, 1917, p. 1.
[9] On the other hand, Congressman Jacob Meeker said they had had "about all the feminist movement" that they could stand. *Congressional Record*, Volume LV, Part 7, 65th Congress, First Session, House, p. 7380, 7373, 7377.
[10] Baker to Dr. Lydia DeBelbins, September 24, 1917, Reel 49, NWPP.
[11] Kettler in Gluck, *Parlor to Prison*, pp. 242-243; Stevens, *Jailed*, p. 177.
[12] The *Suffragist*, September 29, 1917, p. 4.
[13] Hilda Blumberg affidavit, October 26, 1917, Reel 51, NWPP.
[14] Samarodin to Pauline Clark, October 22, 1917, Reel 51; and September 14, 1917 statement, Reel 91; NWPP.
[15] Doris Stevens to Alice Paul, September 16, 1917, Reel 49; NWP photograph on Reel 97, NWPP.
[16] Irwin, *Alice Paul and the NWP*, pp. 251-256, Alice Paul to her mother, Mrs. William Paul, October 22; Arnold letter to Mabel Vernon, October 23, 1917, Reel 51, NWPP. "Black Maria" refers to the police wagon.
[17] Stevens, *Jailed for Freedom*, p. 215, Kettler in Gluck, *Parlor to Prison*, p. 247.
[18] Stiehm, *Nonviolent Power*, p. 17; Katzenstein, *Suffrage in Pennsylvania*, p. 314; Alice Paul to Dora Lewis, November 1917, Reel 53, NWPP.
[19] Florence Boeckel to Anne Martin, November 7, 1917; Dora Lewis to Honorable Gwynne Gardener, DC District Commissioner, November 7, 1917; Gertrude

Crocker for the prisoners, to Beulah Amidon, November 8, 1917, Reel 52, NWPP.

[20] Gallagher, Paul interview, p. 91; Stevens, *Jailed*, pp. 220-223; *New York Times*, November 7, 1917, p. 13; November 9, 1917, p. 13.

[21] Lewis to Gardener, November 7, 1917, Reel 52; Beulah Amidon, NWP Press Release, October 19, 1917, Reel 50, NWPP.

[22] Zane is said to have saved a besieged fort in West Virginia (in a final Indian attack of the war) by carrying gunpowder to its defenders. Stevens, *Jailed*, p. 195; Irwin, *Paul and the NWP*, pp. 257-258; Alva Belmont from Dora Lewis, November 13, 1917, told her the crowds were "coming around." To Gilson Gardner's point of view, it was because of the pickets' "nerve" and because the press was becoming less negative. Reel 52, NWPP.

[23] *Salt Lake City Tribune*, November 14, 1917. On November 17 Anna Kelton Wiley, Elizabeth Kent and Elizabeth McShane also got 15 days for their November 10 picket. Irwin, *Paul and the NWP*, p. 260.

[24] *Salt Lake Telegram*, November 11, 1917, p.1; Quay to Alice Paul, February 2, 1919, Reel 68, NWPP.

[25] Eleanor Calnan to Agnes Morey, December 12, 1918, Reel 66; Julia Emory to Paul, February 18, 1918, Reel 56, NWPP; *Niagara Frontier*, January 17, 1974, p. 20, states Juengling ran for Congress in the 1920s to make sure a woman was on the ballot.

[26] Stafford affidavit, November 28, 1917, Reel 53, NWPP.

[27] Irwin, *Paul and the NWP*, p. 280; Eunice Brannan affidavit, November 23, 1917, Reel 53; Beulah Amidon, NWP Press Release October 19, 1917, Reel 50; Robertson affidavit, November 28, 1917, Reel 53; on Burns' speech, FBI File 108-250, Document 25025, Reel 108, report of May 1, 1919, p. 5. Burns added, "Even the President himself wouldn't take that responsibility [of having them die]."

[28] Swing quote in papers of Camilla Whitcomb, N. D. *Worcester Telegram* article. Affidavits of November 23, 28 and 30, 1917 of Eunice Brannan, Mary Nolan, Alice Cosu, Belle Sheinberg, November 30, Reel 52, NWPP.

[29] Cosu affidavit, November 28, 1917, Reel 53, NWPP.

[30] Week affidavit, November 1, 1920, Reel 83; Week to Burns, August 21, 1917, Reel 46, NWPP.

[31] Emory affidavit, November 1917, Reel 53; Burns' November 1917 statement, Reel 52; Greiner affidavit, November 1917; Day affidavit, November 28, 1917; Kruger affidavit and Robertson affidavit, November 28, 1917; Sheinberg affidavit, November 30, 1917, Reel 53, NWPP.

[32] Day, *The Long Loneliness*, pp. 89-90.

[33] Lucy Daniels affidavit, November 30, 1917, Reel 53; and Kathryn Lincoln's affidavit, November 28, 1917, Reed, 53, NWPP.

[34] Catharine Flanagan to Mary Ingham, November 22, 1917, Reel 52, NWPP.

[35] Winslow's notes to NWP headquarters and to her husband, quoted in Stevens, *Jailed*, pp. 189-191.
[36] Louise Page, "Dora Lewis, Political Prisoner," unpublished manuscript; NWP Press Release, November 27, 1917, Reel 92, NWPP.
[37] Burns, in Irwin, *Paul and the NWP*, p. 289.
[38] McShane to Mary Ingham, November 26, 1917, released to press, Reel 91; McShane, November 28, 1917 affidavit, Reel 53, NWPP; Stevens, *Jailed*, appendix.
[39] NWP Press Release, November 27, 1917, Reel 92, NWPP. Many were told if they did not eat, they could not appear in court when their cases were heard. So were some thus persuaded, to their later chagrin. Lincoln affidavit, November 28, 1917, Reel 53. When hunger strikes occurred in 1918 and 1919 the authorities would make sentences shorter, therefore the use of forcible feeding to ostensibly prevent the starvation of the hunger strikers, would have been indefensible.
[40] NWP Press Release, November 27, 1917, Reel 92, NWPP.
[41] *Ibid.*
[42] See Christine Lunardini, *From Equal Suffrage to Equal Rights*. Lunardini has seen much of the same evidence as I have, but still sees Wilson in a more complimentary light than I believe the record warrants.
[43] Wilson to Catt, October 13, 1917, Reel 210, Wilson Papers on Microfilm.
[44] W. Flynn, New York Secret Service head, to Wilson and Wilson's reply, October 26, 1917, Reel 210, Wilson Papers on Microfilm.
[45] November correspondence to Wilson on Reel 210; Gardener to Wilson Report, November 9, 1917, Reel 210, Wilson Papers on Microfilm; Brownlow, *Anonymity*, p. 79
[46] *Salt Lake City Republican*, November 13, 1917, p. 1; Wilson to Tumulty, November 12, 1917, Reel 210, Wilson Papers on Microfilm.
[47] Vera Whitehouse, New York NAWSA, to J. Tumulty, November 16, 1917; Wilson to "WFJ, Secretary," November 16, 1917, Reel 210, Wilson Papers on Microfilm.
[48] Doris Stevens, put in charge when Lewis went to jail, to Ethel Adamson, November 16, 1917, Reel 52, NWPP.
[49] 1917 NWP handbill, Reel 93, NWPP.
[50] At that time, the Secret Service was part of the Treasury Department, and competing with it was a separate Bureau of Investigation under the Justice Department, headed by Chief Bruce Bielaski. William R. Corson, *The Armies of Ignorance: The Rise of the American Intelligence Empire* (New York: The Dial Press, 1977), pp. 585-586. November 16, 1917, Reel 210, Wilson Papers on Microfilm. Harrison sent the letter on to "Mr. Polk" at State and then William MacAdoo, Secretary of the Treasury and Wilson's son-in-law, received it.
[51] Flynn to Harrison letter, November 16, 1917, Reel 210, Wilson Papers on Microfilm.

52 Dorothy Bartlett to Catharine Flanagan, November 30, Reel 53; Florence Manion to Agnes Morey, November 1, 1917, Reel 51, NWPP. Gertrude Stevenson, a writer for Newspaper Enterprise Association, was replaced by a man after a pro-suffrage article. *Suffragist*, September 8, 1917, p. 5.

53 Hourwich to Beulah Amidon, October 24, 1917, Reel 51; Calderhead to Henrietta Baldwin, September 5, 1917, Reel 48, NWPP.

54 *New York Tribune*, November 22, 1917 on Reel 95; Stevens to Paul, November 22, 1917; Margaret Long to Lucy Burns, November 9, 1917, Reel 52, NWPP. Long wanted to stand by Kessler but feared it was not NWP policy.

55 Only local officials could enforce espionage laws--under local statutes. Corson, *Armies*, p. 586. Joan M. Jensen, *The Price of Vigilance* (New York: Rand McNally Co., 1968), p. 12; September 29, 1917 *Sun* article, FBI File 108-250, Document 25025, Reel 108, National Archives, 1981; Paul to Iris Calderhead, October 11, 1917, Elizabeth Stuyvesant to Paul, October 12, 1917, Reel 50, NWPP.

56 FBI "Secretary Sweeter" to Attorney General, N. D., FBI File 108-205, Reel 108. The Bureau received "hundreds of unsolicited reports" from citizens regarding "German spies," Corson, *Armies*, p. 589. Many also appear on File 108-205. Gardner letter, November 1917, and Schanberg to Wilson, November 13, 1917 in FBI File 108-250. Gardner letter, November 1917, and Schanberg to Wilson, November 13, 1917 in FBI File 108-250, Reel 108.

57 Ford, Reyher interview; Thompson to Lucy Burns, August 8, 1917, Reel 46, Report of New Jersey branch, October 29, 1917, Reel 51, NWPP.

58 Anne Martin to Pauline Clarke, October 31, 1917 and November 19, Reel 51; Martin to a Eugene, Oregon editor, November 1, 1917, Reel 51, NWPP.

59 *New York Tribune*, November 22, 1917 and November 23, 1917, Reel 95, NWPP.

60 See Reels 48-51, October and November correspondence, NWPP.

61 The *Philadelphia Jewish World*'s A. Sussman gave the NWP two columns an issue, saying children would someday read about the NWP in their school books. Anne Martin to Pauline Clarke, October 31, 1917, Reel 51, NWPP; *Suffragist*, October 27, 1917, p. 5; Katzenstein *Lifting the Curtain*, p. 128. She also says Quakers were the only religious sect to endorse woman suffrage. Hennacy to Alice Paul, November 8, 1917, Reel 52, NWPP.

62 Report on Reel 54, NWPP. Many NWP pickets were also members of the labor group, the WTUL, and when two of them were jailed Paul wrote Rose Schneiderman, thinking "labor women would want to picket." Alice Paul to Rose Schneiderman, September 21, 1917, Reel 49, NWPP. Mary Beard told Paul, however, that the WTUL's Schneiderman and Mary Dreier were "dead set against us in every way," September 25, 1917, Reel 49, NWPP.

63 *Suffragist*, July 7, 1917, p. 5; late June correspondence; Eastman to NWP, June 21, 1917, Reel 44, NWPP; Reed breakfast speech, *Suffragist*, June 27, 1917, p. 9;

Reed, "An Arraignment of the Police," June 30, 1917, pp. 6-7. See *New York Times*, September 8, 1917, p. 1, for socialist arrests.

[64] Mabel Vernon to John Spargo, July 23, 1917, Reel 46, NWPP.

[65] On *The Call* coverage, Allison Hopkins to Pauline Clarke, November 3, 1917, Reel 51; Stuyvesant in *New York Call*, August 12 and November 23, 1917 on Reels 48 and 52, NWPP.

[66] Patrick Renshaw, *The Wobblies: The Story of Syndicalism in the United States* (Garden City, NY: Doubleday and Co., Anchor Book, 1967), pp. 160, 172-186; Peterson and Fite, *Dissenters*, pp. 257-258.

[67] Lillian Kerr to *Colorado Gazette* editor, August 30, 1918, Reel 64, NWPP; *New York Times*, February 10, 1919, p. 1.

[68] Fall Organizing Report, Reel 52, NWPP.

[69] Henri Fink Zinnard to Alice Paul, June 22, 1917, Reel 44, NWPP; Ford, Reyher interview.

[70] Organizer to Mrs. Lee Brock, November 21, 1917; Pauline Adams to Virginia Arnold, November 18, 1917, Reel 52, NWPP.

[71] In October the NWP lost 49 and gained 294, and in November they lost 48 and gained 208. The total membership was about 30,000. Executive Secretary Report, October and November 1917, Reel 87; Advisory Board Report of 1921, Reel 87, Beard to Rogers, November 17, 1917, Reel 52, NWPP, for "anti-letters."

[72] The man sounded like an advertisement for soap! Parke Upshur to Paul, November 7, 1917; George Burton to Lucy Burns, November 1917, Reel 52; Unsigned letter to Lucy Burns, November 1917, Reel 52, NWPP.

[73] Concluding with her major grievance against the NWP--their militancy--Shaw said that every step of the CU/NWP was "in imitation of Mrs. Pankhurst's methods in England, where they were such a flat failure, just as they are in this country." Shippen Lewis to Anna Shaw, November 20, 1917, Reel 52; Shaw to Lewis, November 28, 1917, Reel 53, NWPP. Shaw thought it good that the WSPU had turned to war work at least.

[74] Cohn to Lucy Burns, November 17, 1917, Reel 52, NWPP; Hopkins to Paul, November 29, 1917, Reel 53, NWPP; *New York Times*, November 9, 1917, p. 13.

[75] Kendall affidavit, November 2, 1920, Reel 51, NWPP.

[76] NWP Press Release, November 27, 1917, Reel 91, NWPP; W. U. Watson told the *Chicago Tribune* that his wife, Madeleine Watson, and Lucy Ewing (both of Chicago) said they were "learning that the old Webster definition--a government by the people and for the people--is not the interpretation for democracy today . . . and they feel that they will have to stand the penalty for giving democracy the ancient translation." *Chicago Tribune*, August 19, 1917, p. 3.

[77] *Putnam Patriot*, August 7, 1917, p. 1.

[78] NWP Press Release, January 12, 1919, Reel 92; Rogers to Burns, N.D. 1917, Chisholm to Wilson, September 19, 1917, copy to Paul, Reel 48; Walker to Dora

Lewis, March 9, 1918, Reel 58; Julia Emory to Paul, September 5, 1917, Reel 48, NWPP.

[79] *Suffragist*, December 15, 1917. In December the NWP lost only nine members and gained 327, showing the sympathy of women to the cause after jailings. December 1917, Report of the Executive Secretary, Reel 87, NWPP.

[80] Leo Kuper, *Passive Resistance in South Africa*, (Yale University Press, 1957), pp. 73-74.

[81] Katherine Muller, "The Making of a Militant: How a New England School Teacher Became a Picketing Suffragette," *Suffragist,* May 13, 1918, p. 7. Stevens said the women knew there could be "no great reform without a downright fight." Doris Stevens, "The Militant Campaign," *Suffragist*, July 19, 1919, p. 9.

Chapter Seven

Jailbirds: A Sisterhood of Struggle, 1917-1919

Really the comradeship and the "soul-shock," if
I may so express it, were compensations for hunger
and other trials.

-Katharine Fisher, Fall 1917

The extraordinary experience of American women reformers, many from sheltered, prosperous backgrounds, suffering imprisonment for picketing the White House, disillusioned and radicalized them. Many of them saw life in prison as a microcosm, in extreme form, of women's status in society. They experienced utter powerlessness in prison, and sometimes were violently attacked by male authorities. In jail, the militant suffragists became painfully aware of their common vulnerability as women, through the reactions of not just those authorities, but friends, family and employers. They also saw even more clearly the injustice of that powerlessness and vulnerability, amplified by a new knowledge of the condition of their fellow women, particularly black women, prisoners. It was at the height of militancy, when demonstrators were being beaten and jailed, that barriers between women of different classes and backgrounds, who may have had conflict between 1913 and 1916, were broken down. A sort of sisterhood of struggle developed. United against a common male enemy, other sorts of divisions seemed unimportant, at least for the duration, and for some, for much longer. Suffrage "jailbirds" left prison with radical, egalitarian feminist beliefs enhanced, certain that militancy and civil disobedience remained women's only avenues to winning the vote.

It was a great shock for Woman's Party suffragists to be found guilty of criminal conduct. Their sojourns in the filthy District of Columbia jail, the infamous Occuquan Workhouse, and the condemned prison workhouse (also in Washington) built over a sewer, were brutal and devastating. Sixty day sentences were meted out in 1917, but in 1918 and 1919 the NWP protesters would receive short sentences of up to 15 days, first for holding public meetings without a permit and climbing on a public statue, and then for building fires. In February 1919, the last group of 16 prisoners would be sentenced to eight days at Boston's Charles Street jail. It is true that fellow dissenters were treated very harshly and given long sentences under the Espionage Act, but the District of Columbia Court of Appeals (in March of 1918) decided that the women arrested in 1917, who had served several months, had been tried and imprisoned completely illegally, *under no law at all.*[1] The NWP demonstrators had been imprisoned in a wave of war hysteria, and their treatment was exacerbated by the sexist hostility the "iron-jawed angels" provoked by being militant and aggressive.

The 168 suffrage militants who served jail sentences in 1917, 1918 and 1919, as noted, included a large number of NWP leaders and organizers; and they would be joined by a group of women from richly varied backgrounds, recruited to demonstrate for women's rights. The notion that the NWP, during suffrage militancy, was just an "elite," conservative, upper to middle class organization is simply untrue. The jailed "recruits" were the largest group of prisoners--88 women--but also represent the smallest proportion of their total number, since probably close to 2,000 women picketed. They are a true cross-section, showing the wide variety of women involved, women representing Paul's "sturdier" pickets, the ones willing to be jailed. Recruited pickets were drawn from every region of the United States, often asked to specifically represent their state, their college or profession, or called upon to increase numbers on certain symbolic holidays. Headquarters sent form letters out to all the NWP districts to encourage members to picket, but Washington would also be flooded with volunteers, from women tourist bystanders to union women journeying to the capitol to stand "in sisterhood" with the NWP.[2]

The data available on the 88 recruits is not as complete as on the other groups, but some traits in socio-economic background do stand out. Ethnically, there was more diversity in recruits than any other group. In 1917 about two-thirds of the 36 demonstrators were native-born, with six, over 16%, from eastern European or Russian Jewish backgrounds. There were nearly the same percentages for 1918-1919 recruited demonstrators, with more than two-thirds of the recruits documented of native-born, western European heritage, and again, six with eastern European/Russian Jewish origins. Data on the recruits' parents are ordinarily unavailable, making family background very difficult to determine for certain. But judging from the women's own or their husband's occupations, the 36 jailed recruits of 1917 drew about one-fourth, ten, of its members from the wealthy or professional classes, half, 18, from the ranks of the self-supporting, greater middle, and five from the working classes. (Three are unknown). Of the 52 recruits of 1918-1919 who were imprisoned, only nine were definitely upper-class women, 14 were working class, and the rest somewhere in the middle. Ten of the 36 1917 recruits were known to have had college educations, and 18 of the 52 of 1918-1919. The recruits tended not to go to women's colleges, but usually to state universities. Nearly half the recruits came from eastern cities, but, unlike NWP leaders (or many organizers) most were not from the cities' upper class strata. (Appendices A, B and C.)

Again, information on recruits' political views is relatively scarce, but 11 of the 36 (30%) 1917 recruits were known to be socialists, and 13 of the 52 (25%) of 1918-1919 recruits were. This statistic, however, may be a bit misleading since if a recruit was socialist, it became an issue as NWP activists were publicly linked with other radical wartime protest groups; whereas other sorts of political views were not as obvious. Still, the number of leftists in this group of jailed NWP members is significant when comparing the nature of the NWP with the more conservative NAWSA. Woman recruits were involved in a wide variety of social reforms from the DAR and Grange through political reform clubs, the WTUL and YMCA, to birth control and peace. NWP recruits were, on the whole, decidedly more politically radical than NWP leaders and drawn from a wide pool of women from all sorts of class backgrounds.

Unfortunately, there is not a lot of evidence, but what there is indicates that at least some recruits were involved in women-related activities, as well as revolutionary ones, before and after joining the NWP. Seven women left NAWSA for the NWP, three worked for the Women's Trade Union League, and two more each for "women's reforms" or birth-control. Although many radical recruits showed ambivalence about the importance of the vote for women's freedom, many of them did work for woman suffrage after their release from jail; some served as organizers and speakers, sharing their prison experience and soliciting help in the cause. At least one recruit was an NWP officer after suffrage was won. However, many more recruits, rather than working for the NWP's new cause, an Equal Rights Amendment, would work for labor reform or world peace.

The women drafted to participate in demonstrations show many "new woman" characteristics, but not as purely as organizers. Again, their function and circumstances must be kept in mind. Women recruited to demonstrate and then quite possibly serve jail terms needed a bit of freedom and mobility to be able to do so. With that in mind, it is amazing (and indicative of the strength of their beliefs) how many women with responsibilities of family and/or job came to participate in protests. About half of the recruits were single and most were self-supporting: 31 of 36 in 1917 (86%) and 38 of 52 in 1918-1919 (73%). It is very clear that single working women were drawn to an assertive struggle to gain their political rights. The "recruits" were eager to join this feminist movement even at the risk of imprisonment. All of the documented single women were self-supporting. About 55% of the married women were, with about 15% of married recruits undocumented on this point. A real difference between jailed recruits and leaders or organizers, was that most of the women who worked were still in middle class "women's" professions like teaching, social work or nursing, but 25%, a fairly large number, were "industrial workers."

Fewer than half of all recruits resided in urban areas of the 1918-1919 group, but in 1917 almost half of the 36 came from New York City and over two-thirds were from urban areas. The makeup of the recruited groups was in part determined by exigencies of transportation and time considerations (and, in part, by which group happened to be picketing on the day police were ordered to arrest demonstrators), as well as by the ability of a woman to take time from family and job responsibilities for protests and prison. Therefore, it was certainly easier for young, single women from the Northeast to come to Washington, although many risked (and some lost) their jobs and/or relationships, in order to demonstrate.

Recruited pickets of 1917 to 1919 represented militant feminists of all stripes. Political leftists like Anna Gwinter, Ernestine Hara or Louise Bryant, were representative of recruits who picketed for women's rights as a radical, civil liberties, cause. The socialist recruits believed that class differences should be overcome, at least temporarily, because of the importance of this militant feminist struggle. Anna Gwinter of the Women's Waistmaker's Union, had been with the woman's movement for eight years. She said she went to prison in 1917 to "help women get their rights." While there, she refused to scrub toilets when ordered to by the matrons, because she said she had to work when she got out and could not afford to "get any of the awful diseases."[3] Socialists were also heavily represented among the prisoners of 1918 and 1919. Philadelphian Reba Gomborov of the WTUL brought with her sister-in-law Rose Fishstein, a "businesswoman," and Rose Gratz Fishstein, a union organizer who had been imprisoned for "revolutionary activities" in Russia. They were joined by the notorious Louise Bryant herself.

Ernestine Hara, jailed in 1917, came from a Rumanian Jewish family with anarchist beliefs; they had arrived in New York in 1907 when she was 11 years old. She soon became a factory worker and then graduated to stenographer. Once told by Eugene O'Neill she had writing talent, Hara instead devoted her energies to socialism and "bohemianism." She said the "excitement" of the NWP picket appealed to her, although having once been jailed she said she "was not courageous enough to go back again." Hara recalled the real political differences between herself and her fellow prisoners, but grew to admire their courage a great deal:

> Most of the women [in the NWP] were liberal-conservative. They were not radicals; their vision was limited to voting rights. That doesn't mean there was no radicals in the group--there were--but they were not effective. . . . It was really a conservative group of women. Many of them came from fine, rich families with very good minds and a willingness to fight for their ideas, to endure prison and the food and even to starve.[4]

Developing a feeling of solidarity with fellow prisoners, the radical Hara was always in the center of action in jail, being there when the decision to demand political prisoner status was made, and in the middle when several prison mélées broke out. Socialist prisoners were sensitive to the issue of the jailed demonstrators' rights being suppressed, had been the first to see the political nature of the incarceration, and wanted to stand in solidarity with all the woman suffragists who had decided to brave prison to fight for justice.

Another sizeable group of jailed recruits was made up of independent working women, women like munitions worker Elsie Vervane (jailed in 1919) whose anger at the government overcame her desire to keep her job. Elsie Unterman, a social worker from Chicago, took her week's vacation to picket in 1919, and found herself in prison. New Jersey teacher and organizer Mary Dubrow, had been brought into the Woman's Party by Rebecca Reyher, who called her "wonderful, lively, interesting, impassioned." She said she could only be with them a limited time because she needed to work. Dubrow stated it was very "important to be economically independent." The 1918-1919 pickets had numerous working women--child labor inspector Anne Herkimer of Baltimore, artist Marguerite Rossette of Chevy Chase, and Estella Eylward of New Orleans, a Stanford graduate, who had practiced law with her father and was known as "honest, self-sacrificing" and a "zealous" suffragist. Airline pilot Kate Boeckh of Washington was jailed for applauding the pickets in court. Berthe Arnold (See Figure 8), the daughter of a "prominent physician," was from Colorado Springs and a graduate of Colorado State University. She was a kindergarten teacher; young, fresh, exactly the sort of woman Alice Paul liked to recruit. Janet and Margaret Fotheringham of Buffalo, two sisters (their mother was an NWP district chairman), both took leaves from work to picket in 1917. Janet Fotheringham was a physical culture teacher, "of age, sound mind and unusually sound body." Margaret Fotheringham, 27, was a graduate of Drexel Institute, a teacher and dietician for the military. She strongly objected to being served raw salt pork in jail! These working women cherished their independence and went to jail because, as Texas housekeeper Lucille Shields put it: "Imprisonment is only endurable because it's for greater freedom."[5] Economic freedom, power to live on their own without dependency on a male, was a prime motivator for self-supporting women, a shared concern of many suffrage pickets in prison.

Other "recruit" prisoners were much like state officers and national advisors; they were mature, "clubwomen" reformers who insisted on rights for all women. Effie Boutwell Main, imprisoned in August 1918, was a member of the Good Government League until thrown out for opposing the draft. She braved her family's censure to demonstrate in Washington. The Quaker Louise Parker Mayo, of Framingham, Massachusetts, was a former teacher and mother of seven, married to the grandson of a former Chief Justice of Massachusetts, a farmer. She was a member of the Equal Suffrage League and described as "a fine type of New England woman . . . a person of ideals." Mayo was opposed to picketing until converted by a Mabel Vernon speech. After her jailing in 1917, she wrote Doris Stevens to share her "boiling indignation" against the Wilson government. Kate Stafford of Oklahoma City, sent to Occuquan in November 1917, was a long-time reformer for women and children's issues, and a mother of six. The 45-year-old Stafford was one of the hunger strikers at Occuquan, and, in addition to that indignity, she was struck by prison Superintendent Whittaker when she told him she "wanted her political rights." He "threw his hands in [her] face" and said he wanted to hear no more of that nonsense.[6] Leftist radicals, social workers, pilots,

Kindergarten teacher Berthe Arnold was one of the youthful, self-supporting women recruited to demonstrate for women's rights.
Figure 8

clubwomen, and homemakers, developed a sense of shared vulnerability--and rage --at the suppression of their feminist protest.

Political rights, economic independence and female solidarity were important elements of NWP militant feminism. The large majority of NWP recruits were self-supporting, even the married ones. And compared to leaders, officers and organizers, many more were of the working classes; and often, political radicals. There were recruits who were youthful, educated "new women," especially the left wing of new womanhood, but there were also older clubwomen/reformers. In other words, jailed recruits seem to have included women of every conceivable background. And all NWP feminists--recruits, organizers and officers--shared in the commonalities created by being "jailbirds."

The militants shared jail's drudgery, oppression and humiliation; as well as the problems jail caused for families, jobs and reputation. The women were constantly made aware they were indeed prisoners. The longest prison sentences were given in 1917 and spent in the Occuquan Workhouse, the fiefdom of Superintendent Raymond Whittaker. According to organizer Kathryn Lincoln, Whittaker was exceedingly unpleasant: "We all know instinctively who he is. He has stiff white hair, blazing little eyes, and a dull purple birthmark on the side of his face. A wave of animosity sweeps the group when we discover his attitude, which is that of the bully." Eunice Dana Brannan insisted that Whittaker "had determined to attack us as part of the government plan to suppress picketing." He particularly disliked the non-cooperative aspect of their nonviolent resistance, actions to win political prisoner status. Brannan said that he edited everything she said in his reports of their conversations. When she decided not to cooperate by refusing to give her name, she was threatened by guards; and when she asked after Kathryn Lincoln's condition, she was told by Whittaker to "shut up." She particularly hated the sound of bloodhounds baying outside the walls. Brannan's health was "undermined" by prison, and she reportedly fought hard to stave off a nervous breakdown after her experience. Mary Nolan, in her 70s, testified that Whittaker, angered she would not give her name or do prison work, would not let her go to the bathroom when she was hospitalized. (The matron there told her the police had insisted the suffragists had guns and pipes.)[7] Whittaker threatened Minnie Quay with the "whipping post," and Lucy Burns with a strait jacket. It was also he who sometimes threatened to kill them.[8] The man in charge of the prison took the lead in trying to terrorize the women into submission.[9]

The conditions of prison life faced by the suffragists were, if not always terrifying, then depressing and dehumanizing, calculated to make them constantly aware of their criminal status. Nineteen-year-old Rhoda Kellogg was a graduate of the University of Minnesota who became an expert in children's art. She said, in gentle understatement, "[A]n experience in jail was anything but pleasant."[10] The atmosphere was one of intimidation, the accommodations were anything but inviting, and daily life dreary. Prisoner Matilda Hall Gardner (See Figure 4) described prison life in the summer of 1917:

> The days were spent in the sewing-room. We were permitted to talk in low tones, two or three being allowed to sit together. While we were there, the sewing was light. We turned hems on sheets and pillow slips and sewed on the machine. There were both white and colored women working in the sewing room. The work was monotonous and our clothing extremely heavy. The great nervous strain came at meal time. All the women ate in one big room. The white women sat at one side. The meal lasted thirty and sometimes forty minutes. The food to us was not palatable, but we all tried to be sensible and eat enough to keep up our strength. The real problem, however, was not the food; it was the enforced silence. We were not allowed to speak in the dining-room, and after a conscientious effort to eat, the silent waiting was curiously unpleasant.[11]

Lack of communication with their fellow inmates deprived them of the comfort of companionship. Annie Arniel reported that the prison officers "treated us as if we were animals instead of human beings." Arniel was a "physical wreck" following her jail term, and had to have an operation as a result.[12]

There were numerous accounts confirming conditions in jail as brutalizing. Virginia Bovee, a matron at Occuquan who was dismissed for her kindnesses to the suffragists in August of 1917, testified in part:

> The blankets now being used in the prison have been in use since December without being washed. Officers are warned not to touch any of the bedding. . . . The prisoners with disease are not always isolated, by any means . . . a few pieces of soap [are] common to all inmates. . . . The beans, hominy, rice, cornmeal. . . and cereal have all had worms in them. Sometimes the worms float on top of the soup.[13]

Dorothy Bartlett testified that "diseased women" shared water with the suffragists. Bartlett was from Putnam, Connecticut, the leader of the State Grange; and on the State "work committee" for the war effort, involved in food production, Liberty Loans and the Red Cross. Bartlett said they had no fresh air and no heat (in November), were given only bread and water as punishment, and could have no counsel or mail. She finally got milk and toast through her doctor's orders. Scientist Agnes Meara Chase's doctor tried to visit her after she was jailed, since she had just been very ill, but the authorities would not let him in. Ada Davenport Kendall testified that she was put on bread and water in solitary for protesting being given floors to scrub after days with no food. Whittaker called her protests "impudent." In her isolation cell she was given an open pail for a toilet, with no new water for four days. She did have some company: large rats were the women's constant companions. Gladys Greiner testified she was never allowed to change clothing in a month, her bed was black with bedbugs, and the rat fights kept her awake. Kate Winston of Chevy Chase, Maryland, wife of an economics professor, also complained of the plentiful "vermin." She also found her old Sunday school teacher was the jail matron! Winston told her she was "obeying her conscience and fighting for the right as she was given it see it."

Women jailed in August 1918 were housed in a former men's workhouse in a swamp, declared unfit for habitation since 1909. It was especially re-opened for them, complete with damp, cold, dark cells, bad water, and sewer gas. The women went on hunger strike except for two elderly women. One of them, "Mrs. J. Irving Gross" was an elderly Massachusetts officer whose father and husband had fought in the Civil War. Unable to hunger strike, she still suffered mightily from her imprisonment, getting "spots all over" and very bad rheumatism as a result. Effie Main fasted for 48 hours and then went into a stupor from the sewer gas in her cell. Elsie Hill smuggled out a furious note to Doris Stevens relating that their "hell-hole" had been prepared for them a week before the verdict, and they all had rheumatic pain from the damp conditions.[14] The weakness of the women's position seemed clear, but they were undaunted, and united, in spite of the intimidation they received in jail.

The brutalizing prison experience, according to Doris Stevens, was made even worse for the "suffrage ladies," compliments of Superintendent Raymond Whittaker. Besides inedible food, rough treatment and unwearable clothing, the women were housed with black women prostitutes and thieves. This was a situation which the prison authorities thought the white protesters would find intolerable, but in fact, the suffragists often developed bonds with black women prisoners. Eunice Brannan stated that they were "put with colored women as an insult, but the colored women were kind to them and indignant at their treatment." The *New York Times* reported that three suffragists--Betsy Reyneau, Julia Hurlbut and Mary Ingham--complained about being with "colored women, drunks and thieves." But Pauline Clarke, *Suffragist* editor, argued that the press was not accurate when it had women "expressing distaste on being jailed with colored women." She said they only objected to diseased women (prostitutes); and that they were "not undemocratic."[15]

An incident that happened in October 1917 illustrates how Whittaker continued to set black women against white. It also clearly shows the helpless condition the women were forced into, the measures they took to try to change the situation, and the distorted accounts of NWP "crazies" which came from the press. On October 5, 1917, the *New York Times* reported a "Pickets' Mutiny in Workhouse--Eighteen Suffragist Prisoners Attack the Superintendent of Washington Institution--Suppressed By Negresses." The article went on to describe a "rough- and-tumble fight" of "militants" versus guards and "negresses." Alonzo Tweedale, workhouse auditor (in charge when Superintendent Whittaker was suspended while an inquiry into the suffragists' treatment was taking place), reported that the suffragists, at least one with "a club," were supposed to have attacked Tweedale, the prison matron and three male guards, as socialist writer Peggy Johns was being removed for "medical treatment" to the Washington Asylum Hospital. The *Times* also stated that Alice Paul denied Tweedale's account.[16] The suffragists involved vehemently refuted Tweedale's version. It is interesting that Inez Haynes Irwin's detailed history of the NWP does not mention the event, perhaps indicating its less-than-heroic aspects. Doris Stevens' book discusses it only briefly, as an example of black woman prisoners "commanded to physically attack the suffragists," which they did "reluctantly and under threats of punishment."[17] Ernestine Hara Kettler, a good friend of Peggy Johns, disagreed, writing that the black women "got the most intense joy out of beating the hell out of the white women"-- so much so that they had to be called off.[18]

Whatever the "negresses' " attitudes really were, and most witnesses tended to agree with Stevens, the prison authorities often tried to fan racial hatred. In this particular case, according to Peggy Johns, she had been very ill and had a hip boil that went untreated for some time before she was finally taken to the prison hospital. Hara, her constant visitor, found Johns missing from the hospital one day and discovered her after a search, dressed, as Johns told her, so she could be taken "to a psychopathic ward," something the women were threatened with repeatedly.[19] The other women present with Hara--Ada Davenport Kendall, New York librarian Maud Malone, Hilda Blumberg and Mary Winsor--wrote an account of the "riot" which said that when

> Mrs. Johns disappeared from the hospital Mrs. Kendall told the women in the sewing room. We sent two letters to Mrs. Herndon [the matron] and Mr. Tweedale but received no satisfactory answer. Five of us [Kendall, Malone, Hara, Blumberg, Winsor] went to the office. The matron tried to hold the door but we went through. We hurried into the kitchen where Mrs. McCampbell [a matron] sat at her desk. She rushed to the door of the corridor and threw herself against it. We went through and saw at the further end of the corridor Mrs. Waters the nurse . . . Mr. Tweedale. . . and Mrs. Johns. . . . We called 'We're here Peggy' and she called 'They are taking me away! Help Me! Save me!,' and ran towards us. We ran after her and took her, bruising Mrs. Kendall's arm. She ran with us towards the sewing room, but three husky guards appeared so we turned towards the colored dormitory.

The women were then attacked, and after a struggle, the five called for the other suffragists to come help. The guards took Johns away while the five women ran to the front of the prison. Lucy Burns tried to call NWP headquarters from the prison office, but was attacked by "five or six black girls who tried to beat and choke her." Margaret Fotheringham, who had been holding Mrs. McCampbell was beaten on the head while the guards watched. The women's report concluded by stating that Mr. Tweedale's report was a lie, Hilda Blumberg had had no pipe.[20] It is obvious that the suffrage prisoners were very far from being cowed, even under the dehumanizing and seemingly insurmountable, powerful foes of husky guards and harsh superintendents.

Starting in the fall of 1917, when the suffrage prisoners began to demand rights as feminist political prisoners rather than common criminals, they were subjected to what Doris Stevens called "administration terrorism," the worst example being the "Night of Terror" of November 15. The hunger strikes that began when the women's demands for political offender status were ignored were met with the punishing violence of forced feeding, adding greater horrors for the suffragist inmates. The consistently brutal methods of the superintendent and his guards astounded and angered many. The sister of imprisoned Nina Samarodin wrote the Russian ambassador that such treatment as the woman suffragists were undergoing was "much worse" than they would suffer in Russia as political offenders. Some police and prison guards carried out their duties with relish. Ada Davenport Kendall wrote that she "resented nothing so much as the constant ugliness and discourtesy and mean manners of the officers." Linda Gordon, in writing about the treatment of women imprisoned for working for birth control, argues that guards were "hostile and violent" to the women because they "seemed to violate every male fantasy about what women should be like." Women were completely under male power in jail. One of the youngest prisoners, Alice Gram, tried to appeal to Whittaker's gentlemanly instincts. She told him she was friends with a friend of his " and did not intend to be treated in any other way than as a lady." The astounded superintendent offered to pay her way home.[!] Male guards came and went constantly among the female prisoners, giving them no privacy. Artist Cora Week testified that male attendants flushed their toilets. One example of misogyny toward the prisoners would be the elderly Mary Nolan's account of hearing a guard yell, "The_____Suffrager! My mother ain't no suffrager. I'll put you through_____." As Estelle Freedman wrote in *Their Sisters' Keepers*, under the control of male jail keepers, women prisoners represent "an extreme case of sexual powerlessness," symbolizing the constraints placed on all women by authoritarian institutions. Just as they were thought of as unnatural members of their sex outside prison, from the mobs in the streets to the President of the United States, so were the NWP militants considered within their prison cells, and so were they punished.

In prison, militant suffragists were under the direct control of oppressive male authorities, but even there they continued to defy those authorities with whatever means possible. They resisted and refused to cooperate even though many of the women had been truly frightened there. Amy Juengling, the educator from Buffalo, stated she was "under a peculiar nerve strain such as I had never previously been owing to the unjust and cruel treatment I had witnessed women subjected to, and realized the power of the law as administered by. . .Whittaker."

She reported that after jail she felt "as in a daze. . .a constant feeling of general weakness and lack of usual vigor."[21] Women came face to face with the stark fact of their lack of power.

Texan Lucille Shields stated afterward that in jail she realized how long women had struggled for their freedom, and "the tasks that they have been forced to leave undone for lack of power to do them." Katharine Rolston Fisher, originally from California, was a teacher, writer and social worker, and worked at the U.S. War Risk Bureau during the war. She had written Alice Paul in July that since she seemed free of her chronic headaches, she wanted to picket. She said: "I'm about as little use as anybody can be," so could go to jail for six months. "It's too bad there is not another way, but the fight must be won." After her jail term, Fisher spoke at a meeting honoring the released prisoners. She saw a parallel between the lives of women in and out of jail: "Five of us. . .have recently come out from the workhouse into the world. A great change? Not so much of a change for women, disfranchised women. In prison or out, American women are not free. . . . Disfranchisement is the prison of women's power and spirit." The knowledge of past powerlessness and lack of freedom did not paralyze these militant feminists. Madeleine Watson of Chicago wrote Catharine Flanagan in December of 1917 that she had seen Superintendent Whittaker on a train, where he almost spoke to her, "but didn't dare." If he had, wrote Watson, she would have held a protest meeting right there.[22] (See Figure 7, Flanagan and Watson pictured.) Woman's Party suffragists painfully realized the common oppression of women while in prison, but they retained their defiant spirit.

The militant women became more aware of their lack of power and liberty under male governance in prison, but the suffragists also came to realize their common lack of freedom through constraints and demands imposed by their families. Agnes Morey once bemoaned the fact that she was not free to act without consulting her husband; women had "to consider other people who think they can't get along without us, which is absurd." Many women never were able to make the trip to picket. Florence Whitehouse wrote Alice Paul, "I want to go and help so much but Mr. Whitehouse is very much opposed to it and I could not go without deeply hurting him, so I must give it up."[23] Family reactions were very difficult for the prisoners. Perhaps the worst problem area was that of reputation. According to Ernestine Hara Kettler, "Jails had a very bad reputation for anyone, especially for women. If you were a jailbird, you were a fallen woman." Indeed, on this point Amelia Walker, for one, "seethed with rage" at the administration and thought the government should pay. Walker, a Quaker NWP officer from Baltimore, wanted "damages," saying she lost many friends because of her status as "jailbird."[24]

Some husbands, especially the "prominent" ones, were not pleased by the notoriety of marriage to a fallen woman. Ann Dorris Chisholm of Huntingdon, Pennsylvania, was 54 when she was jailed. Chisholm was a stained glass designer, who had studied in Dresden, Germany--she had done a window for the Women's Building at the Chicago Exposition in 1896. Chisholm's husband insisted he would pay her bail, but she refused. Her husband then apparently had a "breakdown" and later lost his race for judge because of his wife's jailing in 1917 for suffrage.[25]

Sarah Colvin's husband, afraid her activities would hurt his career (as a surgeon), very much disapproved of her protesting for her "principles." She said they discussed it once and never again. Dr. John Rogers, a "delicate husband," got "ulcers of the stomach" over "this prison business"; prompting Elizabeth Selden Rogers to consider being arrested as "Eliza White" to protect his reputation.[26] A very high price was paid by Effie Boutwell Main, Topeka reformer turned antiwar and suffrage activist. Her husband "filed suit for a divorce on account of the 'disgrace' I had brought upon his name on account of former demonstrations." Hazel Hunkins had a half-brother who felt similarly. He put an ad in the *Billings* (Montana) *Gazette* that said his sister "had been deluded by people in Washington" and "was not that kind of girl." The ultra-wealthy Louisine Havemeyer reported that it was hard for her children to read about her on the front page, and that she sometimes received "cruel telegrams" from relatives. (To her grandson, however, she remained "a real sport.")[27] It was difficult enough to suffer prison's indignities, but to then suffer the stigma of having been there was doubly cruel.

There were husbands of militants who were concerned not only with reputation, but who were opposed to their wives' or daughters' views of women's freedom. Mothers had added worries. Beatrice Kinkead, a New Jersey NWP officer, was one of the first women to graduate from the University of California, and had taught at Vassar and Bryn Mawr. She once suggested to Alice Paul that she picket with her four boys. Her husband was "opposed to the whole thing. It adds a complication." Ada Davenport Kendall found her husband got "upset, nervous and ill" over her activities, saying the Woman's Party was "breaking up families." He reputedly did not believe "in any freedom for women," and insisted his wife was "morally responsible to him and obliged to obey his wishes."[28] Twenty-nine-year-old Betsy Graves Reyneau from Detroit was a portrait painter. Her portraits of Florence Bayard Hilles and Anna Kelton Wiley are at NWP Headquarters today. Apparently, her painter husband was not supportive of her actions. Headquarters wrote Paul Reyneau that "your wife was superb . . . [and] looked like a wild rose" when sentenced, and was "perfectly all right." Apparently Reyneau was not assuaged by the letter. It was followed by Betsy Reyneau's abject apologies to Lucy Burns for having to cancel a suffrage meeting in Detroit because her husband "acted like a spoiled boy." They were divorced shortly after the war. Pauline Adams' was a "prominent" clubwoman from Norfolk, Virginia: "bilingual, diligent and friendly," according to her son. Adams' doctor husband feared for her health in October and wanted organizer Virginia Arnold to loan her money to get home, as he was a busy doctor who could not leave his practice. He expressed an understanding of why the women had to fight at this point, although he thought "you are trying to do too much." But by November, he wrote Arnold, insisting any sacrifice involved with her jailing was his, "as she left home when she was needed very badly." Adams hoped she would learn by the jailing that "a woman's place is in the home."[29]

Not only husbands, but fathers disowned their "jailbird" daughters. Hilda Blumberg was the woman who wrote so movingly about the impossibility of imprisoning thought in the Bastille. Her father also hearkened back to the French in describing his opposition to his daughter's actions:

> The picketing methods resemble the Jacobin methods that unseated the Girondin party--not by representative rights but by nearness to the Capitol. Such methods have in all historical times drawn nations into anarchy similar to the Reign of Terror in France and present conditions in Russia. It is therefore eminently wise to prevent the Capitol from being swayed by clamorous crowds.[30]

Militancy did not serve to bind the Blumbergs. Katharine Fisher's father supported and admired the pickets, but he "opposed [his daughter's] going," because of her health. Betsy Reyneau, whose husband was already making scenes about her political activities, was also disowned by her father in a letter to President Wilson. He wrote that women must prove themselves worthy, and that it would be a sorry government if it were "controlled by such unbalanced individuals." Even Alice Paul had to contend with her Uncle Mickle. He did not approve of Paul's style of reform, and wished she would "stop militant methods" which were "alienating" her friends, in favor of the more Quaker-like "power of persuasion."[31] If women faced such attitudes from family members, they could hardly expect understanding from prison officials.

Naturally there were other more tender concerns that caused husbands and families to oppose a loved one's imprisonment. Alice Paul carefully answered many, many letters from friends and relatives of the prisoners, trying to calm their fears.[32] Margaret Wood Kessler's husband, for instance, was frightened that since his wife's health was so frail, she might die in prison. Mary Winsor's mother did not know where her daughter was jailed, wanted her to know of her uncle's death, and feared how much the jailing would distress Mary's father. Clara Hamilton "forbade" her daughter Elizabeth to be allowed to hunger strike or undergo violence because of her poor health. "Her spirit is willing but the flesh exceedingly weak." But her daughter did go on hunger strike for seven days and was then released through her father's efforts. She remained at NWP headquarters under care of a nurse, ". . .in a very weakened and emaciated condition." Henry Butterworth thought a "week's discomfort" was long enough to register a protest and wanted to get his wife out, whether she liked it or not. Katherine Fisher's father felt she could only stand a week in prison "health-wise," although he supported the picketers and admired their courage. Families tried hard to pay the fines of the prisoners, but in most cases were adamantly forbidden to do so by the women. Although admiring her spirit, Camilla Whitcomb's sister-in-law wanted to pay her fine, thinking "the women [had] gone far enough." Whitcomb did suffer some rough treatment, she was taken to the men's prison hospital because as a political prisoner she would not work and suffered through a long hunger strike. Tearfully, Florence Bayard Hilles' husband and daughter pleaded with her to let them pay her fine, but she refused. But, against her "passionate protest" Abby Scott Baker's husband paid her fine anyway.[33] Some families, then, strongly fought to keep their wives, mothers, sisters and daughters from prison.

All families did not oppose or interfere with the militants' activities. According to Rebecca Hourwich Reyher, husbands and families were really very supportive considering that the problem of a wife in jail, a cause of considerable anguish, was "a first" for them. Reyher herself had recently married, and some of the other prisoners were also newlyweds: organizer husbands, "in every instance suffragists," were already used to rarely seeing their wives. One of them said, "It's got to be love at first sight, for you're not likely to get a second." Examples of husbandly support abound. Josephine Bennett's husband, M. Toscan Bennett, a lawyer and writer, sent her a telegram upon her arrest, reading: "Good luck to you --we are proud of our fighter for democracy." Rebecca Winsor Evans' husband, Edmond C. Evans, became, according to his wife, a "red-hot" suffragist after cooking his own meals while she was in jail. When asked if he paid his wife's fine, Gilson Gardner said his wife was "an absolutely free woman. I won't interfere with her. This is her job, and she is going through with it with a great deal of courage." Gardner, along with onetime Wilson advisor, J.A.H. Hopkins, John Milholland and Dudley Field Malone, continually protested to Wilson and government friends about their loved ones' jailing. The Hopkins had a very odd relation with the President. Indeed, just weeks before her arrest, Allison Turnbull Hopkins had had dinner with Wilson. After being released, she wrote him that she did not desire his pardon, but "American justice," and upon finishing the letter took this message on a banner to the White House. Wilson saluted her as she stood there.[34] Hopkins, in spite of her husband's closeness to the president, would not be spared jail.

Although wishing she could keep her safe, Helen Paul supported her sister. An NWP activist in New Jersey herself, Helen wrote Alice in 1917: "If at any time thee thinks there is any way I can be of use please let me know and I will come at once. . . .we think of thee with much love constantly and want to do anything we can to help. . . . Mama sends much love." Worried about her sister's frail health, a week later Helen wrote her sister wanting to have Alice "safe where those cruel people could not touch thee. Thy beautiful selfless spirit is an inspiration to me."[35] Burns' close-knit family were very much involved in suffrage activity. Like Helen Paul, Burns' sisters Janet and Helen both worked for their NWP branch, in New York. Her army lieutenant brother Edward anxiously awaited news of her jailing, although "knowing the recital will make me boiling mad." The family of Dora Lewis, although "worried to death" and thinking of her constantly, were immensively supportive. Recruit Dorothy Bartlett regretted the sacrifice of separation from her family "but they're ready to make it, too."[36] The publicity gained by the newspapers' exploitation of the human interest element of jailed suffragists was invaluable to the NWP.

Reporters expected irate husbands to be annoyed at their wives' antics. In Boston, attorney George Roewer told the *Boston Sunday Post* in 1919 that he saw nothing to be "peeved" or "shocked" about his 33-year-old wife, Rosa Heinzen Roewer, being in jail. Anyway, he went on, besides agreeing with her on her suffrage views, with an "efficient pair of servants who will attend to the house and mind the kiddies, and cook the food, there is little room for [a husband] to be disgruntled over a little matter like his wife being in jail, especially when she wants to be there." Both R.B. Quay and C.T. Robertson of Salt Lake City, ardent suffragists, told the press they were "outraged" at the "crime" of authorities' jailing their wives in Washington, vowing to stand by the women "'til the last ditch."[37] For women whose husbands did not share their views, going to prison had innumerable consequences at home; but for those lucky women whose husbands and families were supportive, the indignities of jail could be healed at home.

Suffrage "jailbirds" paid another dear price for demonstrating: they faced possible dismissal from employers. Margaret Fotheringham lost her teaching job in Buffalo. Nell Mercer, who had family dependents, feared she might lose her clerical job since her employer was much opposed to the protests. Elizabeth McShane, so violently forced fed, resigned her job in order to join the demonstrations. Edna M. Purtell, from Hartford, Connecticut, not only suffered a broken finger, but lost her job at the Travellers Insurance Company as a result of her joining the August 1918 demonstrations. Purtell wrote Burns she would like to demonstrate in 1919, but had just got a job again: "Others are involved, or I would."[38]

The distinguished Agnes Meara Chase had difficulty at her place of employment because of her participation in the August protests as well. Chase was a botanist who was an expert on grasses, with 70 publications (one 1922 book indexed 80,000 kinds of grasses) and later honorary fellow of the Smithsonian. The 48-year-old Chase was originally from Illinois, the daughter of an Irish blacksmith who died young, leaving six children to the care of his widow. Chase taught herself the sciences, along with Spanish, French, German and Portuguese. She said, "Girls didn't get to go to college," [so] "I had to pick up as I went along." Eventually she studied at Chicago's Museum of Natural History. Under five feet tall, Chase had married in 1889, but her husband died a year later. She was an ardent prohibitionist and non-smoking advocate, beyond her feminist activities. Chase had been enthusiastic about picketing since it began. She had tartly written the NWP in 1917, however, that she was not "shirking" by not doing it herself, but had to earn money, as she had since the age of 17. In 1918 she did demonstrate and therefore "Der Hauptmann" of her department, the U.S. Department of Agriculture (where she was doing research), was "laying for her," since she had "disgraced" herself and the department.[39]

Pickets who were professional women shared the "disgrace" with women who held less lofty positions. Amid hostility from much of the public, the NWP continued to draw staunch support from "laboring women."[40] Sometimes those laboring women sacrificed a great deal in joining with the NWP to make a feminist protest. In January 1919, led by Elsie Vervane (the president), representatives of the Woman Machinists Union of Bridgeport, Ruth Scott, Helen Chisaski and Eva and Carrie Weaver, came to Washington to protest as women and as workers. Three of them would lose their jobs for coming. Elsie Hill had spoken to the group when they were out on strike in 1917, as had NWP national advisor and Connecticut officer, Josephine Bennett. In September of 1918 the machinists went on strike; Wilson himself threatened the workers with blackballing and the draft. They went back to work, but in December government contracts were cancelled, leading to thousands of layoffs. During the strikes, the *Machinist Monthly Journal* reflected conflicting sentiments about women workers, wanting on the one hand to "protect" women and get them out of the factory as soon as the war was over, but insisting on equal pay for them (even if they did not "need" it) when there.[41] So it was that the women had grievances against Wilson, the government and men in general that January. They took part in the Washington protests and were jailed.

Working women paid a high price for their protests, but did gain the experience of fighting for a cause in solidarity with all sorts of women. In February Elsie Vervane was unable to find factory work, writing Lucy Burns that she had been speaking for suffrage, but with no work "felt quite hard up." As for the government, she said, "I hope they will get theirs for it sometime."[42] Carrie Weaver was fired the month before coming to Washington for participating in local NWP actions.[43] Ruth Scott also lost her job for going to the protests, but said, "It didn't worry me at all" because there was no work at home anyway. She wrote Burns that her mother, "some scrapper," would have come, too, if strong enough, and she "talks suffrage to death" with everyone. When Scott went to Washington her landlady "was wild" and put her things out on the street. She said her friends there tried "to get her goat," but she only laughed at them and said she was "doing their bit" while they stayed home. They "got wild" over her daughter's "Votes for Women" button, but Scott shrugged it off, saying her girl was "mama's little suff." She wrote Burns to say what a wonderful time she had had there, including jail, and that she missed them all. She particularly enjoyed going for "a delightful drive" in Mrs. [Elizabeth] Kent's automobile. (Scott sent money for the *Suffragist*.)[44] Vervane, Weaver and Scott exemplify the real sacrifices women were willing to make for the suffrage struggle. As Scott's letter shows, prison brought a blurring of class lines between women making personal sacrifices. Society woman Amelia Walker, after her summer in prison, started going to socialist meetings to discuss the militants' campaign. Working women were jailed alongside the "prominent"; all were joined in a woman's fight for rights.

Jail created a sisterhood. The women were united in anger and disbelief at the government; but also in exhilaration that they were fighting an important feminist battle. During the "Night of Terror" there were countless incidents of women trying to care for each other. Lucy Burns suffered beatings for insisting on calling out the names of other prisoners to see how they were. Alice Cosu showed "extraordinary thoughtfulness and tenderness" in tending the elderly Mary Nolan and others. Aviator "Mrs. L.H." Hornsby tried mightily to get a guard off Dorothy Day. Anna Kelton Wiley could have been pardoned but chose to go to jail so Elizabeth McShane would not have to go alone. Julia Emory fought to stay in jail with her comrades: "I am heart-broken. I hate to breathe the free air. The other twelve are in and I am out and that fact just sears my very soul." Organizer Kate Heffelfinger said she suffered constant "anxiety for my comrades. It was hard to bear."

The person most often cited as caring for her sister prisoners was 44-year-old organizer Edith Ainge, "Aingy," of Jamestown, New York, who "handled everything" in jail. Ainge came from a family of British emigrants, her father was an auditor and accountant, which "she ran" with "charm, character and persuasion." She had eight brothers--at least one fighting in France in 1917. She came to Occuquan in November in perfect health, but after six weeks had lost 23 pounds, and was unable to walk. She had been "manhandled" by Warden Zinkham and unnerved by male guards who took off her shoes while she was sleeping. [!] She nursed Dorothy Bartlett and Peggy Johns in their illnesses, and kept everyone's spirits up with her "fine, dignified presence."

One of the understandable immediate effects of the experience of imprisonment was bitterness and desolation, emotions all the jailed women shared. Lucy Branham called being locked up "a suffocating process"; "You lie awake at night and think and think and think." Branham felt prison was "a WASTE," as she may well have, being worried about her history doctoral thesis with Columbia's Charles Beard. She contacted him for a list of readings! Kathryn Lincoln described days in jail as "an eternity." She said she felt she was "gradually losing my hold upon life." Kate Heffelfinger wondered if NWP speakers were able to "make you feel and taste and smell this place! Imagination could never have done it for me." Thoroughly disillusioned, singer Lillian Ascough asked herself in jail, "What have I done that I am going to be shut away from the rest of the world?"[45] Many women paid for the physical ordeal of prison long after their release--Mrs. Henry Butterworth had one serious illness after another after Occuquan. Nellie Barnes, NWP officer in Indiana, told the Woman's Party officer who requested she picket, that her husband had had a "slight stroke" but was better and had told her he could "get along" if his wife felt it her duty to go. She did go and said she "came home from Washington sick and have been in bed ever since: am now only able to sit up part of the day." She missed her comrades, and ". . .would be pleased to hear from any of the ladies."[46] Perhaps the most pointed commentary on the suffragists' jailing came from Louisine Havemeyer. She wrote that in jail "the sparks of indignation snapped within" her: "Where was my Uncle Sam? Where was liberty and democracy?" Havemeyer felt she finally understood the courage of Jael to kill Sisera and Charlotte Corday to kill Marat: her "very soul was out of joint."[47]

If disillusion with the American government and anger at its injustice was one effect of jail which made the women more militant, camaraderie and inspiration from their fellow women to keep on fighting, was another. Newspaper writer and University of Oregon graduate Clara Wold came to the demonstrations because, after Louise Bryant had told her about them, she "felt mean." Wold was of Norwegian ancestry, and related to Ibsen. She wrote Paul that "all the passion [she] accumulated in jail" had "made a grand slaying," but when she collected her wits she would write "for the cause" in the *Suffragist*. To Kathryn Lincoln, "Prison bars mean only freedom. . . The cause of women must advance."[48] Many of the prisoners tried to encourage their fellow suffrage inmates. Lucy Branham, with actress Vida Milholland, led songs in prison like "Shout the Revolution of Women," or perhaps "Alive-Oh":

> Awake to the dawning! We conquer! We conquer!
> The sky is ablaze with the fire of our day;
> The morning has risen--
> In triumph we hail it--
> For justice, for freedom,
> Alive, Alive, OH!

In a lighter vein, the women would do a rendition of "We Worried Woody Wood as We Stood" or, to the tune of "We've Been Working on the Railroad":

> We've been starving in the workhouse all the livelong day,
> We've been starving in the workhouse
> Just to pass the S.B.A. -
> Don't you hear old Zinkham calling -
> Rise up so early in the morn -
> Don't you see the Senate moving?
> Woodrow, Blow your horn![49]

Hilda Blumberg, not one to give in to depression, organized courses in Russian, French, English literature, Spanish, German and physical culture for the prisoners. In addition to those offerings, Nina Samarodin taught Russian; Pauline Adams, French; Lucy Burns, English literature; and Margaret Fotheringham taught physical culture. (This was before the period of "terrorism.")[50] Such measures helped maintain the women's sanity, and created a stronger bond between them.

It was not only their fellow suffragists that the NWP connected with in jail. The militants felt gratitude, sympathy and solidarity with fellow women prisoners. Often they were moved to help them as individuals. According to Caroline Katzenstein, the suffragists' "comrade" prisoners wanted to hunger strike, too, to gain overall better conditions, but were told that without organization they would fail. The NWP still did what it could to help them.[51] Although the *New York Times* had reported that the suffragists resented being housed with "colored women," the NWP always denied that, saying they were placed with black women "as an insult" but that the black women were kind and sympathetic to them.[52] Kate Heffelfinger wrote Beulah Amidon from jail, where she was put in and out of solitary, that she was "wild with madness or mad with wildness . . ." She sometimes cried remembering "the dear funny, sickening little kindnesses prisoners showed me--for it was penalty of solitary for them if they were seen talking to me. . . . Especially the Negroes are good to us."[53] Ernestine Hara voiced concern that the black women had fewer blankets than the whites and *no* exercise. Dorothy Bartlett reported that when sick, it was the black prisoners who cared for her. She, in turn, asked permission to play the piano for the "colored department." Bartlett, who specialized in "Billy Sunday Hymns," said: "I have opened the 'Smile Box' there."[54] Some NWP women tried to help their fellow black prisoners. Mary Winsor wrote to Dudley Field Malone, NWP lawyer, to help a black girl who was whipped by Whittaker.[55]

Prison was a real eye-opener for the relatively sheltered suffragists, and they reacted with compassion to fellow inmates. Ada Davenport Kendall wrote in her Buffalo newspaper column, that out of prison she would "think of all the unfortunates there and wish to help them. My bed will not be soft nor my food pleasant, nor will any of the comforts of life be mine until the suffering of these people is ended. So long as man persecutes man, I am persecuted."[56] Clearly, the position of women was personified in its extreme in the lives of these unfortunates. A black prostitute told Doris Stevens she was helpless, constantly picked up by the police. She hoped they got the vote " and fix SOMETHINGS for women." Stevens said she came out of prison "hot with indignation."[57] Margaret Sanger wrote Anne Martin, saying she, too, had been jailed, for advocating birth-control. Sanger hoped that Martin would help her in changing conditions for women prisoners. "There is hope today for women's emancipation because she has desired something & will suffer for it. A new spirit has arisen!"[58] Prison served to point to the need for feminist agitation, to help all women, as it underscored the helplessness of women without power in society.

Rather like Christabel Pankhurst, some women were exhilarated even in the face of adversity, because they were fighting for their rights with other women, involved in an important and worthwhile cause. And, of course, they were honored within the NWP for their prison ordeal, with prison pins, banquets and prestige. At the top, Alice Paul, upon the day of her release from jail, called her time there "the most thrilling, absorbing life I have ever experienced." NWP Advisor Anna Kelton Wiley once said that the "jailing was the highlight of my life."[59] Testifying to the positive side of prison, Baltimore physician Anna Kuhn felt lonely and desolate after returning home from jail, missing the fellowship of her fellow suffragists. Dr. Caroline Spencer wrote Paul she would "treasure the memory of those picket lines and my few minutes in jail the rest of my life." And Pennsylvania officer Mary Carroll Dowell stated that "for variety of interest and depth of heart no other experience of my life can be compared to my five days in prison." Calling jail her "spiritual uplift," Dowell thanked "God and Alice Paul, our intrepid leader, for inspiration. We would have gone on until the millennium except for the handful of fearless women who broke loose from old conventions to secure liberty for all the women of the nation. . . . I am thrilled with pride to be a part." Student Rhoda Kellogg called her trip to Washington "the leading inspiration for all my life. . . how glorious it was to meet so many splendid people."[60] Belle Sheinburg of New York, also a student recruit, wrote Betty Gram in December of 1917, "Just now my spirit moves me to get up and cry 'three cheers for all of us' and tell the world of the glory of the entire affair. . . . ["I'll] continue to spread the Gospel of Freedom and Liberty for all." Katharine Rolston Fisher wrote that the "comradeship and the 'soul-shock' . . . were compensations for hunger and other trials. . . . [T]he joyous moments of the long days when we daringly waved a greeting to our eleven friends across the dining room, or pressed our faces against our window screens and exchanged hurried words."[61] The sort of commitment necessary to be willing to be a militant, to defy the laws of men and go to jail, required sacrifice; but it also had its rewards. The camaderie of the cause made the suffering almost worth it.

In spite of privations, in spite of deeply felt injustice, physical injury and illnesses, the majority of the suffrage prisoners were not daunted by their jail experience. On the contrary, the effect was the opposite. Jail emphasized for the NWP their lack of liberty and status in society, the hypocrisy of their government, their vulnerability through their family ties, and the problems they shared with their sister prisoners--all those realizations making them more radically feminist. As Dorothy Day wrote, "Never would I recover from this wound, this ugly knowledge I had gained of what men were capable in their treatment of each other."[62] The militants came out of jail convinced their radical methods were the only way women could ever gain power. The "ugly knowledge" they gained in prison did not discourage, but only boosted their crusade for political equality for women. Overcoming their social and political differences, they forged a strong sisterhood of militancy and of feminist radicalism in prison, persuaded that America's male-run government was thoroughly unjust. As known "jailbirds" and established radicals, the NWP faced the final stage of militancy--the last campaigns of 1918, 1919 and 1920--determined to carry their struggle to success without turning back.

---

[1] Doris Stevens, *Jailed*, p. 229; Irwin, *Paul and the NWP*, pp. 267-268, 418; Peterson and Fite, *Opponents of War*, p. 257, details the horrible treatment the IWW received in jail.

[2] Many form letters were sent out; members were also asked, if they could not come themselves, to secure a substitute. See, for example, Reel 51, October

correspondence, NWPP. Information on the prisoners in this section come from the same variety of sources listed in notes in Chapter Three.
[3] Gwinter statement, October 13, 1917, Reel 50, NWPP. She wrote to socialist Congressman Meyer London to complain about conditions.*Suffragist*, September 29, 1917, p. 4.
[4] Kettler in Gluck, *Parlor to Prison*, pp. 228, 246; Stevens, *Jailed*, appendix.
[5] Stevens, *Jailed*, p. 153, appendix; Vivian Pierce to Paul February 8, 1919, Reel 93; on Fotheringhams, Hill to Baker, July 12, 1917, Reel 45; Margaret Fotheringham statement, October 1917, Reel 51; Fry, Reyher interview, p. 37; *Shreveport Times*, February 10, 1919; Shields in NWP news release, January 18, 1919, Reel 92, NWPP.
[6] Alice Belcher to Abby Scott Baker, July 3, 1917, Reel 45, NWPP; Stafford affidavit, November 28, 1917, Reel 53, NWPP.
[7] Lincoln affidavit, November 28, 1917, Reel 53; Irwin, *Paul and the NWP*, p. 282; Brannan's affidavit, November 23, 1917, Reel 81; Dr. John Brannan to Paul, November, 1917; Doris Stevens to Dora Lewis, December 5, 1917, Reel 53; Nolan affidavit, November 23, 1917, Reel 52, NWPP.
[8] Quay affidavit, November 28, 1917, Robertson affidavit, November 28, 1917, Reel 53, NWPP; FBI File 108-250, Document 25025, Reel 108, report of May 1, 1919, p. 5, Re: Prison Special.
[9] According to matron Virginia Bovee, brutal beatings at the "whipping post" were carried out by Whittaker and his son, but that particular punishment was not dealt to the suffrage prisoners, so far as we know. Bovee affidavit, August 28, 1917, Reel 47, NWPP.
[10] Kellogg to author, March 24, 1983.
[11] Irwin, *Paul and the NWP*, p. 274.
[12] Arniel's statement, October 3, 1917, Reel 49, NWPP.
[13] Bovee affidavit, August 28, 1917, Reel 47, NWPP. All the NWP affidavits affirm the tainted food, lack of exercise, and so on.
[14] Bartlett to Dr. Paul Pearson, September 8, 1917 (from Occuquan); to Mr. Bartlett, September 1917, and from George Hamilton to Dorothy Bartlett, September 15, 1917, Reel 64; Bartlett affidavit, November 5, 1917, Reel 51; Kendall affidavit, November 2, 1920, Reel 83; Chase to Paul, September 11, 1918, Reel 64; Greiner affidavit, November 1917, Reel 52; Winston in January 9, 1919 NWP Press Release, Reel 92; Winston affidavit, November 2, 1920, Reel 83; Elsie Hill to Doris Stevens, August 1918, Reel 64, NWPP; *Suffragist*, August 31, 1918, p. 5; Stevens, *Jailed*, appendix.
[15] *New York Times*, July 20, 1917, p. 1; July 27, 1917, p. 9; Clarke to Lester Walton, August 1, 1917, Reel 46, NWPP. Still, Virginia Arnold okayed a letter sent by a friendly attorney, W.H. Clarke of New York, to Mrs. James Laidlaw trying to persuade her not to criticize the NWP in the press, which read in part: "There is many a time when the conservatives are helped out of a hole or a deadlock

by having a band of radical Indians to dump tea in Boston Harbor, or an army of KKKers to stop outrages which would have been long drawn out under calmer methods." This is another example of casual racism, as in Irwin's use of "association with colored prisoners" as the telling example of prison indignities. W.H. Clarke to Laidlaw, August 1, 1917, Reel 46, NWPP; Irwin, *Paul and the NWP*, p. 300. Also, in her affidavit of October 1, 1920 (Reel 92), Elizabeth Kalb felt mixing Negro and white prisoners was bad.
[16] *New York Times*, October 5, 1917, p. 11.
[17] Stevens, *Jailed*, p. 155.
[18] Kettler in Gluck, *Parlor to Prison*, p. 245. Johns tried to pass the hours in jail by reading, asking Dora Lewis to get her Freud and Jung. October 1917 Lewis memo, Reel 51, NWPP.
[19] Johns' affidavit, October 26, 1917, Reel 51, NWPP; Gluck, *Parlor to Prison*, p. 244.
[20] Account of "Riot" of October 1917 at Occuquan, Reel 51, NWPP. According to Hara, after the battle, Tweedale did allow them to call headquarters. A lawyer then met Johns with her guards in Washington, and she was taken to a hospital, not a mental institution, for treatment. Gluck, *Parlor to Prison*, p. 245.
[21] Vera Samarodin to "Russian ambassador," N.D. in Stevens, *Jailed*, p. 179; Kendall, "Garrett Philosopher, *Buffalo Times*, September 1917; Linda Gordon, *Woman's Body, Woman's Right,* p. 233. Gordon also states that birth control leader Agnes Smedley was once told by a police officer he wished they were in the South, because there she would be "strung up to the first lamp post." Greiner affidavit, November 1917, Reel 52; Alice Gram, November 23, 1917 statement, Reel 52; Week Affidavit, November 1, 1920, Reel 83; Nolan affidavit, November 23, 1917, Reel 52, NWPP; Freedman, *Their Sisters' Keepers: Woman's Prison Reform in America, 1830-1930* (Ann Arbor: University of Michigan Press, 1981), p. 1; Juengling affidavit, November 30, 1917, Reel 53, NWPP.
[22] Shields, in a January 18, 1919 NWP Press Release, Reel 92, NWPP; Fisher quote in Stevens, *Jailed*, p. 156; Watson to Flanagan, December 12, 1917, Reel 53, NWPP.
[23] Morey to Paul, February 8, 1917, Reel 39; Whitehouse to Paul, October 25, 1917, Reel 51, NWPP.
[24] Kettler, in Gluck, *Parlor to Prison*, p. 250; Walker to Dora Lewis, March 9, 1918, Reel 58, NWPP.
[25] Chisholm to Dora Lewis, December 1917, Reel 54, NWPP.
[26] Colvin, *A Rebel in Thought*, p. 142; Dr. John Rogers to Doris Stevens, November 20, 1917, Reel 52; Elizabeth Rogers to Paul, September 25, 1916, Reel 33, and February 6, 1919, Reel 69, NWPP.
[27] Effie Boutwell Main to Doris Steven, August 25, 1918 and to Paul, August 24, 1918, Reel 64, NWPP; Hunkins, "Talk to Women's Press Club"; Louisine

Havemeyer, "The Prison Special: Memories of a Militant," *Scribner's Magazine*, June 1922, p. 672.

[28] Beatrice Kinkead to Paul, September 15, 1917, Reel 48, NWPP; Elizabeth Stuyvesant to Paul, October 5, 1917, Reel 50, NWPP.

[29] Headquarters to Reyneau, July 17; Reyneau to Lucy Burns, July 17, 1917, Reel 45. In light of the *Times* report that Reyneau objected to black women prisoners, it is interesting that she later painted portraits of "distinguished Negroes" and was involved in the civil rights movement of the 1950s. *New York Times* obituary, October 21, 1964, p. 63. Dr. Walter J. Adams to Virginia Arnold, October 26, 1917, Reel 50 and November 1, 1917, Reel 51, NWPP.

[30] Irwin Blumberg to "Secretary of the NWP," November 25, 1917, Reel 52, NWPP.

[31] Fisher to Mabel Vernon, July 11, 1917, Reel 45; Henry Graves to Wilson, September 2, 1917, Reel 210, Wilson Papers on Microfilm; Mickle Paul to Alice Paul, October 8, 1917, Reel 12; and August 16, 1918, Reel 63, NWPP.

[32] See especially October 1917, Reel 49, NWPP.

[33] Mr. Kessler to Paul, October 4, 1917; Mrs. James Winsor to Paul, September 5, 1917, Reel 49; Clara Hamilton to "Miss Small," Headquarters, November 16, 1917; Catharine Flanagan to Mary Ingham, November 22, 1917, Henry Butterworth to Virginia Arnold, November 15, 1917, Reel 52; Katharine Fisher to Mabel Vernon, July 11, 1917, Reel 45; Ellen Clary to Headquarters, November 20, 1917, Reel 52; NWP Report November 27, 1917; Whitcomb affidavit, November 28, 1917, Reel 52; *New York Times*, July 19, 1917, p. 2; Abby Scott Baker to Ruth Pickering, January 14, 1918, Reel 55, NWPP.

[34] Reyher in Ford interview; Florence Boeckel, April 1919 NWP Press Release, Reel 92, NWPP. Non-prisoner organizers Clara Louise Rowe and Beulah Amidon also married between 1917 and 1919. M. Toscan Bennett telegram, January 10, 1919, Reel 92, Rebecca Winsor Evans to Paul, January 21, 1919, Reel 69, NWPP; Gardner in *New York Times*, July 19, 1917, p. 2; on Hopkins, Irwin, *Paul and the NWP*, p. 234.

[35] Helen Paul to Alice Paul, November 22, 1917, Reel 52; and November 29, 1917, Reel 53, NWPP.

[36] Bland, "Suffrage Militancy of Lucy Burns," p. 16; Shippen Lewis to Dora Lewis, November 1917, Reel 52; Dorothy Bartlett to Dr. Paul Pearson, September 8, 1917, Reel 48, NWPP.

[37] *Sunday Boston Post*, March 2, 1919, p. 1; *Salt Lake Telegraph*, November 11, 1917, p. 2.

[38] *Buffalo Express* clipping, August 9, 1917 on Reel 48; Nell Mercer to Lucy Burns, February 3, 1919, Reel 68; on Purtell, Katharine Houghton Hepburn to Elizabeth Flanagan, August 29, 1918, Reel 64; Elizabeth McShane to Virginia Arnold, November 2, 1917, Reel 51; Purtell to Lucy Burns, January 8, 1919, Reel 67.

[39] Chase obituary, *New York Times*, September 26, 1963, p. 35; *Notable American Women*, p. 148; Chase to Paul, May 26, 1917, Reel 43 and September 11, 1918, Reel 64; Chase to Burns, December 13, 1918, NWPP. According to Josephus Daniels, he and MacAdoo were in favor of Civil Service women employees participating in suffrage demonstrations and Wilson agreed to it. He also said the NWP gave Wilson "many an uncomfortable hour," but that Wilson was converted by women's war work. Daniels, *The Wilson Era: The Years of Peace, 1910-1917* (Chapel Hill, 1947), p. 458.

[40] William P. Harvey of the War Labor Board wrote that there was an analogy between the methods of the NWP and those of labor: pickets, an "undaunted front" when illegally imprisoned, and collective bargaining based on political (as opposed to labor's economic) strength. *Suffragist*, July 5, 1919, p. 9.

[41] In 1915 Remington Arms had built a factory in Bridgeport employing 15,000 workers. The machinists union there was solidly socialist. In July of 1917, IWW leader Samuel Lavit led a walkout to protest women being hired to do the more menial chores of metal polishing, but by 1918 tool makers led a strike which listed among its demands "equal pay for women who did equal work." Tenzer, Elsie Hill interview, part V, p. 22; David Montgomery, *Worker's Control in America* (Cambridge University Press, 1979), pp. 127-132; *Machinists Monthly Journal*, February 1918, Volume 30, pp. 161-162; September 1919, Volume 31, p. 853; January 1920, p. 20 and April 1920, Volume 32, p. 363.

[42] When she was released from jail, Vervane sent a telegram to Samuel Gompers of the AFL, asking Gompers to confer with Wilson about passing woman suffrage. NWP Press Release, January 18, 1919, and January 23, 1919, Reel 92. The latter release said Vervane was working with union leaders to secure the provision that girls under 18 should not receive back pay and wage increases that had been won, showing the limits of feminist power in unions. See also Vervane to Burns and Edith Ainge, February 2, 1919, Reel 68, NWPP.

[43] Both Eva Weaver and Helen Chisaski came to Washington to protest Josephine Bennett's arrest, as well as make their own statement of solidarity with the suffragists. NWP Press Release, January 23, 1919, Reel 92, NWPP.

[44] Scott to Burns, January 23, 1919 and February 3, 1919, Reel 68, NWPP.

[45] On Weaver, Emory to Paul, September 1917, Reel 48; On Cosu, Irwin, *Paul and the NWP*, p. 281; Hornsby incident in Dorothy Day affidavit, November 28, 1917, Reel 52; Wiley in November 12, 1917 Picket Report, Reel 87; Emory to Paul, September 5, 1917, Reel 48; Heffelfinger affidavit, December 1917, Reel 54; On Ainge, Biographical material, Jamestown Historical Society; Doris Hazard to Paul July 24, 1916, Reel 33; Ainge affidavit, November 16, 1917, Reel 13; NWP Press Release, September 4, 1917, Reel 91, NWPP; *Suffragist* editor to Charles Beard, September 6, 1917, Reel 48, NWPP. *Suffragist*, September 22, 1917, p. 7; Lincoln affidavit, November 28, 1917, Reel 53, NWPP; Kate Heffelfinger to Beulah Amidon, November 8, 1917, Reel 52; Ascough in NWP

Press Release, August 20, 1918, Reel 91, NWPP. Ascough was very ill in prison and had to leave after two days, paying her fine. NWP member Annie Porritt complained to organizer Catharine Flanagan that Ascough "didn't stick it out" and left her comrades, but Katharine Hepburn defended her as being dangerously ill. Porritt to Flanagan, August 26, 1918 and "Treasurer" to Hepburn, August 18, 1918, Reel 64, NWPP.

[46] Cora Week to Alice Paul, August 1918 (Butterworth was imprisoned in November of 1917), Reel 64; Nellie Barnes to Betty Gram, November 3, 1917, Reel 51, NWPP; Blanche Spellman to Paul, November 17, 1917, Reel 51, NWPP.

[47] Havemeyer, "Prison Special." p. 666.

[48] Wold to Paul, August 28, 1918, Reel 64, NWPP; Lincoln affidavit, November 28, 1917, Reel 53, NWPP.

[49] *Suffragist*, February 9, 1918, p. 13; August 31, 1918, p. 9. See songs in Appendix C.

[50] Katharine Fisher statement, September 1917, Reel 49, NWPP.

[51] *Lifting the Curtain*, p. 250.

[52] *New York Times*, July 20, 1917, p. 1; July 27, 1917, p. 9.

[53] November 8, 1917, Reel 52, NWPP.

[54] Hara affidavit, October 26, 1917, Reel 51; Dorothy Bartlett to Dr. Paul Pearson, September 8, 1917, to Mr. Bartlett, September 1917, Reel 46; Bartlett affidavit, November 5, 1917, Reel 51.

[55] This was interesting from Mary Winsor--Ellen Winsor had complained about CU racism in 1915. Mary Winsor once founded a Limited Suffrage League to keep the "criminal and illiterate" from voting. But she did once scoff at suffragists "who were no feminists"--perhaps her strong feminism became more inclusive in jail. Krone, "Dauntless Women," p. 12; Katzenstein, *Suffrage in Pennsylvania*, p. 58. Winsor affidavit, November 23, 1917, Reel 52, NWPP.

[56] Kendall, in her column, "The Garrett Philosopher," *Buffalo Express*, N.D., fall 1917.

[57] *Suffragist*, August 11, 1917, p. 7.

[58] July 19, 1917, Reel 45, NWPP. The treasurer of the New York Birth-Control League, Frederick Blossom, also wrote Abby Baker on their "splendid fight . . . your group has the real rebel techniques, the only ones that can win." August 2, 1917, Reel 46, NWPP.

[59] NWP Press Release, for Paul statement, November 27, 1917, Reel 91, NWPP; Wiley in *New York Times* obituary, January 7, 1964, p. 33.

[60] Kuhn to Paul, August 10, 1918, Reel 63; Spencer to Paul, January 12, 1918, Reel 55; Dowell to NWP Headquarters, February 19, 1919, Kellogg to Paul, February 15, 1919, Reel 69, NWPP.

[61] Sheinburg to Gram, December 4, 1917, Reel 54; Katharine Fisher to Anne Martin, October 18, 1917, Reel 50; Fisher statement, September 1917, Reel 49, NWPP.
[62] Day, *The Long Loneliness* (New York: Harper and Row, 1952), p. 90.

Chapter Eight

A Victory for Militancy 1918-1920

> Did you expect us to turn back? We never turn back . . . and we won't until democracy is won!
>
> -Elsie Hill, 1919

The significance of militancy for the winning of the vote is twofold: it is important firstly because win or lose, a broad cross-section of American women literally fought for their rights in an egalitarian feminist, militant campaign; and secondly, because militant tactics *were* effective in successfully achieving a national woman suffrage amendment. Woman's Party feminists organized to use women's power in a brilliantly conceived, nonviolent resistance against the intractable Wilson government, pushing them to action. It was the aggressive Congressional Union which started an energetic campaign for a national amendment, and which pushed NAWSA to more national action. And it was the NWP which would continue to keep suffrage in the headlines and keep pressure on the national government with new actions to create public sympathy between 1918 and 1920. As the militants kept pushing, at the peak of their militancy, against a still indifferent male government, they were met yet again with misogynous rhetoric and violence, which they skillfully countered with symbolically "female," nonviolent actions, until they won their victory.

In the process of headline-making, the militant suffragists had to contend with their by then, widely acknowledged reputation as radical feminists and seditious political dissenters. In the context of America's full involvement in the first World War, this was very difficult for individual Woman's Party "outlaws," but they thought their sacrifice a painful necessity. In spite of their unsavory reputation, the Woman's Party continued to attract a wildly varied lot of women; and from Louise Bryant to Louisine Havemeyer, they were all quite willing to see their struggle through to the finish. Anathema to the DAR, but heroic to socialist allies, the militant demonstrators found original ways to shock the public and keep suffrage alive and controversial. The peak stage of militancy, of "administration terrorism" and hunger strikes for political prisoner status, was followed by victory in the House. But seeing no movement in the Senate, the NWP mustered its forces in pressure on that body, late in 1918, a campaign met with antifemale rhetoric, violence and no Senate action. In the final campaign, Paul and her forces concentrated yet again on the President himself, dogging his every step, burning him in effigy, making use of pure, nonviolent resister moral suasion in different theaters around the country, and finally winning victory in the Senate, and then (rather anticlimactically) in the several states. Militancy provided the telling pressure on Washington politicians, and provided its practitioners with well-deserved pride in their own female strength. The feminists of the Woman's Party had nothing but contempt for a male-run government which had beaten and imprisoned them rather than allow them a share in American democracy. Their belief that the American government sorely needed the participation of women was only strengthened by such experiences, as was the conviction that theirs was necessarily a woman's fight.

The feminists' militant actions had created public sympathy for woman suffrage. There had been enormous public pressure created by their treatment in prison. That pressure helped force Wilson and the House--the most representative American legislative body--to act on the issue the Woman's Party had made urgent and unavoidable. All of the NWP accounts of progress made in January and February describe the political action taken as directly attributable to their actions. And there was political action on suffrage in 1918. On January 9, President Wilson publicly endorsed national woman suffrage, and on January 11, the House passed the amendment 274 to 136, with the necessary two-thirds majority. In February the National Committees of both major parties endorsed woman suffrage. The *Suffragist* described the pickets as "winning" the House; and Caroline Katzenstein, Pennsylvania state officer, stated that "1918 brought the capitulation of President Wilson." Wilson was given little credit for his endorsement, characterized by the NWP as tardy and a surrender, rather than a positive step. According to Abby Scott Baker, the President had only helped the House vote in order "to help Woodrow Wilson." Not only was the President's action not praised, the NWP did not publicly acknowledge NAWSA's efforts at this point. Although NAWSA and the President certainly deserve credit for their efforts in the House victory, both *had* been pushed by a determined NWP strategy.[1]

Even though House members had to acknowledge the Woman's Party tactics made suffrage an unavoidable issue, many of them, during the fascinating debate, would not credit the NWP with serving the cause of suffrage, quite the contrary. Congressman Scott Ferris of Oklahoma disapproved of picketing the White House "or any other wild militancy, hunger strikes, and efforts of that sort." Ferris, like so many of his countrymen, equated the NWP with the British WSPU, even bringing up Emily Davison's run at the King's Derby horse. Ferris did not like

> . . . the course of those women that throw themselves in front of horses, become agitators, lay off their womanly qualities in their efforts to secure votes. I do not approve of anything unwomanly anywhere, anytime, and my course today in supporting this suffrage amendment is not guided by such conduct on the part of a very few women here or elsewhere. [Applause][2]

Ferris was concerned with unwomanly behavior, as was Republican Congressman Edward Gray of New Jersey, who feared that giving women equal political rights would lead to the "deterioration of manhood" and "male vitality." Congressman William Gordon of Ohio called the NWP "militant Amazons" who had been "coaxing, teasing and nagging the President of the United States for the purpose of inducing him by coercion to club Congress into adapting this joint [suffrage] resolution."[3] Abby Scott Baker reported that after this speech, the Republicans started shouting, "They did it and they got him," creating a roar and a din joined by the Democrats.[4] The outburst reflects how emotional Congressmen became over having their male virility threatened by the Women's Party.

Support was voiced by men like Republican Congressman John Langley of Kentucky. Langley spoke not "in criticism or commendation," but wondered if promises made to the NWP were broken, then "whether in that silent, peaceful protest that was against this broken faith there can be found sufficient warrant for the indignities which the so-called 'pickets' suffered." Langley most objected to

> cultured, intellectual women arrested and dragged off to prison because of their method of giving publicity to what they believed to be the truth. I will confess that the question sometimes arose in my mind whether when the impartial history of this great struggle has been written their names may not be placed upon the roll of martyrs to the cause to which they were consecrating their lives in the manner that they deemed most effective.[5]

NWP militancy had created a situation where action had to be taken. Woman's Party leaders believed that their "martyrdom" had been very effective thus far, but that winning the Senate and keeping pro-suffrage public pressure on Wilson would be difficult.

The question for the NWP in 1918 was how, as established "seditious" radicals, they could still court support for their cause. After the House victory, they postponed further demonstrations, but not lobbying, organizing, speaking and doing whatever else necessary to keep suffrage in the public eye. The NWP was sure that it had been the public protests over their jailing that helped lead the House to act on the amendment. It was therefore very important to them "to convert as much of the press as possible, so that it makes the cause its own, and as for the rest, to give it such compelling news that not even a European war or an attempted boycott by the government will keep it off the front pages." But, as in the past, the "seditious" Woman's Party could not always be sure in 1918 that news of their actions would reach local papers, news they hoped would win more converts to the militant cause. In New Orleans, NWP state officer Alice Cosu complained that the papers were not publishing NWP articles: "It is dreadful how few women are aware to the big results that Alice Paul's sacrifice has brought."[6] It would be up to NWP organizers and speakers to make women aware.

It would be far from easy to enlist support, but the NWP had the advantage of charismatic speakers like Rebecca Hourwich, Lucy Burns, Doris Stevens, Abby Scott Baker--and Dudley Field Malone. Malone was highly dramatic, telling his audiences: "But to the women who have endured torture and public scorn . . . remember it is only those who have dared first to suffer who hear the paean-cry of immortality." [7] Hundreds of new members came in during the period of greatest militant activism. By March of 1918 the Woman's Party had 29,405 members.[8] The NWP gained endorsements and petitions to the Senate from groups as diverse as the WTUL, Russian writers, women munition workers, and the Farmers' Open Forum, that spring.[9] Still ambiguous on including black women, southern organizer Vivian Pierce wrote Paul that she "did not want to be undemocratic" and so did speak to groups of black women. Pierce thought black women should join the NWP (but not come to luncheons). According to Rebecca Hourwich Reyher, membership was technically open to all women, but each state did what it wanted in terms of exclusion. A 1918 article in the *Suffragist* did explore the question of whether woman suffragists should look for solidarity with blacks, because black women were "forced to take men's places as street cleaners" during the war, and thus needed the ballot.[10] Although seeking sympathy everywhere, the NWP was not quite ready to join forces with their black sisters, although they were more than willing to maintain alliances with leftist political radicals.

Socialist women continued to join NWP protest demonstrations in droves in 1918. As fellow dissenters who had had their civil rights ignored during the Wilson war administration, the NWP and anti-war leftists became allies. The socialist *Liberator* gave them full credit for suffrage passage in the House, "definitely an NWP victory." The "patient persuaders" [NAWSA] did not play "the political game" like the "militant idealist" did, "with a certain hardness of grain that enabled her to see and meet the facts of human nature as a political fighter must." Not only were the militants savvy political fighters, but "Alice Paul and her young army of militants were one of three of the *leading radical forces* in American politics in the near future," along with the Non-Partisan League and the socialists. A list of members of NWP "comrades" was sought by Upton Sinclair when he started his new "little radical paper," dealing with liberal peace terms and post-war social reconstruction.[11] Having achieved some success on suffrage--the House vote--by using militant protests, the NWP gained alliances and was lionized by other dissenters as a true, "radical" force. Militancy brought public attention and favor in some circles, but it also created enmity.

NWP radicals still had to contend with the mainline suffrage organization. Clara Louise Rowe, organizing in Ohio, wrote Paul that NAWSA was very strong there, "but doing no work." According to Rowe, NAWSA was rather like an exclusive woman's club, hostile to a competing group coming in.[12] NAWSA leaders, as is obvious from NAWSA's Anna Shaw's indifference about her friend Dora Lewis's jailing, were not at all sympathetic to the NWP.

A case in point is that of Sue Shelton White, in 1917 a member of NAWSA and the Tennessee Equal Suffrage Association. The thirty-year-old White was the youngest daughter of a lawyer/minister from Jackson, Tennessee, a descendent of Thomas Jefferson. Jackson was in every Tennessee women's club imaginable, a court reporter, and appointed by the governor in 1918 to be Secretary of the Tennessee Commission for the Blind. (In 1923 she earned her degree and then practiced law.) Lucy Branham called White "a most unusual woman, capable and brilliant and sincere." White had already interceded for Rebecca Hourwich and Maud Younger when they had trouble securing audiences in Tennessee. White told Hourwich that she had doubted the wisdom of picketing, but did not "understand the spirit that would deny a hearing" to the NWP. Carrie Chapman Catt was horrified when White, one of NAWSA's best young leaders, decided to go over to the militants. White wrote Catt that when she heard that Maud Younger was called "pro-German" she knew it was not true and must defend her. If necessary, she wrote, "I would have to join the pickets at the White House gates and take the consequences, not so much for equal suffrage as for freedom of speech, which is not only essential to our cause, but to every other step in human progress."[13] The dangerous militants even made converts from NAWSA that spring.

By the summer of 1918, the radical suffragists decided they must act to pressure the Senate. The atmosphere for militant protest remained hostile. Some Congressional action had been taken in the spring: in May of 1918 they passed the Sabotage and Sedition Acts which prescribed tough punishment for those expressing antigovernment and "disloyal" opinions. The National Woman's Party, as a threat to national security, had definitely helped inspire some legislators to pass those laws. Nevertheless, the NWP had pushed the government to a partial victory through its militant actions. They then retreated to lobby, propagandize and organize, hoping the Senate would soon pass woman suffrage. For seven months they were silent, but by the end of summer 1918, the women decided to end the truce. In May woman suffrage had twice been called for a vote, but delays prevented it. On the 27th, Democrats had threatened a filibuster against it and the amendment died. One senator told Maud Younger the Senate was tired of being "nagged" on the issue. President Wilson did write to recalcitrant senators, but the Woman's Party did not think he was firm enough; it was "good public relations" for him, but nothing for women. They decided that after seven months of no militant action, they would have to take matters into their own hands.

With the period of retreat over, the NWP planned dramatic demonstrations throughout the rest of the year, actions which would bring forth a stern reaction from the administration and antiwoman rhetoric on the Senate floor. The initial proceeding was a series of protest meetings starting on the anniversary of the birth of Inez Milholland Boissevain, each theatrically staged across from the White House, in front of the statue of Lafayette, the fighter for American liberty. When she appealed to members to join the August demonstrations, Paul stressed it was not her intent for them to be arrested. She believed that if enough "prominent women" were there, they would not be, but could not guarantee anything. Paul also thought it crucial to include women workers, especially munitions and Red Cross workers, for their very considerable "war service" publicity value.[14] Paul had little difficulty recruiting militantly impatient women to protest Senate inaction.

The August demonstrations against the Senate only yielded hostility against the women demonstrators. On August 6th, 100 women gathered at the Lafayette monument bearing banners protesting their continued unenfranchisement and condemning Wilson and the Democrats. One banner would particularly anger the Senate: "We Deplore The Weakness Of President Wilson In Permitting The Senate To Line Itself With The Prussian Reichstag By Denying Democracy To The People."[15] The authorities were forewarned about the demonstrations. The administration could always count on NAWSA's Helen Gardener to inform them of Paul's plans. She warned Wilson that the Woman's Party was trying to prevent the Democratic party from getting credit for passing woman suffrage. Perhaps Wilson believed that, since he reportedly "smiled at the women's arrest" in the park.[16] Dora Lewis, and then Hazel Hunkins attempted to speak, but were immediately arrested. Altogether 48 women were arrested and several hurt, many while climbing the statue of Lafayette and attempting to make speeches, and others, including Alice Paul, while simply listening.

Government authorities refused to tell the imprisoned militants on what charge they were being held, but just ordered them to appear in court the next day. The *Suffragist* reported that the women were arrested "by order of the President's military aide, Colonel Ridley." The District Attorney said he "had had no orders" initially, about their sentencing. Soon the charges of "holding a meeting on public grounds with no permit" and for some, "climbing a statue," were decided upon. The case was twice postponed. At their trials, the nonviolent resisters pleaded not guilty, refused to recognize the court because they were an "unenfranchised class," protested their arrests as unlawful, and then refused to answer questions. All decided not to pay the fines, and 26 were sentenced to from 10 to 15 days in jail. At the other two protest demonstrations held in August (on the 12th and 14th), some of the women did succeed in making speeches showing their resentment at government suppression, before being arrested.[17] Many of the demonstrators had suffered broken and sprained wrists from vainly trying to hold to their purple, gold and white sashes, or their banners: Connecticut member Ruby Koenig's arm was sprained by the police; Edna Purtell suffered a broken finger; Lucy Burns, Hazel Hunkins, Julia Emory and Gladys Greiner were also injured. But the worst suffering came, as in 1917, in the district jail, filled with sewer gas and rats. After visitations by members of the legislature and a rousing public protest, the women were released after five days. The *Suffragist* insisted the action signified a government admission it had erred in still trying to suppress legitimate protest.[18]

Paul and her followers had not succeeded in forcing a Senate vote with the Lafayette Park demonstrations, so another action was carried out on September 16--a burning of the "hollow phrases" of the President, on the day the Senate Rules

Committee informed the NWP that the Senate would recess without taking action on woman suffrage. President Wilson told a delegation of Democratic women that day he was in sympathy with woman suffrage and would do all he could to urge an early vote. But since the Senate had already recessed, the women realized the President had been simply "uttering more fine words," to cover his inaction, so they took his words and burned them in Lafayette Park. The demonstrators called on Lafayette to speak for them, because they had "no power but justice and right"; they said they based their action upon those of the Crusaders who burned phrases of "those responsible for injustice." The crowd roared its approval and the police made no arrests.[19]

Historian David Morgan gives entire credit to Carrie Chapman Catt for a sudden reversal and scheduling of a vote for woman suffrage on October 1, but the NWP's "direct action" demonstrations also helped keep suffrage a burning issue. After long debate and a presidential appeal for passage, a Senate vote was taken. Militant feminists made Senators as nervous as Congressmen had been. The banner linking the Senate with the Prussian Reichstag was unfavorably mentioned. Senator Kenneth McKellar, Democrat from Tennessee, chastised the NWP for its "unseemly protest" which was "very hurtful indeed." McKellar insisted senators would not change their minds "out of unlawful assemblages or attacks upon the President." Senator Miles Poindexter, however, thought it was the NWP that had changed Wilson's mind on suffrage. The nature of the NWP battle seemed to fascinate male politicians. Many of the senators made sure in debate that the NWP should not be confused with the more "womanly" and moderate NAWSA (although some of them were still unsure which was which). Senator Charles Thomas of Colorado, for example, cautioned his fellows not to "mix Mrs. Catt up with the outfit which had one of its periodic outbreaks on the streets a few days ago."[20] Anti-suffrage Democrat, Senator James Reed from Missouri, insisted women should concentrate on keeping the home:

> There are some women today who think that is an ignoble calling. . . . [T]hose women at least never ought to be permitted to vote. The woman who thinks that the keeping of the home is beneath her sex is not fit to vote and is not fit for anything else. . . . There are some differences between men and women that were ordained by the Almighty and that all the cranks and agitators of earth can never remove.

Reed thought that the "cranks" of the NWP had probably been influenced by Bolsheviks (if not by the Republicans). Republican Senator Cumins did defend the agitators, saying they had committed no crime and were entitled to demonstrate. He had little sympathy with their methods, but said "their treatment in confinement is a disgrace to the civilized world."[21] The militants were not worried about senatorial

Burning the President's "Hollow Phrases." Women pictured include Lucy Branham in the middle, Ernestine Hara to her right, and Lucy Burns on the far right.
Figure 9

censure about their femininity; they only wanted to press them to action on suffrage.

At this point Woodrow Wilson made what turned out to be a futile plea to the Senate for passage, which the Woman's Party thought a "beautiful appeal" although a bit late. The NWP felt he had "protected" the Senate opposition for too long for it to break down because of one speech. Wilson implored the Senate to make America a true democracy and reward women for their war services. The war services argument had always proved effective with Wilson, one of the reasons Paul liked to use munitions workers in demonstrations. He certainly was not about to publicly credit the "madwomen" of the NWP. In fact, in his speech he said "the voices of foolish and intemperate agitators do not reach me at all!" Like fellow Liberal Herbert Asquith of England, Wilson would not admit to listening to "outdoors agitation," although obviously the agitators' voices had reached him. Woman's suffrage was defeated (short of a two-thirds majority) 62 to 34. Maud Younger described the women suffragists as stunned, "some with a dull sense of injustice, some with burning resentment."[22] To Alice Paul, it was clear another militant action must commence at once.

The NWP 1918 fall campaign took the shape of a picket of the Senate and a campaign battle waged to defeat Democratic senators in the West *and* to support two pro-suffrage Democrats in the East. This strategy was prompted by the situation of needing just two votes to win suffrage, the two eastern Democrats being pledged to support the amendment. The Woman's Party took some credit for the subsequent election of a Republican Congress and for Wilson's inclusion of woman suffrage as part of his administration's program in December. The women also began another picket, this time a picket of the Senate, conducted throughout October and November. The Senate pickets were detained by police but not formally charged: authorities wanted no more hunger strikes. But this by no means meant they would not aim to discourage the militant "crazies." The NWP protesters were repeatedly rushed and beaten by capitol police. The police confiscated their banners denouncing the Senate's inaction, and became (with the crowd) particularly incensed by the ones that read "Germany Has Established 'Equal, Universal, Secret, Direct Franchise.' The Senate Has Denied Equal Universal Suffrage To America. Which Is More Of A Democracy, Germany Or America?" Top Secret Service officials debated about whether to give that banner back to the NWP, and decided finally to "take no action" against them. Meanwhile, the *Chicago Tribune* called the Senate demonstrators "petticoat Bolsheviks." On October 28, Annie Arniel was thrown to the ground and knocked unconscious. A week later, a group of women wore black arm bands to commemorate "the death of justice" in the Senate. The war had ended on November 11, and the Congress was about to recess. The Woman's Party attacked the government for going to the peace conference with "unclean hands," not yet representing true democracy. The "unclean hands" banners drove the crowd to a frenzy and the radical women were again badlv beaten, particularly Alice Paul.[23] The war in Europe had ended, but the Woman's Party's war with Congress and the administration had not.

It was obvious at the end of 1918 that the "iron-jawed angels" of the Woman's Party were not growing more patient. Their demands for women's political freedom had not yet been met. The women were especially furious that the President had sailed to France without securing the two votes needed in the Senate. Thus the NWP executive committee decided at their December meeting to burn all of Wilson's past speeches on "freedom and democracy," to try to embarrass him as a "champion of world liberty." Speeches were made from LaFayette's statue and then Wilson's words burned. Louise Bryant felt utter frustration during her participation in the December demonstrations: "The only emotion I had all the time I was walking along and after I had climbed unto the statue was one of shame. I felt red in the face. I had an almost overpowering un-ladylike desire to break somebody's head, by way of relief. It seemed so degrading to me to have to plead for suffrage!"[24] Even ultraradical Louise Bryant had rallied to the militant suffrage cause in the wake of the violent suppression of their protests. Alienated and defiant, woman recruits kept coming to Washington.

The NWP still attracted a large number of women who were willing to lose their reputations as sane members of their communities. These militants did not need much urging to express their fury with the Wilson government. All sorts of women faced the public disgrace of being involved in the 1918 militant demonstrations. About half the women arrested were veteran demonstrators--NWP leaders, state officers and organizers--but the other portion were brand new to demonstrating. The *Suffragist* reported in mid-September that the NWP had 47,842 members, close to the highest number it would ever have. (And the Woman's Party quoted several newspapers crediting Alice Paul and the NWP with any success woman suffrage had had, and which protested their "harassment by the government.") Most women asked to participate readily accepted. As Minnesota state officer Bertha Moller impatiently put it, the "next step in human freedom" had to come from Washington. Rebecca Winsor Evans promised Paul she would come if it were not too hot, since she once had had a heat stroke: the "spirit is willing, but the flesh is weak." Evans was sister to Mary and Ellen Winsor; a native of Ardmore, Pennsylvania. She felt she "*had* to go" demonstrate--"others should not sacrifice for me." Evans also informed Paul in August that she wanted "to exterminate" reporter David Lawrence of the *Washington Post*. Lawrence, wrote Evans, was "an impertinent little chit" for stating that women of the future would revere Woodrow Wilson.[25] The "prominent" Dr. Sarah H. Lockrey, a Congressional District "Chairman," was head of the gynecological clinic of Philadelphia's Interne Women's Hospital and surgeon at West Philadelphia Hospital for Women and Children. Lockrey could not understand why she was arrested since she went to make "a dignified, womanly . . . and legal protest." Ironically, Lockrey, who had often offered her (medical) services to the government, would eventually be released from jail in order to do emergency surgery for a doctor in France.[26]

Newspaperwoman Clara Wold wrote about her statue climbing exploit, on her first day in Washington, for the *Suffragist*. She had no time to sightsee, although she recognized the Capitol building. She was appalled by her arrest: "For once a distinct sense of protest rose within me."[27]

The government's treatment of woman demonstrators continued to shock them and motivate them to further militancy. Young Elizabeth Green Kalb, whose mother, Benigna Kalb, was the president of "Texas Farm Women," insisted that if the women of Texas knew of the situation in Washington:

> They would come in a body to join the protest of and for American womanhood. [That women] should be fallen upon by a set of ruffianly police, mauled about, dragged and struck in the most outrageous manner . . . is absolutely unthinkable. It makes one sick with shame for our boasted democracy.[28]

Incarceration for setting fire to Wilson's words only inflamed the women's anger. Bertha Moller was married to a Minneapolis educator and had two uncles in the Swedish parliament. Moller said she felt "a great deal more than $10.00 [her fine] worth of contempt for a court which would jail American women for asking for freedom."[29] Mary Nolan, the "oldest picket," wrote Paul: "We must be free or die." NWP women knew they had to go to extremes to press their case. Woman's Party leaders felt arrests and prison were still part of the strategy.

Burns was not as active in 1918 as previously, but Paul more than took up the slack. The militants were quite willing to keep following the inspirational leadership of Alice Paul. They shared her conviction about their protests: "My feeling about our movement, you see, is that it is pregnant with possibilities, that it is worth sacrificing everything for, leisure, money, reputation, and even our lives."[30] However, Dudley Field Malone, no enemy of the NWP, but worried about Doris Stevens, questioned Paul's methods. Malone was fearful lest Stevens "get into a bad nervous condition because [you] literally *feel* the suffering in jail of each of those women. This is once I wish you were indifferent as Alice Paul always is to others' suffering." This was unfair criticism, but it is true that Paul's followers were willing to suffer for her. Julia Emory's mother wrote Paul that August that Emory was "a dear child with more energy than strength," but so "completely loyal to Alice Paul" that only she could tell her to rest.[31]

As for Anne Martin, she felt she could serve the cause of women in other ways than the suffrage struggle, in 1918. Anne Martin ran for senator in 1918. Paul did not approve of Martin's campaign or of her members' working for Martin when they should have been concentrating on suffrage. Paul felt there were too few suffrage workers, and without more general political influence women would never be effective on issues of war, peace or anything else. Mabel Vernon and Margaret Whittemore both campaigned for Martin, to their chief's displeasure. Martin had felt somewhat estranged from the NWP for some time, since Maud Younger was actually heading the lobbying effort, although Martin was titular "chairman." She also felt optimistic about woman suffrage's imminent success. So when Senator Francis Newlands died, she decided to run for his seat as an independent. She stood for Wilson's war policy, prohibition and "public ownership of public utilities." Martin did not win, but thought her efforts had nonetheless been a "gesture to women."[32] Early in 1919, the Woman's Party decided to fight to gain more than "gestures" to women, from the President.

In 1919, in a final militant push for suffrage, the NWP used the shock value of new publicity stunts and nonviolent resistance techniques of moral martyrdom to keep suffrage a burning public issue and one Wilson would not be able to avoid resolving in their favor. The first months of 1919 therefore, brought an all-out NWP attack on the President to force him to secure the two votes they still needed for Senate passage of the suffrage amendment. The dramatic new measures would include lighting watchfires, burning images of Wilson in effigy, sponsoring a touring "prison train" and more anti-Wilson demonstrations in Boston and New York. After Congress passed the amendment, the nitty-gritty battles of winning ratification would begin.

In January, beginning on the birthday of Joan of Arc, the Woman's Party lit "watchfires for freedom" in a final push for suffrage. The first fire was lit in honor of Joan of Arc, because she was "denied by the King after serving him," and then burned at the stake by her enemies. Joan had fought for the French King Charles in the 1430s, against pro-English forces in her own country, during the 100 Years War. Pro-English churchment at the University of Paris had her tried for heresy, and then burned her for lying and "being of evil spirits." The King she had crowned stood by and never raised a ransom for her. "The history of Joan of Arc is the history of women and government throughout the ages of the world. They offer sacrifice and service and are humiliated and denied."[33]

Besides recalling the martyrdom of Joan of Arc, the NWP also cited the precedent of "The Great Illumination" of 1832, fires lit to show approval for the British 1832 Suffrage Reform Bill. To symbolize their desire for a suffrage reform amendment for women, the NWP had wood brought from all over the country: the first batch was taken from a tree in Philadelphia's Independence Square. The original plan of the executive committee, (made up of the same women as in 1917) was to keep a fire going constantly, and couple that with the ringing of an enormous bell on the hour until the amendment passed. Unfortunately the bell proved impracticable. There were complaints; among them was that Senator Medill McCormick's babies were being kept up by the bell. But the women did keep the fires going. Paul remembered that whenever the President would make "some wonderful, idealistic statement that was impossible to reconcile with what he was doing at home," the text would be burned in a cauldron.[34] With the watchfires, the suffrage radicals took dramatic, attention-getting steps beyond the LaFayette Square protest meetings of 1918.

THE SUFFRAGE WATCHFIRE BEFORE THE WHITE HOUSE.

Figure 10

As with earlier demonstrations, the authorities were not about to sit still for this phase of militant action. The following days brought a series of fires, speeches, new banners; and then riots and arrests. A crowd had gathered to watch on New Year's Day, as Edith Ainge started a fire in the cauldron for Dora Lewis. Ainge burned words taken from a speech Wilson had given in Manchester, England: "We will enter into no combinations of power which are not combinations of all of us." When Helena Hill Weed's turn came to put another Wilson speech to ashes, a group of soldiers suddenly overturned the burning urn and stamped out the fire. The women quickly relit it. A small riot ensued, followed by the arrest of Paul and organizers Ainge, Julia Emory and Hazel Hunkins. In the next few days more of the protesting women were arrested for "building a bonfire on a public highway between sunrise and sunset." On January 5, Emory, Mary Dubrow, Phoebe Munnecke and state officer Annie Arniel were sent to prison; some firestarters got five days, other ten. When they got there, they promptly started a hunger strike.[35]

Meanwhile the NWP women became quite adept at keeping the fire going in front of the White House in spite of attempts by police and crowd to douse it. Mildred Morris, a newspaper writer and investigator for the War Labor Board from Denver, became very good at lighting asbestos coils, the fires matching her flaming red hair. She once almost set off the White House trees. Hunkins described Morris as "cynical, thin and wiry, her hair red with streaks of white as it stood out in all directions. . . . [She] stopped at nothing . . . she slept where she happened to be . . . ate when she had money, drank too much and smoked endlessly." She had to be carried out of her jail cell on a stretcher. Hunkins herself once vaulted the White House fence and lit two fires on the lawn before being caught.[36]

On January the 8th, the well-to-do Josephine Bennett of Hartford, Connecticut, burned a speech of Wilson's which claimed that "being free, America desired to secure freedom for other nations." Bennett said women resented such a claim, and vowed to keep the "flame of liberty" burning until his words became reality. She was jailed, joining ten others sentenced on the 5th and 7th, and she, too, went on a hunger strike.[37] All told, 22 women were arrested and sentenced to up to five days for setting fires on the 13th; two on the 24th and five more on the 27th and 31st. The women insisted in court that by burning Wilson's "hypocritical words" they were expressing the "unmistakable impatience of American women," who "demand action."[38] Twenty NWP supporters were detained one to two days for refusing to stop applauding the defendants in court.

The federal courts gave the women short sentences in 1918 and 1919, but their time in prison was still grim and still newsworthy. The attacks on the government in the winter of 1919 were launched by a group of militant feminists who were alternately frightened and enraged at the United States government. Barnard student Bertha Wallerstein wrote Rebecca Hourwich from Precinct Number 3:

> I am under arrest! Aren't you ashamed of me?. . . . It's all such a lot of waiting and so little happening but of course when you reflect what it's for, you feel better. . . . Seriously, I have enjoyed the

> experience, tho I can't say it's exciting or terrifying. I have a fiendishly healthy young appetite, and it's going to be the dickens with the hunger strike![39]

That was written before being in jail, however. All the January prisoners went on hunger strikes. Sarah Colvin called prison "indescribably revolting" and said that the judge had limited their sentences to five days only so no one would die of a hunger strike. Organizer Phoebe Munnecke from Detroit, thought maybe her suffragist colleagues exaggerated the horror of jail, but once there she knew the stories "did not begin to equal the actual horrors of the District prison." Josephine Bennett said the vile jail smells "relieved my contemplated hunger strike of its martyrdom." Bennett's Senator visited her, but would not change his vote: he only wanted to get her out.[40] Rebecca Winsor Evans thought the Senate should be arrested for their hypocrisy, not the NWP demonstrators. The women had been in jail "fighting against cockroaches, bedbugs and lice, such an insignificant thing as an anti-suffrage Senator can never daunt them." Elizabeth Kalb voiced the commonly held sentiment: "As long as women are not free we are going to protest at the cost of health and strength against our political bondage."[41] The women felt the United States Senate would rather see women imprisoned than give them the vote, but they would not surrender.

As February began, Paul decided, according to Louisine Havemeyer, they had to do something more "drastic" or the administration would "refuse to fight" them; woman suffrage would die as an issue of public debate.[42] Wilson's speeches had been burned; now Wilson himself would be burned in effigy. Abby Scott Baker listed the President's failings for the *New York Times*: he had never demanded a party caucus on woman suffrage, as he had on other issues; he had campaigned for "anti" Democratic Congressmen in 1918; and his floor leader led the opposition to suffrage. Paul thought that intellectually Wilson may have been for woman suffrage, but not emotionally, hence his hesitation to use all his powers.[43] Havemeyer argued that they were "opposed by a President who felt himself absolute, and to whom the thought of mobilized womanhood was as a red rag to an infuriated bull." Concern about the turmoil created by the NWP helped cause President Wilson (still in France) to cable balking senators. He convinced Senator William Pollack of South Carolina to finally decide to support suffrage. As suffrage was about to be again voted upon in the Senate, Dudley Field Malone melodramatically wrote Stevens that if the amendment did not pass it "would be the end of the Democratic party."[44] The militants tried to make sure that it would pass.

With one vote lacking and only two weeks left in the Congressional session, the militants saw the President's efforts as still inadequate, and so on February 9, in a highly controversial move, burned his portrait in effigy, "even as the Revolutionary fathers had burned a portrait of King George." New banners proclaimed Wilson's deception: "President Wilson Is Deceiving The World When He Appears As The Prophet Of Democracy."[45] The marchers gathered about the urn as former

NAWSA leader Sue White burned Wilson's figure. White said she burned the figure of "the leader of an autocratic party organization whose tyrannical power holds millions of women in political slavery"; she burned the effigy in the name of her own southern Jefferson/Jackson tradition.[46] Louisine Havemeyer then started to speak, but was immediately arrested. Havemeyer later related that she "never had such a struggle for poise in my life." At first the chief of police did not want to arrest the wealthy dowager and had to call the White House for instructions. Havemeyer confided to Lucy Burns, "I believe I will have to kick him to get in the game."[47] Obviously, Paul and the NWP wanted the administration to "fight" their nonviolent protest in order for them to gain proper publicity and political leverage. Altogether 39 were arrested that day, and 26 then sentenced to two to five days for setting fires. On the same day woman suffrage lost in the Senate, Senator Edward Gay castigating "the militant suffragists, who seek notoriety and bring reproach upon the cause."[48] The women had certainly made a sensation, but still lacked the vote.

A great deal of feeling, much of it hostile, was generated by the watchfires and Wilson effigy burnings, even within the Woman's Party itself. Lavinia Dock did not approve of burning the President in effigy, saying it looked too much like lynching. Organizer Elizabeth McShane "could not see the watchfires working." Although the *Suffragist* ran an article in 1919 explaining that the Daughters of the American Revolution was born because the Sons of the Revolution excluded women, the same group dropped Berthe Arnold from its membership because of her NWP activities.[49] Keeping her sense of humor, Berthe Arnold wrote, "We are cordially disliked and disowned ever since we burned Woody Wood's whiskers in Washington."[50] Julia Emory wrote Paul she did not want to pay her taxes to Wilson's government, "by jinks!" Sue White wrote Lucy Burns that after coming home from the "bonfires," she "was lucky to escape tar and feathers. . . . I have become a real dangerous character."[51] Anyone associated with the NWP in 1919 was likely to be considered a real dangerous character, perhaps even a Bolshevik.

When asked if the NWP "favored Bolshevism" and why it was militant, Josephine Bennett replied that Woman's Party actions were "for political purposes and our experiences in the past have demonstrated to us that they are effective. . . . [We] are not satisfied with words and promises."[52] She did not bother to answer the charge of "Bolshevism." Of course, Bolshevik sympathizers did often ally themselves with the NWP. The most visible remained Louise Bryant. The famed radical Bryant, then wife of John Reed, and just back from Petrograd and the Revolution, saw the NWP fight as part of a world struggle for freedom. In her testimony before the Congressional (Overman) "Propaganda Committee" in February 1919, Bryant defended her Woman's Party connection by commenting: "I believe in equality for women as well as men, even in my own country." Writing for the *Suffragist*, Bryant noted that women were free in Russia, but not in America. Bryant wrote to Alice Paul to arrange to "do a sentence" for the NWP in February. Her first commitment was to speaking out against American intervention on the side of the anti-Bolsheviks in Russia, but, "If you can arrange an arrest for me after--?"[53] In the eyes of the public, militant suffragists were, like Bryant, seditious radicals.

Still, Elizabeth Rogers noted that the Washington crowd observing the effigy burning was "not too hostile"; some of them even clapped. The *Miami Metropolis* predicted that NWP women "will be eulogized by history like the men of 1776" and a Washington writer admired the militants for withstanding public insult. The women themselves were comforted by their sense of purpose: "Lookers-on blame the militant women because they themselves lack a sense of proportion. They think a bother is bigger than a principle. They don't know a world struggle when they see it."[54]

In February, the "world struggle" moved North in yet another attempt to put pressure on the President to secure that last Senate vote before the session ended on March 3rd. "Freedom or Jail" was the cry of Boston NWP militants as they met President Wilson upon his return to the United States from Europe on February 24, 1919. Alice Paul and Agnes Morey had arranged the details of what was a classic instance of nonviolent resistance to authority. NWP members marched through a line of Marines trying to hold the crowds back, bearing banners reminding Wilson that he had told the Senate the government would "deserve to be distrusted" if it did not enfranchise women. Agnes Morey, leading the demonstrators with daughter Katharine, cautioned the women:

> Ladies, I think it would look more dignified to be as sober as possible. It is better not to smile. . . . Don't be provoked to discussion. If you are arrested, offer no resistance and prefer no arguments. If an inquisition should take place as to the aims of our party, refuse to talk on any subject save the enfranchisement of women.[55]

The crowd seemed much amused by the demonstrators; one man got the throng's approval by yelling, "They ought to be home, darning their husbands' socks." Twenty-one were quickly arrested for "loitering" and most were sentenced to eight days in the Charles Street jail. Although not "resisting" physically, all insisted they would "not be like lambs being led off to slaughter," but would show "their eternal defiance."[56] Betty Gram refused to cooperate when arrested, and had to be carried bodily into the patrol wagon.

It is difficult to know exactly who was imprisoned after this demonstration since the nonviolent resister militants refused to identify themselves except as Jane Doe. Little is known about many of the identified prisoners. Boston's Francis Fowler and "Mrs. George Hill," state NWP officer Ruth Small and art student Berry Pottier served sentences, as did "household assistant" Betty Connoly of West Newton. Josephine Collins, owner and manager of a Framingham Center village store, went on hunger strike in jail, along with several others. Collins later encountered "serious opposition" from some of her customers. Vassar and Radcliffe alumna Lois Warren Shaw, mother of six, was "chairman" of the New Hampshire NWP. She met Elsie Hill, there to help organize Wilson's welcome home, for the first time in years; after being her roommate at Vassar, they were roommates in jail. Rosa Roewer, a Radcliffe alumna as well, was an attorney's wife and a descendant of German revolutionary exile Karl Heinzen. These New Englanders took their feminism very seriously.

Many of the Boston prisoners, as in Washington, were associated with political radicalism. Socialists Martha Foley and Jessica Henderson were among the jailed. Boston NWP member Foley was accused by the FBI of being a "comrade" of the Socialist Party who attended meetings of "radicals and Bolsheviks" at the Boston "Golden Rooster," allegedly financed by the NWP's Katharine and Agnes Morey. Henderson was a 53-year-old feminist and mother of six, who believed that husband and wife should "incorporate each other's names"; she was also an antivivisectionist, vegetarian and pacifist. Rebecca Reyher reported that Henderson kept her pacifist literature hidden in toilet paper rolls.[57] Henderson and the radical woman militants had spent their last days in prison, but they would not forget or forgive the jailing in Boston. Agnes Morey thought it "a most extraordinary thing to arrest women who are making use of their right of petition for the adjustment of their grievances. . . ."[58] The militants then carried their campaign to adjust grievances into what turned out to be its final phase.

Watchfires and burned speeches and effigies, had not yet created enough public pressure to ensure passage of the suffrage amendment, so the Woman's Party arrived at a publicity scheme which made use of their former prison martyrdom. The very radicalism of the NWP seemed to have made the public wary of them, and in some places, they were hard-pressed to find a constituency by the spring of 1919. To counter this negative impression, the NWP collected a group of its most "prominent" and colorful suffrage prisoners to tour the country on a train called the "Prison Special." The former prisoners would try to secure badly needed goodwill by visiting a series of cities throughout the nation, while along the way suffrage literature would be thrown out the windows to farm communities. On the program, Elizabeth Selden Rogers told the history of woman suffrage and the NWP; Louisine Havemeyer spoke of party methods and the dramatic arrests; and Vida Milholland sang a rendition of the Women's Marseillaise. Then, Mary Winsor told of the terrible conditions in jail. For the finale, Josephine Bennett spoke on the status of the amendment and then Mabel Vernon asked for contributions. The train's slogan was "From Prison to People," and their appearances were really quite successful. In Syracuse, for example, the NWP gained a large sum of money and strong supporters from the train visit. The Syracuse audiences were shocked that such obviously upstanding women could be clothed in prison gear, much less have suffered the treatment they reputedly had.[59]

As people came face to face with the "lunatic Bolsheviks," they turned out to be perfectly respectable women. Many were won over to the NWP and many did press Wilson to try to secure the last Senator. Of course, not everyone was impressed. Lena Smith, the female Secret Service agent following the train, reported that the "prison specialists" were saying "derogatory things" about the government, although even she was surprised at these "genteel, refined, courteous" women. The agent reported that the IWW, anarchists, socialists and pacifists had representatives among the audience at the prison special's luncheon in Los Angeles. Smith reported to her superiors a Lucy Burns speech which decried the six-month sentence given to Paul, but the agent, in defense of the government, said Paul's "Pankhurst proclivities" might have influenced the sentence. Smith was particularly alarmed by Burns saying that the hunger strike was a way out of jail, and compared the NWP's declaration that they could not be crushed, to the defiance of the IWW.[60] The train was met by great acclaim, but the public response would not be as amenable to the next Woman's Party action.

What turned out to be the last militant, antigovernment/anti-Wilson protest, provoked the most violent response yet. It was held outside the New York Metropolitan Opera House in March. The Woman's Party still hoped to pressure the President to call a special session of Congress. When Woodrow Wilson stopped in New York to speak at the Opera House, Alice Paul planned to immediately burn a copy of anything he said about democracy in his address there. Bearing banners protesting Wilson's "autocracy" at home, the women marched toward the Opera House; and they were soon met by the police. The police officers, assisted by soldiers, rushed the pickets, and the ensuing battle went on for hours. Doris Stevens, a participant, said:

> Not a word was spoken by a single officer of the 200 policemen in the attack to indicate the nature of our offense. Clubs were raised and lowered and the women beaten back with such cruelty as none of us had ever witnessed before. . . . Women were knocked down and trampled under foot, some of them almost unconscious, others bleeding from the hands and face; arms were bruised and twisted; pocket-books were snatched and wrist-watches stolen.[61]

Called a "bunch of cannibals and bolsheviks" by the police, the militants were charged with "assaulting the police," but then released. The *Times'* headline read "200 Maddened Women Attack Police With Banners and Fingernails" and its editorial said they were "maniacs who should be institutionalized."[62] Elsie Hill bravely shouted at the crowd of attackers that they should be ashamed for such brutality and should know that the NWP would never quit. "Did you expect us to turn back? We never turn back. . . and we won't until democracy is won!"[63] Until victory was finally secured, the militants had doggedly moved from one action to another, keeping pressure on the President and Congress continually.

New York was the last major battle because victory was in sight for the militants. In May Senator Nathaniel Harris of Georgia was finally secured by

Wilson to vote for suffrage, and a special session of the Congress was called for May 19. The embarrassment of NWP demonstrations, their constant presence, and the pressure they generated on the President directly and indirectly from the public, did have an effect on Wilson. They definitely helped, as Lunardini has also argued, move him to take the last step. Wilson the politician, reading the public tide and avoiding any more political embarrassment, finally acted to ensure the woman suffrage amendment by persuading the last Senator and calling a special session. The House again passed woman suffrage on the 21st, and on June 4th the Senate finally passed a woman suffrage amendment to the Constitution with the necessary majority.

Another long lobbying campaign faced the NWP before the Susan B. Anthony Amendment was finally ratified by a sufficient number of states in August of 1920. Paul said, "We went to work . . . right away and worked continuously for the fourteen months it took."[64] The ratification campaign involved marshalling the NWP's forces to go from state to state, joining NAWSA in traditional lobbying and petitioning, in an all-out attempt to finally win the vote. Wisconsin and Michigan were the first states to ratify. Lucy Burns made thousands of speeches for ratification in Massachusetts and New York, as did all NWP officers and organizers in their various states. New York ratified right after Michigan, with Kansas and Ohio on June 16; and Massachusetts ratified soon after Pennsylvania, on June 25. Burns may have won her two states, but a year later, a very impatient Woman's Party was still waiting on a sufficient number of states--they lacked one. They therefore picketed the Republican national convention in Chicago, hoping to encourage Republican-run Vermont and Connecticut to ratify. But it was Tennessee's legislature, encouraged by Wilson himself, in special session, which finally became the 36th state.[65] The women had won.

The NWP took full credit for the suffrage victory: Doris Stevens said the Wilson administration had "yielded under the gunfire" of the NWP. Historians, however, have differed in the amount of credit they give to the NWP. Christine Lunardini, in her excellent, detailed study, credits their aggressive tactics, not NAWSA's. Inez Haynes Irwin credited the NWP's element of "brook no delay" for suffrage success, but thought the amendment "just squeaked through" in the brief liberal outburst after the war. Eleanor Flexner has argued that the dramatic NWP brought woman suffrage to a Congressional vote, but credited NAWSA and its two million members and Catt's "winning plan," with carrying suffrage though ratification. Similarly, David Morgan wrote that the Woman's Party was "vital to the success of suffrage by galvanizing not politicians and parties, but suffragists."[66]

The NWP did move the great "center" of the woman suffrage movement toward greater activity by its own radical actions. The *Suffragist* said they were "a new squad that carried militancy ahead," making a new middle ground for the foot draggers of the "other" group [NAWSA]. The Woman's Party insisted on the vital importance of woman's right to participate in the political life of society; it demanded attention for the issue and it got it. The Congressional Union revived the dead issue of a national amendment, revitalized the entire movement and made political figures very aware of women's potential power. The militants' stubborn protests, their non-violent resistance to the administration's authoritarian measures, reviled though they may have been, created a situation in which something had to be done. Alice Paul concluded that the militant demonstrations had been very effective in moving Wilson in particular. Each act of overt militancy was followed by government action--militancy worked. The NWP claimed the victory, but in analyzing the struggle, even they admitted that they had won it together with NAWSA. (NAWSA never reciprocated this credit.) Women had been forced to "meet men and defeat them on their own political ground."[67] Woman's Party militants had demanded suffrage and they triumphed.

The significance of gaining the vote has been another issue debated, and ordinarily derided, by historians. But the vote was only considered a symbol and tool by Woman's Party feminists, not any sort of final step. David Morgan has complained, much like William O'Neill and William Chafe, that women have "had no impact on politics." Rheta Childe Dorr and others at the time, did argue that women should vote as a group on social and political problems, to try to make "improvements."[68] But Mabel Vernon, refuting O'Neill specifically, stated that "women's impact" was beside the point. The NWP did not stress that women would bring purity or whatever to government, but simply that women had a *right* to vote, no matter their views. Or, as Rebecca Reyher has stated, the Woman's Party, as straight, egalitarian feminists, unlike NAWSA, did not see women necessarily bringing any specific reforms, but fought so that "all women, as citizens, could participate." On their terms, then, the winning of the vote was very significant, but it was only one step in women's full emancipation. "The ballot is the symbol of a new status in human society, it is the greatest possible single step forward in the progress of women, but it does not in itself complete their freedom." In the *Suffragist*, articles reported that women clearly were not yet on an equal basis with men in legislation, industry and the professions.[69] The vote was merely the beginning.

But the importance of NWP suffrage militancy goes well beyond the gaining of the vote. The significance of the NWP for the history of women's rights is not only that suffrage was a feminist goal for them, but because as militants they acted on their belief that it was important for them--as strong, whole human beings--to act to help themselves. Charlotte Perkins Gilman's "Chant Royal--Woman Are Free At Last in All the Land," written for the *Suffragist* in honor of the victory, expressed this sentiment:

> Gone are the ages that have held us bound
> Beneath a master, now we stand as he,
> Free for world-service unto all mankind,
> Free of the dragging chains that used to bind. . . .

No longer pets or slaves are we, for lo!
Women are free at last in all the land.[70]

Gilman envisioned newly empowered women free to change the world for the better. Gilman was not the NWP's only admirer, a woman from Dayton, Ohio, wrote Doris Stevens: "You know I can't say how much I thank you for interesting me in the woman movement. It has meant much to me. I feel much more respect for myself . . . and for all the human kind."[71] Stevens saw the import of the militant campaign in its use of power, its summons to women to "stop being such good and willing slaves."[72] According to the *Suffragist*, the NWP's militancy had consisted of "aggressive tactics along political and publicity lines." And the "women's" brand of militancy used, the nonviolent resistance of civil disobedience, was seen as superior to men's sort--war.[73]

In light of NWP activism, it is ludicrous to argue simply that Wilson "gave" women the vote "for their war services." As E. P. Thompson has written regarding (male) workers, women in history are still often seen as passive; "the degree to which they contributed, by conscious efforts, to the making of history" is omitted.[74] No one gave more "conscious effort" to a political fight than NWP militants. The suffrage militants waged their struggle in the context of a war atmosphere, and were among the first to bear the brunt of violent suppression of their political rights under the Wilson administration. And that government repression came as a response to their stubborn acts of nonviolent civil disobedience, the use of which was another first for American politics. Alice Paul said on the day the amendment passed in the Senate, "Freedom has come not as a gift but as a triumph, and it is therefore a spiritual as well as a political freedom which women receive."[75] The iron-jawed angels of the National Woman's Party carried out their campaign, from political action, through escalating stages of militant protest, as strong women who "themselves would strike the blow" for women's rights. The suffrage struggle was a victory for feminist militancy, for women's refusing to allow the men in government to get away with ignoring or bullying them, for resisting that indifference and hostility, and winning.

---

[1] Irwin, in *Paul and the NWP*, wrote about the "surrender" of Congress and Stevens ascribed the "thick and fast" political events to the militant protests. Irwin, pp. 344, 345-349; *Jailed for Freedom*, p. 248. Also see *Suffragist*, January 30, 1918, p. 13; Katzenstein, *Suffrage in Pennsylvania*, p. 234. Abby Scott Baker quote in letter to Ruth Pickering, January 14, 1918, Reel 55, NWPP. In 1918, Wilson was obviously much more a friend to woman suffrage than ever before. He did not credit the NWP with his change of heart. Indeed, according to his medical biographer, Edwin Weinstein, in 1918 because of advancing arteriosclerosis, Wilson was increasingly tense, irritable and intolerant of opposition. Weinstein, "Woodrow Wilson's Neurological Illness," *Journal of American History*, p. 336.

[2] *The Congressional Record*, 65th Congress, Second Session, January 10, 1918, p. 779.
[3] Gray quoted in Stevens, *Jailed*, pp. 255-256. On more practical grounds, Congressman William Greene complained women who "flaunt banners" threatened to oppose his re-election. The *Congressional Record*, 65th Congress, Second Session January 10, 1918, pp. 764, (Greene) 775 (Gordon).
[4] Many other arguments used to oppose suffrage surfaced in the debate, particularly those of race and states' rights. Gordon insisted woman suffrage should be a states' issue and resented the "lawless" suffragette invasion. Jeanette Rankin countered the rights concern with the black vote by bringing up the "more white women than black" argument, and also stressing women's invaluable war work, (strange for her) an increasingly effective debating point. Baker to Ruth Pickering, January 14, 1918, Reel 55, NWPP; *Congressional Record*, 65th Congress, Second Session, January 14, 1918, p. 771.
[5] *Congressional Record*, as above, p. 780.
[6] *Suffragist*, February 23, 1918, p. 8; (Cosu's grammar is unchanged.] Cosu to Mary Gertrude Fendall, January 15, 1918, Reel 55, NWPP. *Suffragist*, February 23, 1918, p. 8.
[7] *Suffragist*, February 9, 1918, p. 9.
[8] Executive Secretary Report, March 1918, Reel 87, NWPP. The highest number ever reached was approximately 50,000, according to Irwin, *Paul and the NWP*, p. 4. This may be a bit high. Also see *Suffragist*, January 5, 1918, pp. 12, 15. There was $132,000 in the treasury in early 1918, $21,000 more than in 1917.
[9] The NWP made another interesting connection when a *Suffragist* article asserted that both Indian women and men should be enfranchised, and gave a history of Iroquois women which emphasized the power they held in matriarchal Iroquois society. *Suffragist*, April 27, p. 7; May 18, p. 10; June 1, p. 11, 1918. The NWP listed "pro" organizations in their journal in the same way the present-day NOW does for pro-ERA groups.
[10] *Suffragist*, September 14, 1918, p. 33. Also see March 29, 1919, p. 7, still using white supremacy arguments. Pierce to Paul, April 1, 1918; Ford, Reyher interview. NWP member Katharine Clemmon Gould, an eccentric widow of the millionaire Goulds, endorsed a black candidate for Congress. According to Rebecca Reyher, who worked with her, Gould been a circus rider and was of "questionable morals," so the NWP "subtly let her go." But her endorsement caused enough publicity to make organizer Anita Pollitzer frantically write to Paul. Ford, Reyher interview; Pollitzer to Paul, March 24, 1918; Paul to Pollitzer, April 1, 1918, Reel 58, NWPP.
[11] Italics mine. The *Liberator* quote in *Suffragist*, March 2, 1918. The *Suffragist* quoted Nathaniel Hervert, "a former newspaper editor," as saying that when the history of woman suffrage is written, the chapter on the militant policies of the

NWP will be the most important. *Suffragist*, January 19, 1918, p. 9. Sinclair to "Comrades," February 6, 1918, Reel 56, NWPP.

[12] Rowe to Alice Paul, July 12, 1918, Reel 63, NWPP.

[13] Sue White to C. Catt, April 27, 1918, Folder 20, Box 2, Sue White Papers, Radcliffe; White to Alice Paul, August 12, 1918, Reel 63; White to Hourwich, November 20, 1917, Reel 52; *Notable American Women*, p. 591; Branham to Paul, September 5, 1918, Reel 56, NWPP.

[14] In fact, it proved not to help, although the *Suffragist* and NWP press releases featured the "most important" women expected among the demonstrators, such as Dora Lewis, Lavinia Dock, physicians Sarah Lockrey and Miriam Bell, and Rebecca Winsor Evans of Philadelphia. Paul to Josephine Bennett, July 23, 1918, Reel 63; *Suffragist*, August 10, 1918, p. 5; Abbott to Paul, August 3, 1918, Reel 63, NWPP.

[15] NWP Press Release, August 6, 1918, Reel 91, NWPP.

[16] Gardener to Wilson, August 2, 1918, Reel 210 Wilson Papers on Microfilm; *Suffragist*, August 24, 1918, p. 9, on the Wilson smile.

[17] New York librarian Alice Kimball and Margaret Oakes, all the way from Idaho, were among those arrested. *Suffragist*, August 17, 1918, p. 5; Irwin, *Paul and the NWP*, pp. 363-370.

[18] *New York Times*, August 31, 1918, p. 9; *Suffragist*, August 31, 1918, p. 5.

[19] *Suffragist*, September 28, 1918, p. 6.

[20] One read a poem in the *Record* called "The Daughters of the Hun," describing the shameless lies and disloyalty of the Woman's Party. David Morgan, *Suffragists and Democrats*, p. 125; *The Congressional Record*, 65th Congress, Second Session, August 5, 1918, p. 9211; September 27, 1918, pp. 10843-10844.

[21] The September debate included Democrats accusing the NWP of working for the Republicans. Many were still bothered as well about the race question. Senator Vardaman of Mississippi was in a frenzy over Mrs. Gould's endorsement of the black Congressional candidate. He vowed that if he had his way no black or yellow person would vote. *Congressional Record*, August 5, pp. 9213-9214; August 12, p. 9226; September 28, 1918, p. 10894. *Congressional Record*, 65th Congress, Second Session, October 1, 1918, p. 10978.

[22] Doris Stevens, *Jailed*, pp. 288-290; *Suffragist*, October 5, 1918 and October 12, 1918. Also see C. K. McFarland and Nevin E. Neal, "The Reluctant Reformer: Woodrow Wilson and Woman Suffrage, 1913-1920," *Rocky Mountain Science Journal*, April 1974. This article is quite unsympathetic to the NWP and also confuses them with NAWSA. NAWSA used the war services argument a great deal. Younger in *Suffragist*, October 12 and 19, 1918.

[23] The *Suffragist*, October 19, 1918, p. 4; November 23, 1918, p. 11; John "Womain" [illegible], Special Deputy Sergeant-At-Arms, U. S. Senate to Bruce

Bielaski, Department of Justice, November 13, 1918, Reel 108, Document 25025, FBI Files.
[24] *Suffragist*, December 14 and 21, 1918. As Lady Constance Lytton said in a letter to Wilson, the President gave splendid speeches, but the world looked to him to give American women freedom. Lytton to Alice Paul, January 5, 1919, Reel 67, NWPP; Stevens, *Jailed*, pp. 302-303. Louise Bryant, "Burning His Majesty's Words," *Suffragist*, December 21, 1918, p. 8.
[25] *Suffragist*, September 14, 1918, p. 8. Newspapers quoted were the *Woman Patriot, Hartford Post, Lexington Herald* and *Buffalo Times*. Bertha Moller to Paul, August 16, 1918, Reel 64; Rebecca Evans to Paul, August 3, 1918, Reel 63; and January 21, 1919, Reel 67, NWPP.
[26] Stevens, *Jailed*, appendix. Lockrey was also a new NWP Council advisor. Alice Paul to Sarah Lockrey, February 8, 1918, Reel 56; NWP Press Release, August 8, 1918 and August 20, 1918, Reel 91, NWPP.
[27] Wold, "Did You Ever Climb a Statue?", *Suffragist*, August 17, 1918, p. 4.
[28] NWP Press release, November 23, 1918, Reel 91, NWPP.
[29] Moller in January 16, 1919 NWP Press Release, Reel 92, NWPP; also see August 16, 1918 Press Release, Reel 92; Nolan to Paul, August 30, 1918, Reel 63. In a letter to Paul of March 22, 1919 (Reel 91), Nolan asked for money. She was very sick, but said she would work for the party " 'til the end."
[30] Paul to Alice Henkle, May 24, 1918, Reel 61, NWPP.
[31] Malone to Stevens, August 20, 1918, Folder 36, Carton 2, Stevens papers, Radcliffe; "Mrs. Emory" to Paul, August 1918, Reel 64, NWPP.
[32] Alice Paul to Alice Henkle, May 24, 1918, Reel 61, NWPP; Howard, *Long Campaign*, Chapter 8, pp. 123-138; Sarah Comstock, editor, *Stanford '96, An Accounting in 1926*, privately printed in 1926, p. 210. (Martin got her B.A. in history from Stanford in 1896.) See Howard, "Anne Martin: Western and National Politics," *Nevada Public Affairs Review 1983*, for an excellent account of the campaign.
[33] NWP Press Release, January 3, 1919, Reel 92, NWPP. Present-day NWP headquarters prominently features a statue of Joan of Arc, a gift to Alva Belmont from her husband. Joan of Arc often graced the cover of the *Suffragist*. Also Elizabeth Evans always addressed Alice Paul as "Joan of Arc"! As in Evans to Paul, May 1, 1915, Reel 16, NWPP. See *Suffragist* March 4, 1916 cover. Christabel Pankhurst claimed to be a "spiritual descendent" of Jeanne d'Arc, *The Suffragette*, June 26, 1914, p. 185. See Marina Warner, *Joan of Arc* (New York: Alfred A. Knopf, 1980), pp. 48, 96, 263 (on Christabel Pankhurst).
[34] Gallagher, Paul interview, p. 93. On the fires, Katzenstein, *Lifting the Curtain*, p. 203; *Suffragist*, January 11, 1919; Stevens, *Jailed*, p. 307. The executive committee were: Paul, Martin, Vernon, Belmont, Brannan, Burns, Fendall, Baker, Gardner, Hooker, Hopkins, Kent, Lewis, Stevens and Younger. *Suffragist*, January 25, 1919.

[35] Irwin, *Paul and the NWP*, pp. 401-402, 404.
[36] Virginia Gardener, *Life of Louise Bryant* p. 332, note 4; Fry, Vernon interview, p. 145.
[37] *Hartford Daily Courant*, January 9, 1919, p. 1.
[38] Irwin, *Paul and the NWP*, p. 413.
[39] Wallerstein to Hourwich, January 1919, Reel 86, NWPP. Others jailed in early 1919 were: Reba Gomborov, Rose and Rose Gratz Fishstein, Lucy Branham (senior), Anne Herkimer, Marguerite Rossette, "Mrs. T. W." Forbes, Kate Winston, Lucille Calmes, Elizabeth and Eunice Huff, Bertha Moller, Rhoda Kellogg, Elise Russian, Berthe Arnold, Willie Johnson, Estella Eylward, Louise Bryant, Bertha Wallerstein, Cora Crawford, Martha Reed Shoemaker, Jennie Bronenberg, Mary Brown, Naomi Barrett, Bertha Walmsley, Harriet Andrews, Elsie Untermann, Phoebe Munnecke, Rebecca Harrison, Nell Mercer, Mary Dubrow, Anna Ginsberg, Palys Chevrier, Martha Moore, Catherine Boyle, Gertrude Murphy, Annie J. Magee. Stevens, *Jailed*, appendix; Mary Dubrow to Paul, February 10, 1919, Reel 69; *Shreveport Times*, February 10, 1919; Vivian Pierce to Paul, February 8, 1919, Reel 69; NWP Press Release, January 23, 1919, Reel 92, NWPP.
[40] Colvin, *Rebel in Thought*, p. 138; NWP Press Releases, January 9 and 17, 1919.
[41] NWP Press Release, January 12, February 18, 1919, Reel 92, NWPP.
[42] Louisine Havemeyer, "The Prison Special: Memories of a Militant," *Scribner's Magazine*, June 1922, p. 662.
[43] *New York Times*, January 27, 1919, p. 13; Irwin, *Angels and Amazons*, p. 36.
[44] Havemeyer, "Memories," p. 664; Malone to Stevens, February 5, 1919, Folder 36, Carton 2, Stevens Papers.
[45] NWP Press Release, February 1, 1919, Reel 92, NWPP; Stevens, *Jailed*, pp. 304, 315-316. The NWP also tried to follow Wilson to France, but first Elsie Hill and Stevens, and then Mildred Morris and Clara Wold had their passport requests denied. (From February 1st release.)
[46] *New York Times*, February 10, 1919, p. 1.
[47] Havemeyer came prepared to jail, with a "warm wrapper and a bottle of disinfectant." Havemeyer, "Memories," pp. 664-666.
[48] *Congressional Record*, 65th Congress, 3rd Session, February 10, 1919, p. 306.
[49] Dock to Paul, February 11, 1919, Reel 69; McShane to Paul, February 3, 1919, Reel 68, NWPP. Vida Milholland left the NWP in 1919 because of its "narrow focus," saying Inez had been for "liberty," not just votes. Milholland was upset because the *Suffragist* would not publish an article she wrote on her new idol--Mary Baker Eddy. Milholland to Paul, N.D. 1919, Reel 75, NWPP. On DAR, *Suffragist*, April 30, 1919, p. 9; DAR Application of membership for Arnold, March 15, 1915, notes she was "Dropped," August 1, 1919, courtesy of DAR archives.

[50] Arnold to Mary Gertrude Fendall, February 17, 1919, Reel 69, NWPP. "Woody Wood" is a reference to their prison song, "We Worried Woody As We Stood." See Appendix C for entire song.
[51] Emory to Paul, March 18, 1919, Reel 70; White to Burns, February 10, 1919, Reel 69, NWPP.
[52] Quoted in *Boston Daily Herald*, February 20, 1919, Reel 69, NWPP.
[53] Granville Hicks, *John Reed: The Making of a Revolutionary*, (New York: MacMillan Co., 1936), p. 333; Bryant to Alice Paul, January 27, 1919, Reel 63, NWPP.
[54] Rogers to Rebecca Hourwich, February 10, 1919, Reel 69, NWPP; *Suffragist*, January 18, 1919, p. 11 and January 25, 1919, p. 11. *Suffragist*, March 29, 1919, p. 8.
[55] *Boston Traveller*, February 25, 1919; *Boston American*, February 25, 1919; *Boston Transcript*, February 24, 1919.
[56] *Boston Record*, February 24, 1919, p. 1; *Boston Traveller*, February 25, 1919; *Boston Record*, February 24, 1918, p. 1.
[57] Stevens, *Jailed*, appendix, p. 324; Betty Connoly to Elizabeth Kalb, May 22, 1919, Reel 79, NWPP; on Foley, June 29, 1919 Secret Service Report, Reel 292B, File 36963, National Archives; *Boston Herald*, November 28, 1952 on Henderson; Ford, Reyher interview; Radcliffe Alumni Autobiographical Record File.
[58] *Boston Record*, February 24, 1918, p. 1.
[59] *Syracuse Herald*, March 8; March 9, 1919, p. 1.
[60] *Suffragist*, February 1, 15 and 22, 1919, March 29, 1919. The women on the Prison Special were Havemeyer, Rogers, Amelia Walker, Lillian Ascough, Mary Nolan, Sue White, Lucy Ewing, Lucy Branham, Cora Week, Mary Ingham, Sarah Colvin, Mary Winsor, Gladys Greiner, Pauline Adams, Elizabeth McShane, Berthe Arnold, Estelle Eylward and Willie Grace Johnson--initially. Four dropped out later, when their voices gave out. NWP Press Release, January 25, 1919, Reel 92, NWPP. *New York Times*, January 28, 1919, p. 8, disapproved of the Special; FBI Files, Reel 108, March 1, 12, 1919. *Syracuse Herald*, March 8, 1919, p. 6, said audiences there thought the NWP a "most accomplished group" with a "just and worthy cause."
[61] Stevens, *Jailed*, pp. 331-332.
[62] *New York Times*, March 5, 1919, pp.3, 10. See the *Suffragist*, March 15, 1919, pp. 4-5. Some soldiers later protested the acts of some of their fellows, the *Suffragist*, March 29, 1919, p. 4.
[63] Stevens, *Jailed*, p. 334.
[64] See Lunardini, *Equal Suffrage to Equal Rights*; Gallagher, Paul interview, p. 93.

[65] Bland, "Suffrage Militancy of Lucy Burns," p. 19; Gallagher, Paul interview, p. 93; Irwin, *Alice Paul and the NWP*, pp. 432-433, 465; *Suffragist*, June 21 and June 28.

[66] Stevens, *Jailed*, p. 329; Irwin, *Angels and Amazons*, pp. 392-393; Flexner, *Century of Struggle*, pp. 278 and 290; Morgan, *Suffragists*, p. 187. Even the *New York Times*, May 25, 1919, gave the NWP credit for winning Congress, with the "main suffrage organization," especially through the use of the Congressional Card Index and effective pressure on state organizations.

[67] *Suffragist*, April 10, 1915, p. 3; June 4, 1919, pp. 10-11; NWP Press Release, March 20, 1920, Reel 92, NWPP.

[68] Morgan, *Suffragists*, p. 179; *Suffragist*, April 1920, p. 36.

[69] Fry, Vernon interview, p. 164; Ford, Reyher interview; *Suffragist*, September 1920, p. 191.

[70] *Suffragist*, September 1920, p. 206.

[71] Grace Edwards to Stevens, N.D., Reel 86, NWPP.

[72] In 1919 the NWP favorably cited the Greek play, "Lysistrata," as another example of women organizing for power. They called their withdrawal of sexual favors "militancy," and applauded them for using the "terrific power of the basic emotions [to] make people realize you were in earnest." *Suffragist*, May 24, 1919, p. 9. Stevens, "Militant Campaign."

[73] *Suffragist*, March 29, 1919, p. 8.

[74] E. P. Thompson, *The Making of the English Working Class*, p. 12.

[75] *Suffragist*, June 14, 1919. p. 9.

Conclusion

Feminist Militancy

We have a long, long way ahead of us.

- Alice Paul, 1972

The significance of American suffrage militancy for women's history is enormous. The strong, feminist militancy of the National Woman's Party had its roots in British and American suffrage tradition and evolved as a logical response to the intransigence of male-centered government in the first decades of this century. Working first as aggressive political lobbyists in an era of progressive reform, the militants brought their struggle on into a period of war hysteria in which they developed a very effective strategy of nonviolent civil disobedience as anti-government dissenters. The militant struggle for suffrage attracted a wide variety of intensely committed women, especially--at the height of militancy--socialist and unconventional, bohemian women. Class barriers broke down temporarily in a sisterhood of struggle. Feminist militancy, the readiness to resist authorities and break the law for women's rights, developed gradually from men's (non)reaction to feminist political aims to join male government. Woman militants were not shy about critiquing male oppression and in turn, male authorities responded to the perceived threat of these unnatural "iron-jawed" females. That female threat was even called "revolutionary." In 1953, British historian Vera Brittain wrote:

> In the British and American militant suffrage campaigns, their courage rose to epic heights of heroism. So substantial were their achievements that the story of women in this century has largely to be related in terms of the revolution which they led.[1]

The militants' winning of the vote and their example as whole, strong women operating so visibly and loudly on the public stage was a "substantial achievement" to say the least!

The new race of strong women who were the American suffrage militants, defy easy characterization, except that--importantly--they encompassed every conceivable sort of early 20th century woman and were all committed feminists. The militants fall outside older suffrage studies' (Campbell, Scotts, Chafe, Kraditor) boundaries of traditional, educated, middle-class clubwomen/wives; often being very liberal, single, working women as well. They are also not quite as elitist as later studies would indicate (DuBois, Cott, Buechler), being very deeply influenced by their left wing, especially in regard to the political prisoner demand.

Specifically, as a whole, the 168 suffrage militants profiled here were not exclusively an upper/upper middle class elite: about 70% *were* from "WASP" northeastern backgrounds; but about 40% were actually of the "elite" classes, 47% from the middle, and 13% from the working classes. At least 25 officers were veteran suffragists and a good percentage were involved in various club and reform activities; but, many, especially the organizers and 1917 influx of recruits, had reform interests including much more radical concerns.

The Woman's Party undeniably attracted independent women. In age, the group of suffrage prisoners varied, with 17% in their early 20s, 39% in their mid-20's or 30s, 22% in their 40s or 50s, and five women, 60 or over (18% are unknown). Young women *were* drawn to the militants, and often they were physically fit, even champion athletes. Woman's Party feminists were highly educated for their time: about 32% college educated. Many of the militants were single women, 58% (94) were single and about 42% (72) were married. (Two are unknown.) The single women, especially organizers, who were 80% single, looked to each other for close relationships, some forming intimate, long-lasting ones.[2] Most striking of all is the large number of the whole who supported themselves: 107 (over 60%) of the 168 in "women's" middle class professions and 14 as "industrial" workers. Women who were in traditionally "male" professions flocked to them--doctors, scientists, artists and aviators (Georgia O'Keeffe and Amelia Earhart were members in the 1920s). These were women who firmly believed in maintaining independence from men, especially economic, while trying to achieve their political independence.

Differing in background, temperament, age and occupation, the feminist militants shared a belief in their combined strength. It is important to note that the history of the Woman's Party is not simply that of Alice Paul, or of Paul, Lucy Burns and the other most prominent leaders. The 168 women militants profiled here and their dramatic experience as feminist protesters make clear their importance to the suffrage fight. It should also be said that Alice Paul was an incredible leader --a brilliant tactician and a fearless warhorse, but she was not a complete autocrat. Rebecca Reyher says she may have appeared "cold," but it was the only way to lead. Paul shared leadership with Burns, and to some extent with Anne Martin, Mabel Vernon, Dora Lewis and others, certainly through 1917, and was scrupulous about clearing policy with other rungs of leadership, including women in the districts. Nevertheless, radical feminist leader Paul should not be overly faulted for displaying "male" leadership qualities. And Paul surely inspired fierce loyalty in her followers. In the early organizing years, there was friction between relatively staid, well-to-do militants and those with socialist inclinations, but at the peak of militancy, with a sense of immediacy and purpose, and some excellent leadership, a sisterhood of struggle was formed. The strongest bonds, both between comrade suffragists and with all fellow female prisoners, were forged during the nightmare sojourn in prison, under the threat of the common enemy of male guards and officials. Life in jail impressed the suffragists as a microcosm of patriarchal society, where violence was invoked to try to take away women's power. As militant rebels, the NWP vowed to keep organizing to use women's power against male authorities.

Feminist militancy against the government to secure votes for women evolved in a particular historical context and so in ways peculiar to the times. At the start, as part of the optimistic pre-war reform age, success for the newly aggressive suffrage campaign seemed logical, right and imminent. And perversely, the period of war madness which followed, and which led to the NWP suffragists' jailing as government enemies, also served their militant method. It is also very important to see the NWP militant demonstrators' connection with the other dissenters having their civil liberties ignored by the Wilson war administration, as well as the "womanly" form their militant protest took. The Woman's Party was the first organized American political protest to use--and use successfully--classic methods of nonviolent resistance, developing along the lines outlined by Judith Stiehm and Richard Gregg, nonviolent strategies arrived at after years of growing resentment, of being "pushed too far," and orchestrated in a series of steps to very publicly defy and coerce male politicians with the skillful "moral jujitsu" of female martyrdom.

Looked upon as the Pankhursts' American counterpart, the NWP never did use "violent" WSPU tactics, but their stubbornly insistent feminism provoked excessive hostility. Woman's Party suffragists were *radical* feminists--making them *political* radicals for women's rights--who went outside the bounds of proper female behavior by insisting on those rights. They resented male domination, desired full equality and actually organized and aggressively acted on their demands: they *took* their rights. Some of the mob violence that rained upon them was caused by their supposed lack of patriotism and their "seditious" statements discrediting the government and President Wilson. However, much of the violence was sexist; sexism evidenced by guards saying their mothers were not "suffragettes," by soldiers calling them "no women" who should be spanked, by Congressmen deriding their short hair and short skirts and calling them unfeminine, Amazons and "iron-jawed angels." Wilson himself was very offended at their demanding unfeminine natures, and convinced himself that they were madwomen, thus paving the way for treating them in a very ungentlemanly manner. Then as now, feminists were seen as crazy and hysterical. As psychoanalytic historian Dianne Hunter has argued, the term "hysterical" has often been used to discredit feminists, hysterical meaning out-of-control, uncooperative and showing unfeminine anger and resentment.[3] Militant, radical feminists would be perceived as even more hysterical. As Mary Beard wrote in 1913: "What is feminine is hysterical, frenzied, or just idiotic . . . in a man's world."[4] As militant feminists, NWP suffragists were stepping out of their prescribed roles and they suffered the consequences.

And what happened to feminist militancy after suffrage? For the NWP, with the vote won, a different situation had arrived for women. As Alice Paul said upon ratification of the amendment:

> . . . American women stand with the vote, won at the cost of millions of dollars, of priceless energy, health and even of life, ready at last to take their share in the burdens and the responsibilities of self government. Our victory cannot be a signal for rest. It is not only the symbol of the new status which women have earned, but also the tool with which they must end completely all discriminations against them in departments of life outside the political realm.[5]

One reason for lessening militancy, to stop resisting authority, was that to the Woman's Party the franchise was the tool with which women could change all else which was wrong--eventually. Without that tool, they were not citizens and *had* to work outside the system, with it, they could work within, as feminist citizens and office holders. When American-born Lady Nancy Astor was elected to Parliament in 1919, Paul said that "the important fact is not what that woman may accomplish in office, it is the complete revolution in the status of women which Lady Astor's success at the polls so brilliantly reveals."[6] Paul hoped her election would be the first victory in a whole series of feminist triumphs to come. (But, in Parliament, the men would not speak to Nancy Astor.) No longer being harsh critics of undemocratic government, or freedom fighters for civil liberties in jail, probably helped undercut leftist support for the NWP in the 20s. Leftist and other potential allies were disappointed in the NWP's lack of interest in birth control or labor reforms, and in their narrow focus on the next major political reform for women. In 1920, Alice Paul's Woman's Party turned its attention to securing an Equal Rights Amendment, the next logical step towards women's complete equality under the Constitution. Paul drafted it herself in "simple ordinary English."[7] But unfortunately for the NWP, the 1920s were hardly an amenable period to continue the revolution for women.[8]

The post-suffrage Woman's Party, stubbornly clinging to purely egalitarian feminism, faced a severe shortage of members, making them seem a small "elite" indeed. They would also confront almost uniformly hostile public opinion, making the ERA very much an uphill fight. Nancy Cott has called the NWP's feminist stand "courting conscious unpopularity," costing them labor people and "social feminists." Susan Becker also criticizes their "narrow," "rigid" feminism.[9] But the NWP's pure, "rigid" feminism was the same as ever--the times had changed. Paul's NWP still insisted on putting women's concerns and issues first, that is how they perceived feminism and the struggle to eradicate sex discrimination. And for Alice Paul, as for Susan B. Anthony, political rights had to come first.

Paul said in 1972 that "[e]verybody went back to their respective homes" after winning suffrage. Most NWP leaders, exhausted, did go home, including Lucy Burns. Burns was not in attendance when Paul unfurled the victory banner from the balcony at headquarters, the balcony where Burns had been shot at trying to secure a suffrage banner two years before. Burns had retired to her family in Brooklyn, to raise her niece and devote her time to the Church; she died in 1966. Anne Martin, after running for the Senate again in 1920, accompanied Alva Belmont as NWP representative to a women's international congress in Paris in 1926. She then wrote feminist essays urging women to lose their "inferiority complex," and worked for the Women's International League for Peace and Freedom; she died in 1951.[10] Young organizers and recruits scattered to other concerns in the 20s, and Paul remembered the "new generation of college women" as "so hopeless" on the subject of equal rights. "Giving up on reform," the 20s found former organizer Lucy Branham in Tiflis in the Soviet Union researching its ancient peoples, and in the 30s exploring Delaware's shores for sunken historical treasures.[11] Ernestine Hara Kettler was living at a social security hotel at last report. After leaving Occuquan, Kettler worked with the IWW in the West, and was arrested with her husband; she then skipped bail and her husband and went to live on a women's farm in Oregon. She settled in Seattle with a second husband; and in the 1930s she was back in New York where she became involved again in socialist politics and union organizing. Still a feminist, in 1969 she joined the National Organization for Women.[12]

Recruits may have been difficult to enlist after 1920, but the NWP continued to stand for strong, insistent feminism. From 1923 to 1990, although passed by Congress, the ERA, which seeks to end "abridgement of women's rights" has not become law. Perhaps the Equal Rights Amendment prevented alliances with women working to save protective labor legislation, but the NWP's constant voice for egalitarian feminism won women access to diplomatic service and a women's equality provision in the 1945 United Nations Charter. The NWP spoke out against fascism in the 30s, and the "back to the home" drives of the 30s, 50s and 60s. Woman's Party spokeswomen supported women candidates throughout the period, as well as working to end economic discrimination against (especially married) women.[13] Alice Paul, in 1972 as in 1912, refused to understand why women could not more easily have equal rights: "[T]o me, there is nothing complicated about ordinary equality." But Paul also saw, "[W]e have a long, long way ahead of us" to gain it.[14]

When I visited Rebecca Reyher in Greenwich Village in 1983, she told me in no uncertain terms, that I should not dismiss the ERA hunger strikes led by Sonia Johnson then going on in Illinois, as ineffective in this day and age. Reyher still believes feminist militancy can work. Recent pronouncements by NOW's Eleanor Smeal and Molly Yard promising a new dedication to helping women candidates win political office in a "feminization of power" would sound familiar to suffrage militants. And in the highly-charge context of an America where women's power over reproductive rights is threatened, feminist militancy may well see a comeback. NWP "iron-jawed angels" were jailed in 1917 for leading a militant nonviolent resistance which stubbornly protested that women were not truly part of American democracy. Militancy proved very useful in their struggle for a "feminization of power," and it may prove useful in struggles to come.

---

[1] Brittain, *Lady Into Woman: A History of Women from Victoria to Elizabeth II* (London: Andrew Dakers Ltd., 1953), p. 2.
[2] Anne Martin and Mabel Vernon provide one good example. See undated 1916 correspondence, Reel 46, NWPP; and Howard, *Long Campaign*, p. 30.
[3] Hunter, "Hysteria, Psychoanalysis, and Feminism: The Case of Anna O," *Feminist Studies*, Fall 1983, p. 485.
[4] Mary Beard, "Have Americans Lost Their Democracy?" October 19, 1913, Reel 5, NWPP.
[5] NWP Press Release, 1920, in Folder 24, Anna Kelton Wiley Papers, Radcliffe.
[6] NWP Press Release, November 1919, Reel 92, NWPP.
[7] Gallagher, Paul interview, p. 94. The exact original wording of the ERA was: "Men and women shall have equal rights throughout the United States and every place subject to its jurisdiction." This was changed in 1943, with Paul's approval, to: "Equality of rights under the law shall not be denied or abridged by the United States or any state on account of sex." Sources are Robert L. Daniel, *American Women in the 20th Century* (New York: Harcourt, Brace and Jovanovitch, 1987), p. 52 and Flexner, *Century of Struggle*, p. 342.
[8] See Susan Becker, *The Origins of the ERA: American Feminism Between the Wars* (Westport, CT: Greenwood Press, 1981), for the story of post-suffrage NWP activities.
[9] Cott, *Grounding of Feminism*, p. 77; and "Feminist Politics in the 1920s: The National Woman's Party," *Journal of American History*, p. 62; Becker, *The Origins*, p. 56.
[10] Gallagher, Paul interview, p. 94; Bland, "Suffrage Militancy of Lucy Burns," p. 19; *Notable American Women: Modern Era*, p. 125. "Martin," *Stanford '96*, editor, Sarah Comstock, p. 209; *Notable American Women: Modern Era*, p. 460. Doris Stevens published *Jailed for Freedom* in 1920, and married Dudley Malone in 1921. They divorced in 1927 after his lengthy trips away from her. She did graduate work at Columbia University in the 1930s and remarried in 1935. She remained involved with international women's work through the NWP. According to Paul, in 1947, angered because her good friend Alva Belmont willed money to the NWP she thought should have been hers, Stevens "invaded" NWP Headquarters to try to wrest power from Alice Paul. Stevens died in 1963. Stevens biographical information, Stevens papers, Carton 2, Folder 36, Radcliffe; Betsy Schmidt and Leah Freed, "A Tribute to Doris Caroline Stevens, '11," *Oberlin Alumni Magazine*, May/June 1977; Paul, in Fry interview, p. 586.
[11] Gallagher, Paul interview, p. 94. Branham also taught at Columbia. Branham in *Baltimore Evening Sun*, August 18, 1928; and June 27, 1938.
[12] Hara in Gluck, *Parlor to Prison*, pp. 257-265.
[13] Gallagher, Paul interview, p. 94; Fry, "Alice Paul and the ERA," OAH Newsletter, February 1983, p. 13. See Becker, *Origins*. I do tend to demur at

Becker's stress of the party's "distrust of men" and "rigidity," pp. 9, 264. On economic discrimination versus married women see Wiley to "Mr. Donnelly" of the National Conference of Business and Industrial Communities, N.D., probably 1930s, and Burnita Matthews to Northern Pacific Railroad, December 19, 1931. The letterhead lists (among others) Alva Belmont (Chairman), Anna Kelton Wiley, Florence Bayard Hilles, Edith Ainge, Eunice Brannan, Elsie Hill, Elizabeth Selden Rogers, Doris Stevens, Margaret Whittemore, Maud Younger, Inez H. Irwin, Lavinia Dock and artist Georgia O'Keeffe, as part of the National Council.

14 Gallagher, Paul interview, p. 94.

APPENDIX A

SUFFRAGE PRISONER DATA

TABLE 1 Class Status

Group	Elite	Middle	Working	Unknown
Leaders (16)	16	0	0	0
Officers (35)	23	7	1	4
Organizers (29)	11	16	2	0
Recruits				
1917 (36)	10	18	5	3
1918-19 (52)	9	17	14	12

TABLE 2 Ethnic Background

Group	English	Irish	French	Dutch	German	Scand.	E.Eur/Russ	Unknown
Leaders	12	2	0	1	1	0	0	0
Officers	21	3	1	0	1	1	0	8
Organizers	20	2	0	0	2	1	1	3
Recruits								
1917	16	0	2	2	4	1	6	5
1918-19	29	3	3	0	4	0	6	7

TABLE 3 Geographic Region of Birth

Group	Northeast	Mid-Atlantic	MidWest	West	South
Leaders	10	4	1	1	0
Officers	17	4	7	3	4
Organizers	12	6	5	4	2
Recruits					
1917	26	5	1	4	0
1918-19	28	7	11	4	2

TABLE 4 Political Views

Group	Lib/Conserv	Prog	Socialist	Farmer/Labor	Unknown
Leaders	12	1	3	0	0
Officers	20	1	3	1	10
Organizers	10	0	13	1	5
Recruits					
1917	11	0	11	0	13
1918-19	12	0	13	0	27

TABLE 5 Reform Activities (Before 1917)

	Suffrage						
Group	NAWSA	WSPU	WPU	Clubs	WTUL	DAR	Other Clubs
Leaders	3	5	4	0	0	1	4
Officers	5	2	0	1	2	0	7
Organizers	3	0	0	0	2	2	2
Recruits							
1917	0	0	0	2	2	0	7
1918-19	0	0	0	2	0	1	2

TABLE 5 Reform Activities (Before 1917) (Continued)

Group	IWW	Birth control	Peace	War work	Labor	Prison Reform
Leaders	0	1	0	1	1	3
Officers	0	0	0	0	1	1
Organizers	1	1	2	0	2	0
Recruits						
1917	0	1	0	0	1	1
1918-19	0	0	1	1	5	0

TABLE 6 Reform Activities after 1920

Group	NWP/ERA	Internat'l Women	Peace	AAUW	Labor
Leaders	6	4	1	1	0
Officers	3	0	1	0	2
Organizers	2	1	5	0	2
Recruits					
1917	1	0	0	0	2
1918-19	0	0	1	0	2

TABLE 7 Age in 1917

Group	Early 20s	Mid 20s-30s	40s-50s	60 & up	Unknown
Leaders (16)	1	6	7	2	0
Officers (35)	2	11	14	2	6
Organizers (29)	9	17	2	0	1
Recruits					
1917 (36)	5	18	7	0	6
1918-19 (52)	12	14	7	1	18

TABLE 8 Education (Known college graduates)

Group	College	Graduate Work
Leaders	8	2
Officers	12	
Organizers	14	6
Recruits		
1917	10	
1918-19	18	

TABLE 9 Occupation

Group	Clubwork/wife	Teacher/librarian	Social work	Nurse
Leaders	9	4	2	1
Officers	14	2	4	1
Organizers	0	5	3	0
Recruits				
1917	5	8	1	1
1918-19	1	2	5	0

Group	NWP Organizer	Writer	Physician	Scientist	Pilot	Singer
Leaders	0	0	0	0	0	0
Officers	0	0	2	0	0	1
Organizers	8	2	0	1	0	1
Recruits						
1917	0	4	1	0	2	0
1918-19	0	2	0	1	0	1

	Artist	Govt. worker	Student	Businesswoman	Clerical
Leaders	0	0	0	0	0
Officers	0	2	1	3	0
Organizers	0	3	2	0	0
Recruits					
1917	3	0	1	3	0
1918-19	1	2	4	5	2

	Household Assistant	Factory Work/Org'er	Unknown
Leaders	0	0	0
Officers	0	0	5
Organizers	0	4	0
Recruits			
1917	0	5	2
1918-19	1	12	13

TABLE 10 Marital Status

Group	Single	Widow	Married	With Children (known)
Leaders	7	2	7	6
Officers	17	0	18	3
Organizers	24	0	5	0
Recruits				
1917	18	0	18	5
1918-19	28	3	21	6

APPENDIX B

SUFFRAGE PRISONERS

Leaders	Residence
Baker, Abby Scott	Washington, DC
Brannan, Eunice Dana	New York, NY
Burns, Lucy	Brooklyn, NY
Dock, Lavinia L.	Fayetteville, PA
Gardner, Matilda Hall	Washington, DC
Havemeyer, Louisine Waldron Elder	New York, NY
Hill, Elsie	Norwalk, CT
Hopkins, Allison Turnbull	Morristown, NJ
Lewis, Dora	Philadelphia, PA
Martin, Anne	Reno, NV
Morey, Agnes	Brookline, MA
Paul, Alice	Morristown, NJ
Rogers, Elizabeth Selden	New York, NY
Stevens, Doris	Omaha, NB
Vernon, Mabel	Wilmington, DE
Wiley, Anna Kelton	Washington, DC

State Officers	Residence
Abbott, Minnie D.	Atlantic City, NJ
Adams, Pauline	Norfolk, VA

Ascough, Lillian	Detroit, MI
Barnes, Nellie	Indianapolis, IN
Bennett, Josephine	Hartford, CT
Brown, Mary E.	Wilmington, DE
Calnan, Elanor	Methuen, MA
Colvin, Sarah Tarleton	St. Paul, MN
Cosu, Alice M.	New Orleans, LA
Daniels, Lucy J.C.	Grafton, VT
Dowell, Mary Carroll	Philadelphia, PA
Evans, Rebecca Winsor	Ardmore, PA
Ewing, Lucy	Chicago, IL
Fisher, Katharine Rolston	Boston, MA
Gray, Natalie	Colorado Springs, CO
Gross, Mrs. J. Irving	Boston, MA
Ingham, Mary Hall	Philadelphia, PA
Jamison, Maud	Norfolk, VA
Johnson, Willie Grace	Shreveport, LA
Kennedy, Mary Ernst	Philadelphia, PA
Kessler, Margaret Wood	Denver, CO
Kinkead, Beatrice	Montclair, NJ
Lockrey, Dr. Sarah H.	Philadelphia, PA
Magee, Annie J.	Wilmington, DE

Moller, Bertha	Minneapolis, MN
Moore, Martha W.	Philadelphia, PA
Nolan, Mary A.	Jacksonville, FL
Short, Mary A.	Minneapolis, MN
Small, Ruth	Boston, MA
Spencer, Dr. Caroline E.	Colorado Springs, CO
Walker, Amelia	Baltimore,MD
Watson, Madeleine M.	Chicago, IL
Whitcomb, Camilla	Worcester, MA
Winsor, Ellen	Haverford, PA
Winsor, Mary	Haverford, PA

Organizers	Residence
Ainge, Edith	Jamestown, NY
Arnold, Virginia	North Carolina
Branham, Lucy G.	Baltimore, MD
Calderhead, Iris (Walker)	Marysville, KN
Crocker, Gertrude	Chicago, IL
Crocker, Ruth	Chicago, IL
Dubrow, Mary	Passaic, NJ
Emory, Julia	Baltimore, MD
Fendall, Mary Gertrude	Baltimore, MD

Flanagan, Catharine M.	Hartford, CT
Gram, Alice (Robinson)	Portland, OR
Gram, Betty (Swing)	Portland, OR
Greiner, Gladys	Baltimore,MD
Heffelfinger, Kate	Shamokin, PA
Hilles, Florence Bayard	Newcastle, DE
Hunkins, Hazel (Hallinan)	Billings, MT
Hurlbut, Julia	Morristown, NJ
Lincoln, Kathryn	New York, NY
McShane, Elizabeth	Philadelphia, PA
Milholland, Vida	Lewis, NY
Morey, Katharine A.	Brookline, MA
Munnecke, Phoebe C.	Detroit, MI
Weed, Helena Hill	Norwalk, CT
White, Sue Shelton	Jackson, TN
Whittemore, Margaret Fay	Detroit, MI
Winslow, Rose	New York, NY
Wold, Clara	Portland, OR
Young, Matilda	Washington, DC
Young, Joy (Rogers)	New York, NY

1917 Recruits	Residence

Arneil, Annie	Wilmington, DE
Bartlett, Dorothy	Putnam, CT
Blumberg, Hilda	New York, NY
Boeckh, Kate J.	Washington, DC
Butterworth, Mrs. Henry	New York, NY
Chisholm, Ann Dorris	Huntington, PA
Day, Dorothy	New York, NY
Dixon, Edna	Washington, DC
Findeisen, Ella	Lawrence, MA
Fotheringham, Janet L.	Buffalo, NY
Fotheringham, Margaret	Buffalo, NY
Green, Frances	New York, NY
Gwinter Anna	Bronx, NY
Hamilton, Elizabeth	New York, NY
Hara, Ernestine (Kettler)	New York, NY
Hennesy, Minnie	Hartford, CT
Hornsby, Mrs. L.H.	New York, NY
Jackson, Mrs. Mark	Baltimore, MD
Jakobi, Paula	New York, NY
Johns, Peggy Baird	New York, NY
Juengling, Amy	Buffalo, NY

Kendall, Ada Louise Davenport	Hamburg, NY
Kruger, Hattie	Buffalo, NY
Kuhn, Dr. Anna	Baltimore, MD
Malone, Maud	Brooklyn, NY
Mayo, Louise Parker	Framingham, MA
Quay, Minnie	Salt Lake City, UT
Reyneau, Betsy Graves	Detroit, MI
Robertson, Laverne	Salt Lake City, UT
Samarodin, Nina	New York, NY
Scott, Phebe Persons	Morristown, NJ
Sheinburg, Belle	New York, NY
Shields, Lucille	Amarillo, TX
Stafford, Kate	Oklahoma City, OK
Stuyvesant, Elizabeth	New York, NY
Week, Cora	New York, NY

1918-1919 Recruits	Residence
Andrews, Harriet U.	Kansas City, MO
Arnold, Berthe	Colorado Springs, CO
Barrett, Naomi	Wilmington, DE
Boyle, Catherine	Newcastle, DE
Branham, Lucy G. (Mrs.)	Baltimore, MD

Bronenberg, Jennie	Philadelphia, PA
Bryant, Louise	New York, NY
Calmes, Lucille A.	Princeton, IA
Chase, Agnes Meara	Washington, DC
Chevrier, Palys L.	New York, NY
Chisaski, Helen	Bridgeport, CT
Collins, Josephine	Framingham, MA
Connolly, Betty	West Newton, MA
Crawford, Cora	Philadelphia, PA
Eylward, Estella	New Orleans, LA
Fishstein, Rose	Philadelphia, PA
Fishstein, Rose Gratz	Philadelphia, PA
Foley, Martha	Dorchester, MA
Forbes, Mrs. T.W.	Baltimore, MD
Fowler, Francis	Brookline, MA
Ginsberg, Anna	New York, NY
Gomborov, Reba	Philadelphia, PA
Harrison, Rebecca	Joplin, MO
Henderson, Jessica L.C.	Boston, MA
Herkimer, Anne	Baltimore, MD
Huff, Elizabeth	Des Moines, IA
Huff, Eunice	Des Moines, IA

Hill, Mrs. George	Boston, MA
Kalb, Elizabeth Green	Houston, TX
Kellogg, Rhoda	Minneapolis, MN
Kimball, Alice	New York, NY
Koenig, Ruby E.	Hartford, CT
Main, Effie Boutwell	Topeka, KN
Mercer, Nell	Norfolk, VA
Morris, Mildred	Denver, CO
Murphy, Gertrude	Minneapolis, MN
Oakes, Margaret	Emmett, ID
Pottier, Berry	Boston, MA
Purtell, Edna M.	Hartford, CT
Roewer, Rosa H. Heinzen	Belmont, MA
Rossette, Marguerite	Baltimore, MD
Russian, Elise T.	Detroit, MI
Scott, Ruth	Bridgeport, CT
Shaw, Lois Warren	Manchester, NH
Shoemaker, Martha Reed	Philadelphia, PA
Unterman, Elsie	Chicago, IL
Vervane, Elsie	Bridgeport, CT
Wallerstein, Bertha	New York, NY

Walmsley, Bertha	Kansas City, MO
Weaver, Carrie	Bridgeport, CT
Weaver, Eva	Bridgeport, CT
Winston, Kate	Chevy Chase, MD

APPENDIX C

SHOUT THE REVOLUTION OF WOMEN (To the tune of "Charlie is My Darling")

Shout the Revolution of women, of women,
Shout the Revolution of liberty
Rise, glorious women of the earth,
The voiceless and the free
United strength assures the birth
Of True Democracy.
Invincible our army, forward, forward,
Strong in faith we're marching
To Victory.

Shout the Revolution of women, of women,
Shout the Revolution of liberty
Men's revolutions born in blood
But our's conceived in peace
We hold a banner for a sword,
'Till all oppression cease,
Prison, death defying, onward, onward,
Triumphant daughters marching
To Victory.

Irwin, *Paul and the NWP,* p. 269.

WE WORRIED WOODY WOOD (To the tune of "Captain Kidd")

We worried Woody-wood,
As we stood, as we stood,
We worried Woody-wood,
As we stood.
We worried Woody-wood,
And we worried him right good;
We worried him right good as we stood.

We asked him for the vote,
As we stood, as we stood,
We asked him for the vote
As we stood,
We asked him for the vote,
But he'd rather write a note,
He'd rather write a note--so we stood.

We'll not get out on bail,
Go to jail, go to jail--
We'll not get out on bail,
We prefer to go to jail,
We prefer to go to jail--we're not frail.

We asked them for a brush,
For our teeth, for our teeth,
We asked them for a brush
for our teeth.
We asked them for a brush,
They said, "There ain't no rush,"
They said, "There ain't no rush--darn your teeth."

We asked them for some air,
As we choked, as we choked,
We asked them for some air
As we choked.
We asked them for some air
And they threw us in a lair,
They threw us in a lair, so we choked.

We asked them for our nightie,
As we froze, as we froze,
We asked them for our nightie,

As we froze.
We asked them for our nightie,
And they looked--hightie-tightie--
They looked hightie-tightie--so we froze.

Now, ladies, take the hint,
As ye stand, as ye stand,
Now, ladies, take the hint,
As ye stand.
Now, ladies, take the hint,
Don't quote the Presidint,
Don't quote the Presidint, as ye stand.

Stevens, *Jailed,* pp. 152-153.

BIBLIOGRAPHY

MANUSCRIPT AND ARCHIVAL COLLECTIONS

Bacon, Nathaniel. Nathaniel Bacon and Hazard Family Papers, James P. Adams Library, Rhode Island College.
Dillon Woman Suffrage Collection, Schlesinger Library, Radcliffe.
Gray, James. James Gray and Family Papers, Minnesota Historical Society Archives, Minneapolis.
Irwin, Inez Haynes. Inez Haynes Irwin Papers, Schlesinger Library, Radcliffe.
Lutz, Alma. Woman Suffrage Collection, Vassar College Library.
Mayo Family. Mayo Family Papers, Framingham, Massachusetts Historical Society.
The National Woman's Party Papers, The Suffrage Years, 1913-1920, Microfilming Corporation of America, 1981 edition.
Pollitzer, Anita. Woman Suffrage Collection, Vassar College Library.
Sedgwick, Charles B. Charles B. Sedgwick and Hazard Family Papers, George Arents Research Library for Special Collections. Syracuse University.
Stevens, Doris. Doris Stevens Papers, Schlesinger Library, Radcliffe.
Taylor, James M. James M. Taylor Papers, Vassar College Library.
Whitcomb, Camilla. Camilla Whitcomb Papers, Schlesinger Library, Radcliffe.
White, Sue Shelton. Sue Shelton White Papers, Schlesinger Library, Radcliffe.
Wiley, Anna Kelton. Anna Kelton Wiley Papers, Schlesinger Library, Radcliffe.
Wilson, Woodrow. Papers of Woodrow Wilson, Library of Congress, Microfilm edition.
Winsor, Mary. Mary Winsor Papers, Schlesinger Library, Radcliffe.
Women's Social and Political Union Papers, Schlesinger Library, Radcliffe.
The Woman Suffrage Collection, Onondaga Historical Society, Syracuse.
Archives of Daughters of the American Revolution, Washington, DC.
Archives of International Union of Machinists, Washington, DC.
Alumni Archives of:

Barnard College
Bryn Mawr University
Johns Hopkins University (The Ferdinand Hamburger, Jr. Archives)
Oberlin College
Radcliffe College
Smith College
Stanford University
University of Kansas
University of Minnesota
Vassar College

PERSONAL AND TELEPHONE INTERVIEWS

Auchincloss, Sarah Hazard. Personal interview. 8 July 1983.
Bowden, Rebecca Baxter. Personal interview. 29 March 1983.
Cooper, Mary. Personal interview. 2 May 1983.
Latham, Leslie Hill. Telephone interview. 24 April 1982 and 4 November 1990.
Reyher, Rebecca Hourwich. Personal interview. 23 April 1983.
Robinson, Alice Gram. Telephone interview. 2 March 1983.

CORRESPONDENCE WITH SUFFRAGISTS AND FAMILIES

Adams, Dr. Walter. 17 November 1982.
Kellogg, Rhoda. 24 March 1983.
Kendall, Davenport. 7 October 1982
Nusbaum, Anne Boissevain. 20 March 1983.
Reyher, Rebecca Hourwich. 18 February and 15 April 1983.

PUBLISHED SUFFRAGIST INTERVIEWS

Hill, Elsie. Interview by Morton Tenzer, July 30, 1968 and August 16, 1968. Center for Oral History, University of Connecticut at Storrs.

Hunkins, Hazel. "A Talk to the Women's Press Club, Washington, DC." Transcribed by Angela Ward. August 23, 1977. Bancroft Library Oral History Project, University of California at Berkeley.

Paul, Alice. "Woman Suffrage and the Equal Rights Amendment." Interview by Amelia R. Fry, 1972-1973. Bancroft Library Suffragists Oral History Project. University of California at Berkeley.

Paul, Alice. "I Was Arrested, Of Course." Interview by Robert Gallagher. *American Heritage*, February 1974, pp. 17-24; 92-94.

Reyher, Rebecca Hourwich. "Search and Struggle for Equality and Independence." Interview by Amelia R. Fry and Fern Ingersoll, 1973. Bancroft Library Suffragists Oral History Project, University of California at Berkeley, 1977.

Vernon, Mabel. "Speaker for Suffrage and Petitioner for Peace." Interview by Amelia R. Fry, 1972-1973. Bancroft Library Suffragists Oral History Project, University of California at Berkeley, 1976.

SUFFRAGIST MEMOIRS AND BIOGRAPHIES

Anthony, Katherine. *Susan B. Anthony*. New York: Doubleday and Co., 1954.

Banner, Lois. *Elizabeth Cady Stanton*. Boston: Little, Brown and Co., 1980.

Blackwell, Alice Stone. *Lucy Stone*. Boston: Little, Brown and Co., 1930.

Blatch, Harriot Stanton and Alma Lutz. *Challenging Years: The Memoirs of Harriot Stanton Blatch*. New York: G. P. Putnam's Sons, 1940.

Brown, Louise Fargo. *Apostle of Democracy: The Life of Lucy Maynard Salmon*. New York: Harper and Bros., Publishers, 1943.

Catt, Carrie Chapman and Nettie R. Shuler. *Woman's Suffrage and Politics*. New York: Charles Scribners, 1926.

Colvin, Sarah Tarleton. *A Rebel in Thought*. New York: Island Press, 1947.

Dorr, Rheta Childe. *Susan B. Anthony* 1928; rpt. New York: Arno Press, 1970.

Duniway, Abigail Scott. *Pathbreaking: An Autobiographical History of the Equal Suffrage Movement in the Pacific Coast States* 1914; rpt. New York: Schocken Books, 1971.

Eastman, Crystal. *On Women and Revolution*. Blanche Weisen Cook, editor. New York: Oxford University Press, 1978.

Ellis, Marc. *A Year at the Catholic Worker*. New York: Paulist Press, 1978.

Gardner, Virginia. *Friend and Lover: The Life of Louise Bryant*. New York: Horizon Press, 1982.

Gilman, Charlotte Perkins. *The Living of Charlotte Perkins Gilman: An Autobiography*. New York: Harper and Row, 1935.

Gluck, Sherna, editor. *From Parlor to Prison: Five American Suffragists Talk About Their Lives*. New York: Random House, 1976.

Harper, Ida Husted. *The Life and Work of Susan B. Anthony*. Indianapolis: Bowen and Merrill Co., 1898.

Howard, Anne. *The Long Campaign: A Biography of Anne Martin*. Reno: University of Nevada Press, 1985.

Katzenstein, Caroline. *Lifting The Curtain: The State and National Woman Suffrage Campaigns in Pennsylvania As I Saw Them*. Philadelphia: Dorrance and Co., 1955.

Lane, Ann J., editor. *Mary Ritter Beard: A Sourcebook*. New York: Schocken Books, 1977.

Mitchell, David. *Queen Christabel: A Biography of Christabel Pankhurst*. London: MacDonald and Jane's, 1977.

Park, Maud Wood. *Front Door Lobby*. Boston: Beacon Press, 1960.

Pankhurst, Emmeline. *My Own Story*. New York: Hearsts International Library Co., 1914.

Pankhurst, Sylvia. *The Suffragettes: The History of the Women's Militant Suffrage Movement, 1905-1910*. New York: Sturges and Walton, 1912.

Saarinen, Aline. *Proud Possessors: The H.B. Havemeyers*. New York: Random House, 1958.

Shaw, Anna Howard. *The Story of a Pioneer*. New York: Harper and Bros., 1915.

Stevens, Doris. *Jailed For Freedom* 1920; rpt. New York: Schocken Books, 1976.

GOVERNMENT PUBLICATIONS

Congressional Record 63rd Congress, Second Session through 65th Congress, Third Session, Washington, 1914-1919.

FBI File 108-250 and 36963, Microfilm Publication of National Archives.

NEWSPAPERS

Amarillo Daily News 1917
Atlantic City Press 1917
Baltimore Evening Sun 1917-1919
Boston American 1919
Boston Sunday Post 1919
Boston Transcript 1919
Boston Traveler 1919
Buffalo Courier Express 1917
Buffalo Evening News 1917*Buffalo Express* 1917
Chicago Tribune 1918
Colorado Springs Gazette 1919
Denver Rocky Mountain News 1920
Glasgow Herald 1909
Hartford Daily Courant 1919
Huntingdon, Pennsylvania Daily News 1982
Indianapolis Times 1919
London Times 1907-1914
Manchester, New Hampshire Daily Mirror and American 1917
Manchester, New Hampshire Union 1917
New York Times 1906-1920; obituaries
Norfolk Virginia Ledger-Dispatch 1969
Omaha Daily News 1919
Putnam Patriot 1917
Salt Lake Republican 1917
Salt Lake Telegram 1917
Salt Lake Tribune 1917
Shreveport Times 1917
South Middlesex (Framingham) News 1917
Syracuse Herald American 1906-1919

Syracuse Herald Journal 1906-1919
Syracuse Post Standard 1906-1919
Topeka Capital 1917
Topeka Journal 1917
Utica Daily Press 1919
Virginian Pilot 1917
Washington Herald 1917
Washington Post 1917-1918
Washington Times 1917

PERIODICALS

The Crisis 1913
The Englishwoman's Review of Social and Industrial Questions 1870-1890
The Forerunner 1911-1916
Machinists' Monthly Journal 1919-1920
The Revolution 1868
The Suffragette 1912-1914
The Suffragist 1913-1921
Woman's Journal 1910-1914

CONTEMPORARY ARTICLES

Beard, Charles. "Woman Suffrage and Strategy." *The New Republic*, December 12, 1914, pp. 329-331.

____________ "The Woman's Party." *The New Republic*, July 29, 1916, pp. 22-23.

Evans, Ernestine. "An Hour on the Suffrage Picket Line." *Town and Country*, March 20, 1917, p. 10.

Havemeyer, Louisine. "The Suffrage Torch: Memories of a Militant." *Scribner's Magazine,* May 1922, pp. 528-539.

________________ *The Prison Special: Memories of a Militant.* Scribner's Magazine, June 1922, pp. 661-676.

Herendeen, Anne. "What the Hometown Thinks of Alice Paul." *Everybody's Magazine,* October 1919, p. 45.

Kirchwey, Freda. "Alice Paul Pulls the Strings." *The Nation,* March 2, 1921, pp. 332-333.

Martin, Anne. "Equality Laws vs. Women in Government." *The Nation,* August 16, 1922, pp. 165-166.

Page, Louise. "Political Prisoner, Dora Lewis." N.D. Unpublished manuscript.

Paul, Alice. "The Church and Social Problems." *Friends Intelligencer,* July 23, 1910.

__________ "The Woman Suffrage Movement in Great Britain." *Annals of the American Academy of Politics and Social Science*, Supplement, May 1910.
Winsor, Mary. "Women in Public Life." *Annals of the American Academy of Politics and Social Science*, November 1914.
Younger, Maud. "Revelations of a Woman Lobbyist." *McCall's*, September November 1919.

SECONDARY ARTICLES AND PAPERS

Bland, Sidney. "Stormy Petrel of Suffragism: Lucy Burns." Paper at Berkshires Conference, Vassar College, June 18, 1981.
____________ "'Never Quite as Committed as We'd Like': The Suffrage Militancy of Lucy Burns." *The Journal of Long Island History*, Summer/Fall 1981, pp. 4-23.
Carroll, Berenice A. "Direct Action and Constitutional Rights: The Case of the ERA." *OAH Newsletter*, May 1983, p. 8.
Cheney, Lynne, "How Alice Paul Became the Most Militant Feminist of Them All." *Smithsonian*, 1972, Volume 3, pp. 93-98.
Crute, Sheree. "The Insurance Scandal Behind the Triangle Shirtwaist Fire." *Ms.* April 1983, pp. 81-83.
DuBois, Ellen. "The Radicalism of the Woman Suffrage Movement," *Feminist Studies*, Fall 1975, pp. 63-71.
____________ "Working Women, Class Relations, and Suffrage Militance: Harriot Stanton Blatch and the New York Woman Suffrage Movement, 1894-1909," *Journal of American History*, June 1987.
Dye, Nancy Schrom. "Feminism or Unionism? The New York Women's Trade Union League." *Feminist Studies*, Fall 1975, pp. 111-125.
Elam, Pamela. "The Miltant State of Mind: Alice Paul, Lucy Burns, and the Militant Woman Suffrage Movement." Unpublished master's thesis, Vassar College, 1978.
Fry, Amelia. "The Divine Discontent: Alice Paul and Militancy in the Suffrage Campaign." Paper at Berkshires Conference, Vassar College, June 18, 1981.
__________ "Alice Paul and the ERA." *OAH Newsletter*, February 1983, pp. 13-16.
__________ "Alice Paul and Nonviolent Resistance." Lecture given to Nonviolent Association, Washington, DC. March 1, 1983.
__________ "Alice Paul and the South." Unpublished manuscript.
__________ "Along the Suffrage Trail." *American West*, 1969, Volume 6, pp. 16-25.
Gornick, Vivian. "Alice Paul." *Essays in Feminism.* New York: Harper and Row, 1978, p. 171.
Hall, Robert. "Women Have Been Voting Ever Since." *Adirondack Life*, Winter 1971, pp. 46-49.

Howard, Anne. "Anne Martin: Western and National Politics." *Nevada Public Affairs Review* 1983, pp. 8-14.

Hunter, Dianne. "Hysteria, Psychoanalysis, and Feminism: The Case of Anna O." *Feminist Studies*, Fall 1983, pp. 465-488.

Jacoby, Robin. "The Women's Trade Union League and American Feminism." *Feminist Studies*, Fall 1975, pp. 126-140.

Johnson, Kenneth R. "Kate Gordon and The Woman Suffrage Movement in the South." *Journal of Southern History*, August 1972, Volume 38, pp. 365-385.

Lunardini, Christine and Thomas Knock. "Woodrow Wilson and Woman's Suffrage: A New Look." *Political Science Quarterly*, December 1980, pp. 655-671.

McFarland, Charles and Nevin Neal. "The Reluctant Reformer: Woodrow Wilson and Woman's Suffrage." *Rocky Mountain Social Science Journal,* April 1974, pp. 33-65.

McGovern, James R. "The American Woman's Pre-World War I Freedom in Manners and Morals," *Journal of American History*, September 1968.

Maddox, Robert. "Mrs. Wilson and the President." *American History Illustrated*, 1973, Volume 7, pp. 36-38.

Marcus, Jane. "Transatlantic Sisterhood: Labor and Suffrage Links in the Letters of Elizabeth Robins and Emmeline Pankhurst." *Signs*, Springs 1978, pp. 744-755.

Masel-Walters, Lynne. "To Hustle With the Rowdies: The Organization and Functions of the American Woman Suffrage Press." *Journal of American Culture*, 3, Number 1, Spring 1980, pp. 167-182.

Morgan, Robin. "Alice Paul: Mother of the Era." *Ms*. October 1977, p. 112.

Ross, Dorothy. "Woodrow Wilson and the Case for Psychohistory." *Journal of American History*. December 1982, p. 662-667.

Schmidt, Betsy and Leah Freed. "A Tribute to Doris Caroline Stevens '11." *Oberlin Alumni Magazine*, May/June 1977, pp. 29-31.

Schneier, Miriam. "Meet the Real Louise Bryant." *Ms*. April 1982, pp. 33-36; 52-93.

Schofield, Ann. "Rebel Girls and Union Maids: The Woman Question in the Journals of the AFL and IWW, 1905-1920." *Feminist Studies*, Summer 1983, pp. 335-358.

Snapp, Meredith. "Defeat the Democrats: The Congressional Union for Woman Suffrage in Arizona, 1914 and 1916." *Journal of the West*, 1975, pp. 131-138.

Strom, Sharon Hartman. "Leadership and Tactics in the American Woman Suffrage Movement: A New Perspective from Massachusetts." *Journal of American History*, September 1975, pp. 296-313.

Taylor, Nancy R. "Ann Dorris Chisholm: Art Glass Specialist." Pennsylvania AAUW Division Project, November 1982.

Thompson, Jocelyn, "The Radicalism of the Woman Suffrage Movement: New York City Woman Suffrage Party." Paper at New York State History Conference, Buffalo, NY, June 1982.

Trecker, Janice Law. "The Suffrage Prisoners." *The American Scholar*, Summer 1972, pp. 409-423.

Weinstein, Edwin and James Anderson with Arthur Link. "Woodrow Wilson's Political Personality: A Reappraisal." *Political Science Quarterly*, Winter, 1978-79, pp. 585-593.

Zacharis, John. "Emmeline Pankhurst: An English Suffragette Influences America." *Speech Monographs*, August 1971, pp. 198-203.

SECONDARY WORKS

Anthony, Susan B., Elizabeth Cady Stanton and Matilda Joslyn Gage. *History of Women's Suffrage*. Volume I. New York: Fowler and Wells, 1881. Volume II and III. Rochester: Charles Mann, 1887.

Anthony, Susan B. and Ida Husted Harper. *History of Women's Suffrage*. Volume IV. Rochester: Susan B. Anthony, 1902.

Baker, Ray Stannard and William E. Dodd. *The Public Papers of Woodrow Wilson*. New York: Harper and Bros. Publishers, 1925.

Bauer, Carol and Lawrence Ritt. *Free and Ennobled: Source Readings in the Development of Victorian Feminism*. New York: Pergamon Press, 1979.

Beard, Mary. *Woman as Force in History: A Study in Tradition and Realities*. New York: The MacMillan Co., 1946.

Becker, Susan. *The Origins of the ERA: American Feminism Between the Wars*. Westport, CT: Greenwood Press, 1981.

Besant, Annie. *A Selection of Social and Political Pamphlets*. New York: Augustus Kelley Publishers, 1970.

Blum, John. *Woodrow Wilson and the Politics of Morality*. Boston: Little, Brown and Co., 1956.

Boone, Gladys. *The Women's Trade Union Leagues in Great Britain and the United States*. New York: Columbia Press, 1942.

Bratfisch, Virginia. *The Non-Violent and Militant Alice Paul*. Santa Monica: Women's Heritage Series, 1971.

Brittain, Vera. *Lady Into Woman: A History of Women from Victoria to Elizabeth II*. London: Andrew Dakers Ltd., 1953.

Brownlee, W. Elliot and Mary M. Brownlee. *Women in the American Economy: A Documentary History, 1675 to 1929*. New Haven: Yale University Press, 1976.

Brownlow, Louis. *A Passion for Anonymity: The Autobiography of Louis Brownlow*. University of Chicago Press, 1958.

Buechler, Steven. *The Transformation of the Woman Suffrage Movement: The Case of Illinois, 1850-1920*. New Jersey: Rutgers University Press, 1986.

Buhle, Mari Jo. *Women and American Socialism, 1870-1920.* Urbana: University of Illinois, 1981.

Campbell, Barbara. *The "Liberated Woman" of 1914: Prominent Women in the Progressive Era.* UMI Research Press, 1979.

Chafe, William. *The American Woman: Her Changing Social, Economic, and Political Roles, 1920-1970.* New York: Oxford University Press, 1972.

Chafee, Zechariah. *Free Speech in the United States.* Cambridge: Harvard University Press, 1946.

Corson, William R. *The Armies of Ignorance: The Rise of the American Intelligence Empire.* New York: The Dial Press, 1977.

Cott, Nancy. *The Grounding of Modern Feminism.* New Haven: Yale University Press, 1987.

Critchley, T.A. *The Conquest of Violence: Order and Liberty in Britain.* New York: Schocken Books, 1970.

Dangerfield, George. *The Strange Death of Liberal England.* London: Constable and Co., Ltd., 1936.

Daniels, Josephus. *The Wilson Era: The Years of Peace, 1910-1917.* Chapel Hill: University of North Carolina, 1947.

Dell, Floyd. *Women as World Builders.* Westport, CT: Hyperion Press, 1913.

Dobkin, Marjorie Housepian. *The Making of a Feminist: Early Journals and Letters of M. Carey Thomas.* Kent, OH: Kent State Unitersity Press, 1979.

Doty, William, editor. *Southwestern (New York State) Annals.* Jamestown Historical Society, 1938.

Dubofsky, Melvyn. *We Shall Be All: A History of the IWW.* New York: Quandrangle Books, 1969.

DuBois, Ellen. *Feminism and Suffrage.* Ithaca, NY: Cornell University Press, 1978.

Dye, Nancy Schrom. *As Equals and As Sisters: The Women's Trade Union League.* University of Missouri Press, 1980.

Eastman, Max. *Heroes I Have Known.* New York: Simon and Schuster, 1942.

Filler, Louis. *The Crusade Against Slavery, 1830-1860.* New York: Harper and Row, 1960.

Flexnor, Eleanor. *Century of Struggle: The Woman's Rights Movement in the United States.* Harvard University Press, 1959.

Florence, Barbara, editor. *Lella Secor, A Diary in Letters, 1915-1922.* New York: Burt Franklin and Co., 1978.

Freedman, Estelle. *Their Sisters' Keepers: Women's Prison Reform in America, 1830-1930.* Ann Arbor: University of Michigan Press, 1981.

Gage, Matilda Joslyn. *Women, Church and State* 1893; rpt. Watertown, MA: Persephone Press, 1980.

Gash, Norman. *Reaction and Reconstruction in English Politics, 1832-1852.* London: Oxford University Press, 1956.

George, Alexander and Juliette George. *Woodrow Wilson and Colonel House: A Personality Study*. New York: Dover Books, 1956.

Gilman, Charlotte Perkins. *The Home*. New York: McClure and Phillips Co., 1903.

____________________ *Women and Economics*. Boston: Small, Maynard and Co., 1900.

Goldman, Emma. *Anarchism and Other Essays* 1917; rpt. New York: Dover Press, 1969.

Gordon, Linda. *Woman's Body, Woman's Right: A Social History of Birth Control in America*. New York: Penguin Books, 1974.

Gregg, Richard. *The Power of Nonviolence*. New York: Schocken Books, 1966.

Halevy, Elie. *A History of the English People*, Volume II. E.I. Watkin, trans. London: Ernest Benn Ltd., 1934.

Harrison, J.F.C. *The Early Victorians, 1832-1851*. London: Weindenfeld and Nicols, 1971.

Hartman, Mary S. *Victorian Murderesses: A True History of Thirteen Respectable French and Englishwomen Accused of Unspeakable Crimes*. New York: Schocken Books, 1977.

Hicks, Granville. *John Reed: The Making of a Revolutionary*. New York: The MacMillan Co., 1936.

Irwin, Inez Haynes. *Alice Paul and the National Woman's Party,* 1921; rpt. Faifax, VA: Denlinger's Publishers, 1964.

________________ *Angels and Amazons: A Hundred Years of American Women*. Garden City, NY: Doubleday, Doran and Co., Inc., 1933.

Jensen, Joan. *The Price of Vigilance*. New York: Rand McNally and Co., 1968.

Jones, E.M. Hugh. *Woodrow Wilson and American Liberalism*. New York: Collier Books, 1962.

Koss, Stephen. *H.H. Asquith*. London: Allen Lane, 1976.

Kraditor, Aileen. *Ideas of the Woman's Suffrage Movement, 1890-1920*. New York: Doubleday and Co., 1965.

Krone, Henrietta. "Dauntless Women: The Story of the Woman Suffrage Movement in Pennsylvania." DISS. University of Pennsylvania 1946.

Lasch, Christopher. *The New Radicalism in America: The Intellectual As a Social Type , 1889-1963*. London: Chatto and Windus, 1966.

Lerner, Gerda. *The Female Experience: An American Documentary*. Indianapolis: Bobbs and Merrill, 1977.

___________ *The Grimke Sisters from South Carolina: Rebels Against Slavery*. Boston: Houghton Mifflin Co., 1967.

Link, Arthur, editor. *The Papers of Woodrow Wilson*. Princeton University Press, 1980.

___________ *Woodrow Wilson: A Biography*. Chicago: Quadrangle Books, 1963.

___________ *Woodrow Wilson and the Progressive Era.* New York: Harper and Row, 1954.

Lohman, Judith Sidnee. "Sex or Class? English Socialists and the Woman Question, 1884-1904." DISS. Syracuse University 1979.

Lunardini, Christine Anne. "From Equal Suffrage to Equal Rights: The National Woman's Party, 1913-1923." DISS. Princeton University 1981. Book of same title, New York University Press, 1986.

Marsh, Margaret. *Anarchist Women, 1870-1920.* Philadelphia: Temple University Press, 1981.

Mitchell, David. *The Fighting Pankhursts.* New York: MacMillan Co., 1967.

Mitchell, Hannah. *The Hard Way Up.* London: Faber and Faber, 1968.

Montgomery, David. *Worker's Control in America.* Cambridge University Press, 1979.

Morgan, David. *Suffragists and Democrats.* Michigan State University Press, 1972.

_____________ *Suffragists and Liberals.* London: Oxford University Press, 1975.

Nugent, Walter. *From Centennial to World War: American Society, 1876-1917.* Indianapolis: Bobbs-Merrill Co., 1977.

O'Connor, Richard and Dale Walker. *The Last Revolutionary: A Biography of John Reed.* New York: Harcourt, Brace and World, 1967.

O'Neill, William L., editor. *Echoes of Revolt: The Masses, 1911-1917.* Chicago: Quadrangle Books, 1966.

Pankhurst, Christabel. *The Great Scourge and How to End It.* London: E.P. Lincoln's Inn House, 1913.

Paul, Alice. "The Legal Position of Women in Pennsylvania." DISS. University of Pennsylvania 1912.

Paulsen, Kathryn, editor and Ryan A. Kuhn. *Women's Almanac.* Philadelphia: J.B. Lipincott and Co., 1976.

Paulson, Ross Evans. *Women's Suffrage and Prohibition: A Comparative Study of Equality and Social Control.* Glenview, IL: Scott, Foreman and Co., 1973.

Paxson, Frederic L. *American Democracy and the World War: America at War, 1917-1918.* Boston: Houghton Mifflin Co., 1939.

Pelling, Henry. *Winston Churchill.* New York: E.P. Dutton Inc., 1974.

Penn, Rosalyn Terborg. "Afro-Americans in the Struggle for Woman Suffrage." DISS. Howard University 1978.

Peterson, H.C. and Gilbert C. Fite. *Opponents of War, 1917-1918.* Madison: University of Wisconsin Press, 1957.

Petengill, Helen M. *History of Grafton, Vermont, 1754-1975.* Grafton Historical Society, 1975.

Porter, Cathy. *Alexandra Kollontai.* New York: The Dial Press, 1980.

Preston, William. *Aliens and Dissenters.* Boston: Harvard University Press, 1963.

Ramelson, Marian. *The Petticoat Rebellion: A Century of Struggle for Women's Rights*. London: Lawrence and Wishart, 1967.

Renshaw, Patrick. *The Wobblies: The Story of Syndicalism in the United States*. Garden City, NY: Doubleday and Co., 1967.

Rosenstone, Robert. *Romantic Revolutionary: A Biography of John Reed*. New York: Alfred Knopf, 1975.

Rossi, Alice, editor. *Feminist Papers: From Adams to DeBeauvoir*. New York: Bantam Books, 1973.

Rover, Constance. *Woman's Suffrage and Party Politics in Britain*. London: Routledge and Kegan Paul Ltd., 1967.

Rosen, Andrew. *Rise Up, Women! The Militant Campaign of the WSPU, 1903-1914*. London: Routledge and Kegan Paul Ltd., 1974.

Sanger, Margaret. *An Autobiography* 1938; rpt. New York: Dover Press, 1971.

Schactman, Thomas. *Edith and Woodrow: A Presidential Romance*. New York: G.P. Putnams and Sons, 1981.

Schneier, Miriam, editor. *Feminism: The Essential Historical Writings*. New York: Vintage Books, 1972.

Scott, Anne Firor and Andrew M. Scott. *One Half the People: The Fight for Woman Suffrage*. Philadelphia: J.B. Lipincott, 1975.

Sochen, June. *The New Woman in Greenwich Village, 1910-1920*. New York: Quadrangle Books, 1972.

____________ *Herstory: A Woman's View of American History*. New York: Alfred Publishing Co. Inc., 1974.

Stiehm, Judith. *Nonviolent Power: Active and Passive Resistance in America*. Lexington, MA: D.C. Heath and Co., 1972.

Suhl, Yuri. *Ernestine Rose and the Battle for Human Rights*. New York: Reynal and Co., 1959.

Thompson, E.P. *The Making of the English Working Class*. New York: Vintage Books, 1963.

Tyler, Alice Felt. *Freedom's Ferment: Phases of American Social History from the Colonial Period to the Outbreak of the Civil War*. New York: Harper and Row 1944; rpt. 1962.

Vicinus, Martha, editor. *Suffer and Be Still: Women in the Victorian Age*. Indiana University Press, 1975.

____________ *A Widening Sphere: Changing Roles of Victorian Women*. Indiana University Press, 1977.

Warner, Marina. *Joan of Arc: The Image Of Female Heroism*. New York: Alfred A. Knopf, 1980.

Weinstein, Edwin. *Woodrow Wilson: A Medical and Psychological Biography*. Princeton University Press, 1981.

Wertheimer, Barbara Mayer. *We Were There: The Story of Working Women in America*. New York: Pantheon Books, 1977.

Wiebe, Robert. *The Search for Order, 1877-1920.* New York: Hill and Wang, 1967.

Wilson, Woodrow. *The New Freedom.* Englewood, NJ: Prentice Hall, Inc., 1961, rpt of 1913.

REFERENCE WORKS

City Directories of Amarillo, Texas 1907; Oklahoma City 1907; and Salt Lake City 1917.

Notable American Women: A Biographical Dictionary, 1607-1950, Volumes I-III and *The Modern Period.* Cambridge: Harvard University Press, 1971 and 1980.

Scannell's New Jersey First Citizens, 1917-1918.

Who's Who Among Minnesota Women, 1924, editor, M.D. Foster.

Who's Who Of American Women, 1914-1915; 1918-19; 1920-1921.